# FROM COLD WARS
# TO STAR WARS

## Debates Over Defense and Detente

**Louisa S. Hulett**
Knox College

UNIVERSITY
PRESS OF
AMERICA

Lanham • New York • London

Copyright © 1988 by

University Press of America,® Inc.

4720 Boston Way
Lanham, MD 20706

3 Henrietta Street
London WC2E 8LU England

British Cataloging in Publication Information Available

**Library of Congress Cataloging-in-Publication Data**

Hulett, Louisa S.
From cold wars to Star Wars : debates over defense and detente /
Louisa S. Hulett.
p. cm. Includes bibliographies and index.
1. United States—Foreign relations—1945–   . 2. United States—
Military policy. 3. United States—Foreign relations—1981–   . I. Title
E744.H86     1988
327.73—dc 19     88–12131 CIP
ISBN 0–8191–6995–1 (alk. paper)
ISBN 0–8191–6996–X (pbk. : alk. paper)

All University Press of America books are produced on acid-free
paper which exceeds the minimum standards set by the National
Historical Publications and Records Commission.

# TABLE OF CONTENTS

## CHAPTER V: EVOLUTION OF NUCLEAR STRATEGY: 179
### DO WE WANT TO BE MAD?

## CHAPTER VI: STAR WARS OR WHAT TO DO IF THE 215
### EMPIRE STRIKES FIRST

## CHAPTER VII: FROM COLD WARS TO STAR WARS 239
### TO NO WARS

# INTRODUCTION

Understanding Soviet-American relations requires answering a series of difficult questions. What is the nature of the Soviet Union: ideological or pragmatic; people's democracy or dictatorship; evil empire or beleaguered defender of national security? What caused the cold war: Soviet expansionism, American interventionism, or aggression by both? Why did the Soviets stalinize or satellize Eastern Europe, reject the Baruch and Marshall plans, and revive anti-Western rhetoric so quickly as World War II ended? What should have been the U.S. reponse to Soviet fears and actions after World War II: George Kennan's counterforce, global confrontation, economic or military pressures, detente, or creation of a more effective international organization? What should have been American priorities after the war: Europe, Japan, China, global economic recovery, or third world political and social development? Why were containment, the Truman Doctrine, and NATO chosen? In what ways did these policies succeed or fail, and why have Soviet-American relations alternated between containment and detente, diplomatic negotiations and freezes, cooperation and hostility? In what senses has Ronald Reagan followed or broken away from the "traditional" veiw of the Soviets? Are his anti-communist rhetoric, preference for containment, and emphasis on the importance of military power radical departures from the orientations of other post war presidencies?

To evaluate Reagan's approach to Soviet-American relations, his administration should be compared with previous administrations in terms of the domestic and international environment in which it found itself, its view of the Soviet system, its design and implementations of foreign policy, and its underlying strategy and declaratory objectives. Since, in my veiw, the Reagan administration can be best understood in terms of its reaction to the events and policies of the 1970s, I will concentrate on the detente and nuclear strategy of that period. However, to give greater scope to the 1970s and 1980s, the genesis of containment, as well as detente, must also be considered. Chapters I and II take on this assignment.

Chapter III presents an often neglected feature of reviews of strategy — a brief description of major Soviet and American strategic weapons involved and their stabilizing and destabilizing characteristics, negotiability, supporters and detractors, and projected costs. A thematic glossary of terms discussed by some of the "best and brightest" students of nuclear strategy is also included. The selections, which will be useful for an understanding of subsequent chapters, reflect the current debates over the deterrent value and ethics of American and Soviet nuclear strategies, the merits of the nuclear winter hypothesis, and the prospects for Soviet-American arms control agreements.

Chapters IV and V trace the evolution of American nuclear strategy and the Strategic Arms Limitation Talks (SALT) process, including its contemporary cousins — the Strategic Arms Reduction Talks (START) and the negotiations over Intermediate range Nuclear Forces (INF) in Europe. The fourth chapter begins the theoretical debate over the merits of Mutual Assured Destruction (MAD) versus countervailing and flexible response by placing Soviet-American arms control negotiations in the context of contrasting strategic options and possible nuclear futures. Aside from reviewing the objectives, terms, and ramifications of the various agreements, the following two questions will be addressed: How have the views of the various administrations affected arms control negotiations and political relations with the Soviets? Has the Reagan administration kept a balance between the need for firmness and deterrent strength and the requirements for detente and arms control?

The issues assembled in Chapter V include the problems of how to deter or compel, how to make the deterrent threat credible and stabilizing, and how to judge Soviet views of deterrence. Western military and political officials, strategists, and scientists have grappled inconclusively with these problems for nearly forty years. Their arguments and policies have created an inchoate and peripatetic history of deterrent options from threats of massive retaliations, to promises of flexible response and a mixture of countervalue (population) and counterforce (silo) targeting, and finally to an approach that renews an insistence on the deterrent value of war-fighting and damage limitations capabilities. I will examine the degree to which the Reagan policy of countervailing (or deterrence based on the ability to deny the Soviets nuclear victory via improved American counterforce and strategic defense capability) differs from deterrence based on MAD.

While engaged in this examination, it is important to try to comprehend the Soviet Union's perspective; in other words, its problems, objectives, fears, and methods. An ethnocentric or xenophobic appraisal of Soviet strategy or of the presumably innate logic of American views of deterrence undermines objectivity and invalidates conclusions. However, there is another possible obstacle or bias to avoid. Much of the literature on strategy and the Soviet Union tends to have a partisan perspective; that is to say, positions often depend on the degree to which scholars subscribe to "liberal" or "conservative" views on the Soviets. Many writers have clear cut positions that they present indirectly in the guise of objective analysis of the advantages and disadvantages of strategy and policy. While I question the logic of MAD and the degree of Soviet commitment to it, I hope to avoid any substitution of opinion for analysis.

Chapter VI focuses on Reagan's intended tour de force contribution to nuclear strategy — the argument for moving the U.S. *and* the Soviet Union toward deterrence based on defense or Ballistic Missile Defense (BMD) rather than on offense. The controversy over what has been labeled Star Wars (the Strategic Defense Initiative or SDI) encapsulates the debate over doctrine and targeting revealed and/or reviled throughout the nuclear era. This chapter explores several key factors including the impact of BMD on strategic thinking, crisis stability, the Soviet Union, NATO, arms control negotiations, and public opinion. The very important question of technological feasibility will also be discussed. However, given the complexity and specialized nature of this issue, the incomplete knowledge about hypothetical BMD systems, and the greater relevance of strategic implications, strategic and political questions will take precedence. The review of the approving and disapproving arguments is followed by a concluding chapter that summarizes and evaluates Reagan's approaches to foreign and strategic policy and places them in the context of comparisons with cold war policies and with alternative orientations suggested by critics of containment in general and Reagan in particular.

Before proceeding, I would like to thank my colleagues and students at Knox College for their encouragement and the Earhart Foundation for its financial support. For guidance over greater distances, I owe a continued debt of gratitude to William Van Cleave of the University of Southern California and David Yost of the U.S. Naval Post Graduate School. In addition, thanks go to former SALT negotiators Albert Carnesale (Harvard) and Sidney Graybeal for their candid exchanges on Star Wars during their 1986 and 1987 visits to Knox. I have also appreciated the active interchanges between Knox and the University of Illinois's Program in Arms Control, Disarmament, and International Security. Most importantly, I thank God for the peace that yet remains in the nuclear age and for whatever insight He provides to world leaders and to those who try to understand their dilemmas and guide their decisions. They might consider the following words: "Justice will bring about peace; right will produce calm and security." (Isaiah 32:17)

# CHAPTER 1

# From Containment to Detente

## Soviet-Watching

Evaluations of policies designed to stabilize, pacify, or in any way modify Soviet-American relations depend on one's view of the Soviet system and the objectives of its political, military, or ideological leaders. The literature on Soviet foreign policy abounds with myriad perspectives and meticulous explanations for the veracity, perspicacity, and relevance of each particular view. Most analysts would agree that the Soviet system is militaristic, nonpluralistic (they differ over whether it is totalitarian or authoritarian), deliberately isolationist and autarkic, and motivated by both fears for its security and hopes to alleviate that insecurity via a rearrangement of the correlation of forces (balance of power in Western jargon) that favors the inevitable installation of a world order consistent with, and reflective of, communist rather than capitalist economic, political, and social structures. However, we do not really know why the Soviets act in these ways, and we wonder to what degree these characteristics influence Soviet foreign policy, which elements take priority, and which (if any) threaten Western interests and international stability.

Some wonder less than others, being blessed with intuitive (or tutored) insight that reveals to them the obvious "truth" about the Soviets. Schools of thought on the Soviets range from those wherein scholars describe and decry the implacable Soviet hostility toward the West and its inherently expansionist, mesianic, and evil nature; to those wherein mirror-imagers see the Soviet Union as driven by the same needs that drive any other nation (namely security, a comfortable balance of power, economic health, public consensus, and so forth); and finally to those wherein Soviet behavior is explained in terms of its reaction to implacable Western hostility and expansionism.

Raymond Garthoff suggests a tri-partite division into essentialists (Reagan and former advisers like Richard Pipes and Caspar Weinberger) who seek to confront and eliminate the evil empire; mechanists (most cold war administrations) who sought to contain, yet live with, Soviet aggression that resulted from security concerns more than ideological motivations; and interactionists who blame the dynamics of the Soviet-American conflict and mutual Soviet and American misperceptions of each other's aims and fears for the hostility of the Soviet Union *and* the U.S.[1] Another typologist, Charles Wolf of RAND, discusses the dominance of two major divisions in Soviet-watching. He disapproves of the "mirror-imagers" who assert 1) that Soviet preoccupation with defense derives from their historical experiences with invasions and anti-communist crusades and 2) that the long term political, economic, social, and defense aims of the Soviet system mirror ours.[2] He approves instead the "power-maximizing" view that Soviet preoccupation with defense derives from the overriding Soviet concern for maximizing political and military power at home and abroad.

While Aaron Wildavsky is undoubtedly correct that the debate over Soviet nature and motives is a surrogate for an American foreign policy debate, each analyst's or official's recommendations for policy choices (containment versus detente, for example, if such a simple dyad exists) reflect his or her impressions about the Soviets.[3] Given this reality, special attention will be paid in this study to the close linkage between policy preferences and underlying views of the Soviets. Having identified various schools of thought, we may now move to a brief examination of the cold war administrations to evaluate their responses to perceived threats and crises.

## The Cold War Begins, 1945 - 1952

The Truman administration, while not sharply divided on its views of the Soviet Union, which it began to see largely as hostile, untrustworthy, expansionist, and dangerous, was somewhat divided on the best way to deal with Soviet leaders. Harry Truman, newly and unexpectedly thrust into the presidential realm of foreign policy in 1945, was a long time opponent of communism and Stalin. While he may have shared Franklin Roosevelt's hope for a continuation of the brief war-time alliance with the Soviets after World War II, what lingering wishes existed soon dissipated as Soviet exclusionary activities in Eastern Europe (a communist party takeover in Poland, for example) appeared to Truman to violate the precepts and promises of the Yalta and Potsdam agreements on free elections and other post-war settlements.

The status of Western Europe especially concerned Truman and advisers like Dean Acheson, W. Averell Harriman, George Kennan, and George Marshall. After nearly four years of fighting German dominance of Europe, was the Soviet Union an eager seeker after the same role? Were Soviet decisions to satellize Eastern Europe, maintain the occupation of Iran, demand territorial concessions from Turkey, support Yugoslavia's (Tito's) intervention in the Greek civil war, and to dishonor obligations regarding Germany indications that the Soviets had an even larger sphere in mind? The Truman administration saw these actions as threats to American interests in a "free Europe" and a "free world." Apparent Soviet attempts to meddle in and exploit crises that appeared promising in terms of expanding Soviet power vindicated American suspicions about Soviet character.

Under the impetus of these now confirmed suspicions, the Truman administration launched a patchwork, improvised policy to meet Soviet force and aggression with threats of counterforce, resistance, and containment. Kennan, the father of containment, who later divorced himself from this particular offspring, argued that the hostile, cruel, paranoid, militaristic, dangerous, and insidious Soviet Union was "committed fanatically to the belief that with US there can be no permanent *modus vivendi,* that it is desirable and necessary that the internal harmony of our society be disrupted, our traditonal way of life be destroyed...if Soviet power is to be secure."[4]

Despite the ominous picture that Kennan often painted for Truman, he maintained that political and economic, rather than military, containment would supply a powerful and, after the long haul, effective and sustainable antidote to Soviet aggression. While in the famous Mr. X article Kennan wrote of the need "to confront the Russians with unalterable counterforce at every point where they show signs of encroaching upon the interests of a peaceful and stable world," he also implied that this task could be achieved without provoking unnecessarily the aforementioned dangerous and insidious, yet cautious and patient, adversary.[5] According to Kennan, "Soviet power, unlike that of Hitlerite Germany, is neither schematic nor adventuristic. It does not work by fixed plans. It does not take unnecessary risks...and it is highly sensitive to logic of force. For this reason it can easily withdraw...when strong resistance is encountered at any point. Thus, if the adversary has sufficient force and makes clear his readiness to use it, he rarely has to do so."[6] In essence, then, carefully chosen and executed shows of force and selective applications of counterpressure would create "situations which will compel the Soviet Government to recognize the practical undesirability of acting on the basis of its present concepts and the necessity of behaving in accordance with precepts of international conduct, as set forth in the...UN Charter."[7] While Kennan thought Truman overcommitted the U.S. with the promise of the Truman Doctrine to assist "free peoples" everywhere, he saw the Marshall Plan, to help stabilize and revitalize the European economies, as a prototype of an appropriately selective response to the dangers posed by Soviet attempts to exploit economic and political turmoil in post-war Europe.

However, Kennan's advice about selectivity and non-provocative counterforce competed with more hard line advice by others in the Department of State and the cabinet (Acheson, Forrestal, Harriman, and Nitze, for example) to upgrade containment to resistance by whatever means possible, during any contingency posed, and in whatever location found. Given assumptions of Soviet ideological and revolutionary fanaticism in its desire to dominate the international system, the "hard liners" and the authors of National Security Council memorandum # 68 (NSC-68) urged acceptance of their version of a containment. Their containment would seek "by all means short of war to 1) block further expansion of Soviet power, 2) expose the falsities of Soviet pretensions, 3) induce a retraction of the Kremlin's control and influence and 4) in general, so foster the seeds of destruction within the Soviet system that the Kremlin is brought at least to the point of modifying its behavior to conform to generally accepted international standards."[8]

To provide evidence that containment enjoyed sufficient teeth to guarantee the above objectives, a strong conventional and strategic military capability (hitherto underfunded and underappreciated) was imperative. Without it the Soviets might undertake "piecemeal aggression," counting on American "unwillingness to engage in atomic war unless we are directly attacked."[9] The authors of NSC-68 feared an American paralysis in the face of Soviet pressures on various areas of vital interest. If the U.S. faced only two choices— capitulating, due to a fear of nuclear war and an inability to respond to piecemeal aggression or minichallenges through conventional means, or precipitating a nuclear war, then the U.S. would appear irresolute and desperate. To avoid this fate and to frustrate Soviet designs on the free world, the U.S. and the free world should rapidly build up their political, economic and military strength. This strength would supply the requisite ingredients for the development and sustenance of a successful political and economic system, deterrence of Soviet expansion, and defeat of Soviet aggression of a limited or total nature. The authors of NSC-68 concluded that:

> We must organize and enlist the energies and resources of the free world in a positive program for peace which will frustrate the Kremlin design for world domination by creating a situation...to which the Kremlin will be compelled to adjust. Without such a cooperative effort, led by the U.S., we will have to make gradual withdrawals under pressure until we discover one day that we have sacrificed positions of vital interests... In summary, we must, by means of a rapid and sustained build-up...of the free world...wrest the initiative from the Soviet Union, (and) confront it with convincing evidence of the determination and ability of the free world to frustrate the Kremlin design of a world dominated by its will. Such evidence is the only means short of war which eventually may force the Kremlin to abandon its present course of action and to negotiate acceptable agreements on issues of major importance.[10]

In view of these assessments, Soviet attempts to upset the status quo forcefully and all challenges to allies and friends (whether to Europe and Japan, the ultimate dominos, or the pheripheral states) must be resisted to signal that the U.S. accepted the task of defending newly engaged commitments. American officials believed that only demonstrative shows of force, embracing of new commitments, and willingness to take risks would eventually persuade the Soviet Union that its behavior was costly and counterproductive. Eventually the Soviet Union would be forced to choose self restraint in face of American "patient and firm" opposition.

The challenges of the early cold war years eventually resulted in American decisions to subsidize the Western European economy; increase military spending (NSC-68 recommended an increase taking up to 20% of the GNP, but only in the mid 1960s did the military budget approach even half that figure); engage in limited military actions (Korea and over 30,000 American lives lost); create and lead alliance pacts, some of which automatically committed the U.S. to direct military intervention (NATO and defense pacts with Japan, Korea, Taiwan, and the Philippines); and assist states facing communist or nationalist insurgencies. The Truman administration and subsequent administrations deemed this effort necessary in the struggle to prevent Soviet dominance of the international system.

However, American leaders also saw no alternative to a semi limited containment. The U.S. did not attempt to eliminate the Soviet system, push the Soviets out of Eastern Europe, risk nuclear war over Korea or Berlin or, more than half-heartedly, attempt to preclude a communist takeover in China. It undertook, however, additional and evergrowing commitments, the defense of which would, in subsequent years, arouse perennial questions about American credibility. Once the U.S. drew lines against Soviet expansion, Soviet challenges or breeches of the lines would involve tests of American resolve. Truman passed one major test with the Berlin airlift in 1948-1949 at relatively low cost, although he engineered no resolution of the conflict over the status of Berlin. A second test over Korea, which also ended in stalemate, cost a great deal more in terms of men and material. And, in demonstrating the credibility of American commitment to defend South Korea against communist aggression (and, by implication, so we thought, to defend Japan, Western Europe, and any other interested party) the U.S. encountered additional choices: should it defend Taiwan against the People's Republic of China (PRC), Indochina against local communists, the Middle East and the so-called Northern Tier against the Soviets, and so on?

Critics of the Truman administration saw this rush to assure credibility leading to a no-win situation in which the U.S. would find the mere presence of the Soviets anywhere to represent an automatic threat to vital national interest. John Gaddis and Robert Johnson, for example, accused the U.S. of preoccupation with credibility and with defining interest in terms of threats, both of which made "interests a function of threats."[11] Both critics would agree that neither concerns for credibility nor the existence of threats should substitute for defining national interests. Nor should, according to Johnson, credibility be so universalized that American "action in one conflict comes to be seen as a test of credibility in all potential or actual conflicts including nuclear."[12] Such a position and/or predisposition left the initiative in Soviet hands, led to confusion in the articulation of priorites for American foreign policy, and involved the U.S. in a potentially never ending battle with the Soviet Union. The greatest danger of an open ended policy of containment lay in its apparently built in tendency to institutionalize and perpetuate cold war hostility rather than to facilitate the goals of acquainting the Soviets with the values of restraint, mutual respect, and peaceful coexistence.

Ironically criticism also emerged regarding the appeasement like qualities of a containment policy that opted for coexistence with the Soviets until they mellowed. Those, like Dulles, who opposed this "treadmill policy" of indefinite coexistence with "godless terrorists," argued for a more active policy that pursued conclusive victory not perpetual stalemate. However, once in office, the Eisenhower team reassessed its objections in the face of Eisenhower's preference for leaner defense budgets, avoidance of costly conventional wars and large standing armies, and his early discovery of the wisdom of Truman's insight about the limits of American power.

# Containment in the 1950s and 1960s

A review of the Eisenhower administration reveals its interesting evolution from a bluff and bluster proponent of rollback to a pragmatic practitioner of "traditional" containment. The Eisenhower/Dulles view of the Korean War stalemate serves as a fine example of the initial, albeit temporary, transition from Trumanesque containment to confrontation in Eisenhower's foreign policy approach. Eisenhower and Dulles blamed the Truman administration's inconsistent and half hearted approach to containment for encouraging the Soviets to probe the vaguely defined line drawn in Asia, primarily around Japan, after the administration abandoned Jiang Gaishek (Chiang Kai Shek). If the Truman administration had warned the Soviets that aggression would not be tolerated and that the U.S. would up the ante for any scavenging for dominos, then Stalin might have hesitated to encourage "proxies" like Kim il Sung in North Korea to make grabs for territory. Once the war started, Truman's haphazard inconsistency regarding war aims led to a decision to accept stalemate rather than to take risks to assure victory and a reunification of Korea. The Eisenhower administration abhored stalemate, but agreed with limiting American objectives, as long as it could force an early end to the war. The administration soon resorted to threats of nuclear attack to persuade the Chinese, the Soviets, and the North Koreans to negotiate an acceptable Korean cease-fire arrangement.

In the meantime, Dulles rhapsodized about a more dynamic, effective, and victory-assuring alternative to Truman's more passive and reactive policy: liberation and rollback. Mere containing or living with the evil empire was "negative, futile, and immoral," according to the 1952 Republican platform. On the other hand, while the American public applauded the platform, it also demanded relief from the physical cost of containment (land wars in Asia and taxes and budget deficits for defense spending.) To satisfy these contradictory inputs, the Eisenhower/Dulles team found relief in rhetorical bluster fortified by deterrent threats of massive retaliation. The administration hoped to restrain the Soviets by consolidating the lines being drawn to hem in Soviet expansion and by threatening nuclear retaliation for any Soviet (or Chinese) crossings of the line. The U.S. enlisted alliance partners to share the burden of defending the "free world." NATO, SEATO (South East Asian Treaty Organization), CENTO (Central Treaty Organization), and the Eisenhower Doctrine projected an image of military solidarity (pactomania according to critics). The U.S. also supported economic integration in Western Europe (the European Economic Community, for example), balanced budgets at home, and economic, military, and technological assistance to third world states potentially vulnerable to communist subversion.

The most important asset in the Eisenhower policy remained the nuclear superiority that the U.S. maintained throughout the 1950s. The U.S. relied on threats of nuclear retaliation to deter Soviet aggression. The administration advertised its intention to carry communist sponsored crises to the brink of war (brinkmanship), confident of Soviet or Chinese retreat as in, presumably, Korea and Quemoy and Matsu (the two islands offshore from Taiwan shelled by the Chinese at various times in the 1950s.) Eventually, as countries behind the lines acquired political and economic stability, once safely removed from the menace of Soviet sponsored aggression or subversion, Soviet expansion would be contained or deflected.

This happy forecast failed to materialize for a number of reasons. 1) Neither Europe nor the third world willingly or effectively shouldered the burden of containment. 2) The Soviets (and the Chinese) discounted the American threat in an age when Soviet retaliation could now damage the American homeland [the lack of American response to the Soviet invasion of Hungary in 1956 confirmed the incredibility of American promises of rollback and retaliation]. 3) As a result of the above, the Soviets or "international communism" crossed, obliterated, or ignored the lines drawn helter skelter throughout the world. Even one of the most unambiguous lines—West Berlin—lay dangling precariously in the late 1950s as Nikita Khrushchev, and many in Western Europe and the U.S., questioned American willingness to risk war over the status of one city in West Germany. From 1958-1960, Khrushchev pressured Eisenhower to retreat from the allied position that the Potsdam agreement on the status of Berlin was not subject to unilateral Soviet interpretation and disposition. While Eisenhower resisted Khruschev's ultimatum, his waffling on the issue of the "abnormality" of an independent West Berlin in the midst of East Germany, called into question American commitment to defending the line drawn through Europe.

Conceptual problems also derailed the Eisenhower policy and led to the failure to "liberate" the enslaved, eliminate the menace, or hold the line against major challenges as in Berlin or South East Asia. Despite the campaign-inspired rejection of the Truman containment, the Eisenhower administration accepted the warnings and prescriptions of the NSC-68. On the other hand, it excluded the calls for economic sacrifice and willingness to engage in conventional combat to demonstrate credibility. These two exclusions held the secret to the failure of rollback and brinkmanship. Without "adequate" defense spending and without a willingness to fight limited wars to avoid potentially empty (or worse, realized) threats of massive retaliation, the U.S. could not persuade adversaries about the teeth behind containment, brinkmanship, and massive retaliation. Or, perhaps the task itself had to change as the international environment of the post-Stalin 1950s changed. As the Soviet Union acquired nuclear retaliatory capability, slowly gained (and the West lost) clients and friends in China and the third world, developed economic and political health after the delayed recovery from the destruction of World War II, and as Khrushchev judged his man—Eisenhower—as willing to compromise and retreat (as over Berlin), Khrushchev began to play the game of brinkmanship more daringly and effectively than American leaders. Or, perhaps containment was indeed a rather geographically limited policy of resisting Soviet expansion—a policy that coincided with or caused the prevention of expansion in Western Europe and Korea, but faltered when applied in the third world as later demonstrated most graphically in Vietnam.

The Republican administration did not have all the answers to these questions and possibilities, but it argued the merits of pursuing a policy that confronted Soviet aggression without bankrupting the nation, going to war, losing public support, or jeopardizing American values through some all consuming passion for amassing a huge military industrial complex. While anxious to retard Soviet aggression, Eisenhower also raised questions about the potential of unacceptable ramifications of an anti-communist crusade conducted with little concern for the niceties of American principles and scruples about the rules of the game in power politics. Eisenhower warned against this possibility in his farewell address to the nation in 1961. Perhaps appreciation of Eisenhower's scruples led many revisionist scholars (and others) to admire, somewhat belatedly, the restrained and cautious Eisenhower approach to military policy and Soviet-American relations.

Stephen Ambrose, for example, reminds us of Dulles' recognition of the limitations of brinkmanship, which he never applied for the purpose of liberation; Eisenhower's outstanding achievement of avoiding war and realizing that security could not be enhanced by an unrestrained and thoughtless arms race; and the pragmatic Eisenhower/Dulles ground rules for Soviet-American conduct—not challenging each other's vital interests, agreeing to keep the threshold of conflicts low, and searching for a way out of the cold war.[13] John Gaddis admired what he termed the "asymmetrical" approach to containment embodied in the Eisenhower "New Look", wherein the administration assumed that "the way to deter aggression is for the free community to be willing and able to respond vigorously at places and with means of its own choosing...(and to shape) our military establishment to fit what is *our* policy, instead of having to meet the enemy's many choices."[14] While Eisenhower intervened in Indochina in the 1950s and in Lebanon in 1958 to block outside interference in domestic civil strife, he rejected this option in Cuba in 1959. He also refused to be bull dozed by advisers into matching every imaginable Soviet military development or into elevating the Soviet challenge over Berlin into a major test of nuclear resolve over the future of American commitment to NATO. Finally, he hoped to install the 1959 Spirit of Camp David as a platform for rapprochement between the two nuclear giants.

The Soviet shoot-down of the U-2 in 1960 and Eisenhower's acceptance of the blame, and insistence on the need, for spying on the Soviet Union, put a premature end to Eisenhower's dream of a more stable and buoyant Soviet-U.S. relationship. Despite this setback, Eisenhower's approval for backing away from confrontation represented a bridge between Truman's visceral antagonism toward the Soviets and the acceptance of a more narrowly defined containment and the imperative nature of detente that emerged in the 1960s and 1970s. In sum, where Truman felt compelled to respond to Soviet challenges almost everywhere and in whatever manner appropriate, the asymmetrical Eisenhower approach consisted of a more selective and limited containment wherein, given finite resources, careful distinctions would be made between vital and peripheral threats and interests.

However, not all segments of the American political scene reached the same conclusions. In the heat of the 1960 presidential campaign, the Kennedy team interpreted the events, policies, and portents of the 1950s differently than the Eisenhower administration and its revisionist acolytes. Kennedy entered office criticizing the relative passivity of the Eisenhower administration and rejecting its apparent willingness to choose between not responding to Soviet challenges, i.e. backing away from or ignoring commitments, or responding with massive retaliation.[15] Full of the spirit of NSC-68 and a deep suspicion of hostile Soviet motives and intentions, officials in the Kennedy administration saw all commitments as symbolically important and therefore demanding a response to maintain American credibility. To not live up to commitments or to fail to resist Soviet attempts to shatter the balance of power as in Berlin, Laos, the Cuban missile crisis, or Vietnam, would create an image or perception of American weakness. In this view, the Soviets, being dedicated to overthrowing the status quo, could be expected to exploit such weakness or test American resolve to discover additional vulnerabilities. In sum, if the U.S. failed to meet each test or respond to challenges on the periphery (Vietnam) or at the center (Berlin or Cuba), containment would fail and, even worse, the prospects for war would increase, especially if the Soviet Union chose to make a direct challenge in the mistaken expectation of American inaction.

To avoid this prospect, Kennedy warned the Soviets against "underestimate(ing) the will and unity of democratic societies where vital interests are concerned."[16] With respect to West Berlin, for example, Kennedy insisted that "We cannot and will not permit the Communists to drive us out of Berlin, either gradually or by force. For the fulfillment of our pledge to that city is essential to the morale and security of Western Germany, to the unity of Western Europe, and to the faith of the entire Free World."[17] Kennedy then backed these warnings up with actions such as tripling the draft call, creating counter-guerilla special forces, and increasing military spending, thus rejecting Eisenhower's vision of a balanced budget and embracing the exhortation of NSC-68 regarding economic sacrifices. He also raised the alert status of American missile and bomber forces; reevaluated the merits of massive retaliation versus flexible response—a capability to respond to Soviet military challenges at whatever level threatened from conventional to nuclear wars; accelerated material and manpower support for NATO; and enjoined the Congress and the public to fight the battle of containment in the third world through economic and military means (The Alliance for Progress in Latin America and military assistance for Vietnam and the Congo, for example). While more willing than Truman to negotiate with the Soviets and to compromise on occasion, in the spirit of quid pro quo, Kennedy also saw the Soviets and the U.S. engaged in a relentless struggle of the free versus the unfree, and he assumed that in this struggle the U.S. could never rest, appear weak, neglect a challenge, or refuse to pay the price for containment.

Kennedy feared that he had appeared indecisive and inconsistent during the American supported invasion of the Bay of Pigs in 1961, weak over the building of the Berlin Wall in 1961, where the West responded weakly with condemnation, and naive in the Laos cease-fire compromise, where the Soviets soon violated an agreement guaranteeing the neutrality of Laos. Khrushchev's obduracy over the status of West Berlin and his 1962 Cuban missile crisis gamble convinced Kennedy that the U.S. could not fail to respond in Cuba. Kennedy believed that the Soviet emplacement of missiles, perhaps encouraged by Khrushchev's low opinion of Kennedy's ability to react effectively or expeditiously, directly and symbolically challenged American physical security, the international military and political balance of power, and the image of American willingness to take risks to defend its national interests. According to Kennedy,

> this secret, swift, extraordinary buildup of Communist missiles in an area well known to have a special and historical relationship to the United States...in violation of Soviet assurances and in defiance of American hemispheric policy—this sudden, clandestine decision to station strategic weapons for the first time outside of Soviet soil is a deliberately provocative and unjustified change in the status quo which cannot be accepted by this country if our courage and commitment are ever to be trusted again by either friend or foe. The 1930s taught us a clear lesson. Aggressive conduct, if allowed to go unchecked and unchallenged, ultimately leads to war.[18]

These beliefs and Kennedy's appraisal of the need to defend the periphery as well as the center, led to his decision to apply the principles of containment to the struggle between the American sponsored government in South Vietnam and its communist guerilla and North Vietnamese opponents. This presumed East-West battle embodied what Gaddis labelled the symmetrical approach of Kennedy and NSC-68. Kennedy believed that, since the balance of power was fragile and volatile and since every domino was interdependent, peripheral interests were as important as vital interests.[19] Thus Vietnam was crucial for the sake of the credibility of America's intention to contain the communists anywhere and protect areas of importance. To neglect, avoid, or dismiss mini or ambiguous challenges might call into question America's overall commitment.

President Lyndon Johnson also refused to abandon American commitments no matter how acquired, how dangerous, or how costly. As Vice President he reported to Kennedy that "the basic decision in Southeast Asia is [in Vietnam.] We must decide whether to help these countries to the best of our ability or throw in the towel in the area and pull back our defenses to San Francisco and a 'Fortress America' concept. More important, we would say to the world in this case that we don't live up to treaties and don't stand by our friends."[20] Later, as president, he argued that "surrender anywhere threatens defeat everywhere."[21] This statement resoundingly re-affirmed the persistent American acceptance of the validity of Kennan's and Truman's contention that the Soviets probed for weakspots until they met resistance. For both Kennedy and Johnson (and later for Kissinger and Nixon), intervention in Vietnam was the major test of American resolve, a symbolic domino, and the offspring of containment.

This "test of resolve and will" mentality drove Kennedy and Johnson to create many tests the U.S. was destined to fail, since it had not the will, resources, patience, or the necessary good wishes of other important states to undertake and sustain containment in places like Vietnam. To complicate matters further, the international balance of power was not rigidly set nor buffeted only by Soviet or Chinese challenges. States in the third world envisioned necessary and urgent changes in such things as resource distribution; ethnic, racial, and national divisions; and Western views on social and political values. In this context of change, challenge, and confrontation, the U.S. as a limited state could not apply containment in an unlimited fashion. While disputes on the periphery might ultimately influence the center, priorities had to be established, losses anticipated and accepted, and solutions other than military ones found.

However, post-war presidents found themselves caught in the probably inescapable dilemma imposed by the need to contain the Soviets without escalating the Soviet-U.S. conflict into war or intervening indiscriminately in the third world, but also without underestimating the linkage between reputation and effective foreign policy. Unfortunately, as Gaddis noted, the United States failed to resolve this dilemma since it "could not even appear to withdraw from what were admittedly overextended positions without setting off a crisis of confidence that would undermine American interests everywhere."[22] While Kennedy sought to extricate the U.S. from the dilemma of choosing between reflexive and sterile containment versus naive appeasement after the U.S. and the U.S.S.R. appproached nuclear catastrophe in the Cuban missile crisis, he could not abandon commitments due to his fear of appearing weak. Not until Nixon and Kissinger does the American position reflect more confidence in negotiations and detente and acceptance of limits to American power.

In this retrospective look at the evolution of containment we see a rather consistent view of the Soviet Union (a relentlessly hostile and dangerous adversary), but only a semi consistent policy toward it. All four administrations sought to contain the Soviets and to inspire American and Western publics to support this agenda, but their choices of where and how to apply containment and what to risk and spend for it differed somewhat during these first 20 or so years of the cold war. All four presidents might agree that containment suffered a massive and debilitating blow in the debacle of Vietnam. They might not agree on the policies, events, and actions responsible. How the Nixon and Carter administrations sought to extricate the U.S. from the debacle and redefine containment to fit the new international environment of the 1970s will occupy the next two sections of this chapter.

## Detente Replaces Containment 1969-76

After two decades of containment, a decade of escalated involvement in Vietnam, and a gradual shift in America's global status from a position of nuclear superiority and political predominance to one of parity and retrenchment, the Nixon administration took office in 1969. The political environment surrounding this shift determined, to a large extent, its foreign policy options. The U.S. encountered a Soviet power that reflected intermittent expansionist ambitions supported by growing military, political, and economic capabilities. On the other hand, Nixon and Kissinger hoped to exploit instabilities within the Soviet Union and the Soviet bloc—instabilities resulting from an infirm economic system, a grumbling and demanding East bloc, and a shattered Sino-Soviet alliance. The emergence of a P.R.C. rapidly shedding its isolationist nature and actively engaged in ideological competition with the Soviets, involved the U.S. in a tri-polar international system. American pro-Israeli involvement in the Middle East, still unsettled over the hostilities of 1967, alienated the U.S. from many Arab and third world nations. The third world, radicalized in its insistence on the responsibility of the developed nations to assist the developing nations, made more demands on American attention. The U.S. faced new dimensions in relations with allies. Western Europe, while stronger than in the past, remained plagued by recurring economic and political disruptions from Gaullist fantasies and economic penetration by American multinational corporations to anxiety over how to deter wihout provoking the Soviets and how to exploit independence from the U.S. without undermining NATO unity. Japan remained uncertain as to its potential leadership role regionally and in the international economic system. Finally the U.S. experienced a domestic crisis of spirit over economic dislocations, lack of public trust in government, and over Vietnam which monopolized American attention and resources.

The evaluation of these international and domestic problems by Nixon and Kissinger played a decisive role in their advocacy of detente. Their advocacy, while primarily consistent with traditional American foreign policy behavior, reflected a turning point in attitudes toward America's global role and its relationship with adversaries, allies, and the non-aligned. Before analyzing the stimuli and expectations for the policy of detente, it is important to note the contradictions in Kissinger's early critique of detente and his subsequent favorable appraisal once he joined the Nixon administration.

Before he became Nixon's national security adviser, Kissinger wrote that the international system was subject to deep-seated structural problems, due to the state of upheaval in the world and dissimilar concepts of the "rules of the game" by the two major powers.[23] He considered the Soviet Union and the P.R.C. revolutionary powers dissatisfied with the status quo and determined to subvert the existing order.[24] In such a revolutionary situation the U.S. faced two choices. It could oppose revolutionary attempts to overturn the existing order, or it could decide to ease and even accommodate the transition of the revolutionary states into the existing order. Kissinger suggested the construction of an international system based on "an agreed concept of order" similar to the 19th century balance of power system, but altered to reflect the changes and demands of the late 20th century.[25]

With respect to basing this concept of order on detente, Kissinger argued that the mutual fear of nuclear war "did not automatically produce detente" and that every past Soviet-U.S. detente had proved stillborn.[26] As late as 1968, he described past detentes as tactical Soviet peace offensives characterized more by atmosphere than substance. He therefore insisted that any future policy be based on specific ground rules. For example, the U.S.S.R. should be penalized for intransigence, negotiations should address only concrete issues, and arms race moderation should be emphasized.[27]

Once Kissinger became Nixon's national security adviser, his public views altered. He began describing the Soviets as less revolutionary, more status quo-oriented, and more interested in a stable relationship with the U.S. [28] Pessimistic about American prospects of coping with the changes in the international system as vigorously as in the past and of containing the U.S.S.R., he hoped to ease the Soviets into a partnership or detente with the U.S. Part of the reasoning behind this hope was the perception that the U.S. was declining strategically, increasingly unable or unwilling to translate military power into political strength, and compelled to coexist with the U.S.S.R. Unfortunately, controversy surrounded the definition of detente. As applied to political relations, it referred to a relaxation of tensions between adversaries. As articulated by Kissinger, it also implied the hope for eventual Soviet reciprocation of Western views of acceptable international behavior. Beyond these general meanings and hopes, Western definitions fell into numerous categories such as detente as rapprochement and as an alternative to the cold war. Western enthusiasts assumed that detente reflected a mutual superpower interest in avoiding confrontation, accepting interdependence and the subsequent necessity of restraint and reaching arms control agreements.

However, despite the presumed universality of the necessity for detente, Soviet and Western definitions differed substantially. In the first place, the Soviets more often employed the term *mirnoe sosushchestvovaniya* or peaceful coexistence rather than *razryadka*, which means relaxation, to describe their concept of the force that regulates East-West relations. The Soviets defined peaceful coexistence as an offensive strategy of class struggle with capitalism that included the necessity of military readiness to survive and win a nuclear war.[29] When defining peaceful coexistence the Soviets referred to the intensification of the pursuit of ideological objectives. Brezhnev, for example, made the following comments shortly after the 1972 summit:

We soberly and realistically evaluate the current situation. Despite the successes in relaxing international tension, a hard struggle against the enemies of peace, national and social liberation faces us...Striving for the confirmation of the principle of peaceful coexistence, we recognize that successes in this important matter in no way signify the possibility of weakening the ideological struggle. On the contrary, it is necessary to be prepared that this struggle will intensify.[30]

In sum, peaceful coexistence required continued support for revolutionary or national liberation movements and the ideological subversion of capitalist states. Given this requirement, the Soviets explicitly denied that peaceful coexistence entailed the acceptance of the status quo. According to a recent Soviet report, "one of the fundamental contradictions between the imperialist ideology and Marxist-Leninist ideology is reflected in their vastly different approach to the status quo. Attempts by Western ideologists to replace the policy of peaceful coexistence with the policy of perpetuating the status quo are incompatible with the objective laws of social development"[31] According to one group of critics, Soviet concept of detente denoted little more than a "strategic alternative to overtly military antagonism against the so-called 'capitalist' countries."[32]

Kissinger, however, explained away discrepancies in Soviet and American definitions, and described the framework for a process of detente to be established under his careful tutelage. He defined detente as "the pursuit of relaxation of tensions" and the "search for a more constructive relationship with the Soviet Union" based on the following principles: 1) The U.S. must resist Soviet pressure and aggression, but respond to moderate behavior. 2) The U.S. must maintain a strong national defence, yet not expect political power to flow automatically from military strength. 3) The U.S. must honor the moral commitment to freedom, yet accept the limited ability to produce internal changes in other countries. 4) The U.S. must recognize that both sides should receive advantages in any constructive relationship.[33] He argued that, while the U.S. and the U.S.S.R. were bound to compete, parallel interests provided real stakes in negotiation.[34] While previously skeptical of a fear-inspired policy, Kissinger now discussed the survival imperative as the primary motivating force behind detente. He assumed that the nuclear threat endangered both powers equally, generated a mutual interest in avoiding a nuclear resolution of Soviet-American competition, and provided a vested interest in stability.[35]

Kissinger argued that the Soviets shared these motivations and concerns. In addition to their fear of war, the complexities of the international system, problems with the P.R.C., economic debility, and incipient social unrest in the Soviet bloc also provided the Soviets with incentives to alleviate international tension. Consequently, Kissinger expected the 1970s to be a propitious time for improved Soviet-American relations.[36]

Nixon agreed. In 1970 he and Kissinger listed the three goals of their agenda: Peace Through Partnership and the Nixon Doctrine, Maintaining America's Strength, and establishing the Era of Negotiation. In these Nixon reiterated America's determination to remain faithful to its treaty commitments, to protect the security of nations vital to American interests, and to deter aggression.[37] However, the U.S. and its allies had to re-order their priorities and obligations. Where American interests and commitments were not directly involved, the American role would be limited to using influence rather than military intervention. Nixon expected allies to share the burden of defense and participate more fully

in the determination of their own fate. According to Nixon, "Neither the defense nor the development of other nations can be exclusively or primarily an American undertaking. The nations of each part of the world should assume the primary responsibility for their own well being."[38] While the administration carefully encouraged the perception that the Nixon Doctrine did not entail a global American retreat, allies, adversaries, and other audiences reacted as if this were precisely the case.

The Nixon Doctrine itself did not alienate American allies, who also realized the need for greater independence. But the callous manner of its announcement alienated Japan and many Europeans. While the Nixon Doctrine did not apply to Europe specifically, many Europeans took it as implied. American posturings while attempting to assure NATO partners of its commitment aroused fears about America's fading credibility and commitment to Europe. Japan also resented abandonment by a U.S. willing to subordinate Japanese interests to detentes with the P.R.C and the U.S.S.R. A genuine lack of dialogue between the U.S. and Japan contributed to a scramble by the Japanese to assert political and economic independence from the U.S. and meet Chinese economic advances. An additional negative result of the doctrine was the impression it evidently made on Soviet leaders, who many times stated the conviction that the Nixon Doctrine demonstrated the decline of U.S. power and the forced adherence to the Soviet policy of peaceful coexistence.[39] However, Nixon and Kissinger believed that the Doctrine, which intended to scale down American commitments and elevate the role of allies, represented a practical adaption to the changes in the international system.

A balance of power between the superpowers was as essential to the Nixon/Kissinger structure of peace, as was a pluralist world of resourceful, powerful, and self-reliant partner states. The Nixon administration's concept of a balance of power differed from the classical definition where five more or less equal states in the balance of power system sought only marginal advantage over each other, and where a "balancer" allied itself in opposition to the strongest or most assertive members. According to Nixon, in a system of only two military superpowers, marginal advantage would be difficult to achieve or maintain over time, since a race for increments of power included risks of nuclear war.[40] In the nuclear age, mutual restraint and accommodation must replace attempts at marginal gain. A balance in the 1970s required that "all nations, adversaries and friends alike, must have a stake in preserving the international system," feel that national interests were secure, and "see positive incentives for keeping the peace."[41] Nixon and Kissinger supported a balance of power-based detente as the best method of introducing the Soviets to the benefits of preserving the global system. They preferred this to a dangerous attempt to contain the Soviets or to reverse, by force, the pattern of American decline and Soviet ascendancy.

Kissinger considered efforts to redress the military imbalance solely through a military response impractical, given public aversion to defense

spending in the wake of Vietnam and the American strategic decline in the late 1960s, and provocative, given expanding Soviet power. However, aware that detente with a compromised military deterrent invited Soviet challenges, Nixon and Kissinger emphasized the *second* goal of their agenda: maintaining military strength. Prevention of Soviet exploitation of American desires for balance and detente required vigilance, firmness, and exertion. Since these rather than good will deterred war, Nixon stressed that

> strong military defenses are not the enemy of peace; they are the guardians of peace. Our ability to build a stable and tranquil world—to achieve an arms control agreement, for example—depends on our ability to negotiate from a position of strength. We seek adequate power not as an end in itself but as a means for achieving our purposes. And our purpose is peace.[42]

As a further warning to the Soviets, Nixon urged maintaining a

> strong military power even as we seek mutual limitation and reduction of arms. We do not mistake climate for substance. We based our policies on the actions and capabilities of others, not just on estimates of their intentions. Detente is not the same as lasting peace. And peace does not guarantee tranquility or mean the end of contention. The world will hold perils for as far ahead as we can see.[43]

Adherence to the philosophy of negotiating from strength departed little from traditional American foreign policy. But this did not eliminate intense congressional debate over the levels of defense spending and the direction, quality, and disposition of the military posture from 1969-1974. In the meantime, declining budgets and military preparedness, and the holding pattern in strategic programs compromised this second goal of the Nixon foreign policy framework. Nixon and Kissinger expected SALT I to remedy this compromised position. In fact, the second goal of maintaining military strength depended on the *third* goal of establishing an era of negotiation.

Nixon and Kissinger counted on a Soviet acquisition of a stake in the process of negotiation because the Soviets now realized that more could be achieved by negotiation—defusing Western hostility, decreasing military expenditures (kept high during arms races), and expanding trade—than by seeking unilateral advantages that only accelerated the suicidal prospects of a nuclear war. They anticipated that cooperation in several substantive areas would lead to other agreements that would encourage new habits of cooperation. In his 1973 Report to Congress, Nixon described his attempts

> ...To create circumstances that would offer the Soviet leaders an opportunity to move away from confrontation through carefully prepared negotiations. We hoped that the Soviet Union would acquire a stake in a wide spectrum of negotiations and would become convinced that its interests, like ours, would be best served if this process involved most of our relations. We sought, above all, to create a vested interest in mutual restraint.[44]

The Nixon administration expressed confidence in the prospects of balancing the negative aspects of superpower interaction with success in dealing with substantive issues like Berlin, SALT, the Middle East, and Vietnam. It assumed that successful negotiation over these issues that divided the U.S. and the U.S.S.R. would profoundly alter the substance of the Soviet-American relationship. The formula known as linkage guided the administration's approach to negotiations over these interrelated issues. The administration rejected the notion of selective detente, and insisted that disturbances in one area would contribute to disillusionment with the entire Soviet-American relationship. However, from the beginning, the Soviets rejected the notion of linkage and insisted on the non-linkage of SALT with extraneous political or ideological matters. In addition, as mentioned earlier, their approach to detente was selective. It applied to avoiding nuclear war, but not to the class struggle, national liberation movements, or internal discipline. Apparently, the administration expected the Soviet interest in detente eventually to override the rejection of linkage.

In 1971 Nixon initiated private exchanges with the Soviet leaders in an effort to break the deadlock over negotiations on SALT and Berlin. Progress in dealing with the legal status of West Berlin which, with the 1971 signing of the Four Power Agreement, opened the way for direct negotiation between East and West Germany on access to the city encouraged Nixon. With this obstacle to rapprochement dealt with, the U.S. and the Soviets prepared for bilateral summit negotiations on the whole pattern of their interaction.

Administration officials envisaged four results of the 1972 summit: 1) Improving political relations would lead to "discussions on a wide range of projects for bilateral cooperation."[45] As cooperation increased and as a series of agreements emerged, the trend toward a more constructive political relationship would be reinforced. 2) Improvement of political relations would make it possible to address economic cooperation. 3) SALT negotiations would be completed. 4) Fundamental principles governing Soviet-U.S. relations could be delineated. In contrast to his earlier skepticism, Kissinger now approved of direct communication between the leaders of the two superpowers to provide a mechanism for resolution of their differences and, as the two powers cooperated in political, economic, and military agreements, to create a network of mutually reinforcing cooperative endeavors.

The Middle East, European security, and Vietnam were also discussed at the summit. While reaching no specific agreements, the administration became convinced that the Soviets shared the desire to manage conflicts in these areas. By discussing these problems face-to-face with the Soviets, the administration hoped to facilitate a basic understanding of each state's position and to remove sources of political tension. However exciting the prospects for cooperation in political areas, the Anti-Ballistic Missile Treaty and in the Interim Offensive Agreement (SALT I) commanded most of the attention of the two powers. (See chapter IV for discussion of the SALT process.)

While the shadow of Watergate, public disillusionment with presidential abuse of power, and economic stagflation plagued Nixon's second term, the effort to regularize superpower interaction continued. During the 1973 summit, Nixon reiterated his belief that there was no alternative to detente in the nuclear age, that the superpowers shared a recognition of their responsibility to limit arms, and that summits brought the superpowers closer together.[46] The two powers signed several, largely cosmetic, agreements on atomic energy, agriculture, the oceans, transportation, and cultural exchanges, and they agreed to work toward removing the danger of nuclear war. However, the two sides failed to replace the "interim" SALT agreement.

Kissinger explained away this failure by pointing to Nixon's and Brezhnev's proven commitment to arms limitation, reducing the danger of nuclear war, and strengthening international security. He saw a special "significance in having the relationship develop on such a broad front, developing on both sides a commitment that is becoming increasingly difficult to reverse."[47] These reflections on the symbolic importance of agreements highlighted the administration's position that the fact of an agreement almost superseded its substance. A reading of the objectives of the agreement on the prevention of nuclear war—to remove the danger of war, avoid crises or threats of force, and to consult during crises—also suggested the importance of promisory symbols.

Nixon and Kissinger believed that detente offered economic as well as political and strategic benefits to the superpowers. Consequently, Nixon and Kissinger began emphasizing the importance of trade as a method of accelerating superpower cooperation. As political relations normalized, the prospects for economic normalization brightened. With this in mind, Nixon promised the U.S.S.R. Most Favored Nation (MFN) status and commercial credits. In return he expected the Soviets to purchase more from, and sell more to, the U.S., thus aiding the American balance of trade picture and opening up access to Soviet natural resources such as liquid natural gas. On the other hand, the administration expected more than financial rewards to result from expanded trade. It hoped that as trade increased political relaxation also would increase.

For critics this hope for general economic and political tradeoffs did not compensate for technology transfers to the Soviets or for the unconditional extension of trading privileges to such a repressive regime. In answer to the first complaint, Kissinger thought it a mistake to limit Soviet-American trade to prevent technology from reaching the Soviets, since Western technology was available from other non-Communist sources. He argued that "Boycott denies us a means of influence and possible commercial gain; it does not deprive the U.S.S.R. of technology."[48] The U.S. also should not limit the flow of credit to the Soviet Union because, while it represented only a fraction of the capital available to the Soviets, it gave the U.S. some influence over the Soviets through the "ability to control the scope of trade relationships." Kissinger hoped that trade with the Soviet Union would "leaven the autarkic tendencies of the Soviet system, invite gradual association of the Soviet economy with the world economy, and foster a degree of interdependence that adds an element of stability to the political relationship."[49]

In answer to the complaint from those who wanted to exchange human rights concessions for expansion of American trade with the Soviets, Kissinger argued that the Soviets could not be expected to exchange internal concessions for MFN privileges. Speaking of the limited efficacy of economic leverage, Kissinger pointed out that "denial of economic relations cannot by itself achieve what it failed to do when it was part of a determined policy of political and military confrontation."[50] The U.S. could not be expected to force the Soviets into political concessions that unilaterally favored the U.S. because "the laws of mutual advantage operate or there will be no trade."[51] The principle of reciprocity, then, dictated the conduct of trade; the Soviets would entertain compromise only so long as economic advantages outweighed political disadvantages.

The administration had to decide whether to insist on Soviet compliance to international standards of human rights or to strive for influence over its foreign behavior by involving the Soviets in agreements designed to create interest in restraint and cooperation. Two factors complicated this decision. First, the administration doubted American ability to change the domestic structure of the U.S.S.R. Second, while the administration deplored Soviet internal repression, it weighed this against the overriding concern for preventing a return to cold war practices. The administration believed that a reversal of detente, inherent in the suggestion that unless the Soviet Union became more democratic the U.S. should forego detente, might not persuade the Soviets to alter their system, but might lead to increased tension. After all, the Soviets might interpret such a suggestion as a Western ploy to undermine Communism. Nixon reminded critics that "We cannot gear our foreign policy to transformations of other societies. In the nuclear age, our first responsibility must be the prevention of a war that could destroy all societies...Peace between nations with totally different systems is also a high moral objective."[52] The attempt to decrease international tension represented a higher moral objective than democraticizing the Soviet domestic system.

However, the belief that the U.S. could not afford to delay detente until the Soviet Union changed its domestic policies did not imply carte blanche for the Soviets. Nixon and Kissinger reminded critics that the Soviets already had made concessions on Berlin and on emigration policies. They also suggested that repression of dissidence indicated that detente had generated increased ferment within the Soviet Union.[53] Kissinger argued that detente, even without the overt pressure demanded by critics, promoted demands for internal freedom in the Soviet Union. Eventually, as contacts increased, the Soviets would fear the West less and have less reason to maintain rigid control over their social and economic system. Thus detente would serve as a catalyst for a gradual transformation of the Soviet system—a transformation not dependent on direct pressure but on subtle influence.

As suggested above, Kissinger's philosophy consisted of a mixture of idealism, egoism, and fatalism. For example, his rhetoric exuded confidence in the construction of a durable peace, and he presumed that the Soviets shared, to a certain extent, American satisfaction with the political status quo. However, overriding these surface characteristics, Kissinger's approach to Soviet-U.S. relations was dominated by his philosophical fatalism, tempered by his apparent conviction that he personally could modify behavior and create a new international order via detente. The following passage from Kissinger's memoirs reflects the mixture of these ingredients.

> We are involved in a delicate balancing act: to be committed to peace without letting the quest for it become a form of moral disarmament, surrendering all other values; to be prepared to defend freedom while making it clear that unconstrained rivalry could risk everything, including freedom, in a nuclear holocaust...A successful policy needs both elements: incentive for Soviet restraint (such as economic links), and penalties for adventurism...To maintain the dual track of firmness and conciliation required a disciplined Executive Branch and a Congress and public with confidence in their government...It was a complex task beyond any previous experience...To some extent my interest in detente was tactical...And yet there was a residue reflecting the unprecedented challenge of our period; a conviction that the moral imperative of leadership in our time was to keep open the prospect, however slim, of a fundamental change, of doing our utmost so that Armageddon did not descend on us through neglect or lack of foresight.[54]

In essence, Kissinger accepted American's political and strategic deterioration and the lack of public will to resist it. With repeated references to the futility of regaining decisive strategic preponderance or insisting on moderate Soviet internal behavior, Kissinger displayed a fatalistic view of American prospects. According to his testimony in the 1974 detente hearings, American efforts to redress this increasingly negative situation through any policy other than detente would be dangerous and provocative, especially at a time when Soviet physical power and influence were greater than ever. In his view, then, the most effective method of dealing with this unfavorable situation was to draw the U.S.S.R. into partnership with the U.S. If the U.S. engaged the Soviets in arms limitation agreements, economic exchanges, and arrangements to control crises, it could protect its interests despite growing Soviet preponderance. With such agreements, Nixon and Kissinger had hoped to reinforce a Soviet orientation toward the maintenance of the status quo, and to provide the Soviets with tangible incentives to seach for additional areas in which to derive benefits unattainable in periods of hostility.

## Detente Falters, 1977-1980

Jimmy Carter hoped to accelerate this orientation even further. Unfortunately he inherited a disintegrating international balance of power and public disillusionment with a faltering detente. Detente

faltered as the Soviets violated what many Americans considered to be the principles of detente (restraint and stability) by their actions in the Middle East in 1973, Angola in 1975, and Vietnam from 1974-75. In addition, since 1972 the Soviet Union moved from a position of strategic parity to partial military superiority, successfully identified itself with third world national liberation forces, and appeared to consolidate its position as the superpower equal of the U.S. The U.S., on the other hand, experienced a more vulnerable strategic force, declining international influence and a continuing political, economic, and social malaise at home. Consequently, in 1977 Carter inherited a fractured detente apparently exclusive of Soviet revolutionary activities in the third world, and perhaps exclusive of Soviet moderation generally. Detente appeared to be as the Soviets defined it—selective and limited to direct Soviet-American interaction.

Given these semantic inconsistencies and international developments, which demonstrated the fragility of detente, the questions facing Carter concerned whether the relative power ratio between the U.S. and the Soviets had changed since 1972, and to what extent the changes affected detente. While it may be impossible to discover completely the relative power positions of the U.S. and the Soviet Union, both the Nixon and Carter administrations acknowledged that the U.S. no longer possessed nuclear superiority nor political predominance. Both reported steady increases in Soviet military capability and expressed varying levels of concern over an expanded Soviet global role. But, aside from the potential threat to American security, how did this changing situation affect detente?

In essence, Carter shared the Nixon/Kissinger belief in three major premises of detente: that the U.S. and the Soviet Union had a mutual interest in avoiding nuclear war, were satisfied with nuclear parity, and were interested in stabilizing the international system. The Carter administration sought to realize these objectives through its negotiations over SALT II. According to national security adviser Zbigniew Brzezinski, SALT II not only "provides an increase in stability" but it also "creates a psychological and political climate that makes nuclear war less likely."[55] The Department of State reaffirmed the administration's faith in the political and strategic hat trick provided by SALT:

> First, any SALT agreement must permit the United States to maintain the strategic forces which are at least equal to those of the Soviet Union. Second, it should maintain and, if possible, enhance the stability of the strategic balance, thereby reducing the possibility of nuclear war. In addition, an agreement should support and give substance to a political relationship with the Soviets which reduces tension and controls competition and, hence, expenditures for strategic forces.[56]

Carter and Secretary of State Cyrus Vance assumed that these objectives were realistic because the Soviets surely appreciated that negotiation to preserve a stable military and political balance was "the surest guarantee of peace" and the only alternative to unrestrained arms races.[57]

In sum, then, Carter accepted many of the Nixon administration's notions about stability, detente, and the SALT process. However, differences existed, and they reflected the more disadvantageous international system that influenced Carter to reverse the cause and effect relationship between SALT and detente. Carter, instead of concentrating on establishing detente in order to facilitate the SALT process, emphasized the role of SALT as a precondition for detente. This represented an interesting derivative of the Nixon/Kissinger assumption that SALT I resulted directly from improving superpower relations. According to Nixon and Kissinger, as relations improved and as the superpowers successfully negotiated over divisive issues, they could build on this pattern of behavior and arrive at a strategic arms limitation treaty. However, Carter, given a more tenuous detente, emphasized the SALT framework, as a catalyst facilitating a more stable Soviet-U.S. relationship.

Carter referred to the SALT treaty as "a fundamental element of strategic and political stability in a turbulent world—stability which can provide the necessary political basis for us to contain the kinds of crises that we face today and to prevent their growing into a terrible nuclear confrontation."[58] In a similar vein, SALT II was to be a continuing process that would provide" a framework for guidance toward new areas of cooperation and for facing peacefully those areas in which we still compete."[59] Detente was subsumed then, within the SALT process and depended upon the passage of SALT II. According to former SALT negotiator Paul Warnke, "if SALT fails, the chances of improved relations and of channeling Soviet-American rivalry into less dangerous areas of competition would be immeasurably damaged...(and) would leave us with a very dismal prospect of achieving (detente.)"[60]

The first major distinction, then, from Kissinger's detente (detente I) concerned Carter's task of reviving detente by concluding SALT II. This reversal of cause and effect may have endangered American security, if it encouraged the sacrificing of strategic objectives for political objectives. To determine the extent of this threat, several questions need to be addressed: 1) Did the U.S. sacrifice strategic objectives for political objectives; i.e., was SALT II an equitable treaty that protected U.S. security? 2) Did the SALT process contribute to the political objective of detente? (These questions will be discussed further in Chapter IV.)

A second major distinction concerned the notion of linkage. Carter, deemphasized linkage of Soviet international activities and SALT, and insisted, as late as October of 1979, that SALT II could not be held hostage to Soviet activities in Africa, Cuba, or Afghanistan. According to Carter, it was "precisely because we have fundamental differences with the Soviet Union that we are determined to bring this dangerous dimension of our military competition under control."[61] However, in 1980 Carter reassessed the idea of linkage and appeared to have realized that his rejection of the linkage aspect of his detente II had invited the Soviet Union's expectation that it could undertake military actions in Afghanistan without fear of an effective American response. He then argued that Soviet behavior in Afghanistan jeoparized detente and SALT

II. A final look at linkage will be made below and in subsequent chapters where an attempt is made to determine the extent to which detente depends upon Soviet behavior in the world.

A third distinction concerned the origins of Soviet-American detente. In essence, detente II derived perhaps its only uniqueness from the fact that the U.S. initiated it. Previous abortive detentes were initiated and terminated almost at will by the Soviets. For example, the Nixon-Brezhnev detente originated from an active Soviet concern for limiting the U.S. ABM program, keeping the U.S. and China apart, and expanding trade. Detente II, however, emerged from Carter's invitation to the Soviets to reduce arms drastically and to live up to the promises of detente. Now that the U.S., rather than the Soviet Union, was approaching a position of weakness compared to the 1960s, Carter sought to use the SALT process to interest the Soviets in an improved Soviet-American relationship. He hoped to persuade the Soviets that their best interest lay in a closer partnership with the U.S. After his first moves in this direction, Carter made verbal overtures to the Soviets and backed these up with salesmanlike vigor. He offered trade deals, MFN status, and elimination of controls over the sale of strategic technology to the Soviets.

In sum, convinced of a greatly altered global system in the 1970s, with the Soviets ascendant but mellowed; the U.S. ready to accept political and military parity; allies increasingly independent; and third worlders insistently non-aligned yet often anti-West, vulnerable to external intervention, and caught in a web of economic dependency on the West, Carter tried to salvage detente in the interest of all these states. Urging escape from the grip of anti-communist paranoia, he elected to tempt, rather than force, the Soviets into self-containment. He offered the enticements of SALT II, increased trade and fewer pesky demands for internal and external changes in Soviet behavior.

Unfortunately for Carter, the events of the late 1970s conspired against the already infirm detente. In addition, contrasting Soviet and American objectives and interests in restraint and the Soviet view of detente as a tool to alter the balance of power in their favor by all means short of war further undercut his endeavor to establish a mutual superpower affirmation that they held certain principles of behavior in common. For example, the justification of detente as a survival imperative, given the nuclear reality, ignored the Soviet commitment to detente guaranteed by Soviet military superiority. In addition, while Carter thought that Soviet willingness to negotiate over SALT II reflected common purposes, Soviet doctrine, weapons deployment, and actions suggested otherwise.

Carter's attempt to re-structure Soviet-American relations also failed for a number of reasons relating to the distinction between detente I and II. In the first area of distinction—the emphasis on SALT II as a precondition for detente—Carter pursued SALT for other than purely strategic reasons. Expecting a reciprocal Soviet view of the imperative of stability, Carter highlighted the hypothetical contribution of SALT to political stability as much as its strategic contributions. Consequently, the failure of SALT II to produce an improved Soviet-U.S. relationship, undermined

Carter's political rationale for urging SALT, as well as detente. This failure relates closely to the second distinction between detente I and II—lack of linkage between Soviet foreign policy behavior and SALT II. Carter's position on linkage fluctuated between insisting on Soviet compliance with international standards of human rights; minimizing the linkage of Soviet activities in Angola, Cuba, and Ethiopia to SALT II; and asserting that the move into Afghanistan jeopardized both detente and SALT. Such inconsistency derived from Carter's initial attempt to separate the pursuit of SALT II from Soviet foreign policy behavior. However, this attempt may have convinced the Soviets that they could undertake military actions, in Afghanistan for example, without much active American resistance.

The third distinction of Carter's detente— its American initiation—may have further convinced the Soviets that the U.S., in its eagerness to negotiate SALT and reestablish detente, would hesitate to respond to Soviet military actions. By persuading the Soviets that he believed there were no alternatives, other than cold war and arms races, to detente and SALT, Carter invited Soviet exploitation. The Soviets in negotiations and crises in the 1970s, exerted considerable pressure in the third world to see how far the U.S. could be pushed, in its unwillingness to jeopardize detente, before it reacted to Soviet challenges. While the U.S.S.R. retained an interest in easing nuclear tensions, its efforts to upset the status quo where possible indicated another interest in exploiting whatever opportunities Soviet supremacy and American weakness provided. This behavior demonstrated the limited nature of detente II and the unchanged Soviet dedication to the overthrow of any status quo oriented balance of power.

This attempt at distinguishing between detentes I and II suggests that Carter's detente II was characterized by more hesitation, more inconsistency, and less effectiveness than detente I and, consequently jeopardized the prospects of international stability and an improvement in Soviet-U.S. relations. During the Carter tenure, the Soviets often acted as if they expected ineffective American responses to Soviet challenges to stability and detente whether in South East Asia, Africa, Yemen, or Afghanistan. If these impressions about Carter and the Soviets were correct, two tasks faced the U.S. after Carter: 1) to remove the Soviet impression of American ineffectiveness, which encouraged risk taking and assertiveness, and 2) to persuade the Soviet Union to abandon its quest for superiority.

Despite this rather bleak portrait of detente (few deny that detente failed in many of its objectives), not all would agree with my assertions about the causes of its decline. Garthoff, for example, blames Soviet *and* American misperceptions of each other's definition of, and expectations for, detente. He also pondered four additional fatal fears and features: (1) failure to devise a regime of crisis management; (2) failure to define a mutually acceptable code of conduct, due to each side's application of a one-sided double standard in perceiving and judging the behavior of the other, (in other words, each side presumably held the other to an idealized view of detente, and then was disappointed when the "partner"

violated the code); (3) mutual fear that the other side was acquiring destabilizing strategic capabilities and thus undermining detente; and (4) failure to appreciate the relationship of detente to internal political pressures.[62] While Garthoff is undoubtedly correct in noting these avoidable failures in perception and wisdom, before accepting his suggestions about resuscitating detente, the Reagan interpretation and preferences must be examined further.

## REFERENCES

[1]Raymond L. Garthoff, *Detente and Confrontation: American-Soviet Relations from Nixon to Reagan*, (Washington: Brookings, 1985): 1120-1122.

[2]Charles Wolf, Jr., "Extended Containment," in Aaron Wildavsky, ed., *Beyond Containment: Alternative American Policies Toward the Soviet Union*. (San Francisco: Institute for Contemporary Studies Press, 1983): 147.

[3]George F. Kennan's "Long Telegram, 1946," quoted in Thomas G. Paterson, ed., *Major Problems in American Foreign Policy: Documents and Essays, Volume II: Since 1914*, (Lexington: Heath, 1968): 278.

[4]Wildavsky, *Beyond Containment*, 16.

[5]Kennan, "The Sources of Soviet Conduct," *Foreign Affairs* 25 (July 1947): 581.

[6]Kennan, "Long Telegram, 1946," in Paterson, *Major Problems in American Foreign Policy*, 279.

[7]Kennan, quoted in John Lewis Gaddis, *Strategies of Containment: A Critical Appraisal of Postwar American National Security Policy*, (New York: Oxford University Press, 1982): 71.

[8]National Security Council Memorandum #68 (NSC-68), 1950, declassified text quoted in the *Naval War College Review* (May-June 1975): 51-108.

[9]NSC-68, 68.

[10]NSC-68, 80 and 107-108.

[11]Robert Johnson, "Exaggerating America's Stakes in Third World Conflicts," *International Security* 10 (Winter 1985-86): 43.

[12]Johnson, "Exaggerating America's Stakes in Third World Conflicts, 44.

[13]Stephen E. Ambrose, *Rise to Globalism: American Foreign Policy Since 1938*, (New York: Viking Penguin, 1985): 132-179; see also *Eisenhower, the President Vol. II*, (New York: Simon & Schuster, 1984.)

[14]John Foster Dulles, "Policy for Security and Peace," *Foreign Affairs* 32 (April 1954): 357-358.

[15]Gaddis, *Strategies of Containment*, 214.

[16]John F. Kennedy, "The President's New Conference of June 28, 1961," in *Public Papers of the President, 1961* (Government Printing Office, (GPO)1961): 477.

[17]Kennedy, "The Presidents News Conference of July 25, 1961," in *Public Papers of the President, 1961*, 534.

[18]Kennedy, October 1962 speech reprinted in the *New York Times* (October 23, 1982): 5.

[19]Gaddis, *Strategies of Containment*, 202-235.

[20]"Report by Vice President Lyndon B. Johnson on His Visit to Asian Countries," in *The Pentagon Papers* (New York: Bantam Books, 1971): 129.

[21]Johnson, speech quoted in *Public Papers of the President, 1963-1964* (Government Printing Office): 494.

[22]Gaddis, *Strategies of Containment*, 235-236.

[23]Henry A. Kissinger, "Central Issues of American Foreign Policy," in *Agenda for the*

*Nation,* ed. Kermit Gordon (New York: Doubleday, 1968): 585-614.

[24]Kissinger, "Reflections on American Diplomacy," *Foreign Affairs* (October 1956): 44.

[25]Kissinger, "Central Issues of American Foreign Policy," 586.

[26]Ibid., 609-609.

[27]Ibid., 610.

[28]Kissinger, Briefing of Congressional Leaders, June 15, 1972, in *American Foreign Policy,* (New York: W. W. Norton 1974): 140-144. (Hereafter, SALT Briefing.)

[29]See Leonid Brezhnev, *Report of the Central Committee of the Communism, Party of the Soviet Union,* 23rd Congress of the CPSU, 1966 and subsequent Congresses; and F. Ryzhenko, "The Limits of Peaceful Coexistence," *Pravda* (August 22, 1973): 3-4, translated in *Current Digest of Soviet Press* 25 #34, p. 5.

[30]Brezhnev speech quoted in Foy D. Kohler, et. al., *Soviet Strategy for the Seventies: From Cold War to Peaceful Coexistence,* (Miami: Center for Advanced International Studies, 1973): 135.

[31]Analysis by the Institute of Philosophy of the USSR Academy of Science quoted in Kohler, *Soviet Strategy for the Seventies,* 124.

[32]Robert Conquest, et. al., "Detente: An Evaluation," *International Review* 1 (Spring 1974): 13.

[33]Kissinger, Address to The Pilgrims of Great Britain, London, December 12, 1973, in *American Foreign Policy,* 276. And, Statement, U.S. Congress, Senate, Committee on Foreign Relations, *Detente,* 93rd Cong., 2nd sess., 1974, pp. 239 and 247-248. (Hereafter, *Detente Hearing.*)

[34]Kissinger, *Detente Hearing,* 141, 143.

[35]*Detente Hearing,* 239-260; SALT Briefing, 140-144.

[36]Most auspicious, of course, was the suddenly apparent, but long festering, Sino-Soviet split. While the administration denied any exploitative motives for improving the atmosphere between the U.S. and the PRC, the potential political advantages of a Sino-Soviet rift were apparent. Soviet and Chinese mutual pre-occupation with each other could take some of the pressure off the U.S.-USSR relationship. A triangular relationship could be an intriguing alternative to a rigid bipolar situation. See Nixon, "Asia After Vietnam," *Foreign Affairs* 47 (October 1967): 111-125.

[37]See *Setting the Course, The First Year: Major Policy Statements by President Richard Nixon,* (New York: Funk & Wagnalls, 1970), 300-307. (Hereafter *Major Policy Statements.*) And, *United States Foreign Policy for the 1970s: A New Strategy for Peace.* A Report to the Congress, February 18, 1970. (Hereafter, *1970 Foreign Policy Report.*)

[38]Nixon, State of the Union Address, January 22, 1970, in *Major Policy Statements,* 373.

[39]Iu. A. Shevedkov, "The Nixon Doctrine: Declarations and Realities," *S. Sh.A., Ekonomica, Politica, Ideolgiia* (February 1971), in *FBIS, Daily Report: Soviet Union* (March 5, 1971): A2-A35.

[40]Nixon, *U.S. Foreign Policy for the 1970s: Shaping a Durable Peace,* A Report to the Congress, May 3, 1973, *Department of State Bulletin (DOSB)* (June 4, 1973): 833. (Hereafter, *1973 Foreign Policy Report.*)

[41]Ibid., 833.

[42]Nixon, *1972 State of the Union Address, DOSB* 66 #1702 (February 2, 1972): 147.

[43]Nixon, *1973 Foreign Policy Report,* 834.

[44]Nixon, *1973 Foreign Policy Report,* 730-731.

[45]Nixon, *1973 Foreign Policy Report,* 732.

[46]Department of State, *The Washington Summit: General Secretary Brezhnev's Visit to the United States,* (June 18-25, 1973): 2.

[47]Ibid., 54.

[48]Kissinger, *Detente Hearings,* 253.

[49]Ibid., 253.

[50]Ibid., 253.

[51]Ibid., 253.

[52]Nixon, Address at the 124th Commencement Ceremony of the U.S. Naval Academy, June 5, 1974, *DOSB* 71 #1827.

[53]Kissinger, Address, Pacem in Terris III Conference, Washington, October 4, 1973, in *American Foreign Policy*, 264.

[54]Kissinger, *White House Years,* (Boston: Little Brown, 1979) : 1254-55.

[55]Statement by Zbigniew Brzezinski, "American Power and Global Change, " reprinted in Department of State Bureau of Public Affairs, *Current Policy* #81 August 2, 1979, pp. 1-2. (Hereafter, this publication will be referred to as *Current Policy*.)

[56]*The Strategic Arms Limitation Talks*, U.S. Department of State: Bureau of Public Affairs, Special Report 46 (Revised) May 1979, p. 1. (Hereafter referred to as Special Report 46 (Revised).

[57]Testimony by Vance, before the Senate Committee on Foreign Relations (July 9 and 10), reprinted in *Current Policy* #72A, pp. 10-11.

[58]Speech by Jimmy Carter, *Department of State Bulletin (DOSB)* 79, #2024, March 1979,
[58]Speech by Jimmy Carter, *DOSB* 79, #2024, March 1979, pp. 22-23.

[59]Carter, *DOSB* 79, #2028, July 1979, p. 51.

[60]Speech by Paul C. Warnke, former Director of ACDA, *"Arms Control: SALT II-The Home Stretch,"* *DOSB* 78, #2019, October 1978, p. 20.

[61]News Conference by Jimmy Carter, *DOSB* 79, #2024, March 1979, p. 23.

[62]Garthoff, *Detente and Confrontation*, 21 and 1073-1089.

# National Security Council
# Paper No. 68 (NSC-68), 1950

....Two complex sets of factors have now basically altered this historical distribution of power. First, the defeat of Germany and Japan and the decline of the British and French Empires have interacted with the development of the United States and the Soviet Union in such a way that power has increasingly gravitated to these two centers. Second, the Soviet Union, unlike previous aspirants to hegemony, is animated by a new fanatic faith, antithetical to our own, and seeks to impose its absolute authority over the rest of the world. Conflict has, therefore, become endemic and is waged, on the part of the Soviet Union, by violent or non-violent methods in accordance with the dictates of expedience. With the development of increasingly terrifying weapons of mass destruction, every individual faces the ever-present possibility of annihilation should the conflict enter the phase of total war.

On the one hand, the people of the world yearn for relief from the anxiety arising from the risk of atomic war. On the other hand, any substantial further extension of the area under the domination of the Kremlin would raise the possibility that no coalition adequate to confront the Kremlin with greater strength could be assembled. It is in this context that this Republic and its citizens in the ascendance of their strength stand in their deepest peril....

Our overall policy at the present time may be described as one designed to foster a world environment in which the American system can survive and flourish. It therefore rejects the concept of isolation and affirms the necessity of our positive participation in the world community.

This broad intention embraces two subsidiary policies. One is a policy which we would probably pursue even if there were no Soviet threat. It is a policy of attempting to develop a healthy international community. The other is the policy of "containing" the Soviet system. These two policies are closely interrelated and interact on one another. Nevertheless, the distinction between them is basically valid and contributed to a clearer understanding of what we are trying to do....

As for the policy of "containment," it is one which seeks by all means short of war to (1) block further expansion of Soviet power, (2) expose the falsities of Soviet pretensions, (3) induce a retraction of the Kremlin's control and influence and (4) in general, so foster the seeds of destruction within the Soviet system that the Kremlin is brought at least to the point of modifying its behavior to conform to generally accepted international standards....

It was and continues to be cardinal in this policy that we possess superior overall power in ourselves or in dependable combination with other like-minded nations. One of the most important ingredients of power is military strength. In the concept of "containment," the maintenance of a strong military posture is deemed to be essential for two reasons: (1) as an ultimate guarantee of our national security and (2) as an indispensable backdrop to the conduct of the policy of "containment." Without superior aggregate military strength, in being and readily mobilizable, a policy of "containment"—which is in effect a policy of calculated and gradual coercion—is no more than a policy of bluff.

At the same time, it is essential to the successful conduct of a policy of "containment" that we always leave open the possibility of negotiation with the U.S.S.R. A diplomatic freeze—and we are in one now—tends to defeat the very purposes of "containment" because it raises tensions at the same time that it makes Soviet retractions and adjustments in the direction of moderated behavior more difficult. It also tends to inhibit our initiative and deprives us of opportunities for maintaining a moral ascendency in our struggle with the Soviet system.

In "containment" it is desirable to exert pressure in a fashion which will avoid so far as possible directly challenging Soviet prestige, to keep open the possibility for the U.S.S.R. to retreat before pressure with a minimum loss of face and to secure political advantage from the failure of the Kremlin to yield or take advantage of the openings we leave it.

We have failed to implement adequately these two fundamental aspects of "containment." In the face of obviously mounting Soviet military strength ours has declined relatively. Partly as a byproduct of this, but also for other reasons, we now find ourselves at a diplomatic impasse with the Soviet Union, with the Kremlin growing bolder, with both of us holding on grimly to what we have and with ourselves facing difficult decisions....

It is quite clear from Soviet theory and practice that the Kremlin seeks to bring the free world under its dominion by the methods of the cold war. The preferred technique is to subvert by infiltration and intimidation. Every institution of our society is an instrument which it is sought to stultify and turn against our purposes....The doubts and diversities that in terms of our values are part of the merit of a free

system, the weaknesses and the problems that are peculiar to it, the rights and privileges that free men enjoy, and the disorganization and destruction left in the wake of the last attack on our freedoms, all are but opportunities for the Kremlin to do its evil work. Every advantage is taken of the fact that our means of prevention and retaliation are limited by those principles and scruples which are precisely the ones that give our freedom and democracy its meaning for us. None of our scruples deter those whose only code is, "morality is that which serves the revolution."....

At the same time the Soviet Union is seeking to create overwhelming military force, in order to back up infiltration with intimidation. In the only terms in which it understands strength, it is seeking to demonstrate to the free world that force and the will to use it are on the side of the Kremlin, that those who lack it are decadent and doomed. In local incidents it threatens and encroaches both for the sake of local gains and to increase anxiety and defeatism in all the free world.

The possession of atomic weapons at each of the opposite poles of power, and the inability (for different reasons) of either side to place any trust in the other, puts a premium on a surprise attack against us. It equally puts a premium on a more violent and ruthless prosecution of its design by cold war, especially if the Kremlin is sufficiently objective to realize the improbability of our prosecuting a preventive war. It also puts a premium on piecemeal aggression against others, counting on our unwillingness to engage in atomic war unless we are directly attacked. We run all these risks and the added risk of being confused and immobilized by our inability to weigh and choose, and pursue a firm course based on a rational assessment of each.

The risk that we may thereby be prevented or too long delayed in taking all needful measures to maintain the integrity and vitality of our system is great. The risk that our allies will lose their determination is greater. And the risk that in this manner a descending spiral of too little and too late, of doubt and recrimination, may present us with ever narrower and more desperate alternatives, is the greatest risk of all. For example, it is clear that our present weakness would prevent us from offering effective resistance at any of several vital pressure points. The only deterrent we can present to the Kremlin is the evidence we give that we may make any of the critical points which we cannot hold the occasion for a global war of annihilation.

The risk of having no better choice than to capitulate or precipitate a global war at any of a number of pressure points is bad enough in itself, but it is multiplied by the weakness it imparts to our position in the cold war. Instead of appearing strong and resolute we are continually at the verge of appearing and being alternately irresolute and desperate; yet it is the cold war which we must win, because both the Kremlin design, and our fundamental purpose give it the first priority....

It is necessary to have the military power to deter, if possible, Soviet expansion, and to defeat, if necessary, aggressive Soviet or Soviet-directed actions of a limited or total character....We must organize and enlist the energies and resources of the free world in a positive program

for peace which will frustrate the Kremlin design for world domination by creating a situation in the free world to which the Kremlin will be compelled to adjust. Without such a cooperative effort, led by the United States, we will have to make gradual withdrawals under pressure until we discover one day that we have sacrificed positions of vital interest....we must, by means of a rapid and sustained build-up of the political, economic, and military strength of the free world, and by means of an affirmative program intended to wrest the initiative from the Soviet Union, confront it with convincing evidence of the determination and ability of the free world to frustrate the Kremlin design of a world dominated by its will. Such evidence is the only means short of war which eventually may force the Kremlin to abandon its present course of action and to negotiate acceptable agreements on issues of major importance. The whole success of the proposed program hangs ultimately on recognition by this Government, the American people, and all free peoples, that the cold war is in fact a real war in which the survival of the free world is at stake....

*Excerpts from National Security Council-68, declassified test quoted in the *Naval War College Review* (May/June 1975): 53-54; 67-69; 78-80; 97-98; and 107-108.

## Henry Kissinger - Detente Testimony, 1974*

Tragic as the consequences of violence may have been in the past, the issue of peace and war takes on unprecedented urgency when, for the first time in history, two nations have the capacity to destroy mankind. The destructiveness of modern weapons defines the necessity of the task; deep differences in philosophy and interests between the United States and the Soviet Union point up its difficulty...(However) if peace is pursued to the exclusion of any other goal, other values will be compromised and perhaps lost; but if unconstrained rivalry leads to nuclear conflict, these values, along with everything else, will be destroyed in the resulting holocaust. There can be no peaceful international order without a constructive relationship between the United States and the Soviet Union. There will be no international stability unless both the Soviet Union and the United States conduct themselves with restraint and unless they use their enormous power for the benefit of mankind. Thus, we must be clear at the outset on what the term "detente" entails. It is the search for a more constructive relationship with the Soviet Union. It is a continuing process, not a final condition. And it has been pursued by successive American leaders though the means have varied as have world conditions.

Some fundamental principles guide this policy: The United States does not base its policy solely on Moscow's good intentions. We seek, regardless of Soviet intentions, to serve peace through a systematic resistance to pressure and conciliatory responses to moderate behavior. We must oppose aggressive actions, but we must not seek confrontations

lightly. We must maintain a strong national defense while recognizing that in the nuclear age the relationship between military strength and politically usable power is the most complex in all history. Where the age-old antagonism between freedom and tyranny is concerned, we are not neutral. But other imperatives impose limits on our ability to produce internal changes in foreign countries. Consciousness of our limits is a recognition of the necessity of peace—not moral callousness. The preservation of human life and human society are moral values, too. We must be mature enough to recognize that to be stable in a relationship must provide advantages to both sides and that the most constructive international relationships are those in which both parties perceive an element of gain...

## Current Period of Relaxation of Tensions

What is new in the current period of relaxation of tensions is its duration, the scope of the relationship which has evolved and the continuity and intensity of contact and consultation which it has produced. We sought to explore every avenue toward an honorable and just accommodation while remaining determined not to settle for mere atmospherics. We relied on a balance of mutual interest rather than Soviet intentions....

Cooperative relations, in our view, must be more than a series of isolated agreements. They must reflect an acceptance of mutual obligations and of the need for accommodation and restraints. To set forth principles of behavior in formal documents is hardly to guarantee their observance. But they are reference points against which to judge actions and set goals. The first of the series of documents is the Statement of Principles signed in Moscow in 1972. It affirms: (1) the necessity of avoiding confrontation; (2) the imperative of mutual restraint; (3) the rejection of attempts to exploit tensions to gain unilateral advantages; (4) the renunciation of claims of special influence in the world; and (5) the willingness, on this new basis to coexist peacefully and build a firm long-term relationship....These statements of principles are not an American concession; indeed, we have been affirming them unilaterally for two decades. Nor are they a legal contract; rather, they are an aspiration and a yardstick by which we assess Soviet behavior. We have never intended to rely on Soviet compliance with every principle; we do seek to elaborate standards of conduct which the Soviet Union would violate only to its cost. And if over the long term the more durable relationship takes hold, the basic principles will give it definition, structure, and hope.

## Question of Economic Relations

During the period of the cold war economic contact between ourselves and the U.S.S.R. was virtually nonexistent. The period of confrontation should have left little doubt, however, that economic boycott would not transform the Soviet system or impose upon it a conciliatory foreign policy. Throughout this period the U.S.S.R. was quite prepared to maintain heavy military outlays and to concentrate on capital growth by using the resources of the Communist world alone. The question then

became how trade and economic contact—in which the Soviet Union is obviously interested—could serve the purposes of peace. We have approached the question of economic relations with deliberation and circumspection and as an act of policy not primarily of commercial opportunity. As political relations have improved on a broad basis, economic issues have been dealt with on a comparably broad front. A series of interlocking economic agreements with the U.S.S.R. has been negotiated, side by side with the political progress already noted.

This approach commanded widespread domestic approval. It was considered a natural outgrowth of political progress. At no time were issues regarding Soviet domestic political practices raised. Indeed, not until after the 1972 agreements was the Soviet domestic order invoked as a reason for arresting or reversing the progress so painstakingly achieved. This sudden, ex post facto form of linkage raises serious questions. The significance of trade, originally envisaged as only one ingredient of a complex and evolving relationship, is inflated out of all proportion: The hoped-for results of policy become transformed into preconditions for any policy at all. We recognize the depth and validity of the moral concerns expressed by those who oppose—or put conditions on—expanded trade with the U.S.S.R. But a sense of proportion must be maintained about the leverage our economic relations give us. Denial of economic relations cannot by itself achieve what it failed to do when it was part of a determined policy of political and military confrontation. The economic bargaining ability of most-favored-nation status is marginal. MFN grants no special privilege; it is a misnomer, since we have such agreements with over 100 countries. To continue to deny it is more a political than an economic act. The actual and potential flow of credits from the United States represents a tiny fraction of the capital available to the U.S.S.R. domestically and elsewhere, including Western Europe and Japan. Over time, trade and investment may leaven the autarkic tendencies of the Soviet system, invite gradual association of the Soviet economy with the world economy, and foster a degree of interdependence that adds an element of stability to the political relationship.

## Strategic Arms Competition-Present Situation

We cannot expect to relax international tensions or achieve a more stable international system should the two strongest nuclear powers conduct an unrestrained strategic arms race. Thus, perhaps the single most important component of our policy toward the Soviet Union is the effort to limit strategic weapons competition. The competition in which we now find ourselves is historically unique: Each side has the capacity to destroy civilization as we know it. Failure to maintain equivalence could jeopardize not only our freedom but our very survival. The lead time for technological innovation is so long, yet the pace of change so relentless that the arms race and strategic policy itself are in danger of being driven by technological necessity. When nuclear arsenals reach levels involving thousands of launchers and over 10,000 warheads, and when the characteristics of the weapons of the two sides are so incommensurable, it

becomes difficult to determine what combination of numbers of strategic weapons and performance capabilities would give one side a military and political superiority. At a minimum clear changes in the strategic balance can be achieved only by efforts so enormous and by increments so large that the very attempt is highly destabilizing.

The prospect of a decisive military advantage, even if theoretically possible, is politically intolerable; neither side will passively permit a massive shift in the nuclear balance. Therefore, the probable outcome of each succeeding round of competition is the restoration of a strategic equilibrium, but at increasingly higher and more complex levels of forces. The arms race is driven by political as well as military factors. While a decisive advantage is hard to calculate, the appearance of inferiority—whatever its actual significance—can have serious political consequences. Thus, each side has a high incentive to achieve not only the reality but the appearance of equality. In a very real sense each side shapes the military establishment of the other. If we are driven to it, the United States will sustain an arms race. But the political or military benefit which would flow from such a situation would remain elusive. Indeed, after such an evolution it might well be that both sides would be worse off than before the race began....

Achieving Strategic Stability

SALT has become one means by which we and the Soviet Union could enhance stability by setting mutual constraints on our respective forces and by gradually reaching an understanding of the doctrinal considerations that underlie the deployment of nuclear weapons. SALT, in the American conception, is a means to achieve strategic stability by methods other than the arms race. We believed when we signed these agreements—and we believe now—that they had reduced the danger of nuclear war, that both sides had acquired some greater interest in restraint, and that the basis had been created for the present effort to reach a broader agreement...

Where Detente Has Taken Us So Far

Detente has helped to place our alliance ties on a more enduring basis by removing the fear that friendship with the United States involved the risk of unnecessary confrontation with the U.S.S.R. The world has been freer of East-West tensions and conflict than in the fifties and sixties. A series of bilaterial cooperative relations have turned the United States-Soviet relationship in a far more positive direction. We have achieved unprecedented agreements in arms limitations and measures to avoid accidental war.

It is too early to judge conclusively whether this change should be ascribed to tactical considerations. But in a sense, that is immaterial. For whether the change is temporary and tactical, or lasting and basic, our task is essentially the same; to transform that change into a permanent condition devoted to the purpose of a secure peace and mankind's aspiration for a better life. A tactical change sufficiently prolonged becomes a lasting transformation. But the whole process can be jeopardized if it is taken for granted. As the cold war recedes in memory, detente can come to seem so natual that it appears safe to levy progressively greater demands on it. The temptation to combine detente with increasing pressure on the Soviet Union will grow. Such an attitude would be disastrous. We would not accept it from Moscow; Moscow will not accept it from us.

Principles To Guide U.S. Detente Course

To be sure, the process of detente raises serious issues for many people. We will be guided by these principles. First, if detente is to endure, both sides must benefit. Second, building a new relationship with the Soviet Union does not entail any devaluation of traditional alliance relations. Third, the emergence of more normal relations with the Soviet Union must not undermine our resolve to maintain our national defense. Fourth, we must know what can and cannot be achieved in changing human conditions in the East. We shall insist on responsible international behavior by the Soviet Union. Beyond this, we will use our influence to the maximum to alleviate suffering and to respond to human appeals. We know what we stand for, and we shall leave no doubt about it. But we cannot demand that the Soviet Union, in effect, suddenly reverse five decades of Soviet, and centuries of Russian, history. Such an attempt would be futile and at the same time hazard all that has already been achieved. Changes in Soviet society have already occurred, and more will come. But they are most likely to develop through an evolution that can best go forward in an environment of decreasing international tensions. A renewal of the cold war will hardly encourage the Soviet Union to change its emigration policies or adopt a more benevolent attitude toward dissent.

Agenda For The Future

Detente is a process, not a permanent achievement. The agenda is full and continuing. Obviously, the main concern must be to reduce the sources of potential conflict. Political competition, especially in moments of crisis, must be guided by the principles of restraint set forth in the documents described earlier. Restraint in crises must be augmented by cooperation in removing the causes of crises. There have been too many instances, notably in the Middle East, which demonstrate that policies of unilateral advantage sooner or later run out of control and lead to the brink of war, if not beyond. The process of negotiations and consultation must be continuous and intense....

We must never forget that the process of detente depends ultimately on habits and modes of conduct that extend beyond the letters of agreements to the spirit of relations. In cataloging the desirable, we must take care not to jeopardize what is attainable. If we justify each agreement with Moscow only when we can show unilateral gain, if we strive for an elusive strategic "superiority", if we systematically block benefits to the Soviet Union, if we try to transform the Soviet system by pressure, and, if, in short, we look for final results before we agree to any results, then we would be reviving the doctrines of liberation and massive retaliation of the 1950's. And we would do so at a time when Soviet physical power and influence in the world are greater than a quarter century ago when those policies were devised and failed.

Soviet actions could destroy detente, as well. If the Soviet Union uses detente to strengthen its military capacity in all fields, if in crises it acts to sharpen tension, if it does not contribute to progress toward stability, if it seeks to undermine our alliances, and if it is deaf to the urgent needs of the least developed and the emerging issues of interdependence, then it in turn tempts a return to the tensions and conflicts we have made such efforts to overcome. We have insisted toward the Soviet Union that we cannot have the atmosphere of detente without the substance. It is equally clear that the substance of detente will disappear in an atmosphere of suspicion and hostility. We have profound indfferences with the Soviet Union—in our values, our methods, our vision of the future. But it is these very differences which compel any responsible administration to make a major effort to create a more constructive relationship....

*Excerpts from Statements, U.S. Congress, Senate Committee on Foreign Relations, *Detente*, 93rd Cong., 2nd sess., 1974, pp. 238-247.

# BIBLIOGRAPHY

## Soviet-American Relations

Alperovitz, Gar. *Atomic Diplomacy: Hiroshima and Potsdam.* New York: Vintage Books, 1967.

Ambrose, Stephen E. *Eisenhower. Vol II: The President.* New York: Simon & Schuster, 1984.
*Rise to Globalism,* 4th ed. New York: Viking Penguin Inc., 1985.

Ball, George W. *Diplomacy for a Crowded World.* Boston: Little, Brown, 1976.

Barnet, Richard. *Roots of War.* New York: Atheneum, 1972.

Bernstein, Barton J., ed. *Politics and Policies of the Truman Administration.* Chicago: Quadrangle, 1970.

Bouscaren, Anthony T. "The Acid Fruits of Detente" *Modern Age* 20 (Fall 1976): 419-430.

Brzezinski, Zbigniew. *Power and Principle: Memoirs of the National Security Adviser, 1977-1981.* New York: Farrar, Straus & Girous, 1983.

Buchan, Alastair. "The Irony of Kissinger," *International Affairs* 50 (July 1974): 367-79.

Carter, Jimmy. *Keeping Faith: Memoirs of a President.* New York: Bantam Books, 1982.

Divine, Robert. *Eisenhower and the Cold War.* New York: Oxford University Press, 1981.

Donovan, Robert J. *Conflict and Crisis: The Presidency of Harry S. Truman, 1945-1948.* New York: Norton, 1977.
*Eisenhower: The Inside Story.* New York: Harper & Row, 1956.

Draper, Theodore. *Abuse of Power.* New York: Viking, 1967.
"Appeasement and Detente," *Commentary,* (February 1976): 27-38.

Eisenhower, Dwight D. *The White House Years, Vol. I: Mandate for Change, 1953-1956.* New York: Doubleday, 1965.

Erickson, John. "Detente: Soviet Policy and Purpose," *Strategic Review* 4 (Spring 1976): 37-43.

Feis, Herbert. *Churchill, Roosevelt, Stalin: The War They Waged and the Peace They Sought.* Princeton: Princeton University Press, 1957.

Fleming, Denna F. *The Cold War and Its Origins. 1917-60.* 2 vols. New York: Doubleday, 1961.

Fulbright, William J. *The Arrogance of Power.* New York: Random House, 1967.

Gaddis, John Lewis. *Strategies of Containment: A Critical Appraisal of Postwar American National Security Policy.* New York: Oxford University Press, 1982.

Graebner, Norman A. *Cold War Diplomacy.* Princeton: Princeton University Press, 1962.

Griffith, William E. *Cold War and Coexistence: Russia, China, and the United States.* Englewood Cliffs, N.J.: Prentice-Hall, 1971.

Halle, Louis, J. *The Cold War as History.* New York: Harper & Row, 1967.

Herring, George C. *America's Longest War The United States and Vietnam, 1950-1975.* New York: John Wiley & Sons, 1979.

Hilsman, Roger. *To Move a Nation.* New York: Dell, 1967.

Hoopes, Townsend. *The Devil and John Foster Dulles.* Boston: Little, Brown, 1973.

Hyland, William. *Soviet-American Relations: A New Cold War.* Santa Monica: Rand, 1981.

Johnson, Lyndon Baines. *The Vantage Point: Perspectives of the Presidency, 1963-1969.* New York: Holt, Rinehart and Winston, 1971.

Karnow, Stanley. *Vietnam: A History.* New York: Viking, 1983.

Kennan, George F. *American Diplomacy, 1900-1950.* New York: Mentor Books, 1952.
    *Memoirs, 1925-1950.* Boston: Little, Brown, 1967.
    *Russia and the West under Lenin and Stalin.* New York: Mentor Books, 1961.
    "The Sources of Soviet Conduct," *Foreign Affairs,* (July 1974): 566-582.

Kissinger, Henry A. *White House Years.* Boston: Little, Brown, 1982.

Kolko, Gabriel. *The Roots of American Foreign Policy,* Boston: Beacon, 1969.

Labedz, Leopold. "Detente or Deception," *International Review* 1 (Spring 1974): 13-28.

Laqueur, Walter. "Pity the Poor Russians?" *Commentary* 71 (February 1981): 13-28.

Legvold, Robert. "Containment Without Confrontation," *Foreign Policy* 40 (Fall 1980): 74-99.

Maddox, Robert James. *The New Left and the Origin of the Cold War.* Princeton: Princeton University Press, 1973.

May, Ernest R. *American Imperialism: A Speculative Essay.* New York: Atheneum, 1968.

Nixon, Richard M. *RN: The Memoirs of Richard Nixon.* New York: Grosset & Dunlap, 1978.

Paterson, Thomas G. et al. *American Foreign Policy: A History.* Lexington: D.C. Health, 1977.
    *On Every Front: The Making of the Cold War.* New York: W. W. Norton, 1979.

Pipes, Richard. "USA-USSR: Preconditions of Detente," *Survey* 21 (Winter-Spring 1975): 43-62.

Podhoretz, Norman. "The Future Danger," *Commentary* 71 (April 1981): 29-47.

Potichnyj, Peter J. and Shapiro, Jane P., eds. *From the Cold War to Detente.* New York: Praeger, 1976.

Ramundo, Bernard A. *Peaceful Coexistence: International Law in the Building of Communism.* Baltimore: Johns Hopkins University Press, 1967.

Rosecrance, Richard, "Detente or Entente?" *Foreign Affairs* 53 (April 1975): 464-481.

Rubinstein, Alvin Z. "The Elusive Parameters of Detente," *Orbis* 19 (Winter 1976): 1344-1358.

Schlesinger, Arthur M., Jr. *A Thousand Days.* Boston: Houghton Mifflin, 1965.

Schwab, George and Friedlander, Henry, eds. *Detente: In Historical Perspective.* New York: Cyrco Press, 1975.

Seabury, Paul. *The Rise and Decline of the Cold War.* New York: Basic Books, 1967.

Sonnefeldt, Helmut. "Russia, America, and Detente," *Foreign Affairs* 56 (January 1978). 275-94.

Steel, Ronald. *Pax Americana.* New York: Viking, 1967.

Stoessinger, John G. *Crusaders and Pragmatists: Movers of Modern American Foreign Policy.* New York: Norton, 1979.

Truman, Harry S. *Memoirs.* Garden City, N.Y.: Doubleday, 1955.

Tucker, Robert W. "Beyond Detente," *Commentary* 63 (March 1977): 42-50.
"The Purposes of American Power," *Foreign Affairs* 59 (Winter 1980-81): 241-273.

Ulam, Adam. *Expansion and Coexistence: The History of Soviet Foreign Policy, 1917-1967.* New York: Praeger, 1968.

Urban, George R. *Detente.* New York: Universe Books, 1976.

Vance, Cyrus. *Hard Choices: Critical Years in America's Foreign Policy.* New York: Simon & Schuster, 1983.

Yergin, Daniel. *Shattered Peace: The Origins of the Cold War and the National Security State.* Boston, Houghton Mifflin, 1978.

## On The Soviets

Albright, David E., ed. *Communism in Africa.* Bloomington: Indiana University Press, 1980.

Arbatov, G. "On Soviet-American Relations," *Kommunist* 3 (February): 101-113. In *CDSP* 25 (May 9, 1973): 1-8.
and Oltmans, Willem. *The Soviet Viewpoint.* New York: Dodd, Mead, 1983.

Aspaturian, Vernon V. *Process and Power in Soviet Foreign Policy.* Boston: Little, Brown, 1971.

Berman, Robert B. and Baker, John C. *Soviet Strategic Forces.* Washington Brookings Institute, 1982.

Bialer, Seweryn, ed. *The Domestic Context of Soviet Foreign Policy.* Boulder: Westview, 1980.

Bogdanov, Radomir and Semeiki, Lev. "Soviet Military Might: A Soviet View," *Fortune* 26 (February 1979): 46-52.

Bradasher, Harry S. *Afghanistan and the Soviet Union.* Durham, N.C.: Duke University Press, 1983.

Brzezinski, Zbigniew. *The Soviet Bloc, Unity and Conflict.* Cambridge: Harvard University Press, 1971.

Carew Hunt, R.N. *The Theory and Practice of Communism, An Introduction.* New York: MacMillan, 1957.

Donaldson, Robert H., ed. *The Soviet Union in the Third World: Success and Failures.* Boulder: Westview, 1980.

Douglass, Joseph. *Soviet Military Strategy in Europe.* New York: Pergamon Press, 1980.
and Hoeber, Amoretta. *Soviet Strategy for Nuclear War.* Stanford: Hoover Institution Press, 1979.

Duncan, W. Raymond, ed. *Soviet Policy in the Third World.* New York: Pergamon Press, 1978.

Dziak, John. *Soviet Perceptions of Military Doctrine and Military Power: The Interaction of Theory and Practice.* New York: National Strategy Information Center, 1981.

Erickson, John. *Soviet Military Power.* London: Royal Institute, 1971 and Edward Fleuchtwanger, eds., *Soviet Military Power and Performance.* London: MacMillan Press, 1979.
"The Soviet View of Deterrence: A General Survey," *Survival* 24 (November-December 1982): 242-251.

Ermarth, Fritz. "Contrasts in American and Soviet Strategic Thought," *International Security* 3 (Fall 1978): 138-55.

Garthoff, Raymond L. *Detente and Confrontation.* Washington, Brookings, 1985.

Glagolev, Igor. "The Soviet Decision-Making Process in Arms Control Negotiations" *Orbis* 21 (Winter 1978): 767-76.

Goure, Leon. *War, Survival, and Soviet Strategy.* University of Miami Press, 1976.

Grechko, A.A. *The Armed Forces of the Soviet State.* Moscow: Voyenizdat, 1974, with revised edition 1975.
*On Guard for Peace and the Building of Communism,* Moscow: Military Publishing House, 1971.

Gromyko, A.A. and Ponomaryov, Boris, eds. *Soviet Foreign Policy, 1917-1980.* 2 Vols. 4th ed. Moscow: Progress Publishers, 1981.

Hoffman, Erik P. and Laird, Robbin F., eds. *Soviet Foreign Policy in a Changing World.* Hawthorne, NY: Aldine, 1986.

Holloway, David. *The Soviet Union and the Arms Race.* New Haven: Yale University Press, 1983.

Horelick, Arnold L. "The Cuban Missile Crisis: An Analysis of Soviet Calculations and Behavior," *World Politics* (April 1964): 363-389.
and Rush, Myron, *Strategic Power and Soviet Foreign Policy.* Chicago: University of Chicago Press, 1966.

Hough, Jerry and Fainsod, Merle. *How the Soviet Union Is Governed.* Cambridge: Harvard University Press, 1979.

Inozemtzev, Nikolai. *Peace and Disarmament: Academic Studies.* Moscow: Progress Publishers, 1980.

Katz, Mark N. "The Soviet Cuban Connection," *International Security* 8 (Summer 1983): 88-112.
*Khrushchev Remembers.* edited by Strobe Talbott. Boston: Little, Brown, 1970.

Kohler, Foy D., et al. *Soviet Strategy for the Seventies: From Cold War to Peaceful Coexistence.* Center for Advanced International Studies, University of Miami, 1973.

Kolkowicz, Roman and Mickiewicz, Ellen Propper. *The Soviet Calculus of Nuclear War.* Lexington, MA: D.C. Heath, 1986.

Kovalev, A.A. "Escalation of Detente and De-escalation of Conflict," *SSHA: Ekonomika, Politika, Ideologiya* 4 (April 1979). Trans. in U.S. Dept. of Commerce, Joint Project Research Service, *USSR Report,* (July 19, 1979): 13-26.

Kulish, Visily. "Detente, International Relations, and Military Might," *Coexistence* 14 #2 (1978): 175-195.

Lambeth, Benjamin S. *How to Think about Soviet Military Doctrine.* Santa Monica: Rand, February, 1978.
"On Thresholds in Soviet Military Thought," *Washington Quarterly* 7 (Spring 1984): 69-76.

Lebednev, Nikolai. *The USSR in World Politics.* Moscow: Progress Publishers, 1980.

Leebaert, Derek. *Soviet Military Thinking.* London: George Allen and Unwin, 1980.

Lockwood, Jonathan. *The Soviet View of U.S. Strategic Doctrine,* New Brunswick: Transaction Books, 1983.

Mackintosh, John M. *Strategy and Tactics of Soviet Foreign Policy.* New York: Oxford University Press, 1963.

Meyer, Stephen M. *Soviet Theatre Nuclear Forces: Part I: Development of Doctrine and Objectives: Part II: Capabilities and Implications.* London: International Institute for Strategic Studies, 1983-1984.

Mil'stein, M.A. and Semejko, L.S. "Problems of the Inadmissability of Nuclear Conflict," *International Studies Quarterly* 20 (March 1976).

Mosely, Philip E. *The Kremlin and World Politics, Studies in Soviet Policy and Action.* New York: Vintage Books, 1960.

Moskvichov, L. "Ideological Expansion Doctrines," *International Affairs* 12 (Moscow, December 1979): 68-76.

Odom, William E. "The Soviet Approach to Nuclear Weapons: A Historical Review," *Annals of the American Academy* 469 (September 1983): 117-135.
"Operational Principles of Soviet Foreign Policy," *Survey* 19 (Spring 1983): 41-61.

Pipes, Richard. "Operational Principles of Soviet Foreign Policy," *Survey* 19 (Spring 1983): 41-61.

Ryzhenko, F. "The Limits of Peaceful Coexistence," *Pravda, (22 August 1973): 3-4. In Current Digest of Soviet Press* 25, #34, p. 5.

Schwartz, Morton. *Soviet Perceptions of the United States.* Berkeley: University of California Press, 1978.

Scott, Harriet Fast, and Scott, William F. *The Armed Forces of the USSR.* Boulder: Westview, 1979.
eds. *The Soviet Art of War.* Boulder: Westview Press, 1982.

Scott, William F. *Soviet Sources of Military Doctrine and Strategy. New York:* Crane, Russak, 1975.

*Selected Soviet Military Writings, 1970-1975.* Translated by the U.S. Air Force. Washington: GPO. 1976.

Shevedkov, Iu. A. "The Nixon Doctrine: Declarations and Realities," *S. SH. A Ekonomika, Politica, Ideologia,* February 1971, in *FBIS, Daily Report: Soviet Union.* (March 5, 1971): A2-A35.

Shulman, Marshall D. *Stalin's Foreign Policy Reappraised.* New York: Altheneum, 1965.

Sidelnikov, I. "Who Needs Military Superiority and Why," *Krasnaya Avezda,* January 15, 1980. Trans. in *Reprints from the Soviet Press.* (Feb. 15, 1980): 18-25.

Siderenko, A. *The Offensive.* Trans. by the U.S. Air Force. Washington: GPO, 1974.

Simes, Dimitri K. "Deterrence and Coercion in Soviet Policy," *International Security* 5 (Winter 1980-81): 80-103.
"The Military and Militarism in Soviet Society," *International Security* 6 (Winter 1981-82): 123-143.

Sokolovsky, Marshal V.D. *Soviet Military Strategy.* edited by Dinerstein, Herbert, et. al., Englewood Cliffs: Prentice-Hall, 1963.

Sovetov, A. "Detente and the Modern World," *International Affairs* 6 (Moscow, June 1979): 3-14.

Talbott, Strobe. *The Russians and Reagan.* New York: Vintage Books, 1983.

Trofimenko, Henry, "Counterforce: Illusion of a Panacea," *International Security* 5 (Spring 1981): 28-48.

Tucker, Robert C. *The Soviet Political Mind, Stalinism and Post-Stalin Change.* Rev. ed. New York: Norton, 1971.

Ustinov, Dmitri F. *Against the Arms Race and Threat of War.* Moscow: Novosti Press, 1981.
"Military Detente—Imperative of the Time," *International Affairs,* (January 1980): 3-9.

Valenta, Jiri, and Potter, William C, eds. *Soviet Decisionmaking for National Security.* London: George Allen and Unwin, 1984.

Vernon, Graham D., ed. *Soviet Perceptions of War and Peace.* Washington: National Defense University Press, 1981.

Weeks, Albert L. "The Garthoff-Pipes Debate on Soviet Doctrine: Another Perspective," *Strategic Review,* (Winter 1983): 57-64.

Whelan, Joseph G. *Soviet Diplomacy and Negotiating Behavior.* Boulder: Westview, 1983.

Wolfe, Thomas. *Soviet Power and Europe 1945-1970.* Baltimore: Johns Hopkins University Press, 1970.

Zakharov, Y. "Ideological Struggle in the International Arena," *International Affairs* 11 (Moscow, November 1979): 92-102.

Zheleznov, R. "Monitoring Arms Limitation Measures," *International Affairs* 7 (Moscow, 1982): 75-84.

Zimmerman, William, "Rethinking Soviet Foreign Policy: Changing American Perspectives," *International Journal* 35 (Summer 1980): 520-47.

# CHAPTER II
# Containment Revisited: Reagan's Approach to Soviet-American Relations

## Reagan: Realism and the Russians

If Central America were to fall, what would the consequences be in Asia, Europe, and for alliances such as NATO? If the U.S. cannot respond to a threat near our own borders, why should Europeans or Asians believe that we are seriously concerned about threats to them? If the Soviets can assume that nothing short of an actual attack on the U.S. will provoke an American response, which ally, which friend will trust us then?

But we take it as part of our obligation to peace to encourage the gradual evolution of the Soviet system toward a more pluralistic political and economic system, and above all to counter Soviet expansionism through sustained and effective political, economic, and military competition.

Soviet power threatens us directly and poses obstacles to the successful conduct of our foreign policy....the critical point in deterring war and preventing aggression is maintaining a balance of forces. History shows us all too often that conflicts occur when one state believes it has sufficiently greater military capability than another and attempts to exploit that superior strength through initimidation or conflict with the weaker state.[1]

These statements by the Reagan administration reveal a political orientation reminiscent of containment in the 1940s. They reflect the skepticism of Soviet intentions found in the policy articulated within the Truman administration and followed with more or less vigor, consistency, and effectiveness ever since. However, containment, as defined by George Kennan during the nascent cold war of the 1940s, was not easily attainable then or now, although some of the principles associated with it still apply. Kennan argued, for example, that containment, or modifying Soviet behavior via counterpressure deterrents followed by rewards for acceptable behavior, would lead to political mutation within the Soviet Union because its deterministic ideology could not survive if the U.S. blocked its 'inevitable" expansion. Kennan assumed that internal forces would then bring about an evolution in Soviet ideology and expansionist tendencies. In contrast, Reagan wants to do more than merely react to Soviet moves to facilitate internal changes in the Soviet Union. He hopes to reinstate a balance of power in which the U.S. can have the time to conduct the "Campaign for Freedom" announced in June 1982.

In this campaign, Reagan anticipates winning the struggle for the hearts and minds of the peoples of the world, which he believes possible if the free world engineers a collective educational-propaganda offensive. Reagan and Secretary of State George Shultz repeatedly hype this theme in an effort to garner public and congressional support for "freedom fighters" in Nicaragua, Afghanistan, and Angola and for overturning the Brezhnev Doctrine which asserts the irreversibility of Soviet gains in the third world. As an example of the bankruptcy of the Soviet claim that shifts in the correlation of forces inevitably favor communism, they refer to the "striking trend toward democracy" in Latin American and the Caribbean where 90% of the populations now live under democratic governments. Reagan wants to use American influence to encourage this trend for the sake of democracy and for the sake of its impact on Soviet-U.S. relations. In his view, "a foreign policy that ignored the fate of millions around the world who seek freedom would be a betrayal of our national heritage. Our own freedom, and that of our allies, could never be secure in a world where freedom was threatened everywhere else."[2] Shultz added that it is prudent to provide military and economic support to democratic forces, in states threatened by Soviet supported subversion, because "the more stable these countries, the fewer the opportunities for Soviet interference in the third world."[3] While similar offensives originated in the anti-communist doctrines of the 1940s and 1950s, the Reagan emphasis on a military application of containment and on winning allies constitutes a significant distinction from Kennan, and fits more easily within the framework of NSC-68.

Another reason for the difficulty in attaining containment, as described by Kennan, has more to do with the different strategic and domestic political environments of the 1980s than with specific contrasts in emphasis. Since the 1940s, the military balance of power between the U.S. and the Soviet Union evolved from one of American superiority to one of tenuous parity by the 1970s. An even more important change occurred in public views of the Soviets. By the late 1940s, the American public accepted the arguments about the need for the U.S. to resist Soviet threats actively and globally. In the 1980s, perceptions of the Soviet Union vary from hostile to friendly, the latter entailing assumptions that the Soviet Union is a status quo power that is as unwilling as the U.S. to risk nuclear war. Reagan spends much of his time attempting to refurbish the former consensus and to remind Americans that there is no safety in isolation, "stop and go commitments," or in failure to maintain military and economic strength. However, many members of the public and Congress agonize over the costs, risks of escalation, and potential violations of American principles involved in the containment effort and its 1980s reincarnation—the Reagan Doctrine (support for movements engaged in low intensity conflicts with communist groups or governments.)

Despite differences in emphasis and atmosphere, both Reagan and Truman chose containment as the most effective way of dealing with the Soviets. Truman, impressed with the consequences of Munich and appeasement, expected similarly disastrous results from accommodation with the Soviet Union. Reagan's similar fear about detente inspires his advocacy of containment, if adjusted to fit the realities of the 1980s. Like Truman and the authors of NSC-68 argued, the Reagan administration argues that Soviet expansion poses a threat to U.S. interests, that only Western firmness and demonstrated willingness to resist all Soviet challenges encourages Soviet awareness of the benefits of self-restraint, and that "a defeat of free institutions anywhere is a defeat everywhere." The Reagan administration emphasizes, as the Truman, Kennedy, and Johnson administrations emphasized, that the U.S. has to have the capacity to respond to Soviet attempts to alter the balance of power to whatever level, region, or cost. Truman discovered that the peripherally important Korea assumed major importance as the test of the credibility of American commitments. Reagan found that a Caribbean micro-state assumed macro-importance in a similar test of American power and willingness to use force to prevent destabilization in that strategic region. Tiny Grenada assumed large stature in the political struggle between American interests in supporting a gradual evolution toward democracy and stability in the third world and the Soviet/Cuban interest in fostering and exploiting the instability that feeds on the frustrations of peoples disillusioned with the slow pace of political and economic development.

Truman, Eisenhower, and Reagan, while pursuing a global containment, also appreciated the limits imposed by domestic and international realities. In fact, the thunderous anti-Soviet and anti-accommodation rhetoric of all three presidents intermingled with hints of compromise, awareness of the limits of American power, and acceptance of the reality that some interests and commitments superseded others. While Truman made statements about defending free peoples everywhere, he primarily directed American efforts toward economic reconstruction in Europe and Japan, gave only limited support to selected allies in key geographic locations, and limited the fighting in Korea and forbade the use of nuclear weapons there. Eisenhower and Dulles practiced an even harsher rhetoric, but softer policy, as rollback turned into rollover vis-a-vis Eastern Europe and Berlin. While Reagan urges replacing detente with containment and unilateral arms restraint with renewed military strength, and while the invasion of Grenada reminded the world that he sees an obligation to counter Soviet or Cuban victories in the third world, he showed signs of compromise over the number and basing made of MX missles, the SALT II treaty he agreed to honor, the Intermediate Range Nuclear Force (INF) zero-option, and the execution of economic and technological sanctions against the Soviets for their activities in Poland (1981-1982) and Afghanistan. In addition arms control talks hardly missed a beat after the 1983 Soviet shootdown of the civilian South Korean airliner (KAL-007) that had strayed over Soviet territory.

Before reviewing the Reagan version of containment further, it is necessary to describe the international environment facing the administration and its evaluation of the decade of detente. The post-detente decade began with Carter's reluctant and disheartened rejection of detente in the aftermath of the Soviet invasion of Afghanistan in 1979. This dramatic addition to what Brzezinski labelled the arc of crisis forced

Carter to withdraw the SALT II treaty from Senate deliberations, announce the institution of the Carter Doctrine, and accept the fact that the Soviet pursuit of strategic geo-political, and ideological objectives in Afghanistan trampled on what remained of American support for detente. Carter's heightened interest in El Salvador, Nicaragua, the Horn of Africa, Poland, and China; support for increasing the defense budget and for draft registration; and economic sanctions and cultural and sporting boycotts against the Soviets reflected his determination to hold a faltering line against the Soviet Union and its global influence. Reagan inherited this belated policy of reaction to Soviet pressures in an era of Soviet political and military ascendency and American military, political and economic decline.

## The Agenda

Interest in redressing these two trends dominated the Reagan foreign policy agenda. However, many factors complicated this agenda. The U.S. faced the delicate task of wooing the PRC without abandoning Taiwan and without compromising the ideological coherence and consistency of Reagan's anti-communist stand, answering European demands for equal rights in NATO planning and for independence from American positions on international finance and detente, and repairing the accumulated damages in Japanese-U.S. trade and defense relations. In the meantime, the administration encountered turmoil in Middle Eastern states, which demanded American adaption to post-Shah, post-Camp David, and post-Sadat events; upheavals in Latin America in the midst of anti-Americanism and marxist revolutionaries and new economic and political demands from important neighbors like Mexico; anger in Africa over American support of South Africa; and storms in South East Asia among fraternal communist states, over civil unrest in South Korea and the Philippines, and in the unexpected cracks in ANZUS (the alliance between Australia, New Zealand, and the U.S.) blasted apart in 1986 by New Zealand's closing of its ports to nuclear-powered or capable U.S. ships. In addition, the often hostile non-aligned movement demanded Western compensation for its economic woes and an end to U.S. (but apparently not Soviet) intervention in third world conflicts. In the 1986 meeting of the non-aligned movement, for example, the final communique condemned the U.S. for the "state-sponsored terrorism" but ignored Soviet actions in Afghanistan and elsewhere. Finally, the war in Afghanistan highlighted the importance of Pakistan and India.

This litany of trouble spots colored the perception of the administration, which sought explanations for many of these problems in the direct and indirect machinations of the Soviet Union and its allies. However, Reagan also accused previous U.S. administrations of inadequate responses to the selective detente practiced by the Soviets. Reagan's indictment rested on his conclusion that contrasting Soviet and American views of detente and Soviet exploitation of these had precluded the emergence of a genuine improvement in Soviet-American relations and made suspect the Soviet declarations of peaceful intentions and American remarks on "irreversible processes." One example of this disparity was the marked difference between the American emphasis on detente as a process of stabilizing Soviet-U.S. relations and Brezhnev's emphasis on peaceful coexistence as a method of continuing the international class struggle.

The Soviet's notion of a correlation of forces shifting in favor of the socialists precluded its acceptance of the inherent value of stability, the status quo, or American stipulations about linkage. Soviet leaders saw no contradiction in welcoming the fruits of detente in Europe, for example, while rejecting limitations on their pursuit of socialist victory elsewhere. These Soviet assessments limited the prospect of employing a detente-inspired balance of power system as a universal conflict-reducing tool. The Nixon administration reduced reliance on the ephemeral crisis management capability of detente in the aftermath of the 1973 Middle East war in which Soviet support of the attacks on Israel violated the "spirit" of the code of conduct presumably embodied in detente. Carter discovered the Soviet-imposed boundaries on the areas in which detente applied and the decidedly parochial Soviet interest in stability after the 1979 invasion of Afghanistan. This action invalidated the notion that Soviet and Western perceptions of detente were similar enough to provide mutual guidelines for acceptable behavior and demonstrated that the expansionist character of Soviet foreign policy was not obsolete, limited to the Eastern European buffer zone, or a myth perpetuated by a hostile, encircling West.

Not everyone, however, blames the Soviets alone for the decline of detente. Garthoff, for example, blamed *both* superpowers for misperceiving the nature of the relationship between Afghanistan and detente. In his view, Carter and Reagan overreacted to a reluctant Soviet defensive move in its security sphere. A more enlightened acceptance of the Soviet action might have saved detente. However, it is difficult to understand this criticism, when juxtaposed with Garthoff's acceptance of the Soviet assertion that they thought Carter's reaction to Afghanistan was just an excuse for abandoning a now repugnant detente in preference for containment and superiority. Garthoff says they were wrong to assume this, I suggest that they did not assume this at all, although they trumpeted this claim to counter hostile Western and third world responses to the invasion. While it seems likely that the extent of Carter's squawking surprised the Soviets, they could not have assumed that he sought an excuse to jettison detente since they had long appreicated his campaign to save it. Instead, due to the awareness of Carter's unflagging support for detente, the Soviets thought they could get away with a little muscle-flexing in the third world. They moved into Afghanistan to settle events there and may have hoped that, once successful, they could use Afghanistan as an example of the validity of the Brezhnev Doctrine and as a reminder to neighboring states of their vulnerability and need to pacify their large neighbor. The muscle-flexing failed to come cheaply not because the Americans preferred containment, as the Soviets claimed, but because Carter finally accepted the significance of the differences in American and Soviet views of detente and, as a result, decided to abandon a policy so defined as to allow an invasion of Afghanistan.

While critical of detente as practiced throughout the 1970s, Reagan reserved special attention for Carter's approach, which he characterized as one of hesitation, inconsistency, and ineffectiveness. According to administration officials, due to Carter's early decisions not "to maintain strategic and conventional capabilities" nor "respond vigorously to the use of Soviet force," detente jeopardized the prospects for international stability and encouraged Soviet behavior that showed "little regard for the ability and/or will of the West to respond effectively to its challenge."[4] Reagan intended to make clear to the Soviets that certain behavior contradicted the requirements of a genuine relaxation of tensions, convince them of American willingness to counter unacceptable behavior, and design a foreign policy that facilitated containment or even reversal of Soviet expansion.

This intended policy incorporated and updated several cold war assumptions about the best way to deal with the Soviets. They included: a conviction that the Soviet Union posed genuine strategic and political threats to the U.S. and the world; a view that the detente of the 1970s (and the accompanying underestimation of the Soviet threat and insufficient defense spending) facilitated Soviet activism just like appeasement in the 1930s facilitated German aggression; a determination to block Soviet ambition; and an assumption that military strength was the most effective tool to deny the Soviets opportunities to exploit international crises, to convince them to negotiate seriously, and to enable the U.S. to stand fast with respect to international commitments. These convictions derived from a simple world view and a simple solution. Reagan recommended no illusions and wishful thinking about the ideological, adventuristic, and "evil" Soviet empire. Given the irreconcilable differences and unbounded Soviet global ambitions, the U.S. had to replace detente and containment, which, based on American economic and military strength, would keep regional conflicts from spreading; convince the Soviets that the expansionist policies of the 1970s would no longer work; and thereby reduce the risk of superpower confrontations.[5] According to Reagan, echoing Truman and NSC-68, "a great deal hangs on America's staying power and steadfast commitment....Backing away from this challenge will not bring peace. It will only mean that others who are hostile to everything we believe in will have a freer hand to work their will in the world."[6]

These interrelated convictions and expectations provided the underlying foundation for former Secretary of State Alexander Haig's outline of the procedures necessary for re-instituting a policy of containment: restoring economic and military strength; renewing the strength and unity of NATO and adding new allies to the Western front; promoting peaceful change in the third world; and pursuing a constructive relationship with the Soviets based on restraint, reciprocity, and realism.[7] Secretary Shultz refined these objectives when he emphasized that the U.S. would *resist encroachments on our vital interest, ...ensure that those who have a positive alternative to the Soviet model have our support,* and *leave Moscow no opportunity to distort or misconstrue our intentions.*[8] Shultz also assured Americans that the emerging policy remained consistent with past policies and objectives. However, he highlighted the administration's determination to compensate for the voluntary or inadvertent American political and military decline during the decade of detente that had encouraged the Soviets to exploit the apparent near impotence of Carter's foreign policy, divisions in the Western alliance, and turmoil in the third world.

## Defense Revisited

The most important items on the Reagan agenda for convincing the Soviets of American ability to respond to challenges were increased defense spending and a restoration of America's deterrent capability. Reagan urged a substantial reinvestment in defense outlays since, in terms of constant dollars, they declined over 20% during the decade of detente from FY 1968-1979, while as a per centage of GNP they declined from 7.8% (FY 1970) to 4.7% (FY 1979).[9] Despite incipient budget battles with Congress, which persistently dissipated support for various elements of his defense plans and priorities (witness the debate over the MX missile and the hesitation over funding for the SDI) Reagan managed about a 30-36% real increase in actual expenditures from FY 1982-1985—an increase rate higher than in any other comparable peace time period.[10] However, by the end of this period, the U.S. spent only 6.2% of its GNP on defense - well below Reagan's hoped for amount. While the money spent represented about one third more, in constant dollars, than Carter spent during his four years, the FY 1982-1985 outlays averaged slightly lower than the Carter projections for FY 1982-1985. However, this resulted partly from incorrect assumptions of high inflation and fuel costs.[11]

Reagan concentrated funding on nuclear modernization, strategic and conventional weaponry, and on research and development for SDI which the Department of Defense projects will take up nearly 10% of the military budget by the early 1990s. Despite accelerated congressional budget bashing (Congress approved less for FY 1986 than it had for FY 1985, reduced the FY 1987 request by 8.8%, and voted similar reductions for FY 1988), budget battles primarily concern the amount of increased allocations and what to buy rather than the necessity of strengthening military and deterrent capability. It is to this necessity that we now turn.

According to Defense Secretary Caspar Weinberger, to maintain a credible nuclear deterrent, the U.S. (1) "must be able to respond in a measured and prudent manner to the threat posed by the Soviet Union" (flexible response and escalation dominance capabilities), (2) complicate the first strike plans of any aggressor and frustrate any temptation to consider launching an attack (degrade Soviet first strike capabilities by offensive and defensive means), (3) "make the cost of nuclear war much higher than any possible benefit" (assured destruction capability), and (4) convince the Soviets "that a nuclear attack on the U.S. would bring swift nuclear retaliation" (invulnerable second strike and victory denial capabilities).[12] Since Reagan assumed that U.S. ability to meet these requirements eroded in the aftermath of the Soviet achievement of nuclear parity (or better) in the 1970s, he urged a modernization of strategic nuclear forces to restore the military balance and the punch, invulnerability, and deterrent value of U.S. weapons systems and strategies. Success in these efforts would depend on accurate Soviet perceptions of the vitality and reliability of U.S. retaliatory forces in answering various levels of threat or attack, on preparing credible responses to a protracted nuclear conflict, and on improving damage limitation capability and the ability to destroy Soviet missile silos (BMD and counterforce capabilities.).

References to "prevailing" in protracted nuclear conflicts, denying the Soviets a nuclear victory, and the possibility of defending American cities and silos against missile attacks, marked a move away from the strategy of Mutual Assured Destruction (MAD), which assumes that fear of nuclear retaliation and the inevitability of escalation and MAD deters rational leaders from considering the use of nucelar weapons. The Reagan administration questions the credibility of MAD which relies on vulnerability to deter and on Soviet subscription to its credo. Reagan urges a consideration of prevailing and flexible response as more suitable deterrent options. These two strategies portray deterrence as delicate and assume that 1) nuclear capabilities and balances change constantly; 2) these changes may impair U.S. ability to retaliate and deter and, as a result, influence Soviet and European perception of American willingness to retaliate; and 3) that the most effective way to deter is to convince the Soviets of American determination to maintain a military balance and a strategic nuclear force capable of blunting any Soviet first strike plan. The administration suggests that this determination, embodied in modernized offensive and defensive forces and healthy defense budgets, also encourages Soviet willingness, since they respect only those who negoitate from strength, to negotiate seriously on arms control. (See chapters III-V for more detailed appraisals of weapons, strategies, and arms control negotiations.)

However, persuading the Soviets to come to terms with the U.S. over desirable military balances, nuclear strategies, and arms control agreements that genuinely enhance security and reduce tensions is not the only problem. The Reagan administration also has to sell American and European publics on the benefits of its approach of negotiating from strength. While Reagan won two elections selling this argument (and other arguments about the benefits of supply side economics and low taxes), these publics, as a whole, fear the prospects of arms races, reject high defense spending, and do not always appreciate that a flawed arms control agreement might be worse than no agreement at all.

Reagan's expedition into the dense and arcane jungle of strategy arouse cries of outrage from proponents of MAD as well as from opponents of nuclear deterrence in general. Those who see Reagan's modernization intentions as part of a plan to achieve nuclear superiority and to push for a war-fighting scheme as a new magic formula for deterrence warn that his risky and provocative strategies, and their accompanying weaponry, will compel similar Soviet responses and thus will escalate chances for a breakdown in deterrence. The Soviets indeed reject the legitimacy of Reagan's violation of the principles of MAD and accuse the administration of undermining the stability imposed by the reality of the rough equality in Soviet and U.S. nuclear capabilities. They promise to prevent, by whatever means necessary, Reagan's efforts to coerce and threaten them. Whether Reagan's strategic plans entail solutions to the dilemma of deterrence in the 1980s or a new impetus for the arms race remains the fundamental bone of contention between supporters and critics of the administration's policy. Opinion divides largely over one question: what prevents nuclear war —deterrence based on mutual vulnerability and threat of retaliation or deterrence based on defense and a damage limitation capability to deny the enemy victory in any first strike scenario. (See chapters V and VI for a review of this question.)

While Reagan's call for deterrence based on defense frightens proponents of MAD, his campaign to educate Americans about the urgency of defense spending, weapons development and testing, and arms control proposals judged primarily on their contributions to stability achieved relative success in recent years. Slow to court the Russians, in preference to being courted, and slow to give in to arms freeze pressures, which it absorbed in build-down and Zero-Option proposals (the proposal to eliminate Soviet and U.S. INF from Europe), the administration is now actively negotiating over reducing what it considers the most destabilizing weapons (ICBM's) in the new rounds of the START talks; eliminating INF deployments; and moving to deterrence based on defense or BMD. Reagan succeeded in placing INF in Europe as a symbolic and blue chip "bargaining chip" counter to Soviet SS-20s; winning public approval for the principle of a population-based defense; and maintaining, until the Iran-Contra connection, unprecedented popular support (68% in one 1986 count). Remarkably, he achieved all of this in the midst of sending mixed signals to the American public about his peacemaker versus "war-mongering" role that demanded high defense spending, retaliation against Libyan sponsored terrorism; funding of Nicaraguan guerrillas (with or without congressional approval) and mining of Nicaraguan harbors; rejection of decisions by the World Court that the mining violated international law; and no moratoria on INF deployments or Anti-Satellite (ASAT), chemical, and nuclear weapons testing.

Reagan's initial arms control and foreign policy success derived, in part, from a number of fortuitous features of the domestic and international system. These included a relatively healthy (if somewhat sluggish and indebted) economy with low inflation and low taxes as promised; Soviet blunders and inertia by Brezhnev and his two revolving door successors; a fractious and frustrated opposition in the U.S. and Western Europe; an Arab world more occupied with falling oil prices, fraticidal Palestinian and Lebanese obsessions, and the alignment-shattering Iran-Iraq war than with American sponsored Israel; and an increasingly dependent and divided third world. However, the flip side of this success story remains to be heard. A generally supportive public may feel betrayed by a stalemated arms control process and a reinvigorated, destabilizing, and expensive arms race; the Soviets under Gorbachev may continue to play successfully on Western fears of wars and arms races; and a decisive defeat for the Nicaraguan Contras or for the U.S. naval presence in the Persian Gulf involving an escalation of American intervention in these two regions may foster a backlash that will further erode Reagan's popularity and the effectiveness of his foreign policy. Finally, the impact of the Iran-Contra affair on the ability of the administration to exercise forceful arms control and foreign policy initiatives may yet reach the heights (or the depths) of the debilitating fallout from the Watergate scandal.

We will investigate these and other possibilities below, in a review of Reagan's attempt to apply containment on a global basis, and in later chapters that evaluate the specifics of U.S. deterrent strategies, arms control objectives, and Soviet reaction to both. The rest of this chapter focuses on three areas that have not escaped imprisonment in the twilight zone of East-West conflict: Europe, Africa, and Latin America. In each area the superpowers drew and crossed lines while locals got squeezed in the process. Europeans opted to replace containment with detente, Africans and Latin Americans most often found themselves with fewer options as they encountered numbing replays of internal and external storms complicated by the harsh and unforgiving dynamics of the cold war. Let us now take a closer look at developments in these regions as they affect, and are affected by, their inevitable and unenviable involvement in Soviet-U.S. relations.

## Detente Revisited: Detente vs Containment in Europe

The focus in this section will be on one of the major political issues dividing the NATO allies—disagreements over the nature and value of containment versus detente. The West Europeans, who received the first Brezhnev invitation to help create detente embraced the policy wholeheartedly in the 1960s. However, with the disappointing breakdown in Soviet-American relations in the 1970s, the lack luster Soviet follow through on the human rights promises of the 1975 Helsinki accords, and Soviet footdragging since 1971 in the Mutual and Balanced Force Reductions (MBFR) talks, Americans and Europeans began to question the Soviet commitment to detente. However, some West Europeans remained determined to perpetuate their side of the detente bargain in the hope of persuading the Soviets to rejoin the aborted partnership.

Several of the smaller members of NATO still wax eloquently over their praise of detente and their fear of Reagan's alternatives. West Germany and Great Britain also prefer detente to containment, but found their enthusiasm tempered periodically as the Soviets violated some of the "rules of the game." Given the influential role of these two states, I will concentrate on their views of Soviet-American relations and how the application of some of these have aroused Reagan's fears about the potential impact of a short-sighted detente on his major European objectives of NATO unity and strength.

The British Conservative government, with its traditionally close association with the U.S., its concern about Soviet challenges to the international balance of power, and its dependence on a re-vitalized NATO, has argued that the detente of the 1970s often favored Soviet objectives and threatened Western objectives. The Thatcher government, while appreciating the potential of East-West trade (essential for its foreign trade dependent economy), concerned about the prospects of an escalating arms race, and aware of Western European military vulnerability (potentially overwhelming if the American deterrent should fade or when all INF are withdrawn from Europe), has criticized Soviet abuse of detente. The Conservatives saw, in the recent phases of NATO disarray, in the ascendency of Soviet strategic capabilities, and in the apparent decline of American commitment and capabilities in the 1970s, a manifest Soviet opportunity to expand its influence. Detente, intended to provide the Soviet Union with a stake in the status quo, appeared to result instead, in a West European acceptance of the status quo in Eastern Europe, Soviet pressure not to use the human rights principles of the Helsinki Accords to interfere in Soviet internal affairs, and accommodation to Soviet interests in Western Europe.

Thatcher and Reagan fear that the Soviet Union, if it could convince the West of its commitment to a relaxation of tensions, status quo in Europe, and arms control, would do much to weaken further the unity of NATO, members of which already question anti-detente measures such as placing upgraded chemical and biological weapons in Europe, replacing INF with shorter range missiles, and increasing military spending. If at the same time Soviet military power continued to improve enough to be overwhelmingly dominant compared to a vulnerable and unreliable American deterrent, the Western Europeans could wake up one day afraid to jeopardize detente and unable to resist Soviet pressure.

This prospect of a Western Europe caught off guard due to misperceptions of detente and an underestimation of the Soviet commitment to dominate Europe prompted Thatcher to insist on a "realistic," reciprocal detente; a detente that entailed 1) an East-West military balance, 2) a cohesive and strong alliance, and 3) firm opposition to Soviet ambitions. As her then Foreign Minister, Lord Carrington, argued, given Soviet expansion of military power and a now questionable detente, the West had no choice but to respond by maintaining weapons to deter, after all if

> arms control negotiations cannot be expected to revive detente, how much more so this is true of unilateralism. A unilateral reduction in our defense effort is not a policy which any government with Britain's interests at heart could pursue....Experience does not suggest that the Russians would respond except to exploit....I cannot ignore the lessons of the 1930s....The truth still is that unilateral disarmament makes it easier for others to use possession of weapons to gain their objectives with or without war, and may even increase the risk of war. I am more than ever convinced that genuine arms control must depend on multilateral efforts.[13]

This obviously did not rule out the vital arms control process. However, the West had to disabuse the Soviets of the notion that negotiation was a "euphemism for talking the West into impotence." The West should be prepared to continue its longstanding NATO decision to maintain an East-West military balance and a viable nuclear deterrent at whatever cost.

This deterrent and a two-way detente were all the more necessary in the aftermath of the Soviet move into Afghanistan. Thatcher, like Reagan, viewed Afghanistan as extremely relevant for East-West detente. First, it illustrated the Soviet expectation that the West would not resist the move. Second, it invalidated the notion that Soviet and Western perceptions of detente were similar enough to provide mutual guidelines for acceptable behavior. Finally, it indicated that even when faced with a common threat, the spectre of Soviet expansion, NATO was in such disarray that a unified posture not only emerged slowly, but it was qualified by divergent Western European and American levels of response.

The British were close to the Americans in their evaluation of the implications of the Soviet move. According to Lord Carrington,

> The Soviet action is a breach of all the conventions which have governed East-West relations for the last decade. It is a vivid demonstration of the Soviet drive to gain wider influence wherever possible, by propaganda, by subversion, and where necessary by force....It is bound to affect our attitude in current and future negotiations between East and West. Though we naturally want these to continue where they clearly serve our interests as well as those of the Soviet Union....One is bound to ask where the Russian drive is to stop. If the Russians are to be deterred, a sustained and significant response will be needed....(The West) itself needs to find ways to make the Russians understand that they cannot break the rules of international behavior with impunity....[14]

However, the British wanted to leave the door open to a renewed detente. The fear of the Soviet Eurostrategic advantage, persistent doubts about American response and responsibility, and the Western European stake in economic relations with the Soviets all provide incentives for the British to anticipate the re-opening of a "fruitful dialogue" with the Soviet Union, especially a Soviet Union led by the reform-minded Gorbachev.

Despite Thatcher's early determination to withhold detente as long as the Soviets remained in Afghanistan, economic constraints, pressures by European Economic Community (EEC) partners to insulate the European-Soviet detente from global Soviet-American conflict, the psychological and military threat imposed by the Soviet military build-up in the European theater, and fears of an inadequate American role in Europe (or perhaps worse, an over-reactive Reagan policy) have prompted less resistance more recently. The British have to decide whether to insist on a realistic detente, or follow the Labour party's advice to disarm, withdraw, and sue for detente at any price. So far, the Thatcher government, despite economic impoverishment, public uncertainty, and military vulnerability, has opted for resistance. Whether the British can afford it in the long run (or after Thatcher leaves office) remains a question. But there is no question that without equally resistant partners Britain cannot go it alone. Consequently, the nature of West German resistance concerns the British as well as the Americans.

## Ostpolitik Revisited

The Federal Republic of Germany (FRG), with its very close ties to the U.S. and NATO (*Westpolitik*), its geographic vulnerability, and its concern for the division of Germany, is torn between dependency on both East and West. The West Germans depend on the West for military protection and European integration and on the East for improving relations with the German Democratic Republic (GDR) and increasing East bloc trade. By the mid 1960s perceptions of a diminishing Soviet threat, concern about the American commitment, and lingering dreams of re-unification persuaded many West Germans, Willy Brandt and the Social Democratic Party (SPD) especially, that Ostpolitik (improved relations with the East), in conjunction with a deterrent NATO force structure, offered a solution for West Germany's geostrategic, political, and economic problems.[15]

Helmut Schmidt, Chancellor from 1974-1983, favored Ostpolitik and a gradual rapproachement between East and West Germany (*wandel durch Annaeherung*). According to Schmidt, in contrast with the perennial crises of the 1940s through 1960s, "we have created a policy of cooperation between West and East Europe. A policy of what one calls detente, a policy of calculability on both sides....One of the necessities of the alliance as well as for us Germans is to get along well with the Eastern power. We don't want to get back into the cold war."[16] The avoidance of the perils of the cold war was not the only reason for the commitment to Ostpolitik. There were more specific objectives behind West Germany's stake in it and the "special relationship" with the East. Benefits included the East-West treaties of the 1970s, the open exit gate for the ethnic German populations of Eastern Europe, reconciliation between East and West Germany, increases in East bloc trade, and a much desired arms control process.

Perhaps the search for an Eastern option reflected more of a change in attitude towards the U.S. than the Soviet Union. For example, the West Germans questioned American strategic capacity and willingness to abide by its commitments to Western Europe. A 1979 survey showed only 12% of West German respondents strongly confident in the American commitment to West German, while 54% had only "some" confidence in this commitment.[17] With this doubt, West Germany had to do what it could to alleviate Soviet pressures on Germany, insulate Europe from Soviet-U.S. conflict, and perhaps even act as power broker/mediator between the protagonists.

Even after Afghanistan, Schmidt was reluctant to jeopardize Ostpolitik. He justified this in terms of priorities: detente in Europe superseded Soviet probing in the third world. In other words, the overwhelming contribution of detente could not be sacrificed for a temporary and essentially peripheral cold war flashback of the Soviet Union. Since detente was a long term policy and subject to periods of increased tension, detente along the European front should not be interrupted simply because of tension over Africa, Afghanistan, or even Poland. Many Germans appeared to be more disturbed at the prospect of an anti-communist crusade, whether rhetorical or interventionary, by Reagan than by Soviet military build-ups or third world invasions. Despite the more conservative credentials of Chancellor Helmut Kohl, his unqualified support for INF deployment, the qualified support for SDI, and his deep skepticism about Soviet intentions, he also downplayed the relevance of Afghanistan and the the Soviet pressure on Poland and the Solidarity labor movement.

Critics of Ostpolitik within the Conservative Christian Democratic Union/Christian Socialist Union (CDU/CSU) asserted that Ostpolitik facilitated Soviet goals in Europe and undermined Western objectives. For example, the apparent Soviet goals of dividing NATO, weakening European trust in the American commitment to Western Europe, and legitimizing Soviet hegemony in Eastern Europe were well represented in Soviet attempts to block American participation in the Conference on Security and Cooperation in Europe (CSCE—the Helsinki Accords), inclusion of Eurostrategic limitations in SALT II, and the formal acceptance of Soviet domination of Eastern Europe and the permanent division of Germany in the Helsinki Accords.

According to conservatives like Franz Josef Strauss, President of the CSU and unsuccessful candidate for Chancellor, as a result of Ostpolitik, the FRG not only accepted the "reality" of an increasingly Soviet dominated balance of power but also began a process of appeasement, pacifism, and accommodation to Soviet interests in Europe. According to Uwe Nerlich, this accommodation or incapacity to withstand Soviet pressure had increased throughout Western Europe, not only because of the increasing Soviet military—useful as a deterrent and as an example (Cuban missile crisis, Czechoslovakia, and Afghanistan)—but also because of a Western desire for detente at almost any price.[18] And if, as Reagan fears, West Germany and Western Europe become more and more reluctant to jeopardize detente (or natural gas pipelines) or to provoke the Soviet Union, Soviet leverage over them could increase. The sluggish West German and Western European reaction to Afghanistan and the attempt to insulate European detente and East-West trade from non-European matters did not indicate accommodation in an absolute sense, but they did indicate acceptance of the Soviet insistence on a selective and divisible detente. While Reagan criticized this acceptance, many Europeans view a divisible and insulated detente as the best way to deal with the Soviets in an age of radical change in the balance of power—with the Soviet Union in ascendency and the U.S. and NATO in decline.

In this new age, the question remains: what is the "best" policy for Western Europeans to pursue towards the Soviet Union and how will their choice affect NATO and U.S. interests? The British under Thatcher urge a "realistic," reciprocal detente, a close partnership with the U.S., a balancing of military forces in Europe as a visible example of NATO's credibility, and a rejection of a paralyzing European acquiescence to a subtle dual Soviet policy of pressure and bribery. The West Germans urge a moderate response to the gradual Soviet overtures towards Western Europe, a NATO guided by a political detente as well as military deterrence, and a careful maturation period for detente so that it might serve as a pre-condition of, rather than a hostage to, East-West relations elsewhere. They suggest insulating Europe from the rest of the East-West struggle and protecting the fragile accord that has already yielded it so many tangible economic, political, and military benefits and offers the prospect of many more. They hope that even a divisible and partially rhetorical detente, however limited in scope and confined geographically, will eventually spillover into other policies and areas. Reagan fears that these expectations and regional priorities might eventually convince Europeans that a more neutral position might provide more security than a junior partnership in a declining bloc.

This fear seems excessive, in view of the continued vitality of NATO despite a history of dire predictions of imminent collapse. In the same vein, we might conclude that this pessimistic portrayal of the saga of detente underestimates more positive features of East-West relations in the 1980s. While Kohl, for example, pursues Ostpolitik in much the same fashion as did the SPD, Reagan supports West German overtures to East Germany. The fact the Kohl pursues NATO unity and strength assertively no doubt relieves Reagan of most of the concerns he may entertain about neutralist tendencies in West Germany. (35% of the voting public and 45% of the SPD favored German neutrality between the two superpowers in a 1984 poll.)[19] In a recent display of reciprocal support, Reagan did not oppose West German credits to the GDR and Kohl extended qualified support for the SDI. The British, under Thatcher, remain the most steadfast, with their interest in SDI research, their gutsy granting of base take-off privileges for Reagan's retaliatory raid against Libya in 1986, and their persistent criticism of Soviet and East bloc breeches of human rights features of the Helsinki Accords.

As for Euro-U.S. relations, the 1980s reflect not only the chronic disarray and acrimony over opposing economic and strategic interests (most recently Western European concerns about American high interest rates and protectionist urges and U.S. concerns about EEC dumping and conflicting approaches to detente and deterrence), but also rays of hope for renewed allied unity. (See chapters IV and V for discussions of deterrence in the European context.) In the 1980s, the Europeans and the U.S. handled INF deployment without shattering public support for deterrence or NATO. A 1984 West German poll reported that, while 37% of the respondents preferred to get rid of nuclear weapons in Europe, 61% believed they were necessary for deterrence.[20] In 1985 the Belgian and Dutch holdouts approved Cruise Missile deployment in their countries, despite spirited opposition by a significant minority of their populations. Spain's 1986 referendum on NATO membership received 51% approval. In 1987 Reagan soft-pedalled his opposition to technology sales to the Soviets (most of Western European trade to the Soviet Union—five times the amount of Soviet-U.S. trade—involves technology and manufactured goods.)

While political tension still plagues the alliance over issues such as Reagan's call for a NATO-backed Persian Gulf policy, his anti-Sandinista and anti-terrorism rhetoric and actions, or the nascent European flirtation with neutralism (primarily in the radical wings of parties like Labour in Britain and the SPD and Greens in West Germany), the alliance hangs on in its healthy, but hypochondriacal middle age. Much of this sturdiness derives from a relatively successful European offensive by the Reagan administration after the hard-learned lessons of the early years of causal references to nuclear wars limited "only" to Europe. Despite Reagan's absent-minded and second thought consultations with allies over summits with Gorbachev, raids on Mediterranean countries, and decisions to undertake new deterrent and arms control strategies, the Europeans see in Reagan's administration a somewhat more purposeful and predictable approach than they witnessed, to their dismay, during the Carter years.

While they disparage Reagan's cowboy aura, they approve the accompanying less flamboyant image of an administration reigned in by caution and realpolitik. They appreciate the steel shown in Reagan's firmness, but they also appreciate the flexibility shown in his willingness to negotiate with Gorbachev, his move toward European views on the problems of the international economy, and his selective rather than indiscriminate use of force or threats of force. While the U.S. and Western Europe remain far apart on many issues (arms control, SDI, the impact of U.S. budget deficits on European economies, and the proper ways to handle terrorism) through mutual need, as much as deliberate choice, they agree that their economic, political and military interests depend on a healthy Atlantic partnership. We find less agreement on U.S. policies in the third world—our next subject.

## Containment Applied: Africa

In the next two sections on Reagan's application of containment, I will focus on Africa and Latin America. Perhaps neither region is as explosive as the Persian Gulf or the Middle East, however their resources and the trade routes around them, the irritation of Cuba, the proximity of Mexico, and the psychological, monetary, and military investment in El Salvador and Nicaragua indicate their importance to the U.S. Also, since Reagan has declared war on Soviet third world adventurism and since we see very clear battle lines drawn in Latin America and Africa, it seems appropriate to focus on these regions.

Africa, while not the focus of attention or recipient of aid that Latin America is, provides an excellent example of why the third world attracts the attention of an administration concerned about America's global role as it competes with the Soviets for influence in the third world. It also provides an example of the nature of the debate over the causes of the conflicts that occur with distressing regularity in the third world.

Did conflicts there derive solely from the legacy of colonialism and the exploitation of neocolonialism? Did they drive from economic underdevelopment or from ethnic, religious, and ideological differences?

To what extent have East-West interventions and consequent arms sale races exacerbated these problems? Which solutions best serve third world interests: scientific socialism or democratic capitalism; non-alignment, anti-imperialist solidarity, or Western dependency; federalist or unitary government; multi or single party system; and regional integration, Libyan-style unions, or tribal/ethnic separatism? It is beyond the scope of this section to address all of these vital areas. But with an eye to discovering what positive role the U.S. can play in the third world—a role that serves third world as well as American interests—the purposes and influences of American intervention, whether in Africa or elsewhere, must be assessed.

The United States has periodically discovered and rediscovered Africa from Tripoli in 1801, to North Africa in 1942, to the Congo in 1960, to Angola in 1975, and the Horn in 1978. In the post World War II years, whether by inadvertence or design, the U.S. considered Africa to be a Western European preserve to be left alone except for occasional prodding about the pace of decolonization and access for American trade. Three concerns prompted the U.S. to reconsider the importance of Africa: Soviet attempts at exploiting local instability, concern over access to markets and natural resources, and massive catastrophes inflicted by climate and man. No comprehensive foreign policy existed, however, until the Carter administration focussed attention on Africa as a sadly overlooked victim of Western colonial (and Soviet) abuse—a victim that merited a re-vitalized American approach. Carter intended to concentrate on issues that Africans believed most crucial: economic development and destroying the remnants of colonialism in southern Africa.

Carter emphasized 1) that internal problems and events, not Soviet schemes, led to revolution and the establishment of radical governments, 2) that American attempts at intervention would be counterproductive, and 3) that African problems should be solved in an African context.[21] He criticized past intervention on behalf of corrupt and right-wing dictatorships threatened by people dissatisfied with their economic and political deprivation. Such interventions perpetuated the image of the U.S. as a reactionary, status quo power ready to support any regime that guaranteed the U.S. access to its economy. American references to the dangers of a Soviet threat or the "non-democratic" nature of national liberation movements had reinforced the additional African impression that the U.S. was blinded by its geostrategic concerns and either unaware of or unconcerned with local problems and factors.

Carter suggested that the best way to contain the Soviet threat was to resolve the local economic and social problems that the Soviets exploited, accommodate African and third world concerns, and use escalated American pressure to end apartheid and free Namibia.[22] This approach, which Helen Kitchen labelled "tempered idealism," assumed that Africans would become increasingly disillusioned with Soviet actions and anxious about future Soviet/Cuban interventions and that the U.S. could nullify Soviet attempts to capitalize on regional instability to establish their presence in Africa by convincing Africans that their interests were best served by economic and political cooperation with the West [23] After all, while the Soviets provided military aid and portrayed themselves as the champions of national liberation struggles, only the West (especially the U.S.) could deal effectively with the problems of economic development. In addition, the U.S. had the advantage of being able to put pressure on the white regimes in South Africa and Rhodesia (now Zimbabwe).[24]

Carter believed that American identification with Africans against South Africa was the key to foreign policy success. On moral grounds this appealed to people like Carter, U.N. Ambassador Andrew Young, and most black and white Americans. In addition, the opposite approach of "busines as usual" with South Africa, for whatever reasons— need for mineral resources, South Africa's strategic location, and so forth—entailed many counterproductive results. Any less than committed stand by the U.S. could result in an increased stature and interventionary role by the Soviets, who supported the African opposition, and in an African backlash against an apparent American indifference to the most emotional issue in Africa—a backlash that could include economic sanctions from Nigeria (one of the largest oil exporters to the U.S.).[25]

The Carter approach, then, consisted of some rather dramatic new policies and assumptions. Carter wanted to see Africa as isolated as possible from the East-West confrontation and its incendiary impact on regional struggles. First steps in this direction included the acknowledgement that local problems did not derive from Soviet inspiration and that local forces might indeed invite Soviet or Cuban assistance against colonial or outside forces as in Angola, where Cubans now protect the Marxist regime against rather powerful resistance forces supported primarily by the U.S. and South Africa, or against invaders as in Ethiopia. Second, it was essential to have both super-powers refrain from transferring their arms race to the African continent. (The U.S. greatly reduced arms sales during this period. From 1974-1978 U.S. arms sales to Africa represented 3.7% of the total in contrast to the Soviet group's 56.5%. Soviet portions of the total have recently been as high as 70%.) (See Tables at the end of the chapter.) A brief look at the Horn of Africa enbroglio demonstrates how this Carter approach fared in the late 1970s.

Somalia reached independence in 1960, but for the next twenty years struggled unsuccessfully to finish the process of incorporating Somalis in Ethiopia, Kenya (NFD), and Djibouti. This endeavor drained the Somali economy, antagonized her African neighbors and the Organization of African Unity (OAU) which adhered to the principle of the sanctity of colonial borders, and resulted in several disastrous military defeats and nearly one and a half million Somali refugees from the Ogaden region of Ethiopia. In the process of this obsession, Somalia, a largely Muslim nation and one of the poorest in the world, sought allies in several worlds—Western, Arab, African, Russian, and Chinese. Spurning Western economic packages encumbered by obnoxious conditions regarding Somali territorial ambitions, Somalia accepted a more lucrative promise from the Soviets who asked for little more than a "minor" presence in Somalia. This minor presence grew after Mohammed Siad Barre took power in a military coup in 1969. Siad Barre concentrated at first on consolidating his power, instituting socialist economic reforms, and institutionalizing alliances by joining the Arab League and signing a Friendship Treaty with the Soviets in 1974 (the first Black African government to do so). However, Siad Barre never discarded the goal of re-gaining lost territory, and by 1977 the Somalis were primed for their largest assault. Given the apparent imminent collapse of the Ethiopian empire after a 1974 coup and given the power of Somali forces well fortified after several years of Soviet military assistance, the Somalis felt ready to liberate the Ogaden.

Ethiopia was indeed experiencing apocalyptic disruptions. The corrupt, regressive, and economically impoverished empire of Haile Selassie ended in a military coup led by a mixture of Marxist and moderate officers who called for social, political, and economic reforms. The subsequent revolutionary in-fighting left tens of thousands killed before Mengistu Haile Mariam controlled the Dergue (Amharic for committee). While Mengistu controlled the Dergue and most of Addis Ababa, he did not control the rest of Ethiopia which suffered from economic dislocations, ethnic factionalism, and two major secessionist movements in Eritrea and the Ogaden.

A poor nation, Ethiopia needed allies and assistance to survive. After the civil war, Ethiopia maintained a tenuous relationship with the U.S., which had been a major supporter of Selassie. (From 1953-1970 Ethiopia received 50% of all American aid to Africa.)[26] However, neither patron nor client were satisfied with current arrangements. The Dergue, uncomfortable receiving aid from capitalists and uncomfortable with American nagging about human rights violations and subsequent reductions in aid in 1977, cast out the Americans and invited the Soviets in as more ideologically appropriate replacements. Mengistu, not unaware of Soviet influence in Somalia and support of Marxist groups in Eritrea, must have entertained the notion that the Soviets, if offered a big enough prize, might use their influence on both Somali and Eritrean nationalist forces. He was correct. The closer the Somalis moved toward intervention in Ethiopia in 1977, the slower Soviet aid to Somalia trickled in. The fence sitting Soviets finally answered Mengistu's prayers when the Somalis, disappointed with the scale of aid and Soviet support for Ethiopia, kicked the Soviets out in 1977 after the Somali attack in the Ogaden.

The 1977-1978 war, fought with American and Soviet weapons (the Ethiopians had both) see-sawed until finally superior Ethiopian manpower, resupplied with Soviet and Cuban equipment and men, routed the Somalis. However, the Eritrean front soon demanded equal attention. The disputed territory, strategically located on the Red Sea (Ethiopia would be landlocked without it), was and still is the focus of local Eritrean demands for independence. Ethiopia, unwilling to allow this territory to slip away, directed its resupplied, retrained, and revitalized forces toward the various Eritrean insurgents, who were supported in large measure by several Arab countries who also supported Somalia. After initial failures, Ethiopia defeated most of the rebel groups and forced the remnants, primarily the Eritrean People's Liberation Front (EPLF), into the mountains where they still conduct rebel activities, and where recently the Dergue used the famine in the region to debilitate the rebel forces further.

In this brief review a certain picture unfolds: Two African countries, locked in a zero sum game of opposing interests, sought the aid of various outside powers to expedite their plans and objectives. And the superpowers, in varying degrees and for varying reasons, accepted the invitations.

The U.S., had maintained very strong ties for years with Ethiopia. As host for a communication command center since 1952, it provided a listening post into the Middle East and the Soviet Union. In addition, the solidly pro-Western Emperor (an island of stability for Africa one might have said) was a vital ally for the U.S. and its allies, in particular Israel. Even after his replacement, the U.S. continued to aid Ethiopia due to fears of Soviet encroachment in areas surrounding the Middle East. Soviet influence in Somalia, Yemen, Libya, and Iraq were of particular concern. However, even after Soviet action in Angola, President Carter cut off aid to the extremely repressive and bloody regime in Ethiopia for "humanitarian" reasons in 1977. And, rather than jumping in to replace the Soviets in Somalia, the U.S., despite an interest in wooing Somalia away from the Soviets, refused to support Somalia's designs on the Ogaden. Only after 1981 did significant American military and economic aid reach Somalia. Carter's hesitancy may also be explained in terms of his hope that Ethiopia could be wooed away from the Soviets. This could be implemented more easily if the U.S. remained "neutral" in the local conflict.

The Soviets, however, reject neutralism in favor of supporting national liberation struggles. Soviet interests in third world liberation movements and in undermining Western influence globally resulted in expanded overtures to key African countries in the 1970s. Soviet involvement in the Horn could meet both of these interests as well as yield strategic benefits due to its geographic location. Access to facilities in Somalia or Ethiopia could, in tandem with Soviet influence in South Yemen, Iraq, and Mozambique, offer splended opportunities for naval deployments and projections of power into Africa, the Mid East, and South West Asia. Sovietologist Alvin Rubinstein suggested that the Soviet military pressed this point hardest:

> the ability to reprovision its submarines in Somali ports meant that they could remain on station for longer periods and thereby better evade Western detection devices at the narrow sea routes that lead to Soviet home bases; second, the range of Soviet anti-submarine warfare capabilities was greatly extended in the Arabian Sea and Indian Ocean areas, thus complicating the U.S. deployment of Polaris and Poseidon submarines; and third, the missile storage, port handling, and repair facilities in Somalia constituted part of an overseas operational infrastructure that was designed to support the Soviet navy's assigned tasks in the Indian Ocean area.[27]

The ports of Somalia or Ethiopia were important despite the fact that the Soviets had carte blanche in South Yemen. (The Soviets feared that a naval concentration on the Arabian peninsula might "abuse the sensibilities" of the Arab states.)[28] However, if a choice had to be made between Ethiopia and Somalia, Ethiopia represented the greater asset due to its size, potential, and ideological commitment. In addition, Ethiopia's ouster of the U.S. in exchange for the Soviets represented a major political coup.

However, once enmeshed in Ethiopia's affairs, the Soviets took on new responsbilities and costs as well as assets. The Soviets helped stem the disintegration of Ethiopia (an Ethiopia without Eritrean ports was not much of an asset) but not without billions of rubles in aid. From 1977 to 1979 the Soviets spent more in Ethiopia than they had spent in all of Africa since the beginning of their aid programs.[29] While expecting little reaction from the Carter administration, especially due to the use of primarily Cuban rather than Soviet forces to fight the Somalis, the Soviets did not want to push the U.S. far enough to scare it out of its lethargy. In this they succeeded until the impact of Afghanistan galvanized American public opinion and the presidency. But in terms of their objectives in Africa, the Soviets succeeded more than they failed. The Dergue, increasingly dependent upon the Soviet Union to maintain its grip on power, articulated support for the creation of a vanguard party, for Soviet foreign policy lines (on Afghanistan, for example), for proletarian internationalism, and for Soviet access to facilities on the Red Sea.

While the Soviets were invited into Somalia and Ethiopia and, in fact, were used by the two countries to expedite their respective objectives, the success of Soviet intervention presented several dangerous precedents that have had major ramifications for U.S. foreign policy. The Soviets used military aid to change the course of power in the Horn (first by supplying Somalia with sufficient military capability to launch a war and then by supplying the other side sufficiently to counter that attack), they encouraged formation of vanguard parties intended to lead the Africans down the path of scientific socialism, and they legitimized their access to facilities in an age where it is less legitimate to serve American forces. The Soviets, with patient activism, projected an image of strength and determination that corresponded with the Soviet assertion that the correlation of forces favored socialist forces.

Despite Carter's good intentions, his Africa policy yielded considerable criticism in the U.S. in the late 1970s as the impact of Soviet moves in Angola, the Horn of Africa, and Afghanistan hit home. Many believed that Carter overcompensated for the past narrow geostrategic approach of American policy in Africa. Many in the Reagan administration believed that the overall flabbiness of the Carter response to Soviet actions in Somalia and throughout Africa may have signalled two messages to Soviets and Africans: 1) that the Soviet assessment about American inability or unwillingness to respond to Soviet challenges was correct and 2) that present allies and clients should take note of American hesitancy, inconsistency, and weakness. Reagan intended to refute the validity of these messages.

The Reagan administration entered office with a different set of assumptions about the nature of Soviet-U.S. relations and how these impinged on Africa. Since the Soviets had demonstrated, via third world adventures (among other things), that detente was limited and not applicable to support for national liberation movements as in Angola or Ethiopia, Reagan believed that the U.S. must reenter the struggle that Carter avoided, especially since this avoidance allowed unpleasant Soviet in-roads. Africa was important for a number of reasons. According to Helen Kitchen,

> Africa is perceived primarily as a theater of operations in Moscow's long-term campaign to extend its area of hegemony into segments of the globe that have historically been within the West's sphere of influence. The current pattern of Soviet behavior in Africa can be characterized as one of opportunism (as contrasted with a step-by-step master plan) only in the sense that the accelerating pace of Soviet intervention there is closely related to the paralyzing mood of suicidal appeasement that has seized the United States since Vietnam.[30]

Most dangerous for the U.S. was the Soviet Union's opportunistic search for conflicts to exploit in attempts to expand its influence while undermining Western influence. Chester Crocker, Assistant Secretary for African Affairs, commented on the security issues in these Soviet attempts:

> Internal instability, often in tandem with external adventurism, plagues many African countries. Border struggles, which have often evolved from uncertain colonial arrangements, create serious regional problems. Ethnic rivalries have precipitated civil wars, sometimes leading to cross-border violence. The mere management of modest security forces overtaxes the meager resources of many states. These circumstances are often exploited by outside powers unfriendly to us, and in this manner a problem having clearly African roots can acquire broader global implications.
>
> Neither we in the West nor African states can gain when one outside power seeks unilateral advantage through the projection or application of military force in Africa. Africa, like the West, is the loser when regional actors are encouraged to pursue violent rather than negotiated solutions. In such circumstances, we believe that unilateral self-denial by Western countries cannot strengthen African security or nonalignment; instead, it erodes the climate of confidence necessary to achieve them. The United States cannot be a credible partner if it ignores friendly African states who turn to us in real defensive need. The solution to conflicts in Africa does not rest with U.S. abstinence while others rush in to exploit regional strife. This Administration stands ready to help bolster the security of countries so affected.[31]

This activist promise coincided with the administration's attempt to direct Western aid to "proven friends" in Africa and those likely to be vulnerable to Soviet or Cuban pressure. The promise to forego abstinence, while admirable vis-a-vis the embattled black African states or movements seeking Western aid, appeared least appealing when applied to South Africa where the Reagan administration supports "constructive engagement."

South Africa, vital to the West in terms of its strategic resources and location, provided the spark, via apartheid and unyielding resistance to "relinquishment" of Namibia (a territory awarded by the League of Nations to South Africa which was to prepare the people for independence), for inevitable violence in southern Africa. The Reagan administration maintained that the U.S., via quiet diplomacy, would secure independence for Namibia without violence. On the other hand, in a "realistic" appreciation of South Africa's (and America's) security concerns, the Namibian settlement depended on Cuban withdrawal from neighboring Angola. However, aware that its "neutral" approach to South Africa displeased many Africans, the U.S. voted in the U.N. to condemn South Africa's presence in Namibia and recently imposed limited sanctions against it. However, Reagan rejects the application of more extensive sanctions that might be ineffective or that might reduce the American capacity to influence the South African government in a more "decent, democratic, prosperous and civilized" direction.

Another development sending mixed signals regarding Reagan's posture towards Africa involves his support for Jonas Savimbi, the leader of Angola's powerful liberation movement. While the Department of State urged cuts in aid to Savimbi, Reagan decided to supply Stinger anti-aircraft weapons to his forces fighting the Cubans. The State Department has succeeded in blocking American aid to the non-communist opposition in Mozambique, in the hope of wooing the Marxist regime away from the Soviet bloc. Obviously the administration remains divided over its policy in southern Africa, except for the vague and probably impossible hope that it can help arrange a final agreement over Apartheid, Namibia, and Angola that will ameliorate some of the sources of conflict in the region without damaging American interests there.

Other key states in Subsaharan and Central Africa are Somalia, the Sudan, and Kenya (facing the Indian Ocean and/or the Red Sea), Nigeria (oil rich, pro-West, but a large debtor and needing reassurance about American credentials vis-a-vis South Africa), and Zaire (resource rich, but institution poor). Three key North African countries—Egypt, Morocco, and Tunisia—receive about 90% of American aid to Africa. Despite American support of these states, foreign aid and security assistance to Africa lags behind similar aid to the Middle East or Latin American (and in some cases behind Soviet military aid). For example, while it took the U.S. almost four years from 1979-1982 to extend 20 million dollars to Somalia, after it left the Soviet camp, the Soviet group extended two billion dollars in aid to its new Ethiopian client. From 1979-1983 it transferred nearly two billion more in arms to Ethiopia. The recipient of most American arms in this latter period was Egypt with $2.4 billion.

The three key states in the Horn of Africa—Somalia, Sudan, and Kenya— are among the poorest and most overpopulated in the third world. They have faced horrible droughts, chronic border disputes, and periodic Marxist and Islamic (among others) stirrings in recent years. Largely as a response to the basic human needs of these nations, American development assistance, food aid, and economic and training grants heavily outweighed military aid. In FY 1984 Sudan received $189 million in economic aid and $60 million in military aid; Kenya received nearly $90 million versus $23 million in economic and military aid; and Somalia received $72 million versus $40 million in economic and military aid. (See tables below.) The Reagan administration, awaiting the FY 1988 knife, plans to increase aid to Somalia, Kenya, and Zaire in another year of draconian cuts in overall foreign aid. However, even these projected increases pale into insignificance compared to aid to Egypt. However, the Soviets win the prize with their arms transfers which ranged from $7.2 billion for Iraq to nearly $6 billion for Libya from 1979-1983. On the other hand, Soviet economic aid remains miniscule compared to aid from the U.S. and Western Europe.

The particulars of aid and arms transfers merely provide some insightful indicators of favored clients and current hot spots in the region. It might be more useful at this point to sum up American objectives in Africa and the problems and costs American policies encounter there. American objectives fall into several economic, strategic, and political categories. Number one on the economic list is access to African goods and markets. Related interests falling into the strategic category include preventing the Soviets from gaining control of countries that mine key and scarce natural resources and that provide, via their locations facing the Red Sea, the Indian Ocean, and the Cape, excellent prospects of interdicting sea lanes. Political objectives include intentions to persuade Africans of U.S. staying power, fairness, and economic largesse. The Reagan administration wants to counter the perception that the balance of power is changing in the Soviet Union's favor, prevent its domination of key states, and use military aid capability to correct regional imbalances of power created by Soviet or Cuban infestations. With respect to the Africans, the administration wants to stabilize vulnerable countries through economic aid and trade, avoid arms sales that might exacerbate local tensions, encourage inter-relationships among moderate Arab and African governments that share economic, security, and political interests with the U.S., and "help Africans achieve a degree of institutional stability that would reduce the incidence of insurgencies, cross border actions, and civil wars."

Perhaps because of the mix of idealism and pragmatism reflected in these objectives, we are not surprised to see obstacles to their realization described in both pragmatic and idealistic terms.[32] The idealists remind us that emphasis on global issues brings the U.S. into close proximity with hated regimes in South Africa and Zaire and causes it to be insensitive to African goals, to stress false priorities (sea lanes over human rights), and to exaggerate the nature of the Soviet threat. They also remind us that constructive engagement and quiet diplomacy have had little impact on moderation in South Africa. Pragmatists question whether economic aid alone can promote stable political conditions or counter Soviet in-roads.

Most of the objectives and problems discussed in this section—concern about Soviet and Cuban interventions, domestic instability, and geostrategic trade routes; attacks on the credibility of American commitments; and the dilemma of choosing between corrupt regimes versus radical revolutionaries and between human rights versus global interests—are found as well in the rest of the third world. A review of a few more hot spots will broaden out understanding of Reagan's view of the necessary American role in the third world.

## Containment Applied: Latin America

From the Monroe Doctrine of 1801 to the Spanish-American War at the end of the 19th century, from the Panama Canal land grab to the several interventions in Nicaragua, Guatemala, Cuba, and the Dominican Republic, and from Franklin Roosevelt's "Good Neighbor Policy" to Kennedy's "Alliance for Progress," Latin America has been a periodic focus of American policy, posturing, and preemption. For reasons of economics (investments, property, resources, and markets); geography (proximity, trade routes, and land and sea bridges to the Western Hemisphere); and credibility (to keep the American sphere of influence inviolate and to defend allies and friends there to maintain credibility of interests elsewhere); every president concerned about the Latin American back yard has maintained a watchful eye over the region.

Reagan follows a traditional balance of power approach to Latin America, an approach often criticized as being characterized more by failure and blunder than by leadership and wisdom. In this balance of power mode, Reagan assumes that Latin America is in America's sphere of influence and, since this sphere experiences greater threats in the 1980s than ever before, it requires expanded efforts to maintain stability there. While Reagan admits that numerous endemic economic, social, and political problems infest and overwhelm the region, and cause most of the unrest and turmoil there, he fears that the Soviets (and Cubans) seek to exploit these problems to increase their influence, infiltrate and manipulate the region, and degrade American influence, prestige, and security. He is determined to roll the Soviets and Cubans out of Latin America (as in Grenada), buttress threatened regimes (as in El Salvador), and advance the cause of democracy, a free economy, and national self determination (as in Nicaragua.)

The Reagan remedy includes money (the Caribbean Basin Initiative, economic aid to the tune of 13% of U.S. bilateral assistance in FY 1988, and increased multilateral and private American lending and investment), military might (the physical presence of U.S. forces and advisers in key areas like the Panama Canal and Guantanamo Bay), and diplomacy. To understand his determination and remedy, it is necessary to place the battle over Latin America in the East-West and third world contexts more generally. The Reagan administration sees Soviet infiltration being conducted in its most subtle and insidious form in the helpless, manipulatable, and incendiary third world, It sees the Soviets, who made great strides in the third world in the 1970s, intent to nibble away at American positions or friends, exploit regional conflicts, and destabilize pro-Western and neutral regimes unless the U.S. erects barriers to Soviet ambitions and makes the cost of Soviet actions expensive and counterproductive. The Soviets now spend over four billion dollars a year to sustain their Cuban outpost—about three times U.S. aid to all of Latin America and the Caribbean—in an attempt to outflank the U.S. in Central America. In Reagan's view this attempt must be met by an unwavering American response—a response based on the acceptance of America's global role in advancing the cause of democracy, resolving regional conflicts, and diminishing the risk of war enhanced by Soviet aggession.[33]

The administration assumes, as have most cold war period administrations, that regional conflicts can not be regarded as peripheral to other issues on the global agenda.[34] Secretary Shultz articulated this Trumanesque view of Soviet challenges at the fringes in the following way:

> Americans must undersatnd...that a number of small challenges, year after year, can add up to a more serious challenge to our interests. The time to act, to help our friends by adding our strength to the equation, is not when the threat is at the doorstep, when the stakes are highest and the needed resources enormous. We must be prepared to commit our political, economic, and, if necessary, military power when the threat is still manageable and when its prudent use can prevent the threat from growing. We have far less margin for error today than we did even thirty years ago. We cannot afford to be complacement about events around the world in the expectation that, in the end, we will have the strength to overcome any challenge. We do not have the luxury of waiting until all the ambiguities have disappeared. This is the essence of statemanship-to see a danger when it is not self-evident; to educate our people to the stakes involved; then to fashion a sensible response and rally support.[35]

This unclear but present danger lurked most visibly in El Salvador, Grenada, and Nicaragua.

Reagan considered the stability of the Jose Napolean Duarte faction (the Christian Democrats) as a number one priority in Central America. Periodically victimized by communist insurgents, El Salvador became a test case for Reagan's pledge to prove that democracy could work in Latin America. In the 1980s it received nearly 1/3 of all U.S. foreign aid to Latin America and the Caribbean. Since 1984 economic and military aid to El Salvador has averaged over $315 million and $125 million per year respectively. (See Table 11.) the electoral success of Duarte in 1985, the defeat of the extreme right wing, the apparent (if reluctant) willingness of the army to support the constitutional government, and the steady decline in numbers and popularity of the communist insurgents (down to five or six thousand), indicates that in El Salvador the centrist forces, with continued U.S. economic and military assistance, may prevail. On the other hand, human rights violations and death squad activities remain and may jeopardize the "victory" of the Reagan Doctrine and the plan of winning the "hearts and minds" of the non-combatants while winning on the battle field in "low intensity conflicts." However, American advice and training and the Salvadoran military's efforts at self-reform and reconstruction in the countryside have, for the moment, yielded encouraging results. For example, according to a 1985 UN human rights commission, death squad activities and arbitrary violations of civil liberties in El Salvador have diminshed in number and frequency. In the meantime, the regime faces attack by forces more deadly than guerrilla terrorism—economic debility. The economic picture for El Salvador and, in fact, for the entire Latin American region shows the underlying causes of social turmoil and the potential for popular explosions.

Excluding Brazil, Latin American experienced a 1.5% drop in per capita income in 1985 and a cumulative 9% decline since 1980.[36] Unemployment and underemployment vary from 30-50%. Inflation averages almost 150% in the region as a whole, while Brazil's inflation rose to over 230% in 1985. Latin American countries face massive debt complicated by disadvantageous trade deficits. Brazil, whose austerity measures to curb inflation stirred up public outcries and strikes, cannot seem to salvage its trade surplus to help service its 1986 foreign debt of $107 billion. Most other Latin American states are behind in interest payments, and they devote nearly 40% of their export earnings to paying interest on outstanding loans. Exports fell steadily throughout the 1980s, while prices for most export commodities fell to their lowest point since the depression of the 1930s. Add to this the overpopulation in much of the region, the slackening in outside investment, unpopular austerity measures, and local corruption or mismanagement, and the prospects for many new democracies (civilian democratic governments rule in over 90% of Latin Americ) appear bleak.

This bleak prospect, the awareness that communism and violence feed on economic unrest, and the Reagan determination to hold the line against Soviet and Cuban meddling in Latin American spawned the creation of a Bipartisan Commission under the leadership of Henry Kissinger. The Commission studied the nature of indigenous and external causes of the social, political, and economic disasters in the region. It found that, while reform and revolution in Latin America did not directly threaten American interests, Soviet and Cuban fueling of the unrest created symbolic and strategic threats to the regional balance of power and American security interest there.[37] According to the commission, a victory by Soviet supported forces, in what the Soviets call the "strategic rear" of the U.S., would indicate American impotence and inability to manage policy or exercise power in the region.

Given the indigenous problems and Soviet exploitation of them, the administration urged a more comprehensive strategy to promote 1) democratization, political legitimization, and national self-determination; 2) human development and social reform; 3) economic growth through doubled economic aid and the creation of institutions like the Central American Development Organization (CADO) to provide a continuous approach to development; and 4) security assistance to states in immediate peril like El Salvador.[38] To respond to both endemic and external threats required both economic development and security assistance. Military aid to El Salvador, for example, was directly linked to the prospects for effective diplomacy and negotiation, since, according to Kissinger, the Soviets and their surrogates "are unlikely to perceive negotiations as anything more than a tactical maneuver as long as they believe they can win power on the field of battle."[39] However, the U.S. imposed conditions on security assistance, such as an end to the violations of human rights in El Salvador in the early 1980s. On the other hand, both Kissinger and the Reagan administration cautioned that such conditions should not be allowed to result in a "Marxist-Leninist victory in El Salvador."

The Caribbean Basin Initiative (CBI), proposed by Reagan in 1983, also undertook the tasks of responding to internal and external threats and of increasing political stability, social tranquility and economic growth in the vulnerable Caribbean. This initiative leapt into existence in the aftermath of the U.S. intervention in Grenada, at the invitation of the Organization of Eastern Caribbean States (OECS). The Grenadans themselves, according to several public opinion polls sponsored by the OECS and the U.S., approved of the operation in overwhelming fashion. One December 1983 OECS poll found an 86% approval rate. The American public, still reeling from the devastating loss of nearly 300 Marines in the terrorist attack in Lebanon in late 1983, rallied behind the president in significantly large numbers. Western allies and many in the third world, excluding the OECS, expressed considerably less public or official enthusiasm. Questions remain as to the impact of the move on Latin American states. Many unofficially appreciated the president's dilemma: to intervene and risk a Latin American and third world backlash of anti-Americanism or to ignore Soviet and Cuban intervention and agitation and risk erosion in the promise to contain or reverse Soviet gains in the third world. The subsequent stability in Grenada quieted many opponents of the intervention.

In his move to put out a small fire in Grenada, Reagan intended to put an end to the turmoil and dangers unleashed by the coming to, and collapsing of, power by the Soviet/Cuban sponsored New Jewel Movement. While the official justification for immediate intervention was the safe and expeditious evacuation of American citizens from the "civil war" zone, the primary objectives seemed to be ousting the rather unpopular, anti-American, and pro-Soviet government; restoring order; demonstrating the importance that the administration attached to the region; and blasting a pregnant message to the Sandinistas and other aspiring Marxist-Leninist groups about potential new applications of the Reagan Doctrine.

The Sandinistas, who came into power in Nicargua in 1979 as one faction of a multifaceted anti-Somoza coalition, had by 1983 purged the more moderate members of the junta, imposed an increasingly repressive regime, and undertaken the task of leading the vanguard of revolution in Latin America. (Even some Anti-Reagan groups, like the International League for Human Rights, have noted the increasing repression by the Sandinistas. [40]) As a consequence of this activity and proclivity, which confirmed Reagan's view of the nature of the communist threat,

Nicaragua quickly superseded El Salvador as the most important place to hold the line against Soviet or Cuban influence.

The administration views the Sandinistas as a great danger to democracy, as they campaign, with considerable Soviet aid (over one billion dollars in the 1980s and one billion in Soviet-bloc aid in 1986) to subvert their neighbors in a self-professed effort to promote "a revolution without borders." Reagan argues that, since democracy is still a fragile root in Latin America, the U.S. should not ignore the long term danger to the region and American interests by a Soviet-backed communist Nicaragua. He urges economic aid and security assistance to the Contras or counter-revolutionaries—many former "children of the revolution" who denounced the radical and repressive direction of the Sandinistas. (The Contras, numbering up to 20,000 by State Department accounts, consist of numerous factions: former supporters of Nicaraguan dictator Somoza, disillusioned Sandinistas, Meskito Indians forceably dispossessed by the government, poor peasants caught up in the struggle over land, members of the middle class seeking an end to economic mismanagement, radicalized Catholics resentful of the cruelty of the Sandinistas to the church, etc.)

While the administration clearly overestimates the threat to the U.S. and the region, the size of Nicaragua's ostentatiously large army, which is the second largest in the region behind only Mexico and which reputedly is scheduled to double in size by the mid 1990s, raises several security issues for the U.S. In addition, Reagan assumes that Marxist groups inevitably seek to disrupt the democratic process because they reject pluralism, power-sharing, and freedom of expression and choice. The active role the Sandinistas play in aiding, training, recruiting, and funding various guerrilla groups reinforces Reagan's convictions. In the meantime, while Reagan may still be uncertain about whether he wants to topple the Sandinistas or merely force them to forego revolutionary activity and repressive domestic practices, he has invoked the precedent of the Truman Doctrine in his campaign to prevent Cuban-like bases or leftist guerrilla sanctuaries on the Latin American mainland. In his attempt to apply a Reagan Doctrine to Latin America, he wants to "support those who struggle to preserve freedom" and to excise or exorcise the "malignancy in Nicaragua" before it spreads and "becomes a mortal threat to the new world."[41]

While the Contadora group (Costa Rica, Mexico, Guatemala, and Panama) have urged a more conciliatory path, El Salvador, Honduras, Costa Rica, and Guatemala have been the most worried about the spread of Sandinista or Soviet inspired and supported revolutionary movements. In the on-again off-again negotiations with the Sandinistas, the Latin American states have been frustrated with both the Sandinistan and American maneuvers to dominate the political agenda. In one last gasp effort to exploit both the economic desperation in Nicaragua and the dramatic divisions within the U.S. over how to deal with Nicaragua, the regional states, in August 1987, promised the Sandinistas withdrawal of support for the Contras in exchange for a cease-fire and democratization in Nicaragua.

The rather vague and hastily formulated plan derived from efforts of the regional states to keep the peace process in Latin American hands, at least on the surface. These same hands rely on American hands to bail them out of economic, political, and military troubles. In the meantime, the Guatemalan Peace Plan (or the Arias Plan, named after the Costa Rican president) puts the Sandinistas in the driver's seat. In exchange for largely cosmetic and easily reversible reforms and actions (amnesties for political prisoners, freedom of the press as of October 1987, renewed promises of free elections, and so forth) the Latin American states and the U.S. pledge to withdraw Contra aid.

Skeptics worry that once the Contra's supplies dry up and they cease to be effective, the Sandinistas could further consolidate power until they could once again end liberalization and democratization as a necessary step in making their control permanent. On the other hand, many in the West, who show distaste for the Contras, show optimism about the prospects of the Marxist-Leninist regime turning itself into a pluralistic democracy willing to bestow equal status on all political groups and to embrace free elections. Others like Kissinger doubt the wisdom of the opponents of Contra aid who have refused to accept that without the Contras there wouldn't have been much movement on the negotiating front and who hesitate to impose security restrictions or human rights provisions on the Sandinistas.[42] Kissinger worries most about the absence in the Guatemalan Plan of references to specific threats to U.S. and regional security and the Soviet and Cuban military aid in the region. The U.S. can not dismiss the possibility that, while the Sandinistas may allow some cosmetic reforms, as they did in 1979, they may reverse course and re-open the door for additional Soviet infiltration once the U.S. abandons the Contras.

Supporters of the plan see an entirely different future. If the Sandinistas carry out their responsibilities under the plan—to open their society to democratic ideas and institutions—a snow ball effect could enhance the prospects of genuine and persistent reform. Without the harassment of the Contras and the U.S., the Sandinistas may live up to the original promises of their revolutionary movement. In addition, if the regional states themselves can create and perpetuate conciliation, negotiation, and democratization in the region, this would bode well as a precedent for regional solutions to other indigenous troubles. Unfortunately, the prospects for peace appear bleak. Denunciations regarding non-compliance flow between the signatories. While Nicaragua has not lifted its state-of-seige laws, extended full political amnesty, nor ended support for guerillas in El Salvador, the U.S. has yet to decide the extent of its support for the plan.

It pledged not to undermine the Arias plan, but this does not mean, according to Shultz, that the U.S. would "permit the peace process to become a shield for the physical elminimation of the Nicaraguan Resistance." However, regarding the Reagan Doctrine and its application in Latin America, the administration has often spoken loudly but carried a small stick. The history of aid to the Contras reflects the administration's inability to find enough aid to achieve its objective of engineering a transformation of the Nicaraguan government into a pluralistic democracy. It has, of course, demonstrated its commitment by mild and wild schemes to generate public approval and funding. More than any recent administration, it has utilized foreign aid as an adjunct to foreign policy. From 1980-1986 foreign aid increased by 85% (unadjusted for inflation.) On the other hand, aid to Latin American represented only about 13% of American bilateral aid. The wilder schemes, such as funding the Contras via secret arms sales to Iran, also demonstrated, more publicly than intended, the administration's concern for the threat to Latin American and American security imposed by Nicaragua's (and the Soviet's) support for revolutionary movements in the region.

In Reagan's view, Nicaragua not only threatens democracies in the region, but it poses a security threat as well in terms of its geostrategic potential as a base for Soviet interruption of vital sea and trading lanes. After all, more than one-half of all American imports and exports traverse the Caribbean basin. While scenarios depicting conventional attacks against commercial or military shipping anticipate the prospect of a limited, conventional war between the U.S. and the Soviet Union and/or Nicaragua (!), either of which seems unlikely, the administration considers it wise to deny the Soviets such a potential capability. More importantly, an unopposed Nicaraguan (Soviet/Cuban) interference in neighboring states poses a more subtle and intangible threat to American credibility. American impotence at restraining Nicaragua might reawaken the doubts of the 1970s about American staying power and commitment. In other words, as the administration asks, "if Central America were to fall, what would the consequences be in Asia, Europe, and for alliances such as NATO? If the U.S. cannot respond to a threat near our own borders, why should Europeans or Asians believe that we are seriously concerned about threats to them? If the Soviets can assume that nothing short of an actual attack on the U.S. will provoke an American response, which ally, which friend will trust us then?"[43] Reagan hopes to escape this fate by convincing the Soviets that the Brezhnev Doctrine (allowing no turnover in communist control in Eastern Europe, Afghanistan, Angola, Nicaragua, and so forth) and the expansionist policies of the 1970s can no longer work.

Nicaragua, then, has represented a major test of the Reagan Doctrine. Economic *and* military aid to Latin America are believed crucial for passing the test and resolving the conflicts there. In yet another rejection of Kennan's advice, the administration has insisted that economic and diplomatic instruments are not effective without sustained and sufficient military aid to help cast an appropriate "shadow of power" across the bargaining table. According to Reagan, in his pleas for congressional approval of military aid for the Contras, "the only way to bring peace and security to Central America is to bring democracy to Nicaragua. And the only way to get the Sandinistas to negotiate seriously about democracy is to give them no alternative."[44] Depriving the Soviets and Nicaraguans of a military victory against the Contras would show them the futility of a military solution and encourage a Sandinistan re-evaluation of their role in the region and their practices at home as well. The administration might assume, as does Kissinger, that the viability of the Contras and the stubborn American support of them did indeed contribute to the Sandinistan willingness to accept a negotiated settlement that included rebel participation. If true, this would vindicate, in part, the administration's claim that the Reagan Doctrine and an active containment policy force appropriate accommodation from the Soviets and their proxies.

These plans, objectives, and remedies of the administration aroused considerable and strident objections by Reagan opponents. Critics complained about the excessive worry about chokepoints, cascading dominos, credibility, and communist challenges. These obsessions, which presumably flow from the myopia of containment-colored glasses, drive Reagan, as they drove Truman, to think in terms of ever expanding vital interests and threats to those interests, the use of forceful counterpressure rather than diplomacy, and global plots rather than endemic unrest. Robert Johnson, for example, asserts that the administration inflated the stakes involved in both El Salvador and Nicaragua due to its outdated geopolitical reasoning and credibility-conscious mentality.[45] James Schlesinger, Nixon's Defense Secretary agrees with this analysis when he compares Nicaragua to Albania rather than Cuba.[46] Raymond Garthoff, argues that the Reagan administration exaggerates the Soviet role in the region and incorrectly assumes the existence of a single minded Soviet master plan to expand power.[47] Such a master plan may exist more in the minds of Western cold warriors than in a Soviet leadership worried about overextension in the third world, the unreliability and burdensome nature of client states, strategic and ideological threats from the U.S. and China, and the stagnation of an economy handcuffed by ideological and bureaucratic inertia.

The focal point of criticism is that containment, as applied by Reagan in Latin America and elsewhere in the third world, concentrates obsessively on the putative involvement of every regional conflict with the global East-West conflict and on unidimensional military solutions that overshadow local ills. As directed toward Nicaragua specifically, this concentration could easily turn the Latin American parts of the third world against the U.S. They already resent past American chauvinism and interference and remain uneasy about American support for opposition groups and the potential danger that this implies for them as future targets. The U.S. might be better off aligning itself with progressive forces, abandoning right-wing clients, and adhering to its own principles regarding the rights of national self determiniation and non-interference in domestic affairs. Indiscriminate American interventions call into question American commitment to these values and may pose a greater threat to credibility than abstention from involvement in Nicaragua.

This emphasis on American responsibility to adhere to its own principles conflicts with Reagan's pursuit of containment seemingly without regard to the nature of the regimes supported. Former Secretary of State Vance insists, for example, that Reagan recognize that anti-communism can not be equated with democracy, and that a dogmatic and automatic support for all those (democratic or undemocratic) caught in the East-West conflict undermines America's moral authority.[48] He suggests limiting intervention to cases where aid promotes human rights, falls under international legal obligations to assist those resisting aggression, or "clearly serves American interests." 'Tis a consummation devoutly to be wished. Surely Reagan would prefer to act only in such clear cut cases, but the games, the players, and the rules are seldom clear enough to meet Vance's criteria. Should the U.S. support less than democratic Turkey; feudal Saudi Arabia (a moderate Arab state); Israel (a partially compromised and retrenching democracy); repressive yet economically healthy South Korea (a jewel of enlightenment compared to North Korea); El Salvador (with Christian Democrats still vulnerable to pressure from the right wing); and Zia's Pakistan (democratic versus front line geo-strategic considerations?) One dilemma, over support for long time ally Marcos of the Phillippines, partially resolved itself in 1986 as Corazon Aquino's democratic coalition replaced the Marcos government with the complete backing of the administration.

To be as pure as Vance's guidelines demand, the U.S. might risk losing more than these few allies or friends. As Shultz argued, in explaining the importance of eliminating third world instability that risked increased East-West tensions,

> In an imperfect and insecure world, of course, we have to cooperate and sometimes assist those who do not share our principles or who do so only nominally. We cannot create democratic or independence movements where none exist or make them strong where they are weak. But there is no mistaking which side we are on. And when there are opportunities to support responsible change for the better, we will be there.[49]

However, even ardent supporters of containment accept the argument that principle must supersede interests. Critics and supporters disagree over the extent to which the U.S. can, should, and does sacrifice principle in the interest of national security.

Whatever individual conclusions on this matter, both supporters and critics question the ability of the U.S. to meet Soviet challenges everywhere in the third world. In urging selective engagement, some call for the establishment of priorities including Western Europe, Japan, and the Persian Gulf, but excluding Angola, Mozambique and Kampuchea because they hold little strategic utility and pose little risk to U.S. credibility; Afghanistan because it resides in the Soviet sphere of influence; and El Salvador or Nicaragua because they are tiny, poor, and distant. Critics also urge selectivity because the issues involved and the threats posed are murky and difficult to explain to the mercurial, self-centered, and Vietnam-scarred American public. This is especially the case with respect to Nicaragua where the public objects to the Sandinista emplacement of an undemocratic, repressive, and hostile regime, but fears that there is little the U.S. can do about it without direct intervention, which it rejects overwhelmingly, according to most public opinion polls. Mere aid to the Contras has aroused public and congressional anxieties about potential escalation of the conflict. But like

Congresses and publics of the past, they hope that injections of dollars and support of local armies or local peace plans will solve problems and elinimate the need for direct intervention.

The Reagan administration faces a constant rear guard action to sustain public support for its containment efforts in Latin America. As long as the costs remain low (or obscure), as long as analogies to Vietnam remain subordinate to comparably abhorrent images of the seeming American impotence and humiliation under Carter, and as long as Reagan achieves modest victories in his attempts to keep Duarte and the Contras floating and the Sandinistas thwarted or bottled up, then a still popular Reagan may continue to find that support.

However, Reagan's precipitous decline in popularity, since the every broadening scope of the revelations about the administration's efforts to circumvent the Congress to fund the Contras, bodes ill for his policy regarding Nicaragua specifically and for the Reagan Doctrine as a whole. The public, already gun-shy, about the costs and risks of intervention in Latin America and the Persian Gulf, may well doubt the urgency, relevance, practicality, and/or legality of Reagan's intention to contain or rollback the Sandinistas, Cubans, or Soviets in the third world.

The high hopes for rollback still founder, then, for a number of reasons:

1) public and congressional intermittent unwillingness to foot the bill in terms of dollars and policy goals;

2) local obstacles resulting from the inability of groups like the Contras or Afghan or Angolan rebels to achieve power;

3) Soviet dexterity in supporting national liberation movements without inflaming third world states or arousing the West;

4) the administration's clumsiness in articulating and executing a coherent plan for containing Soviet aggression without reinstituting the cold war and/or alienating allies and third world states.

## Conclusions:

Reagan has embraced containment as the best way to resist the Soviet Union's manipulation of third world turmoil in its attempts to facilitate the growth of Marxist-Leninist parties, legitimize Soviet participation in third world controversies, and expedite access to facilities in key countries to provide logistical support for a global projection of power. If the U.S. fails to react to the Soviet activism, this may suggest, in the symbolic language of cold war politics, that the U.S. is too weak or unwilling to play the superpower game; confirm Soviet boasts about the shifting correlation of forces; and encourage additonal Soviet moves. With mixed signals of American support for those threatened by internal or external Marxist forces, few third world leaders or groups could count on sufficient or expeditious assistance from the U.S. While Reagan's gun-toting image may be too much for the Soviets, some third worlders, and some Americans to swallow, it may be necessary to demonstrate firmness of purpose by backing up selective and, one would hope, respectable clients and friends. In this way, American interests in countering Soviet moves, denying the validity of the Brezhnev Doctrine, encouraging stability in the third world, and reasserting itself as a responsible and responsive global power may be best served.

While these remarks reflect a "cold war mentality," perhaps this is appropriate given the cold war drama playing in much of the third world. This is not to suggest that the Soviets caused the problems in the third world, nor that ethnic, social, economic, or ideological problems can be solved solely by removing the Soviet presence. Indeed, as the U.S. actively engages in the struggle with the Soviets, it must pay attention to the underlying problems that cause many in the third world to look for radical cures for their ills. However, while the imposition of the superpower struggle in these regions often exacerbates local difficulties, a unilateral American abstention from intervention merely invites full and cheap play by the Soviets. The U.S. can not count on "morally correct" abstention, antiseptic isolation, indiscriminate injections of dollars, and the "example" (no matter how salutory) of the American experience to combat third world problems or Soviet exploitation of them.

In this review of Soviet-American competition in Western Europe and the third world and of Reagan's perceptions of the issues at stake and the most effective remedies for dealing with them, we saw the unfolding of Reagan's approach to containment. The Reagan administration chose containment because of its suspicions that "the Soviet Union is the greatest source of international insecurity today. Soviet promotion of violence as the instrument of change is the greatest danger to peace."[50] According to Shultz, the U.S. should "stand up to the problems that we confront around the world and the problems imposed on us by the military strength of the Soviet Union and the demonstrated willingness of the Soviet Union to use its strength without any compunction whatever."[51]

This 1980s version of containment depends on securing a military balance, convincing the Soviets that there "are penalties for aggression and incentives for restraint," and forging an American consensus on the need to manage Soviet power, defend Western interests, and re-establish a U.S. global presence.[52] The underlying premises of Truman's containment—that the Soviet Union is an expansionist state, that Soviet activism falters when met by resistance, and that Western military power and unity of purpose prompt and reinforce Soviet caution—remain in full force in the Reagan policy.

One of the most comprehensive re-statements of the need for containment came from Shultz in a 1983 Senate hearing. He spoke of the obligation to counter Soviet encroachments, the assumption "that the Soviet Union is more likely to be deterred by our actions that make clear the risks their aggression entails than by a delicate web of interdependence," and the "expectation that, faced with demonstration of the West's renewed determination to strengthen its defenses, enhance its political and economic cohesion, and oppose adventurism, the Soviet Union will see restraint as its most attractive, or only, option."[53] He also suggested what we might call pre-emptive containment: "where it was once our goal to contain the Soviet presence within the limits of its immediate post-war reach, now our goal must be to advance our own objectives where possible foreclosing and when necessary actively countering Soviet challenges wherever they threaten our interests."[54] Unfortunately, the subtle, ambiguous, and uncertain political threat from the Soviets has often been a difficult concept to relay to Western publics fearful of arms races, escalating regional conflicts, and the prospect of nuclear war. Complicating this situation, American officials have had difficulty deciding which issues and areas were important enough to demand a response. For example, Truman and Acheson wrote off China and Korea in 1950 only to find in retrospect that, for the sake of the credibility of other commitments, they had to respond to the North Korean invasion. In rhetoric and style the Eisenhower administration pursued containment, while it sacrificed conventional military strength for a balanced budget and abandoned liberation and rollback by 1956. More consistency between rhetoric and action might have added more consistency in the pursuit of containment.

On the other hand, for people like Dulles words were better than nothing. But not so for Kennedy and Johnson who reverted to what Gaddis called a symmetrical containment. However, it might be more appropriate to describe their policy as both symmetrical and asymmetrical. While both undertook to maintain commitments everywhere for appearance's sake, the failure in Vietnam may be attributed to local conditions, military tactics, and a hostile public as well as to a symmetrical containment. In addition, limitations in the American response to Soviet moves did occur during this period (over Berlin, Laos, Cuba, Czechoslovakia, and in Africa), as did limits on the conduct of the Vietnam war. While it is beyond the scope of this chapter to discuss these events further, it is interesting to note that Gaddis preferred the asymmetrical approach to the selective containment of the Nixon period, a period ending in American retreat on all fronts—economic, military, and political.

Garthoff, on the other hand, disapproves of the Nixon and Kissinger handling of detente which, in his view, resulted from their failure to appreciate Soviet perceptions, interests, and expectations. A clearer and more open minded approach to the Soviets might have avoided the breakdown of detente that followed Carter's even more disastrous handling of Soviet-U.S. relations. Garthoff holds little hope that the Reagan administration, which lets anti-communist assumptions and narrow minded geostrategy and realpolitik drive its foreign policy, will find an intelligent replacement for detente cum containment.

My appraisal of Reagan's containment offers a more hopeful set of conclusions: 1) While Reagan's containment most closely resembles that of Truman, it reflects a pragmatic appreciation of the intrusive strategic, political, and economic realities that all post-war administrations faced. While Reagan lectures the Soviets and concentrates on rebuilding American strategic and conventinal military strength, refostering Western allied unity, and reinstituting the mission of the free world to persuade the Soviets of the benefits of restraint and reciprocity, he also recognizes the limits of American power and the need to accept gradual changes in the international balance of power. 2) Given that Soviet strategic and political goals conflict with American objectives of security and a stable world order basically friendly to the U.S. and a free market economy, the policy of containment and demonstrating that Soviet attempts at upsetting the status quo will fail seems a more effective policy than detente as practiced by Carter. A policy devoid of excessive wishful thinking about the prospects that arms freezes and accommodation alone enhance security or automatically lead to Soviet moderation will provide reminders that the U.S. is determined to resist Soviet expansion, cold war probings, unequal arms treaties, and a selective detente. To the extent that Reagan convinces both the Soviets and Western public opinion of this determination, to that extent the Soviets may be deterred and contained.

The next several chapters focus on the attempts over the years to convince the Soviets of the rewards of foreign policy restraint, equitable arms treaties, and strategic theories that enhance international security and stability. Before getting into the details of treaties and strategies, we need to acquire familiarity with the terms used and the character of the weapons and technologies that have made the discovery of strategies of deterrence and war-avoidance so urgent.

### Table 1*
### Federal Budget Trends

| Fiscal Year | Federal Outlays as a % of GNP | DoD Outlays as a % of Federal Outlays | DoD Outlays as a % of GNP | Non-DoD Outlays as a % of GNP | DoD Outlays as a % of Net Public Spending[1] |
|---|---|---|---|---|---|
| 1950 | 16.0 | 27.5 | 4.4 | 11.6 | 18.5 |
| 1955 | 17.6 | 51.5 | 9.1 | 8.6 | 35.6 |
| 1960 | 18.2 | 45.0 | 8.2 | 10.0 | 30.3 |
| 1965 | 17.5 | 38.8 | 6.8 | 10.7 | 25.2 |
| 1970 | 19.8 | 39.4 | 7.8 | 12.0 | 25.5 |
| 1972 | 20.0 | 32.6 | 6.5 | 13.5 | 20.7 |
| 1973 | 19.1 | 29.8 | 5.7 | 13.4 | 19.0 |
| 1974 | 19.0 | 28.8 | 5.5 | 13.5 | 18.3 |
| 1976 | 21.9 | 23.6 | 5.2 | 16.7 | 15.4 |
| 1977 | 21.1 | 23.4 | 4.9 | 16.2 | 15.5 |
| 1979 | 20.5 | 22.8 | 4.7 | 15.8 | 15.4 |
| 1980 | 22.2 | 22.5 | 5.0 | 17.2 | 15.3 |
| 1981 | 22.7 | 23.0 | 5.2 | 17.5 | 15.8 |
| 1982 | 23.7 | 24.5 | 5.8 | 17.9 | 16.7 |
| 1984 | 23.1 | 25.9 | 6.0 | 17.1 | 17.6 |
| 1985 | 24.0 | 25.9 | 6.2 | 17.8 | 17.6 |
| 1986 | 23.3 | 26.4 | 6.2 | 17.2 | 17.6 |
| 1987 | 21.8 | 27.5 | 6.0 | 15.8 | 17.9 |

[1]Federal, state, and local net spending excluding government enterprises (such as the postal service and public utilities) except for any support these activities receive from tax funds.

*Source: Caspar Weinberger, Annual Report to the Congress, FY 1987

**Table 2\*** *Million US $*
**USSR: Economic Credits and Grants Extended to Non-Communist LDCs**

| | 1954-84 | 1980 | 1981 | 1982 | 1983 | 1984 |
|---|---|---|---|---|---|---|
| **Total** | **30,305** | **2,605** | **600** | **1,015** | **3,360** | **2,350** |
| North Africa | 3,580 | 315 | 50 | NEGL | 280 | NEGL |
| Algeria | 1,345 | 315 | 50 | | 250 | |
| Morocco | 2,100 | | | | | |
| Sub-Saharan Africa | 4,645 | 330 | 155 | 745 | 310 | 545 |
| Angola | 560 | | | 450 | | 50 |
| Congo | 75 | NEGL | 30 | | | |
| Ethiopia | 1,255 | 190 | 60 | 230 | 250 | 250 |
| Ghana | 110 | | 1 | 10 | NEGL | 5 |
| Guinea | 400 | 5 | | | | 165 |
| Madagascar | 85 | 50 | | 5 | | 10 |
| Mali | 135 | 1 | 5 | 20 | | 15 |
| Mozambique | 220 | 85 | 45 | 5 | 15 | 5 |
| Nigeria | 1,205 | | | | | |
| Somalia | 165 | | | | | |
| Sudan | 65 | | | | | |
| Tanzania | 45 | | | 5 | | |
| Uganda | 35 | | | | 10 | |

\*Source: Tables 2-8 are from *World Military Expenditures and Arms Transfers* 1985 (Arms Control and Disarmament Agency, Washington:GPO, 1985). Totals reflect other states not listed.

**Table 3** *Million US $*
**USSR: Economic Credits and Grants Extended to Non-Communist LDCs**

| | 1954-84 | 1980 | 1981 | 1982 | 1983 | 1984 |
|---|---|---|---|---|---|---|
| Latin America | 2,105 | 250 | 175 | 175 | 280 | 210 |
| Argentina | 295 | | | | 65 | NA |
| Bolivia | 190 | | | 2 | 70 | |
| Brazil | 160 | | 55 | | 15 | |
| Chile | 240 | | | | | |
| Columbia | 215 | | | | | NA |
| Grenada | 10 | NEGL | 1 | 10 | | |
| Nicaragua | 570 | NA | 85 | 165 | 115 | 210 |
| Peru | 275 | 250 | | | 1 | |
| Middle East | 11,505 | 210 | 110 | | 1,630 | 1,270 |
| Egypt | 1,440 | | | | | |
| Iran | 1,165 | | | | | |
| Iraq | 2,225 | | | | 1,000 | 500 |
| North Yemen | 195 | | 55 | | | |
| South Yemen | 800 | 210 | | | | |
| Syria | 1,575 | | 55 | | 250 | 500 |
| South Asia | 8,210 | 1,505 | 110 | 95 | 860 | 325 |
| Afghanistan | 3215 | 705 | 25 | 90 | 370 | 325 |
| Bangladesh | 435 | | 70 | | 75 | |
| India | 3,220 | 800 | | | 140 | |
| Pakistan | 1,210 | | 10 | | 275 | NA |

**Table 4**  *Millions of Current Dollars*
**Soviet-Bloc Arms Deliveries to Sub Saharan States**

|  | 1974-1978 |
| --- | --- |
| Angola | 440 |
| Chad | 10 |
| Congo | 30 |
| Madagascar | 20 |
| Mali | 100 |
| Mozambique | 135 |
| Nigeria | 80 |
| Somali | 300 |
| Sudan | 30 |
| Tanzania | 110 |
| Uganda | 120 |
| **Total** | **2870** |

**Table 5**  *Million US $*
**Eastern Europe: Economic Aid Extended to Non-Communist LDCs**

|  | Total | Marxist Client States | Other LDCs |
| --- | --- | --- | --- |
| **Total** | **14,915** | **1,550** | **13,365** |
| 1954-78 | 9,495 | 665 | 8,830 |
| 1980 | 1,325 | 190 | 1,135 |
| 1981 | 725 | 175 | 550 |
| 1982 | 560 | 95 | 465 |
| 1983 | 415 | 270 | 145 |
| 1984 | 1,750 | 60 | 1,690 |

**Table 6**  *Millions US $*
**Sub-Saharan Africa: Economic Credits and Grants from Warsaw Pact Countries**

|  | USSR | Eastern Europe |
| --- | --- | --- |
| **Total [a]** | **4,645** | **2,360** |
| 1958-70 | 765 | 250 |
| 1971-79 | 1,795 | 1425 |
| 1981 | 155 | 105 |
| 1982 | 745 | 115 |
| 1983 | 310 | 100 |
| 1984 | 545 | 80 |

[a] Because of rounding, components may not add to the totals shown.

**Table 7**  *Number of persons*
**USSR and Eastern Europe: Economic Technicians in Non-Communist LDCs, 1984**

|  | Total | USSR | Eastern Europe |
| --- | --- | --- | --- |
| **Total** | **125,960** | **39,570** | **86,390** |
| North Africa | 67,315 | 10,965 | 56,350 |
| Sub-Saharan Africa | 16,020 | 9,080 | 6,940 |
| Latin America | 1,410 | 680 | 730 |
| Middle East | 33,110 | 11,365 | 21,745 |
| South Asia | 7,970 | 7,465 | 505 |

**Table 8**  *Million US $*
**Central America and the Caribbean: Economic Credits and Grants From Warsaw Pact Countries**

|  | USSR | Eastern Europe |
| --- | --- | --- |
| **Total** | **640** | **1,095** |
| 1971-79 | 45 | 405 |
| 1981 | 85 | 95 |
| 1982 | 175 | 95 |
| 1983 | 125 | 255 |
| 1984 | 210 [b] | 230 |

[b] Excludes oil originally provided under commercial contracts that we now believe will be repaid under long-term agreements.

**Table 9\***          *Million current dollars*
## U.S. Economic-Support-Fund Programs for Africa, FY 1961-1980

| | 1961-1965 | 1966-1970 | 1971-1975 | 1976-1980 | Total 1961-1980 |
|---|---|---|---|---|---|
| Worldwide | a | 3,226 | 3,686 | 10,140 | a |
| Africa | 387.3 | 117.9 | 283.4 | 4,305.4 | 5,094 |
| Worldwide (percentage) | a | 4 | 8 | 42 | a |
| North Africa | 153.1 | — | 261.3 | 3,939.7 | 4,354.1 |
| Africa (percentage) | 40 | — | 92 | 92 | 85 |
| Egypt | 30.0 | — | 261.3 | 3,939.7 | 4,231 |
| Libya | 27.8 | — | — | — | 27.8 |
| Morocco | 76.7 | — | — | — | 76.7 |
| Tunisia | 17.3 | — | — | — | 17.3 |
| Sub-Sahara | 234.2 | 117.9 | 22.1 | 365.7 | 739.9 |
| Africa (percentage) | 60 | 100 | 8 | 8 | 15 |
| Botswana | — | — | — | 39.3 | 39.3 |
| Ethiopia | 3.0 | .3 | — | — | 3.3 |
| Guinea | 24.0 | — | — | — | 24.0 |
| Kenya | — | — | — | 14.5 | 14.5 |
| Liberia | — | — | — | 10.2 | 10.2 |
| Nigeria | — | 53.7 | 21.6 | — | 75.3 |
| Somalia | — | — | — | 5.0 | 5.0 |
| Sudan | — | — | — | 40.0 | 40.0 |
| Zaire | 198.3 | 54.5 | — | 42.0 | 294.8 |
| Zambia | — | — | — | 74.0 | 74.0 |
| Zimbabwe | — | — | — | 22.9 | 22.9 |
| Southern Africa Regional | — | — | — | 93.2 | 93.2 |

\*Source: U.S. Agency for International Development, *U.S. Overseas Loans and Grants*, annual, various issues; FY 1980 data from *Congressional Presentation: Security Assistance Programs, FY 1982*, p. 265.

a Cannot be determined due to reporting and aggregating procedures used in various issues of *U.S. Overseas Loans and Grants*.


**Table 10-A\***          *(million current dollars)*
## Principal Recipients of U.S. Military Transfers to Africa, FY 1950-1980

| | 1950-1955 | 1956-1960 | 1961-1965 | 1966-1970 | 1971-1975 | 1976-1980 | Total 1950-1980 |
|---|---|---|---|---|---|---|---|
| Total Africa | 5.72 | 39.7 | 120.6 | 192.9 | 191.5 | 1,329.7 | 1,880.1 |
| North Africa | .12 | 5.75 | 43.4 | 93.8 | 77.4 | 952.2 | 1,172.7 |
| Africa (percentage) | 2 | 14 | 36 | 49 | 40 | 72 | 62 |
| Egypt | .12 | .06 | .16 | .02 | .03 | 474.8 | 475.2 |
| Libya | — | 2.6 | 7.02 | 31.35 | 36.6 | 1.0 | 78.6 |
| Morocco | — | .39 | 20.5 | 48.1 | 22.8 | 405.4 | 497.2 |
| Tunisia | — | 2.7 | 15.7 | 14.3 | 18.0 | 71.0 | 121.8 |
| Sub-Sahara | 5.6 | 33.9 | 77.2 | 99.1 | 114.1 | 377.5 | 707.4 |
| Africa (percentage) | 98 | 86 | 64 | 51 | 60 | 28 | 38 |
| Ethiopia | 5.2 | 32.7 | 57.4 | 67.7 | 64.8 | 96.7 | 324.5 |
| Kenya | — | — | — | — | 5.6 | 64.0 | 69.6 |
| Nigeria | — | — | .72 | .84 | 11.1 | 59.3 | 72.0 |
| South Africa | .24 | .09 | .42 | 2.4 | 3.4 | 15.2 | 21.8 |
| Sudan | — | .003 | .12 | .57 | .03 | 62.7 | 63.5 |
| Zaire | — | — | 11.0 | 20.4 | 22.9 | 48.3 | 102.6 |

Source: U.S. Defense Security Assistance Agency, *Fiscal Year Series, 1980.*

*Notes: Figures represent actual value of deliveries/expenditures, not programmed or pipeline costs.*

# Table 10*
## Economic and Military Assistance as Percentage of Total Assistance

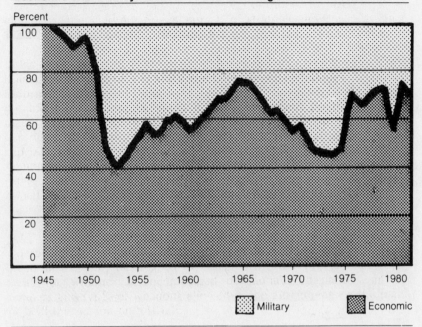

Percent

Military      Economic

Source*: Department of State - Special Report 108.

# Table 11*            *$ millions*
## U.S. Assistance to Central America, FY 1983-1987

| | Economic Assistance | Military Assistance | | Economic Assistance | Military Assistance |
|---|---|---|---|---|---|
| **Costa Rica** | | | **Honduras** | | |
| 1983 | 212.4 | 2.63 | 1983 | 101.2 | 37.30 |
| 1984 | 107.5 | 2.13 | 1984 | 90.3 | 40.94 |
| 1984 supplemental | 67.1 | 7.00 | 1984 supplemental | 79.8 | 36.50 |
| 1985 | 195.1 | 11.23 | 1985 | 130.8 | 67.40 |
| 1986 allocation | 154.5 | 2.58 | 1986 allocation | 122.8 | 79.71 |
| 1987 request | 184.0 | 3.35 | 1987 request | 158.8 | 88.80 |
| **El Salvador** | | | **Panama** | | |
| 1983 | 241.9 | 81.3 | 1983 | 7.2 | 5.45 |
| 1984 | 212.4 | 64.80 | 1984 | 11.7 | 5.50 |
| 1984 supplementals | 111.1 | 131.75 | 1984 supplemental | 34.0 | 8.00 |
| 1985 | 314.3 | 136.25 | 1985 | 34.3 | 10.59 |
| 1986 allocation | 308.9 | 126.81 | 1986 allocation | 22.9 | 8.23 |
| 1987 request | 377.7 | 136.25 | 1987 request | 46.1 | 14.55 |
| **Guatemala** | | | | | |
| 1983 | 26.6 | 0.00 | | | |
| 1984 | 16.0 | 0.00 | | | |
| 1984 supplemental | 15.6 | 0.00 | | | |
| 1985 | 80.3 | 0.46 | | | |
| 1986 allocation | 102.5 | 0.29 | | | |
| 1987 request | 133.7 | 10.50 | | | |

*Source for Tables 11-12 Department of State, Special Report #148 "The U.S. and Central America," Pages 4, 26-27.

**Table 12**
**U.S. Bilateral Assistance to Central America, FY 1983-89**

*U.S. $ Billions*

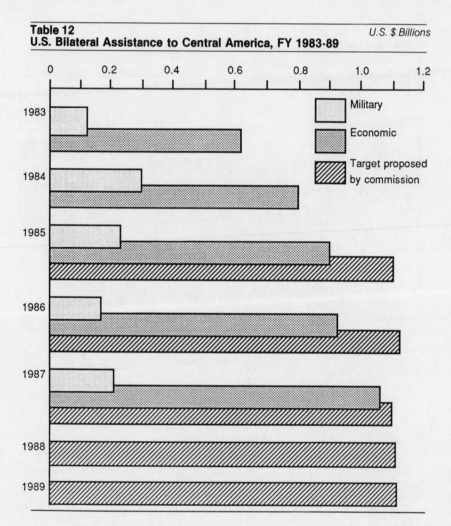

**Table 13***
**Soviet Aid to Nicaragua**

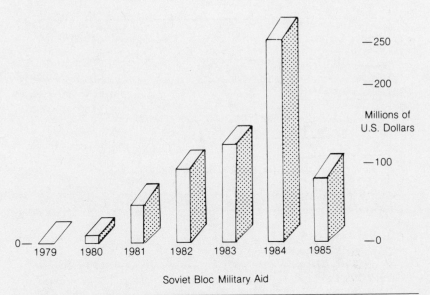

Soviet Bloc Military Aid

*Source: Department of State. *Current Policy 797,* (February 27, 1986):2.

## REFERENCES

[1]Ronald Reagan, address before Congress, in *Current Policy* 482 (April 27, 1983): 4; George P. Schultz, *Testimony,* Senate Foreign Relations Committee, June 15, 1983, Department of State Delivery Copy, p. 5; and Caspar Weinberger, *Annual Report to Congress, FY 1984 Budget and FY 1984-88 Defense Program,* (February 1, 1983): 1.

[2]Reagan, "Freedom, Regional Security, and Global Peace," message to Congress, *Current Policy* 143 (March 14, 1986): 1.

[3]Shultz, "Moral Principles and Strategic Interests," *Current Policy* 820 (April 14, 1986): 3.

[4]Alexander Haig, speech *Current Policy* 292 (March 1981): 1.

[5]Reagan, "Freedom, Regional Security and Global Peace," 3-5.

[6]Ibid., 5-6.

[7]Haig, "A Strategic Approach to American Foreign Policy" *Current Policy* 305 (August 11, 1981): 1-2.

[8]Shultz, *Testimony,* 8.

[9]Weinberger, *Annual Report to Congress FY 1987* (February 5, 1986): 15-19, 58-59, 93-101, and 313-315.

[10]Robert W. Komer, "What 'Decade of Neglect'?" *International Security* 10 (Fall 1985): 79-82.

[11]Ibid., 76.

[12]Weinberger, letter to U.S. newspapers, August 1982 and *Annual Report FY 1984,* p. 34.

[13]Lord Carrington, speech quoted in *British Information Services* (October 27, 1980): 2-5.

[14]Carrington, speech in *Keesing's* (May 9, 1980): 30241.

[15]Pierre Hassner, "Western European Perceptions of the USSR," *Daedalus* (Winter 1979): 116-126.

[16]"Interview with Helmut Schmidt," *Economist* (October 16, 1979): 47 and 54.

[17]Lewis J. Edinger, "The German-American Connection in the 1980s," *Political Science Quarterly* 95 (Winter 1980-81): 589-95.

[18]Uwe Nerlich, "Change in Europe: A Secular Trend?" *Daedalus* (Winter 1981): 73-75.

[19]See polls quoted in Gebhard Schweigler, "Anti-Americanism in Germany," *Washington Quarterly* 9 (Winter 1986): 77.

[20]Ibid., 82.

[21]Jon Kraus, "American Foreign Policy in Africa," *Current History* 80 (March 1981): 98.

[22]Donald Rothchild and John Ravenhill, "From Carter to Reagan: The Global Perspective on Africa Becomes Ascendant," in Kenneth Oye et. al., *Eagles Defiant: US Foreign Policy in the 1980s, (Boston: Little, Brown, 1983): 342; and Scott W. Thompson "U.S. Policy in Africa," Orbis* 25 (March 1982): 1012.

[23]Helen Kitchen, *Options for US Policy Towards Africa,* (Washington: American Enterprise Institute, 1979): 34.

[24]Russell W. Howe, "United States Policy in Africa," *Current History* 76 (March 1979): 97-98.

[25]Kraus, "American Foreign Policy in Africa," 138.

[26]Gerard Chiland, "The Horn of Africa's Dilemma," *Foreign Policy* 30 (Spring 1978): 116-121.

[27]Alvin A. Rubinstein, preface in Marina Ottaway, *Soviet and American Influence in the Horn,* (New York: Praeger, 1982): v.

[28]John Spencer, *Ethiopia, the Horn of Africa and US Policy,* (Cambridge: Institute for Foreign Policy Analysis, 1977): 57.

[29]W.A.E. Skurnik, "Continuing Problems in Africa's Horn," *Current History* (March 1983): 137.

[30]Kitchen, *Options for US Policy in Africa,* 4.

[31]Chester A. Crocker, address, *DOSB* 83 (December 1982): 22.

[32]Rothchild, "From Carter to Reagan," Stephen Solarz, "Rapprochement with Racism," *Orbis* 25 (Winter 1982): 872; and Raymond Copson, "African Flashpoints," *Orbis* 25 (Winter 1982): 916.

[33]Reagan, "Freedom, Regional Security, and Global Peace," message to Congress, in *Current Policy* 805 (March 16, 1986): 1.

[34]Ibid., 2.

[35]Shultz, "Low-Intensity Warfare: The Challenge of Ambiguity," in *Current Policy* 783 (January 15, 1986): 2.

[36]See Agraham F. Lowenthal, "Threat and Opportunity in the Americas," *Foreign Affairs* (America and the World 1985): 546-548, for these and the following statistics.

[37]See the Bipartisan (Kissinger) Commission on Latin America and reports on its findings in the *New York Times* 8-12 January 1984.

[38]Langehorne A. Motley, statement, Subcommittee on Foreign Operations of the House Committee on Appropriations, in *Current Policy* 559 (March 27, 1984): 2-5.

[39]Kissinger, testimony, Senate Foreign Relations Committee, reported in the *Wall Street Journal* (February 8, 1984): 6.

[40]See the 1986 International League for Human Rights document, "Report on Human Rights Defenders in Nicaragua," prepared by Director, Patricia Derian.

[41]Reagan, "Promoting Freedom and Democracy in Central America," in *Current Policy* 952 (May 3, 1987): 2-3.

[42]Kissinger, "Nicaragua: When Compromise Serves No Purpose," *Los Angeles Times* (Sept. 6, 1987): Part V, page 1.

[43]Reagan, address in *Current Policy* (April 27, 1983): 4.

[44]Reagan, "Why Democracy Matters in Central America," address to the nation, in *Current Policy* 850 (June 24, 1986): 3.

[45]Johnson, "Exaggerating America's Stakes in Third World Conflicts," *International Security,* (Winter 1985-86): 64-65.

[46]James R. Schlesinger, "The Eagle and the Bear: Ruminations on Forty Years of Superpower Relations," *Foreign Affairs* (Summer 1985): 958.

[47]Garthoff, *Detente and Confrontation,* 1050-1052.

[48]Cyrus R. Vance, "The Human Rights Imperative," *Foreign Policy* (Summer 1986): 12.

[49]Shultz, "Moral Principles and Strategic Interests," 3.

[50]Haig, "New Direction in U.S. Foreign Policy," *Current Policy* 275 (April 24, 1981): 1-3.

[51]Shultz, address, *Current Policy* 457 (Feb. 24, 1983): 1-3.

[52]Haig, "American Power and American Purpose," *Current Policy* 388 (April 27, 1982): 2.

[53]Shultz, *Testimony,* 11 and 35.

[54]Shultz, 11 and 35.

# Reagan Address to Congress
# March 14, 1986

I. America's State in Regional Security

...Both the causes and consequences of World War II made clear to all Americans that our participation in world affairs, for the rest of the century and beyond, would have to go beyond just the protection of our national territory against direct invasion. We had learned the painful lessons of the 1930s, that there could be no safety in isolation from the rest of this hemisphere, in Europe, in the Pacific, in the Middle East, and in other regions that require strong, confident, and consistent American leadership....we have acted in the belief that our peaceful and prosperous future can best be assured in a world in which other peoples, too, can determine their own destiny, free of coercion or tyranny from either at home or abroad.

Our foreign policy in the postwar era has sought to enhance our nation's security by pursuit of four fundamental goals: We have sought to defend and advance the cause of democracy, freedom, and human rights throughout the world. We have sought to promote prosperity and social progress through a free, open, and expanding market-oriented global economy. We have worked diplomatically to help resolve dangerous regional conflicts. We have worked to reduce and eventually eliminate the danger of nuclear war....

A foreign policy that ignored the fate of millions around the world who seek freedom would be a betrayal of our national heritage. Our own freedom, and that of our allies, could never be secure in a world where freedom was threatened everywhere else. Our stake in the global economy gives us a stake in the well-being of others. A foreign policy that overlooked the dangers posed by international conflicts, that did not work to bring them to a peaceful resolution, would be irresponsible—especially in an age of nuclear weapons. These conflicts and the tensions that they generate are, in fact, a major spur to the continued buildup of nuclear arsenals. For this reason, my Administration has made plain that continuing Soviet adventurism in the developing world is inimical to global security and an obstacle to fundamental improvement of Soviet-American relations. Our stake in resolving regional conflicts can be simply stated: greater freedom for others means greater peace and security for ourselves. These goals threaten no one, but none of them can be achieved without a strong, active, and engaged America.

## II. Regional Security in the 1980s

...Murderous policies in Vietnam and Cambodia produced victims on a scale unknown since the genocides of Hitler and Stalin. In Afghanistan, the Soviet invasion led to the terrified flight of millions from their homes. In Ethiopia, we have witnessed death by famine and more recently by forced resettlement....Other outgrowths of Soviet policies have been the colonial presence of tens of thousands of Cuban troops in Africa, the activities of terriorists trained in facilities in the Soviet bloc, and the effort to use communist Nicaragua as a base from which to extinguish democracy in El Salvador and beyond. These are not isolated events. They make up the distrubing pattern of Soviet conduct in the past 15 years. The problems it creates are no less acute because the Soviet Union has had its share of disagreements with some of its clients or because many of these involvements have proved very costly. That the Soviet leadership persists in such policies despite the growing burden they impose only testifies to the strength of Soviet commitment. Unless we build barriers to Soviet ambitions and create incentives for Soviet restraint, Soviet policies will remain a source of danger....

I have made clear the importance the United States attaches to the resolution of regional conflicts that threaten world peace and the yearning of millions for freedom and independence—whether in Afghanistan or in southern Africa. For the United States, these conflicts cannot be regarded as peripheral to other issues on the global agenda. They raise fundamental issues and are a fundamental part of the overall U.S.-Soviet relationship. Their resolution would represent a crucial step toward the kind of world that Americans seek....

*Joining Others' Strength to Ours.* The second reality that shapes America's approach to regional security is the need to join our own strength to the efforts of others in working toward our common goals. Throughout the postwar period, our country has played an enormous role in helping other nations, in many parts of the world, to protect their freedom. Through NATO we committed ourselves to the defense of Europe against Soviet attack....We sent American troops to Korea to repel a communist invasion. America was an ardent champion of decolonization. We provided security assistance to help friends and allies around the world defend themselves....

Despite our economic and military strength and our leading political role, the pursuit of American goals has always required cooperation with like-minded partners. The problems we face today, however, make cooperation with others even more important. This is, in part, a result of the limits on our own resources, of the steady growth in the power of our adversaries, and of the American people's understandable reluctance to shoulder alone burdens that are properly shared with others. But most important, we want to cooperate with others because of the nature of our goals. Stable regional solutions depend over the long term on what those most directly affected can contribute. If interference by outsiders can be ended, regional security is best protected by the free and independent countries of each region.

*The Democratic Revolution.* If American policy can succeed only in cooperation with others, then the third critical development of the past decade offers special hope: it is the democratic revolution, a trend that has significantly increased the ranks of those around the world who share America's commitment to national independence and popular rule. The democracies that survived or emerged from the ruins of the Second World War-Western Europe, Japan, and a handful of others-have not been joined by many others across the globe. Here in the Western Hemisphere, the 1980s have been a decade of transition to democracy....Ours is a time of enormous social and technological change everywhere, and one country after another is discovering that only free peoples can make the most of this change. Countries that want progress without pluralism, without freedom, are finding that it cannot be done. In this global revolution, there can be no doubt where America stands. The American people believe in human rights and oppose tyranny in whatever form, whether of the left or the right. We use our influence to encourage democratic change, in careful ways that respect other countries' traditions and political realities as well as the security threats that many of them face from external or internal forces of totalitarianism....

Peoples on every continent are insisting on their right to national independence and their right to choose their government free of coercion. The Soviets overreached in the 1970s, at a time when American weakened itself by its internal divisions. In the 1980s the Soviets and their clients are finding it difficult to consolidate these gains—in part because of the revival of American and Western self-confidence but mainly because of the courageous forces of indigenous resistance. Growing resistance movements now challenge communist regimes installed or maintained by the military power of the Soviet Union and its colonial agents—in Afghanistan, Angola, Cambodia, Ethiopia, and Nicaragua...

....the failure of these Soviet client regimes to consolidate themselves only confirms the moral and political bankruptcy of the Leninist model. No one can be surprised by this. But it also reflects the dangerous and destabilizing international impact that even unpopular Leninist regimes can have. None of these struggles is a purely internal one. As I told the UN General Assembly last year, the assault of such regimes on their own people inevitably becomes a menace to their neighbors. Hence the threats to Pakistan and Thailand by the powerful occupying armies in Afghanistan and Cambodia. Hence the insecurity of El Salvador, Costa Rica, and Honduras in the face of the Nicaraguan military buildup. Soviet-style dictatorships, in short, are an almost unique threat to peace, both before and after they consolidate their rule—before, because the war they wage against their own people does not always stay within their own borders, and after, because the elimination of opposition at home frees their hand for subversion abroad. Cuba's foreign adventures of the past decade are a warning to the neighbors of communist regimes everywhere....

III. The Tools of American Policy

....Soviet power and policy cannot be checked without the active commitment of the United States. And we cannot achieve lasting results without giving support to—and receiving support from—those whose goals coincide with ours. These realities call for new ways of thinking about how to cope with the challenge of Soviet power. Since Harry Truman's day, through administrations of both parties, American policy toward the Soviet Union has consistently set itself the goal of containing Soviet expansionism. Today, that goal is more relevant and more important than ever. But how do we achieve it in today's new conditions?

First of all, we must face up to the arrogant Soviet pretension known as the Brezhnev doctrine: the claim that Soviet gains are irreversible; that once a Soviet client begins to oppress its people and threaten its neighbors it must be allowed to oppress and threaten them forever. This claim has no moral or political validity whatsoever. Regimes that cannot live in peace with either their own people or their neighbors forfeit their legitimacy in world affairs. Second, we must take full account of the striking trend that I have mentioned: the growing ranks of those who share our interests and values. In 1945 so much of the burden of defending freedom rested on our shoulders alone. In the 1970s some Americans were pessimistic about whether our values of democracy and freedom were relevant to the new developing nations. Now we know the answer. The growing appeal of democracy, the desire of all nations for true independence, is fully consistent with our values—because we know free peoples never choose tyranny.

To promote these goals, American has a range of foreign policy tools. Our involvement should always be prudent and realistic, but we should remember that our tools work best when joined together in a coherent strategy consistently applied. Diplomacy unsupported by power is mere talk. Power that is not guided by our political purposes can create nothing of permanent value. The two tools of U.S. policy without which few American interests will be secure are our own military strength and the vitality of our economy....The failure to maintain our military capabilities and our economic strength in the 1970s was as important as any other single factor in encouraging Soviet expansionism. By reviving both of them in the 1980s, we deny our adversaries opportunities and deter aggression. We make it easier for other countries to launch sustained economic growth, to build popular institutions, and to contribute on their own to the cause of peace.

*Security Assistance and Arms Transfers.* When Soviet policy succeeds in establishing a regional foothold....our first priority must be to bolster the security of friends most directly threatened....By supporting the efforts of others to strengthen their own defense, we frequently do as much for our own security as through our own defense budget. Security assistance to others is a security bargain for us. We must, however, remember that states hostile to us seek the same sort of bargains at our expense. For this reason, we must be sure that the resources we commit are adequate to the job....

*Economic Assistance.* In speaking of Central American in 1982, I said that "...economic disaster (had) provided a fresh opening to the enemies of freedom, national independence, and peaceful development." We cannot indulge the hope that economic responses alone are enough to prevent this political exploitation, but an effective American policy must address both the short-term and long-term dimensions of economic distress. In the short term, our goal is stabilization; in the long term, sustained growth and progress by encouraging market-oriented reform...Over the long term, America's most effective contribution to self-sustaining growth is not through direct aid but through helping these economies to earn their own way. The vigorous expansion of our own economy has already spurred growth throughout the Western Hemisphere, as well as elsewhere. But this healthy expansion of the global economy—which benefits us as well as others—depends crucially on maintaining a fair and open trading system...

*Support for Freedom Fighters.* In all these regions, the Soviet Union and its clients would, of course, prefer victory to compromise. That is why in Afghanistan, in Southeast Asia, in southern Africa, and in Central America, diplomatic hopes depend on whether the Soviets see that victory is excluded. In each case, resistance forces fighting against communist tyranny deserve our support....our help should give freedom fighters the chance to rally the people to their side....America cannot fight everyone's battle for freedom. But we must not deny others the chance to fight their battle themselves....Communist rulers do not voluntarily or in a single step relinquish control and open their nations to popular rule. But there is no historical basis for thinking that Leninist regimes are the only ones that can indefinitely ignore armed insurgencies and the disintegration of their own political base. The conditions that a growing insurgency can create—high military desertion rates, general strikes, economic shortages, infrastructural breakdowns, to name a few—can, in turn, create policy fissures even within a leadership that has had no change of heart. This is the opportunity that the freedom fighters of the 1980s hope to seize, but it will not exist forever, either in Central America or elsewhere. When the mechanisms of repression are fully in place and consolidated, the task of countering such a regime's policies—both internal and external—becomes incomparably harder. That is why the Nicaraguan regime is so bent on extinguishing the vestiges of pluralism in Nicaraguan society. It is why our own decisions can no longer be deferred.

IV. Regional Security and U.S.-Soviet Relations

....Our policy is designed to keep regional conflicts from spreading and thereby to reduce the risk of superpower confrontations. Our aim is not to increase the dangers to which regional states friendly to us are exposed but to reduce them. We do so by making clear to the Soviet Union and its clients that we will stand behind our friends. Talk alone will not accomplish this. That is why our security assistance package for Pakistan-and for Thailand and Zaire—is so important, and why we have increased our help to democratic states of Central America. We have made clear that there would be no gain from widening these conflicts. We have done so without embroiling American forces in struggles that others are ready to fight on their own. Our goal, in short—indeed, our necessity—is to convince the Soviet Union that the policies on which it embarked in the 1970s cannot work. We cannot be completely sure how the Soviet leadership calculates the benefits of relationships with clients. No one should underestimate the tenacity of such a powerful and resilient opponent.

## V. Conclusion

...If America stays committed, we are more likely to have diplomatic solutions than military ones. If America stays committed, we are more likely to have democratic outcomes than totalitarian ones. If America stays committed, we will find that those who share our goals can do their part and ease the burdens that we might otherwise bear alone. If America stays committed, we can solve problems while they are still manageable and avoid harder choices later. And if America stays committed, we are more likely to convince the Soviet Union that its competition with us must be peaceful. The American people remain committed to a world of peace and freedom. They want an effective foreign policy, which shapes events in accordance with our ideals and does not just react, passively and timidly, to the actions of others. Backing away from this challenge will not bring peace. It will only mean that others who are hostile to everything we believe in will have a freer hand to work their will in the world...

## *U.S.-Soviet Relations*
## *In the Context of U.S. Foreign Policy*

### Statement by the Honorable George P. Shultz
### Before the Senate Foreign Relations Committee
### June 15, 1983

The management of our relations with the Soviet Union is of utmost importance. That relationship touches virtually every aspect of our international concerns and objectives—political, economic, and military—and every part of the world. We must defend our interests and values against a powerful Soviet adversary that threatens both. And we must do so in a nuclear age, in which global war would even more thoroughly threaten those interests and values...

We and the Soviets have sharply divergent goals and philosophies of political and moral order; these differences will not soon go away. Any other assumption is unrealistic. At the same time, we have a fundamental common interest in the avoidance of war. This common interest impels us to work toward a relationship between our nations that can lead to a safer world for all mankind. But a safer world will not be realized through good will. Our hopes for the future must be grounded in a realistic assessment of the challenge we face and in a determined effort to create the conditions that will make their achievement possible. We have made a start. Every postwar American president has come sooner or later to recognize that peace must be built on strength; President Reagan has long recognized this reality. In the past two years this nation—the President in partnership with the Congress—has made a fundamental commitment to restoring its military and economic power and moral and spiritual strength. And having begun to rebuild our strength, we now seek to engage the Soviet leaders in a constructive dialogue—a dialogue through which we hope to find political solutions to outstanding issues. This is the central goal we have pursued since the outset of this Administration. We do not want to—and need not—accept as inevitable the prospect of endless, dangerous confrontation with the Soviet Union....

(Our strategy)...takes account of the facts of Soviet power and of Soviet conduct, mobilizes the resources needed to defend our interests, and offers an agenda for constructive dialogue to resolve concrete international problems. We believe that, if sustained, this policy will make international restraint Moscow's most realistic course, and it can lay the foundation for a more constructive relationship between our peoples.

## I. The Soviet Challenge

It is sometimes said that Americans have too simple a view of world affairs, that we start with the assumption that all problems can be solved. Certainly we have a simple view of how the world should be—free people choosing their own destinies, nurturing their prosperity, peaceably resolving conflicts....Certainly there are many factors contributing to East-West tension. The Soviet Union's strategic Eurasian location places it in close proximity to important Western interests on two continents. Its aspirations for greater international influence lead it to challenge these interests. Its Marxist-Leninist ideology gives its leaders a perspective on history and a vision of the future fundamentally different from our own. But we are not so deterministic as to believe that geopolitics and ideological competition must ineluctably lead to permanent and dangerous confrontation....

A peaceful world order does not require that we and the Soviet Union agree on all the fundamentals of morals or politics. It does require, however, that Moscow's behavior be subject to the restraint appropriate to living together on this planet in the nuclear age. Not all the many external and internal factors affecting Soviet behavior can be influenced by us. But we take it as part of our obligation to peace to encourage the gradual evolution of the Soviet system toward a more pluralistic political and economic system, and above all to counter Soviet expansionism through sustained and effective political, economic, and military competition. In the past decade, regrettably, the changes in Soviet behavior have been for the worse. Soviet actions have come into conflict with many of our objectives. They have made the task of managing the Soviet-American relationship considerably harder, and have needlessly drawn more and more international problems into the East-West rivalry.

...the following developments...have caused us the most concern: *First is the continuing Soviet quest for military superiority even in the face of mounting domestic economic difficulties.* In the late 1970s the allocation of resources for the Soviet military...came even at the expense of industrial investment on which the long-term development of the economy depends. This decision to mortgage the industrial future of the country is a striking demonstration of the inordinate value the Soviets assign to maintaining the momentum of the relentless military buildup underway since the mid-1960's. This buildup consumed an estimated annual average of at least 12 percent of Soviet GNP throughout this entire period, and has recently consumed even more as a result of the sharp decline in Soviet economic growth. *The second disturbing development is the unconstructive Soviet involvement, direct and indirect, in unstable areas of the Third World.* Arms have become a larger percentage of Soviet exports than of the export trade of any other country. The Soviets have too often attempted to play a spoiling or scavenging role in areas of concern to us, most recently in the Middle East. Beyond this, the Soviets in the 70's broke major new ground in the kinds of foreign military intervention they were willing to risk...the Soviet Union has tried to block peaceful solutions and has brought East-West tensions into areas of the world that were once free of them. *Third is the unrelenting effort to impose an alien Soviet "model" on nominally independent Soviet clients and allies....*Moscow clearly remains unwilling to countenance meaningful national autonomy for its satelleties, let alone real independence. Elsewhere in the world, the coming to power of Soviet-supported regimes has usually meant (as in Afghanistan) the forcible creation of Soviet-style institutions and the harsh regimentation and represion of free expression and free initiative...*Fourth is Moscow's continuing practice of stretching a series of treaties and agreements to the brink of violation and beyond...*

II. The American Response: Beyond Containment and Detente

....If we are concerned about the Soviet commitment to military power, we have to take steps to *restore the military balance,* preferably on the basis of verifiable agreements that reduce arms on both sides, but if necessary through our own and allied defense programs. If we are concerned about the Soviet propensity to use force and promote instability, we have to make clear that we will *resist encroachments* on our vital interests and those of our allies and friends. If we are concerned about the loss of liberty that results when Soviet clients come to power, then we have to *ensure that those who have a positive alternative to the Soviet model receive our support.* Finally, if we are concerned about Moscow's observance of its international obligation, we must *leave Moscow no opportunity to distort or misconstrue our own intentions.* We will defend our interests if Soviet conduct leaves us no alternatives; at the same time we will respect legitimate Soviet security interests and are ready to negotiate equitable solutions to outstanding political problems....Today Moscow conducts a fully global foreign and military policy that places global demands on any strategy that aims to counter it.

Where it was once our goal to contain the Soviet presence within the limits of its immediate postwar reach, now our goal must be to advance our own objectives, where possible foreclosing and when necessary actively countering Soviet challenges wherever they threaten our interests.

The policy of detente, of course, represented an effort to induce Soviet restraint. While in some versions it recognized the need to resist Soviet geopolitical encroachments, it also hoped that the anticipation of benefits from expanding economic relations and arms control agreements would restrain Soviet behavior. Unfortunately, experience has proved otherwise. The economic relationship may have eased some of the domestic Soviet economic constraints that might have at least marginally inhibited Moscow's behavior. It also raised the specter of a future Western dependence on Soviet-bloc trade that would inhibit *Western* freedom of action towards the East more than it would dictate prudence to the USSR. Similarly, the SALT I and SALT II processes did not curb the Soviet strategic arms buildup, while encouraging many in the West to imagine that security concerns could now be placed lower on the agenda. Given these differences from the past, we have not been able merely to tinker with earlier approaches. Unlike containment, our policy begins with the clear recognition that the Soviet Union is and will remain a global superpower. In response to the lessons of this global superpower's conduct in recent years, our policy, unlike some versions of detente, assumes that the Soviet Union is more likely to be deterred by our actions that make clear the risks their aggression entails than by a delicate web of interdependence. Our policy is not based on trust, or on a Soviet change of heart. It is based on the expectation that, faced with demonstration of the West's renewed determination to strengthen its defenses, enhance its political and economic cohesion, and oppose adventurism, the Soviet Union will see restraint as its most attractive, or only, option. Perhaps, over time, this restraint will become an ingrained habit; perhaps not. Either way, our responsibility to be vigilant is the same.

III. Programs to Increase Our Strength

*Building Consensus.* From the beginning of this Administration, the President recognized how essential it was to consolidate a new consensus, here at home and among our traditional allies and friends....After the trauma of Vietnam, he sought to bolster a realistic pride in our country and to reinforce the civic courage and commitment on which the credibility of our military deterrent untimately rests. The president also felt that the possibility of greater cooperation with our allies depended importantly on a reaffirmation of our common moral values and interests. There were, as well, opportunities for cooperation with friendly governments of the developing world...As Secretary of State I am acutely conscious of the strength or weakness of American power and its effect on our influence over events. Perceptions of the strategic balance are bound to affect the judgments of not only our adversaties but also our allies and friends around the world who rely on us. As leader of the democratic nations, we have an inescapable responsibility to maintain this pillar of the military balance which only we can maintain. Our determination to do so is an important signal of our resolve, and is essential to sustaining the confidence of allies and friends and the cohesion of our alliances....To deter or deal with any future crisis, we need to maintain both our conventional capabilities and our strategic deterrent....and our collective defence....

*Reassessing the Security Implications of East-West Economic Relations.* The balance of power cannot be measured simply in terms of military forces or hardware; military power rests on a foundation of economic strength. Thus, we and our allies must not only strengthen our own economies but we must also develop a common approach to our economic relations with the Soviet Union that takes into account our broad strategic and security interest. In the past, the nations of the West have sometimes helped the Soviets to avoid difficult economic choices by allowing them to acquire militarily relevant technology and subsidized credits....

*Peace and Stability in the Third World.* Since the 1950's, the Soviet Union has found in the developing regions of the Third World its greatest opportunities for extending its influence through subversion and exploitation of local conflicts. A satisfactory East-West military balance will not by itself close off such opportunities. We must also respond to the economic, political, and security problems that contribute to these opportunities. Our approach has four key elements: First, in the many areas where Soviet activities have added to instability, we are pursuing peaceful diplomatic solutions to regional problems, to raise the political costs of Soviet-backed military presence and to encourage the departure of Soviet-backed forces....Second, we are building up the security capabilities of vulnerable governments in strategically important areas. We are helping our friends to help themselves and to help each other....Third, our program recognizes that economic crisis and political instability create fertile ground for Soviet-sponsored adventurism... Finally, there is the Democracy Initiative, an effort to assist our friends in the Third World to build a foundation for democracy...

IV. Negotiation and Dialogue: The U.S.-Soviet Agenda

Together these programs increase our political, military and economic strength and help create an international climate in which opportunities for Soviet adventurism are reduced. They are essential for the success of the final element of our strategy—engaging the Soviets in an active and productive dialogue on the concrete issues that concern the two sides. Strength and realism can deter war, but only direct dialogue and negotiation can open the path toward lasting peace. In this dialogue, our agenda is as follows: to seek improvement in Soviet performance on human rights; to reduce the risk of war, reduce armaments through sound agreements, and ultimately ease the burdens of military spending; to manage and resolve regional conflicts; and to improve bilateral relations on the basis of reciprocity and mutual interest....

## V. Prospects

....Let us not be misled by "atmospherics," whether sunny or, as they now seem to be, stormy. In the mid-50's, for example, despite the rhetoric and tension of the Cold War—and in the midst of a leadership transition—the Soviet Union chose to conclude the Austrian State Treaty. It was an important agreement, which contributed to the security of Central Europe, and it carries an important lesson for us today. The Soviet leadership did not negotiate seriously merely because Western rhetoric was firm and principled, nor should we expect rhetoric to suffice now or in the future. But adverse "atmospherics" did not *prevent* agreement; Soviet policy was instead affected by the pattern of Western actions, by our resolve and clarity of purpose...

There is no certainty that our current negotiations with the Soviets will lead to acceptable agreements. What is certain is that we will not find ourselves in the position in which we found ourselves in the aftermath of detente. We have not staked so much on the prospect of a successful negotiating outcome that we have neglected to secure ourselves against the possibility of failure. Unlike the immediate post-war period, when negotiating progress was a remote prospect, we attach the highest importance to articulating the requirements for an improved relationship and to exploring every serious avenue for progress. Our parallel pursuit of strength and negotiation prepares us both to resist continued Soviet aggrandizement and to recognize and respond to positive Soviet moves.

....President Brezhnev's successors will have to weigh the increased costs and risks of relentless competiton against the benefits of a less tense international environment in which they could more adequately address the rising expectations of their own citizens. While we can define their alternatives, we cannot decipher their intentions. To a degree unequaled anywhere else, Russia in this respect remains a secret. Her history, of which this secrecy is such an integral part, provides no basis for expecting a dramatic change. And yet it also teaches that gradual change is possible. For our part, we seek to encourage change by a firm but flexible U.S. strategy, resting on a broad consensus, that we can sustain over the long term whether the Soviet Union changes or not. If the democracies can meet this challenge, they can achieve the goals of....defend(ing) freedom and preserv(ing) the peace.

# BIBLIOGRAPHY

## The Reagan Round

Ball, George W. "The Erosion of U.S. Foreign Relations" *Bulletin of the Atomic Scientists* 41 (August 1985): 110-113.

Bell, Cora. "From Carter to Reagan," *Foreign Affairs, America and the World 1984* 63 (1984): 490-510.

Bialer, Seweryn and Afferica, Joan. "The Genesis of Gorbachev's World," *Foreign Affairs, America and the World 1985* 64 (1985): 605-644.
"Reagan and Russia," *Foreign Affairs* 61 (Winter 1982-1983): 249-271.

Brzezinski, Zbigniew. *Game Plan.* New York: Atlantic Monthly Press, 1986.

Caldwell, Lawrence T. and Legvold, Robert. "Reagan Through Soviet Eyes," *Foreign Policy* 52 (Fall 1983): 3-21.

Dallek, Robert. *The American Style of Foreign Policy.* New York: Mentor, 1983.

Gaddis, John Lewis. "The Rise, Fall and Future of Detente," *Foreign Affairs* 62 (Winter (Winter 1983-1984): 354-377.

Gelb, Leslie H. and Lake, Anthony. "Four More Years: Diplomacy Restored?" *Foreign Affairs, America and the World 1984* 63 (1984): 465-489.

George, Alexander L. *Managing U.S.-Soviet Rivalry: Problems of Crisis Prevention.* Boulder: Westview Press, 1982.

Haig, Alexander M. Jr. *Caveat: Realism, Reagan and Foreign Policy.* New York: MacMilan, 1982.

Hersh, Seymour M. *The Price of Power.* New York: Summit Books, 1983.

La Feber, Walter. *America, Russia, and the Cold War 1945-1984,* fifth ed. New York: Alred A. Knopf, 1985.

Laqueur, Walter. "Reagan and the Russians," *Commentary* 73 (January 1982): 19-26. "U.S. Soviet Relations," *Foreign Affairs, America and the World 1983 62 (1983): 561-586.*

Luard, Evan. "Superpowers and Regional Conflicts," *Foreign Affairs* 64 (June 1986): 1006-1025.

Nitze, Paul H. "Living with the Soviets," *Foreign Affairs* 63 (Winter 1984-85): 360-374.

Nye, Joseph S. Jr. "Can America Manage Its Soviet Policy?" *Foreign Affairs* 62 (Spring 1984): 857-878.

Podhoretz, Norman. "The Reagan Road to Detente," *Foreign Affairs, America and the World 1984* 63 (1984): 447-464.

Quester, George H. *American Foreign Policy: The Lost Consensus.* New York: Praeger, 1982.

*Report of the President's Bipartisan Commission on Central America.* Forward by Henry Kissinger. New York: MacMillan, 1984.

Shulman, Marshall. "A Rational Response to the Soviet Challenge," *International Affairs* 61 (June 1985): 375-383.

Simes, Dimitri K. "America's New Edge," *Foreign Policy,* (Fall 1984): 24-43. "Clash Over Poland," *Foreign Policy* 46 (Spring 1982): 49-66.

Steinbruner, John. "U.S. and Soviet Security Perspectives," *Bulletin of the Atomic Scientists* 41 (August 1985): 89-93.

Tatu, Michael. "U.S.-Soviet Relations: A Turning Point?" *Foreign Affairs, America and the World 1982* 61 (1982): 591-610.

Vance, Cyrus. *Hard Choices: Critical Years in America's Foreign Policy.* New York: Simon & Schuster, 1983.

Wildavsky, Aaron, ed. *Beyond Containment.* San Francisco: ICS Press, 1983.

# Africa

Abdi, Awaleh, Jama. *Basis of the Conflict in the Horn of Africa.* Mogadishu: 1978.

Albright, David, ed. *Africa and International Communism.* London: MacMillian Press, 1980.

Al-Izzi, K. *The Shatt Al-Arab Dispute: A Legal Study.* London: Third World Centre, 1982.

Arlinghaus, Bruce E. *Arms for Africa.* Lexington, Mass: D.C. Heath, 1983.

Bender, Gerald J. "The Continuing Crisis in Angola" *Current History* (March 1983): 124-125.

Bienen, Henry. "Soviet Political Relations with Africa" *International Security* 6 (Spring 1982): 153-173.

Clough, Michael, "Beyond Constructive Engagement," *Foreign Policy* 61 (Winter 1985-86): 3-24

Coker, Christopher. "Reagan and Africa" *World Today* 38 (April 1982): 123-130.

Crocker, Chester A. "South Africa: Strategy for Change." *Foreign Affairs* 59 (Winter 1980/81): 323-351.

Crocker, Chester; Roger Fountaine and Dimitri Simes, *Implications of Soviet and Cuban Activities in Africa for U.S. Policy.* Washington: Georgetown University Center for Strategic & International Studies, April 1979.

Current History, See entire issues March 1984 and May 1986.

Desfosses, Helen. "North-South or East-West? Constructs for Superpower African Policy in the Eighties" Journal of International Affairs (Autumn 1981): 369-393.

Dominiguez, Jorge I. "Political & Military Limitations and Consequences of Cuban Policies in Africa" Cuban Studies 10 (July 1980): 1-35.

Dougherty, James E. The Horn of Africa Cambridge, Mass.: Institute for Foreign Policy Analysis, 1982.

"Forum: U.S. Policy Toward Sub-Saharan Africa" Orbis 25 (Winter 1982): 853-879.

Gann, L. H. Africa South of the Sahara. Stanford: Hoover Institution Press, 1981.

Gilpin, Susan. "Minerals and Foreign Policy" Africa Report May-June 1982): 16-21.

Grabendorff, Wolf. "Cuba's Involvement in Africa" Journal of Inter-American Studies & World Affairs, 22 (Feb. 1980): 3-29.

Henze, Paul. "Eritrea: The Endless War," The Washington Quarterly 9 (Spring 1986): 23-36.

Henriksen, Thomas H. Communist Powers and Sub-Saharan Africa. Stanford: Hoover Institution, 1981.

Katz, Mark N. The Third World in Soviet Military Thought Baltimore: John Hopkins, 1982.

Kitchen, Helen. "Six Misconceptions of Africa" Washington Quarterly 5 (Autumn 1982): 167-174.

Klinghoffer, Arthur J. The Angolan War: A Study in Soviet Policy in the Third World Boulder: Westview, 1980.

Kraus, Jon. "American Foreign Policy in Africa" Current History 80 (Mar. 1983): 97-110, 115.

Legum, Colin and Lee, Bill. The Horn of Africa in Continuing Crisis NY: Africana Publ, 1979.

Leogrande, William M. "Cuban-Soviet Relations and Cuban Policy in Africa" Cuban Studies 10 (Jan 1980): 1-37.

Maitama-Sule, Alhaji Yusuff. "Africa, the United States and South Africa" Africa Report (Sept-Oct 1982): 10-13.

Marcum, John H. "Lessons of Angola" Foreign Affairs 54 (April 1976): 407-25.

Noer, Thomas J., Gerald K. Haines & Samuel J. Walker. Non-Benign Neglect: the United States and Black Africa in the 20th Century Westport, Con n. Greenwood Press, 1981.

Nolutshungu, Sam C. "African Interests & Soviet Power" Soviet Studies 34 (July 1982): 397-417.

Obasanjo, Olusegun. "Africa's Needs," Foreign Policy 57 (Winter 1984-85): 80-91.

Puddington, Arch. "Ethiopia: The Communist Uses of Famine," Commentary 81 (Aril 1986): 30-38.

Selassie, Bereket Habte. Conflict & Intervention in the Horn of Africa NY: Monthly Review Press, 1980.

Shaw, Timothy M. (ed). Alternative Futures for Africa Boulder, CO: Westview 1982.

"Soviet Power & Policies in the Third World: The Case of Africa" Prospects of Soviet Power in the 1980's: Part II Adelphi Papers, No. 152 International Institute for Strategic Studies, London, Summer 1979.

Thompson, W. Scott. "U.S. Policy Toward Africa: at America's Service?" Orbis 25 (Winter 1982): 1011-1025.

Valenta, Jiri "Soviet-Cuban Intervention in the Horn of Africa" Journal of International Studies 34 (Fall/Winter 1980): 353-368.

Valkenier, Elizabeth Kridl. "Great Power Economic Competition in Africa" Journal of International Studies 34 (Fall/Winter 1981): 259-268.

Whitaker, Jennifer Seymour, ed. Africa & the United States: Vital Interests NY: N.Y. University Press, 1978.

Zartman, I. William. "Issues of African Diplomacy in the 1980's" Orbis 25 (Winter 1982): 1045-1052.

## Latin America

Anderson, Thomas D. Geopolitics of the Caribbean. New York: Praeger, 1984.

Arnson, Cynthia. *El Salvador: A Revolution Confronts the United States.* Washington D.C.: Institute for Policy Studies, 1982.

Baloyra, Enrique A. "Dilemmas of Political Transition in El Salvador," *Journal of International Affairs* 38 (Winter 1985): 221-242.

Betts, Richard K. and Huntington, Samuel P. "Dead Dictators and Rioting Mobs: Does the Demise of Authoritarian Rulers Lead to Political Instability?" *International Security* 10 (Winter 1985-1986): 112-146.

Black, George. "Garrison Guatemala," *NACLA Report on Guatemala* 17 (January-February 1983):

Blasier, Cole. *The Giant's Rival: The USSR and Latin America.* Pittsburgh: University of Pittsburg Press, 1976.

*The Hovering Giant: U.S. Responses to Revolutionary Change in Latin America.* Pittsburgh: University of Pittsburgh Press, 1976.

Bolin, William H. "Central America: Real Economic Help Is Workable Now," *Foreign Affairs* 62 (Summer 1984): 1096-1106.

Booth, John A. *The End and the Beginning: The Nicaragua Revolution.* Boulder: Westview, 1985.

Coleman, Kenneth M. and Herring, George C., eds. *The Central American Crisis.* Wilmington: Scholarly Resources, 1985.

Cruz, Arturo J. "Nicaragua's Imperiled Revolution," *Foreign Affairs* 61 (Summer 1983): 1031-1047.

Dickey, Christopher. "Central America: From Quagmire to Cauldron?" *Foreign Affairs, America and the World 1983* 62 (1983): 659-694.
*With the Contras.* London: Faber, 1986.

Dominguez, Jorge I. "It Won't Go Away: Cuba on the U.S. Foreign Policy Agenda," *International Security* 8 (Summer 1983): 113-128.

Erisman, H. Michael. *Cuba's International Relations.* Boulder: Westview, 1985.

Fagen, Richard, ed. *Capitalism and the State in U.S.-Latin American Relations.* Stanford: Stanford University Press, 1979.

"Nicaraguan Harvest," *Commentary* 80 (July 1985): 21-18

Farer, Tom J. "Breaking the Deadlock in Central America," *Washington Quarterly* 7 (Spring 1984): 100-113.
"Contadora: The Hidden Agenda," *Foreign Policy* 59 (Summer 1985): 59-72.

Feinberg, Richard E., ed. *Central America: International Dimensions of the Crisis.* New York: Holmes and Meier, 1982.
*U.S. Human Rights Policy: Latin American.* Washington, Center for International Policy, 1980.

Garfinkle, Adam M. "Refections on 'Salvadorians, Sandinistas, and Superpowers'," *Orbis*, (Spring 1981): 3-12.

Gettleman, Marvin E. et al. eds. *El Salvador: Central American and the Cold War.* New York: Grove Press, 1981.

Gleijeses, Piero. "The Case for Power Sharing in El Salvador," *Foreign Affairs* 61 (Summer 1983): 1048-1063.
*Tilting at Windmills: Reagan in Central America.* Washington: Johns Hopkins Foreign Policy Institute, 1982.

Gonzalez, Edward. "Cuba, Confrontation or Findlandization?" *Washington Quarterly* 7 (Fall 1984): 28-39.

Horowitz, David. "Nicaragua: A Speech to My Former Comrades on the Left," *Commentary* 81 (June 1986): 27-31.

"Islands of Discontent: The Caribbean Today," *Contemporary Marxism*, entire issue, no. 10 (1985).

Katz, Mark N. "The Soviet Cuban Connection," *International Security* 8 (Summer 1983): 88-112.

Kenworthy, Eldon. "Central America: Beyond the Credibility Trap," *World Policy Journal* 1 (Fall 1983): 181-200.

Kirkpatrick, Jeane J. "The U.N. and Grenada: A Speech Never Delivered," *Strategic Review* 12 (Winter 1984): 11-18.

"U.S. Security in Latin America," *Commentary*. (January 1981): 29-40.

Leiken, Robert S. "Eastern Winds in Latin America," *Foreign Policy* 42 (Spring 1981): 94-113.

"*Soviet Strategy in Latin America*. Washington Papers, vol. 10, no. 93. New York: Praeger, 1982.

Leogrande, William M. "Cuba Policy Recycled," *Foreign Policy* 46 (Spring 1982): 105-119.

"A Splendid Little War," *International Security* 6 (Summer 1981): 27-52.

Lowenthal, Abraham F. "Threat and Opportunity in the Americas," *Foreign Affairs, America and the World 1985* 64 (1985): 539-561.

Millet, Richard. "Central American Paralysis," *Foreign Policy* 39 (Summer 1980): 99-117.

Montaner, Carlos Alberto. "Containment in Central America: Obstacles and Possibilities," *Washington Quarterly* 7 (Fall 1984): 20-27.

Montgomery, Tommie Sue. *Revolution in El Salvador*. Boulder. Westview, 1982.

Novak, Michael. "El Salvador: Rule by Ballot," *Orbis* 26 (Summer 1982): 317-321.

Payne, Anthony. *Grenada: Revolution and Invasion*. New York: St. Martin's Press, 1985.

Pearce, Jenny. *Under the Eagle: U.S. Intervention in Central America and the Caribbean*. London: Latin America Bureau, 1982.

Purcell, Susan K. "Carter, Reagan, and Central America," *Orbis* 26 (Summer 1982): 322-326.

Radu, Michael. "The Structure of the Salvadoran Left," *Orbis* 28 (Winter 1985): 673-683.

Rangel, Carlos. "Mexico and Other Dominos," *Commentary* 71 (June 1981): 27-33.

Robbins, Carla A. *The Cuban Threat*. New York: McGraw-Hill, 1983.

Rogers, William D. "The United States and Latin America," *Foreign Affairs, America and the World 1984* 63 (1984): 560-580.

Rojas, Antonio Cavalla. "U.S. Military Strategy in Central America: From Carter to Reagan: *Contemporary Marxism* 3 (Summer 1981): 114-130.

Ronfeldt, David, F. *Geopolitics, Security, and U.S. Strategy in the Caribbean Basin*. Santa Monica: Rand, 1983.

"Rethinking the Monroe Doctrine," *Orbis* 28 (Winter 1985): 684-696.

Schultz, Donald E. and Graham, Douglas H., eds. *Revolution and Counterrevolution in Central America and the Caribbean*. Boulder: Westview, 1984.

Treverton, Gregory F. "US Strategy in Central America," *Survival*, (March-April 1986): 119-127.

Ullman, Richard. "At War with Nicaragua," *Foreign Affairs* 62 (Fall 1983): 39-58.

Valenta, Jiri. "The USSR, Cuba, and the Crisis in Central America," *Orbis* 25 (Fall 1981): 715-746.

Varas, Angusto. "Ideology and Politics in Latin American-USSR Relations," *Survival* 26 (May-June 1984): 114-121.

Walker, Thomas, ed. *Nicaragua in Revolution*. New York: Praeger, 1981.

Wiarda, Howard J. *The Continuing Struggle for Democracy in Latin America*. Boulder: Westview, 1980.

# CHAPTER III:
# Weapons and Words

## Introduction: Weapons, Wrath, and Rationality

This chapter provides background on the relationship between nuclear weapons, deterrent strategies, and arms control efforts to keep weapons within certain categories and numbers so that they contribute to crisis and arms race stability. This vital relationship, although sometimes obscure, reveals itself in military posture statements and deployments. We find that decisions on weapons; fears about vulnerability, first strike intentions, or potential technological breakthroughs; and identification of priority targets and sanctuaries all lead to new strategies or reappraisals of old ones. For example, realization of nuclear vulnerability led to the strategy of Mutual Assured Destruction (MAD), and elevating the condition of MAD to strategic preference led to banning Ballistic Missile Defense (BMD) and civil defense to guarantee the continuation of this condition. The Soviet development of large ICBMs (SS-18s) capable of prompt, "hard target (silo) kills" led to an American consideration of circumventing ICBM vulnerability via a strategy of "MAD-plus" or countervailing. This option called for selective counterforce (silo) and countervalue (city) targeting, and more invulnerable weapons such as quieter and longer range nuclear submarines (eventually with counterforce capability); large multi-warhead missiles (the MX) deployed in a more survivable mode; and small, numerous, and single warhead missiles (SICBMs or the Midgetman) in hardened launchers. All three types of weapons either complicate arms control treaties or raise questions about the nuclear balance and the strategic intentions of the U.S.

The issues of which weapons and strategies bought or will buy the most or least security and contributed or will contribute the most or least to arms control will be discussed in an applied setting in chapter IV on the arms control process and in a more theoretical setting in chapter V on American nuclear strategy. In the meantime, the review undertaken in this chapter includes the rationale for the American triad (the combination of strategic nuclear forces into three delivery systems: the ICBM, SLBM, and intercontinental bombers), the advantages and disadvantages of various systems (the MX, the Trident II missile, and the B-1 bomber, in particular), a brief look at Soviet systems and doctrines, a thematic compendium of contrasting American strategies and targeting options, and related concerns such as the problems of credibility and rationality, perceptions and misperceptions, and nuclear winters and arms control-inspired thaws. The controversy over the sacredness of the triad and the 15 year debate and delay over the MX missile, intended originally as a response to ICBM vulnerability, begins our weapons story.

# From Minute to Midgetmen: ICBMs

According to the Reagan administration, the 1983 Scowcroft Commission, and the originators of the plan to compensate for bomber vulnerability with the addition of two more invulnerable components of strategic nuclear forces, the existence of a triad poses debilitating obstacles for any enemy first strike plan.[1] Without the ICBM leg, the Soviets could concentrate research efforts on overcoming the other components, for example, by concentrating on Anti-Submarine Warfare (ASW) or air defense. Thus, the triad permits each component to function as a hedge against possible Soviet breakthroughs in weapon technology. The triad also complicates any Soviet first strike plan by forcing them into unpalatable attack choices. If the Soviets were to attack bomber and submarine bases and ICBM silos simultaneously—by delaying launches from offshore submarines so that SLBMs would arrive at bomber bases at the same time that ICBMs (with a longer 30 minute flight time) would arrive at U.S. silos—then a high proportion of U.S. bombers would be able to take off prior to missile impact because of the ability to order bombers to take off within moments after the discovery of Soviet ICBM launches. If, on the other hand, the Soviets were to launch ICBMs and SLBMs simultaneously (hoping to destroy a higher proportion of bombers with offshore SLBMs—5 to 15 minutes to impact) there would follow a 15 minute interval before Soviet ICBMs hit U.S. silos. The Soviets could not assume that the U.S. would not fire its missiles in that interval. Thus the bomber and ICBM forces are more survivable together than either would be alone. Thus, each component makes a contribution to deterrence even if survivability depends on the existence of the other legs of the triad. This time frame and connectivity could be complicated in the future if (and when) the Soviets develop a counterforce SLBM capability.

The triad also deters as it relies on the unique advantageous properties of each component. For example, nuclear submarines, provided free access to Soviet targets as long as the Anti-Ballistic Missile Treaty (ABMT) bans BMD, remain hidden in the oceans for months at a time. Thus their survivable missiles are always ready for retaliation without the pressure of "use them or lose them" in crisis. Bombers, vulnerable on the ground, slow, and opposed by air defenses, may be launched on warning of attack but retrieved without initiating war. ICBMs, increasingly vulnerable to counterforce attack, are highly accurate, reliable, penetrable, and retargetable, and have an advantage in command, control, and communication ($C^3$). Thus they deter all-out war and Soviet conventional or limited nuclear attacks because they could respond promptly, and in a limited fashion, against military targets and, thereby, disrupt a counterforce attack on the U.S. and its allies without necessarily escalating the conflict to all nuclear war. In sum, the diversity of the tripartite dispersal of warheads provides an interlocking combination of strengths that compensate for weaknesses in individual components. However, the development of more accurate ICBM and SLBM guidance systems, and hence ICBM vulnerability, raised a number of questions for the administrations of the 1970s and 1980s.

The Reagan administration, which worries about appearing weak, vulnerable, and unable to offset growing Soviet military power and its potentially greater willingness to exploit military advantages, announced its intention to acquire the MX to redress the Soviet's destabilizing advantage in hard target kill ICBMs. According to the administration, the U.S. needed its own prompt, hard target capability to place Soviet forces and leadership at risk.[2] In its view, vulnerable Minuteman missiles, slow bombers, and relatively inaccurate SLBMs did not provide this capability, but the addition of 100 MX missiles would do so and, in the process, it would require the Soviets to worry about the vulnerability of their forces and their ability to dominate a crisis and emerge successfully from a nuclear conflict.

The Scowcroft Commission cautiously backed Reagan's position and enumerated a number of arguments in favor of MX deployment as an interim strategic measure. It supported the MX in terms of its symbolic value to the U.S. arms control team. The Commission assumed that a unilateral U.S. termination of its only ongoing ICBM program could persuade the Soviets that, since the U.S. was unwilling and unable to neutralize the Soviet advantage in counterforce capability, they need not consider reductions in their forces nor compromises in arms negotiations. The MX would show resolve, and it could be exchanged, in negotiations, for Soviet agreements to reduce forces. Critics on the other hand, doubt the "blueness" of a bargaining chip that will be deployed in numbers so few as to be largely irrelevant to the military balance and which the administration hesitates to consider as a bargaining chip anyway. However, for the administration and the Scowcroft Commission, symbolic signaling is most important. To cancel the MX might communicate that the U.S. did not have the will essential for effective deterrence. Instead, the ominous hard target kill capability imbalance had to be redressed to show resolve and to reinforce Soviet caution about initiating war.

While the administration intended to fortify deterrence with the means for controlled, prompt, and limited attacks on Soviet hard targets, it compromised with Congress on the numbers of MX required for this assignment. It initially wanted 200, then agreed with the Scowcroft recommendation of 100, and grudgingly accepted the congressional limit of 50. All three groups assumed that 100 (or less) MX and their limited throwweight and megatonnage, about the same as the full contingent of Titan missiles retired by 1987, would not provide a sufficient number of warheads to threaten enough Soviet hardened ICBM silos to instill any genuine fear of an American first strike intention. On the other hand, critics hope to see the MX cancelled because they deem counterforce weapons destabilizing and provocative in principle or because they prefer the development of SLBMs and mobile, single warhead missiles. Critics also point out that the counterforce imbalance would erode further with the deployment of only 100 MX and with the ballistic missile warhead cuts outlined in Reagan's START proposals. Most scenarios can not escape the fact that 50 or 100 MX missiles, especially if based in vulnerable Minuteman silos, represent 50-100 sitting ducks with huge clusters of first strike warheads (10 per MX) that might invite Soviet preemption in crisis much more so than the 1000 or so Minuteman missiles and their 2000 plus warheads.

However, this critique overemphasizes Soviet first strike pressure and undervalues its counterforce threat. In the first place, 50 or 100 MXs pose no practical first strike threat, and hence no Soviet incentive to preempt. Second, if the current Soviet counterforce inventory of 600-700 missiles equivalent in size to the MX does not frighten critics into fearing a Soviet first strike, then the MX should merit the same acquiescence. Third, since fear of retaliation deters each side from a first strike, the MX will add to deterrence: first, by placing Soviet silos at risk from our retaliation, hence eroding Soviet confidence in successful limited counterforce attacks, and second, by symbolically encapsulating the American determination to match Soviet capability.

The main problem with the MX involves its deployment in vulnerable Minuteman silos—an ironic fate for a missile intended to solve ICBM vulnerability. If the Soviets contemplate a counterforce strike, placing the MX in Minuteman silos might not deter such a strike. While Reagan accepted the Scowcroft conclusion that the triad compensated, in part, for this vulnerability, he hoped to avoid this problem with a more survivable basing mode and missile defense. However, only the interim deployment of MX into operational silos received congressional support.

The Scowcroft commission envisioned an escape hatch for the basing dilemma. It recommended the development of a small (Congress imposed a 33,000 pound weight limit) single warhead ICBM (SICBM) deployed on hardened mobile launchers that could be located on military bases until warning of attack when they could be dispersed onto U.S. highways. Such a force structure would complicate Soviet first strike plans because SICBMs would be more survivable, due to mobility and deceptive basing; less inviting as individual targets; and hence more stabilizing and deterring. In other words, an SICBM would deny the attacker the chance to destroy more than one warhead with one attacking warhead as it could if aimed at an MX. The Soviets would have to expend many warheads in redundant barrage attacks trying to find the dispersed SICBMs. While critics fear that barrage attacks with more numerous and sophisticated warheads could erode even mobile ICBM invulnerability, especially if the Soviets increased warheads beyond SALT II limits, proponents envision a transition to a more stable deterrent wherein both sides would opt for more survivable mobile missiles and reductions in the number of warheads. However, while the Soviet move to the SS-24 and SS-25 indicates an interest in mobility, they are unlikely to give up their counterforce advantage in exchange for smaller, single warhead missiles. In the meantime, the Soviets insist that SALT II prohibits U.S. development of a new ICBM system.

Not everyone, then, sings the praises of the SICBM, including an increasingly ambivalent Pentagon, which encouraged Reagan to object to the concept of mobile missiles, as Carter objected to it earlier when he attempted to persuade the Soviets to agree to a ban in SALT II. Military planners (Soviet and U.S.) may appreciate their hard to find missiles and launchers, but they dislike the enemy's. Planners and arms controlers worry about the hornet's nest involved in trying to count and monitor small, hidden, and relocatable SICBMs. In addition, it would be difficult to distinguish between conventional or threater and intercontinental missiles. Third, the single warhead missile entails enormous cost in terms of its warhead per missile ratio. The SICBM will cost approximately 100 million dollars per warhead as opposed to the Trident II missile cost of 13 million dollars per warhead, the B-1B at 16 million per warhead, and the MX at 20 million per warhead. Finally, there remain questions about its vulnerability, in the aftermath of Soviet improvements in warhead accuracy and sensor technology, and about its size, payload, and guidance and control system effectiveness. The SICBM may be desireable as a lower value target than the MX, but if it can not reach its target because of system malfunction or an inability to carry enough penetration aids to foil Soviet defenses, then it loses value. Some suggest putting more warheads on an enlarged Midgetman to increase its penetrability, contribution to force capability, and cost effectiveness. But, in the process, it would become a higher value target.[3] Although, as long as it retained mobility, neither its survivability nor the cost to the Soviets of countering it should be affected.

Despite the technical, cost, and arms control complications anticipated for the SICBM, its merits—the contribution to stability via its survivability, made greater if the two sides agree on warhead reductions, and its high "cost-to-attack" character— standout compared with the deployment of Minuteman and MX missiles in vulnerable silos. But the vulnerability dilemma remains, as both the costly and SALT II prohibited mobile SICBM and the more cost effective MX face improved Soviet ICBM accuracy. While acknowledging that the U.S. can not abandon the ICBM leg of the triad for political (credibility and perception), strategic (high reliability, penetrability, and lethality), and financial (low cost) reasons, many analysts, senators, and naval officers make a plea for increased reliance on the most survivable (but most costly) leg of the triad—the Submarine Launched Ballistic Missile (SLBM).

## Sink Or Swim with the SLBM

While nuclear submarines with SLBMs suffer from command and control weaknesses, they represent the most survivable, post-attack-responsive, and hence most stable and attractive leg of the triad. Until recently, the U.S. relied on Polaris and Poseidon submarines with relatively inaccurate and short range missiles on board. They posed a countervalue threat against Soviet cities. As a hedge against potential Soviet BMD, ASW, and ICBM accuracy breakthroughs, the U.S. built longer range and quieter Trident submarines and longer range, more accurate and penetrable SLBMs and warheads. The Trident force, with 8 subs holding 24 missiles apiece, represents the first bridge to a force of 12-16 Tridents by the late 1990s with from 6000-7000 D-5 warheads on Trident II missiles. The missile and warhead package will include, by December 1989, a range of up to 5000 miles and a potency comparable to the MX. Cost estimates for this deployment range from 75-100 billion dollars.

In the new age of ICBM vulnerability, the force will soon represent the major survivable counterforce deterrent to a Soviet first strike. Even if the Soviets attempted to eliminate American ICBMs in a strike with its SS-18s, the Trident II missiles with their D-5 warheads would, by the early 1990s, enable the U.S. to retaliate, selectively or massively, with its accurate counterforce at sea. However, this very capability inspires fear of a hypothetical American first strike potential. Critics in the U.S. and the Soviet Union point to the shortened 15 minute launch time, the hard target capability, and the great increases in numbers of warheads in an enlarged Trident II contingent as evidence of a potential ability to strike first and perhaps decapitate the Soviet command and control structure and thus preclude an effective Soviet retaliation—unless it resorted to a hair trigger or Launch on Warning (LOW) strategy, which it has threatened as a response to the U.S. modernization program.

Proponents of the Trident II respond by suggesting that the limited number of American forces facing Soviet ICBMs, mobile missiles, and SLBMs do not pose a disarming first strike threat. They also contend that survivability contributes more to stability and deterrence than a hard target capability detracts from them. In other words, the Soviets could have no incentive to preempt, for they would gain nothing by it because retaliation, which would be unimpaired since the Soviets could not take out the subs, would either devastate the remaining Soviet military apparatus or population depending on the nature of Soviet preemption. Even in crisis, the cost of going first would be too high. The difference for the U.S. with the Trident IIs would be that it could retaliate selectively against silos, with the chance of deterring escalation with the threat of reserve nuclear forces, something it could not do with the Trident I countervalue missiles.

In addition since technology has reached a point where most strategic and even conventional weapons systems will soon have hard target capability, it would be foolish to forego this capability.[4] Finally, if a counterforce capability is to deter a first strike, then the threat should be located in the most survivable leg of the triad. Proponents also dismiss the LOW scenario since, in their view, the best answer to vulnerability is not LOW (which may nonetheless be unavoidable on occasion), but an investment in a more survivable force. Both the Soviets, with their expansion of mobile ICBM and SLBM inventories, and the U.S., with its perennial preference for SLBMs, show that they intend to invest in just that.

However, even this survivable Trident force faces an uncertain future. Both naval planners and their critics worry about ASW breakthroughs such as global detection systems employing advanced radar or sonar (acoustical) devices capable of locating submarines with sufficient accuracy to launch barrage attacks on them at sea. While the U.S. leads in the ASW area, as well as in radar and sonar deceiving technologies, leads tend to dissipate, and new devices, such as detection via lasers or a satellite-supported ability to discriminate between natural ocean waves and waves created by subs as they move through the water, may present even more unwelcome possibiities. In the meantime, with the known ICBM vulnerability and the only theoretical vulnerability of nuclear submarines, the Reagan administration wants to hedge its bet by concentrating on large submarines with more potent missile and warhead forces. Debate still occurs over the comparative advantage of a few (16-24) large submarines (the Trident is over 200 yards long) versus more numerous smaller subs with a greater dispersal of warheads and hence lower target value. Another issue is the relative worth of heavier missile payloads for counterforce assurance compared to lesser payloads but greater range for warheads and missiles.

While the administration considers the SLBM, with all its flaws in terms of cost, counter force complications, and potential vulnerability to ASW breakthroughs, to be the most survivable and deterring element in the military balance, many partisans of the triad persist in their support of the manned bomber—the original, quite fragile leg of the triad.

## Bombers, Bombast, and Budget Busters

The manned bomber attracts supporters because of its great flexibility and "recallability." Bombers launched in crises, can be recalled if necessary. Their readiness is enhanced by having a great percentage of aircraft (60-70 percent) on airborne alert. The bomber force, however, entails many obstacles as well, including facing increasingly sophisticated air defenses, finding hard to locate and relocatable (mobile) targets, and overcoming the vulnerability of the B-52 which shows up like a "burning barn door" on radar screens. Concern for these weaknesses inspired the Air Force to modernize the B-52s with the deployment of Air Launched Cruise Missiles (ALCMs) on them. The ALCMs extend the attack range and effectiveness of the B-52 by allowing it to stand off further from Soviet territory to direct ALCMs at Soviet targets. The 1986 conversion of the 131st B-52 with ALCMs threw the U.S. over the SALT II Treaty limits on MIRVed launchers; i.e. launchers of ballistic missiles with three to ten MIRVs or warheads. Reagan, as a part of his "proportionate response" to alleged Soviet violations of SALT II, decided to continue outfitting B-52s with ALCMs.

However, the aging B-52s, despite fancy upgrading, remain questionable in terms of endurance, reliability, and penetration. The U.S. intends to replace the B-52 with the B-1 as its primary strategic bomber until the deployment of the Advanced Technology Bomber (ATB or "Stealth" bomber) sometime in the 1990s. Reagan's decision to deploy the B-1, a program cancelled by Carter in 1977, rather than wait for the ATB, aroused almost as much controversy as the MX decision. The advantages of the B-1, or rather the modified B-1B, include its many "stealth" technology features such as forward looking-radar, terrain hugging flight, computer communications, radar-jamming systems, and other electronic countermeasures that enable the bomber to fly at high speed and low altitude to deceive enemy defenses. However, many flaws stand out as well, including high cost (some estimate that the B1-B will cost up to 400 million dollars per plane), early obsolescence (the B1-B seems to be a very temporary interim between the B52 and the ATB), and its vulnerability to attack on the ground and on its mission.

Despite these flaws, the Reagan administration plans a B-1B contingent of at least 100 aircraft by the mid 1990s. In the meantime, research and development on the ATB—a high speed, high technology, and low radar-observable bomber continues at a fast, but quite secret pace. ATB technology reputedly consists of electronic and advanced avionic designs and countermeasures and non-metallic materials to reduce the plane's radar image (or "cross section") and its infrared detectability to negate or deceive present and projected Soviet air defense radars and sensors. Both the B-1B and the ATB will carry nuclear and conventional cruise missiles and payloads. While both also will encounter more sophisticated and extensive Soviet air defenses and early warning systems, the Air Force scientists expect to overcome these defensive obstacles with the increased accuracy, penetrability, and maneuverability of the two new bombers.

## Cruises: Solution to Vulnerability or New Blow to Arms Control

As indicated above, the latter two legs of the triad have improved capability as a result of the deployment of cruise missiles, which fly more slowly than ballistic missiles, but considerably faster than jets and in a similar low level trajectory that makes them difficult to shoot down. Long range, highly maneuverable, and terrain hugging missiles, they are cheaper than most aircraft and missiles and hard to find on radar. The cruises may be air, ground, or sea-launched. Deployed on B-52s, FB-111s (forward-based tactical bombers), or B-1Bs, they extend the effectiveness of the bombers by allowing them to deliver cruise missiles at targets while outside of Soviet air space. While the congressional and budget crunch of the 1980s cut ALCM plans by about one third, the Air Force expects to purchase about 3000 ALCMs by the mid 1990s. NATO started deploying several hundred, slow-flying Ground Launched Cruise Missiles (GLCMs) in Western Europe, along with the Pershing II intermediate range missiles (INF), to counter Soviet SS-20s in December 1983. The Submarine Launched Cruise Missile (SLCM), the most costly, but also the most survivable of the cruise missiles, provides a deadly adjunct to American retaliatory forces. The Navy plans about 3000-4000 cruises, including 750 with nuclear warheads, for use on submarines and surface ships in order to make several hundred of them potential nuclear attack vessels.

Cruises, in particular the SLCMs, contribute to deterrence since they serve as "stabilizing" weapons more suited for retaliation against cities in a second strike than as weapons aimed at silos in a first strike. However, as Advanced Cruise Missile (ACM) lurks on the horizon that might possess sufficient accuracy and lethality to destroy Soviet silos which, in the Soviet view, would obscure the distinction between American first and second strike intentions. In addition, placing ACMs on hundreds of ships and submarines, while frightening to the Soviets in and of itself, becomes more complicating since it will be impossible to distinguish between ships and cruise missiles that carry nuclear warheads and those that do not. This will create a major headache for arms controllers on both sides (the Soviets lag only about 5 years behind the U.S. in terms of cruise missile technology): 1) you/they can not distinguish between conventional and nuclear warheads, and 2) since these weapons are small and easy to hide, you/they can not count them. If the cruise missiles were purely second strike weapons, these verification problems would not loom so ominously. However, the quite accurate, more powerful, and relatively speedy ACM, especially in conjunction with other nuclear offensive and defensive systems, could pose a possible first strike threat if deployed in very large numbers. Whether and how to control ACMs will be a major new complication in arms control negotiations in the late 1980s.

## How to Defend and Coordinate the Triad

While chapter VI covers the debate over the merits of SDI, this section consists of a brief review of several defense components such as air, space, and ballistic missile defense; the LOW alternative to defense; and C³. The assembled or composite weaknesses of these components form the basis of debate over hypothethically stabilizing versus destabilizing remedies.

Starting with the least controversial defense component, air defense, we find an underfunded, eroded, and permeable remnant of the 1960s. The continental U.S. air defense system, defends against strikes by employing interceptor aircraft and radars manned by the North American Air Defense (NORAD.) Soviet developments in intercontinental bombers, like the Backfire and Blackjack, and in Long Range Cruise Missiles (LCMs) have accelerated concerns for improved air defense in the 1980s. Many scientists and military planners expect anti-satellite (ASAT) and BMD technologies, weapons, and C³ capabilities to apply to air defense and vice versa. While the Reagan administration welcomes this interrelationship, its procurement record shows a higher priority for strategic nuclear forces, conventional equipment, and SDI rather than air defense, although the linkage between air defense and conventional missions still attracts considerable support from the Pentagon.

Space defense, much more controversial than air defense, concerns, in part, the renewed American interest in ASAT capability to deter a Soviet ASAT attack and to deny them an uninhibited use of space in a protracted nuclear war. Critics fear that tests of ASAT weapons, which the Congress conditionally limited in 1985, could be viewed by the Soviets as an adjunct to an American attempt to circumvent the ABM Treaty bans on testing BMD systems. The Soviets worry that, as American scientists explore ASAT technologies and test various devices in space, they could learn quite a bit about technologies applicable to hitting incoming warheads as well as orbiting satellites. In the meantime, while the Soviets already possess a relatively primitive ASAT system and demand a moratorium on, and a testing ban of, ASAT weapons, Reagan refuses to forego research and testing in this area. The U.S. tested the Air Launched Miniature Vehicle launched by an F-15 aircraft against a low altitude satellite in 1985.

Critics of ASAT, who want to avoid the militarization of space, recommend banning ASAT testing and development. Many point out that the U.S. should prefer to prevent Soviet ASAT capability since it is much more dependent on inherently fragile satellites than the Soviets. Ashton Carter argues that arms control in this area would be difficult because ASAT attack is easy and tempting, not all uses of space are benign and deserving of protection, and bans on research would be unverifiable. He recommends the following courses of actions: improvements in satellite survivability, avoidance of dependence on vulnerable satellites, employment of survivable backups to satellites, segregation of "benign" from "threatening" missions and nuclear war-related from conventional war-related missions on different satellites, and plans to attack certain Soviet satellites since the U.S. should demonstrate the ability to give "threatening" Soviet satellites, such as BMD battle stations, a rough time in low earth orbit.[5] In the meantime, the U.S., due to congressional constraints, has not tested an ASAT weapon since the successful 1985 firing of an F-15 borne missile.

While the ABM treaty strictly outlines the limits on testing and deployment of BMD, certain provisions allow for silo defense and for BMD research. While the allowable defense around U.S. silos has all but disintegrated and while the rather exotic possibilities for destroying missiles and warheads prior to atmospheric entry are decades or more away, the U.S. does possess a number of defense options available now or in the near term. Some "off the shelf technology" applies to both boost and terminal phases of missile and warhead flight. Another example of current options is the low altitude defense system, LOADS. LOADS is deployable at silo sites to attack incoming vehicles, and relies on high acceleration missile interceptors (with or without nuclear warheads) to destroy incoming targets. There are problems with this system, such as handling an overwhelming first strike or overcoming sensor vulnerabilities, as both critics and proponents of BMD point out. However, the Reagan administration emphasizes the high priority of defending retaliatory forces.

Other alternatives to ICBM vulnerability already exist, such as mobility and invulnerable basing. Another option, one of the least stabilizing, is to put American forces on LOW status. Few advocate this remedy, although both superpowers may feel so pressured by their ICBM and $C^3$ vulnerability that they might reluctantly adopt this high alert, but precarious, arrangement. At best, the enhanced uncertainty about the prospects of a successful first strike against an opponent depending on a LOW status provides some added deterrence. However, the hair trigger nature of this option pleases no one.

The pressure for moving to LOW also derives from each side's concern for the vulnerability of its $C^3$ capability which is so necessary to discern attack promptly, respond appropriately, and to terminate hostilities as quickly as possible. However, again, each side prefers enhancing the physical invulnerability of its $C^3$ to adopting LOW. In a sense, $C^3$ capabilities comprise the heart and brain of deterrence and retaliation. Each side needs to be able, should deterrence fail, to react rapidly, initiate response commands, link early warning systems (EWS) and radars to the National Command Authority (NCA), and manage hostilities in such a way as to control escalation and terminate conflict on as favorable terms as possible. An effective $C^3$ relies on the following: attack warning and assessment through satellites and ground and air-based sensors, ground and air-based command centers, and a communication network to integrate EWS with battle management facilities, the NCA, and strategic forces. An effective $C^3$ capability provides a key link in the deterrent chain.

The protection of this vital link against a decapitating Soviet first strike falls largely to a creative mixture of early warning measures to extricate decision makers from targeted areas, to lift all air-based commands out of harm's way, and to alert the $C^3$ network of impending attack. Command and communication centers can be hardened, dispersed, and multiplied to provide a more secure, endurable, interoperable, and redundant system. However, the nature of sensors, sensitive computers, fragile satellites, and immobile command centers inhibit easy defense and therefore $C^3$ remains the weakest link, and perhaps priority target, in the deterrent chain.

Most analysts would argue that the U.S. command structure could not survive even a limited Soviet attack with enough effectiveness to direct a coherent response, and thus it possesses the highest "use it or lose it" quality of any segment of the deterrent. Critics differ over suitable remedies. While most urge improving $C^3$ survivability, John Steinbruner pointed out a painful paradox: 1) Vulnerability is destabilizing because a decapitating strike might make sense in a crisis, where war appeared inevitable, even though it would preclude a bargained end to war, because it would reduce the opponent's effective retaliation and would offer a slim chance of complete decapitation and no retaliation.[6] 2) On the other hand, attempts to reduce vulnerability could also be destabilizing, if they persuade the Soviets that such efforts indicated an American willingness to initiate war. Steinbruner concluded that since attempts to improve $C^3$ could only be marginally effective anyway, they were not worth it, especially if they provoked the Soviets. Another paradox occurs to many who note the mutuality of vulnerability: should the U.S. consider decapitation, in the hope, however slim, that it could degrade a Soviet third strike? Or should it abandon this notion, and assume that the Soviets would also, in the hope of finding someone left in command, after deterrence failed, to end the hostilities? This seems a rather fragile and insufficient insurance against attack. Or should we chalk this dilemma up as one more contributor to the overall deterring effect of the inevitability of escalation? If neither weapons, nor efforts to manage nuclear war, will prevent escalation, then both sides will be deterred from initiating war. Here lies another frail hope, but it is one we have relied on throughout the decades of MAD.

These sections on weapons and systems to coordinate and protect their use were intended to provide some insight into the controversies over which best serve deterrence. While all recent administrations noted the importance of assured retaliation and abstaining from provocative threats that might encourage preemption, debate surrounded their weapon preferences, targeting priorities, and willingness to send billions on forces that may be expendable bargaining chips, obsolete prior to deployment, sops to interservice rivalry, or fanciful dreams of individual presidents. More elaborate discussion of the arms control and strategic ramifications of these preferences follows in the last four chapters. Before turning to these, we should take a quick look at Soviet systems and then some of the strategic concepts that reflect and dictate Soviet and U.S. weapons choices.

## Soviet Strategic Weapons
## Source: Soviet Military Power 1986
## (Department of Defense)

The operational Soviet ICBM force consists of some 1,400 silo and mobile launchers, aside from those at test sites. Some 818 of the silo launchers have been rebuilt since 1972; nearly half of these silos have been refurbished since 1970. All 818 silos have been hardened against attack by currently operational U.S. ICBMs. These silos contain the SS-17 Mod 3 (150 silos), the SS-18 Mod 4 (308), and the SS-19 Mod 3 (360), which were the world's most modern deployed ICBMs until the more modern, mobile SS-25 was deployed.

Each SS-18 and SS-19 ICBM can carry more and larger MIRVs than the Minuteman III, the most modern deployed U.S. ICBM. The SS-18 Mod 4 carries at least ten MIRVs, and the SS-19 Mod 3 carries only three. The SS-18 Mod 4 was specifically designed to attack and destroy ICBMs and other hardened targets in the U.S. The SS-18 Mod 4 force currently deployed has the capability to destroy about 65 to 80 percent of U.S. ICBM silos, using two nuclear warheads against each. The remaning Soviet ICBM silos are fitted primarily with the SS-11 Mod 2/3s and SS-13 Mod 2s. These ICBMs of older vintage (most of which will be dismantled by mid 1990s) are housed in less-survivable silos and are considered less capable. The most recent development in the Soviets' operational ICBM force occurred with the deployment of their road-mobile SS-25 missile, in violation of SALT I and SALT II. It carries a single reentry vehicle and is being deployed in a road-mobile configuration similar to that of the SS-20. As such it will be highly survivable with an inherent refire capability. Activity at the Soviet ICBM test ranges indicates that two additional new ICBMs are under development. A new ICBM to replace the SS-18 is nearing the slight test stage of development. Additionally, a solid-propellant missile that may be larger than the SS-X-24 will begin flight-testing in the next few years. Both of these missiles are likely to have better accuracy and greater throwweight potential than their predecessors.

## Submarine-Launched Ballistic Missiles

The Soviets maintain the world's largest ballistic missile submarine force. As of early 1986, the force numbered 62 modern SSBNs carrying 944 SALT-accountable nuclear-tipped missiles. Neither total includes the 13 older GOLF II SSBs with 39 missiles which are currently assigned theater missions. The GOLF III SSB and HOTEL III SSBN are only SALT-accountable for their missile tubes. Twenty SSBNs are fitted with 336 MIRVed submarine-launched ballistic missiles (SLBMs). These 20 units have been built and deployed within the past nine years. Two-thirds of the ballistic missile submarines are fitted with long-range SLBMs, enabling them to patrol in waters close to the Soviet Union. This affords protection from NATO antisubmarine warfare operations...

## Strategic Aviation

The assets of the air armies include some 180 BEAR and BISON bombers, 145 BACKFIRE bombers, 397 medium-range BLINDER and BADGER bombers, and 450 shorter range FENCER strike aircraft. Soviet Naval Aviation assets include some 125 BACKFIRE and 230 BLINDER and BADGER bombers. The Soviets have been producing the BACKFIRE, their most modern operational bomber, at a rate of about 30 per year. Several modifications have been made to the aircraft and further modifications are likely to upgrade performance. The BACKFIRE can perform a variety of missions including nuclear strike, conventional attack, antiship strikes, and reconnaissance. Additionally, the BACKFIRE can be equipped with a probe to permit in-flight refueling to increase its range....The BLACKJACK, a new long-range bomber larger than the U.S. B-1B, is still undergoing flight-testing. The BLACKJACK will be faster than the U.S. B-1B and may have about the same combat radius. The new bomber will be capable of carrying cruise missiles, bombs, or a combination of both and could be operational as early as 1988.

## Long-Range Cruise Missiles

The AS-15, a small, air-launched, subsonic, low-altitude cruise missile, became operational in 1984. It is similar in design to the U.S. Tomahawk and has a range of about 3,000 kilometers. It is currently deployed with the BEAR H and is expected to be carried on the BLACKJACK when that aircraft becomes operational. The Soviets have a sea-launched version and a ground-launched version of the AS-15 under development. The ground-launched cruise missile variant, the SSC-X-4, will probably become operational this year. Its mission will be to support operations in the Eurasian theater since the Soviets are unlikely to deploy it outside the USSR and its range is too short for intercontinental strikes. All of these cruise missiles probably will be equipped with nuclear warheads when first deployed and will be capable of attacking hardened targets. These systems could be accurate enough to permit the use of conventional warheads.

## Intermediate-Range Nuclear Forces

The Soviets began a vigorous effort to modernize and expand their intermediate-range nuclear force in 1977 with the deployment of the first

SS-20 LRINF missiles. Each SS-20 is equipped with three MIRVs....The survivability of the SS-20 is greatly enhanced because of the difficulty in detecting and targeting this system when it is field deployed. Further, the SS-20 launcher can be reloaded and refired, and the Soviets stockpile refire missiles.

## Soviet Ballistic Missile Defense

The world's only operational ABM system is maintained around Moscow. In 1978, the Soviets began to upgrade and expand that system to the limit allowed by the 1972 ABM Treaty. When completed, the modernized Moscow ABM system will be a two-layer defense composed of silo-based, long-range, modified GALOSH interceptors; silo-based GAZELLE high-acceleration endoatmospheric interceptors designed to engage targets within the atmosphere; associated engagement, guidance and battle management radar systems; and a new large radar at Pushkino designed to control ABM engagements. The silo-based launchers may be reloadable. The new system will have the 100 ABM launchers permitted by the ABM Treaty and could be fully operational by 1987.

The Krasnoyarsk radar is designed for ballistic missile detection and tracking, including ballistic missile early warning. It violates the 1972 ABM Treaty as it is not located within a 150-kilometer radius of the national capital (Moscow) as required of ABM radars, nor is it located on the periphery of the Soviet Union and pointed outward as required for early warning radars. The Soviet Union has claimed that the Krasnoyarsk radar is designed for space tracking, rather than ballistic missile early warning, and therefore does not violate the ABM Treaty. Its design, however, is not suited for a space-tracking role, and the radar would, in any event, contribute little to the existing Soviet space-tracking network. Indeed, the design of the Krasnoyarsk radar is essentially identical to that of other radars that are known—and acknowledged by the Soviets—to be for ballistic missile detection and tracking, including ballistic missile early warning. The growing Soviet network of large phased-array, ballistic missile detection and tracking radars, of which the Krasnoyarsk radar is a part, is of particular concern when linked with other Soviet ABM efforts. Such radars take years to construct and their existence might allow the Soviet Union to move rather quickly to construct a nationwide ABM defense if it chooses to do so.

In addition, the Soviets have probably violated the prohibition on testing surface-to-air missile (SAM) components in an ABM mode by conducting tests involving the use of SAM air defense radars in ABM-related testing activities. Moreover, the SA-10 and SA-X-12 SAM systems may have the potential to intercept some types of strategic ballistic missiles. Taken together, all of the Soviet Union's ABM and ABM-related activities are more significant—and more ominous— than any one considered individually. Cumulatively, they suggest that the USSR may be preparing to deploy rapidly an ABM defense of its national territory, contrary to the provisions of the ABM Treaty.

### Laser, Beam, and Energy Weapons

The Soviets are conducting research on three types of gas lasers considered promising for weapons application—the gas-dynamic laser, the electric discharge laser, and the chemical laser. Soviet achievements in this area, in terms of output power, have been impressive. The Soviets also are aware of the military potential of visible and very short wavelength lasers. They are investigating excimer, free-electron, and x-ray lasers and have been developing argon-ion lasers for over a decade. Since the late 1960s, the Soviets have been involved in research to explore the feasibility of space-based weapons that would use particle beams. We estimate that they may be able to test a prototype particle beam weapon intended to disrupt the electronics of satellites in the 1990s. The Soviets also have a variety of research programs underway in the area of kinetic energy weapons, using the high-speed collision of a small mass with the target as the kill mechanism. In the 1960s, the USSR developed an experimental "gun" that could shoot streams of particles of a heavy metal such as tungsten or molybdenum at speeds of nearly 25 kilometers per second in air and over 60 kilometers per second in a vacuum. Long range, space-based KEWS for defense against ballistic missiles probably could not be developed until the mid 1990s or even later.

### Computer, Sensor, ASAT, and Space Technology

Advanced technology weapons programs—including potential advanced defenses against ballistic missiles and ASATs—are dependent on remote sensor and computer technologies, areas in which the West currently leads the Soviet Union. The USSR has had for more than a dozen years the world's only operational antisatellite system, which is launched into the same orbit as its target satellite and, when it gets close enough, destroys the satellite by exploding a conventional warhead. The Soviets operate several space systems that support both military and civil users. These include manned spacecraft, reconnaissance and surveillance vehicles, new space boosters, and a variety of other support systems. The primary focus of Soviet space operations is military, as evidenced by the fact that at least 70 percent of Soviet space launches are purely military in nature and support both offensive and defensive operations.

### Passive Defenses

In the more traditional areas of strategic defense, Soviet military doctrine calls for passive and active defenses to act in conjunction to ensure wartime survival. Physical hardening of military assets to make them more resistant to attack is an important passive defense technique. The USSR has hardened its ICBM silos, launch facilities, and key command and control centers to an unprecedented degree. Much of the current U.S. retaliatory force would be ineffective against these targets.

### Air Defense

The Soviet Union has since the 1950s invested enormous resources in a wide array of strategic air defense weapons systems. Currently, the

Soviets have more than 9,000 strategic SAM launchers, over 4,600 tactical SAM launchers, and some 10,000 air defense radars. More than 1,200 Air Defense Forces interceptor aircraft are dedicated to strategic defense. In additional 2,800 interceptors assigned to Soviet Air Forces (SAF) will be drawn upon for strategic defense missions....The Soviets maintain the world's most extensive early warning system for air defense. It is composed of a widespread network of ground-based radars linked operationally with those of their Warsaw Pact allies.

## Strategic Offensive Forces (1-86)

| US | Soviet |
|---|---|
| **ICBMs** | |
| TITAN.....................17 | SS-11......................450 |
| MINUTEMAN II............450 | SS-13.......................60 |
| MINUTEMAN III............550 | SS-17......................150 |
| 1,017 | SS-18......................308 |
| | SS-19......................360 |
| | SS-25.......................45 |
| | 1,373 |

| US | Soviet |
|---|---|
| **SLBMs** | |
| POSEIDON (C-3)............288 | SS-N-5......................39 |
| TRIDENT I* (C-4)...........360 | SS-N-6.....................304 |
| 648 | SS-N-8.....................292 |
| | SS-N-17.....................12 |
| | SS-N-18....................224 |
| | SS-N-20*....................80 |
| | SS-N-X-23...................32 |
| | 983 |

| US | Soviet |
|---|---|
| **Bombers** | |
| B-52G....................167 | BEAR.....................130 |
| B-52H.....................96 | BISON......................30 |
| FB-111....................61 | BACKFIRE.................270 |
| B-1B.......................3 | 430 |
| 327 | |

### Approximate Totals

| Delivery Vehicles | U.S. | Soviet |
|---|---|---|
| *Missiles | 1,165 | 2,356 |
| *Bombers | 327 | 430 |

*Includes SLBMs potentially carried on TRIDENT and TYPHOON on sea trials.

*This chart in the FY 1987 Joint Chiefs of Staff (JCS) Military Posture Statement places the Soviet Union within the SALT II Treaty limit of 2,504 strategic nuclear delivery vehicles (SNDVs). The Soviet SS-N-5s and Backfires are not SALT II-accountable.*

**Table 1**
# Department of Defense U.S. Strategic Forces Highlights

| | FY 1980 | FY 1984 | FY 1985 | FY 1986 | FY 1987 |
|---|---|---|---|---|---|
| **Strategic Offense** | | | | | |
| **Land-Based ICBMs[1]** | | | | | |
| Titan | 52 | 32 | 21 | 8 | 2 |
| Minuteman | 992 | 990 | 990 | 988 | 963 |
| Peacekeeper | - | - | - | 2 | 27 |
| | | | | | |
| **Strategic Bombers (PAA)[2]** | | | | | |
| B-52D | 75 | - | - | - | - |
| B-52G/H | 241 | 241 | 241 | 241 | 234 |
| FB-111 | 59 | 56 | 56 | 56 | 52 |
| B-1B | - | - | 1 | 18 | 60 |
| | | | | | |
| **Fleet Ballistic Launchers (SLBMs)[1]** | | | | | |
| Polaris | 80 | - | - | - | - |
| Poseidon (C-3 & C-4) | 368 | 416 | 368 | 352 | 336 |
| Trident | - | 72 | 120 | 144 | 192 |
| | | | | | |
| **Strategic Defense** | | | | | |
| **Interceptors (PAA/Squadrons)[2]** | | | | | |
| Active | 127/7 | 90/5 | 90/5 | 76/4 | 54/3 |
| Air National Guard | 165/10 | 162/10 | 198/11 | 198/11 | 195/11 |

[1]Number on-line
[2]Primary Aircraft Authorized

Source: Weinberger, *Annual Report to the Congress, FY 1987*, (February 5, 1986): 13.

# Selected Definitions of Terms and Issues*

**Antiballistic Missile Defense (BMD):** All measures to intercept and destroy hostile ballistic missiles, or otherwise neutralize them. Equipment includes weapons, target acquisition, tracking and guidance radars, plus ancillary installations.

**Command, Control, Communication (C[3]):** An arrangement of facilities, equipment, personnel, and procedures used to acquire, process, and disseminate information needed by decision makers in planning, directing, and controlling operations.

**Commitment, Communication of:** Deterrence is about intentions—not just estimating enemy intentions but influencing them. The hardest part is communicating intentions....Nations have been known to bluff; they have also been known to make threats sincerely and change their minds when the chips were down....A persuasive threat of war may deter an aggressor; the problem is to make it persuasive, to keep it from sounding like a bluff.[7]

**Counterforce:** The employment of strategic air and missile forces to destroy, or render impotent, military capabilities of an enemy force.

Bombers and their bases, ballistic missile submarines, ICBM silos, ABM and air defense installations, command and control centers, and nuclear stockpiles are typical counterforce targets. See Deterrence, Requirements of.

**Countervailing:** According to which the United States seeks to maintain military (including nuclear forces, contingency plans, and command-and-control) capabilities to convince Soviet leaders that they cannot secure victory, however they may define it, at any stage of a potential war. That is, the United States seeks a situation in which the Soviets would always lose more than they could reasonably expect to gain from either beginning or escalating a military conflict....The countervailing strategy implies no illusion that nuclear war once begun would likely to stop short of an all-out exchange. But it does acknowledge that such a limited war could happen, and it seeks to convince the Soviets that if a limited nuclear attack by them somehow failed to escalate into an all-out nuclear exchange, they would not have gained from their aggression.

Operationally, the countervailing strategy requires that plans and capabilities be structured to emphasize U.S. ability to employ strategic nuclear forces selectively as well as in all-out retaliation for massive attacks. This means having the necessary forces and evolving the detailed plans to ensure that Soviet leaders know that if they choose some intermediate level of nuclear aggression, the United States will exact an unacceptably high price in things that the Soviet leaders appear to value most, using large and selective but still less than maximal nuclear responses. The targets of such an attack could be military forces, both nuclear and conventional; the industrial capability to sustain a war; political and military leadership and control structures; and industrial capability.[8] See Flexible Response.

**Countervalue:** A strategic concept which calls for the destruction of selected enemy population centers, industries, resources, and/or institutions which constitute the social fabric of a society. See MAD.

**Credibility and Rationality:** It is a paradox of deterrence that in threatening to hurt somebody if he misbehaves, it need not make a critical difference how much it would hurt you too -- *if* you can make him believe the threat....Another paradox of deterrence is that it does not always help to be, or to be believed to be, fully rational, cool headed, and in control of oneself or of one's country....All of this may suggest that deterrent threats are a matter of resolve, impetuosity, plain obstinancy, or....sheer character....It is not easy to change our character; and becoming fanatic or impetuous would be a high price to pay for making our threats convincing. We have not the character of fanatics and cannot scare countries the way Hitler could. We have to substitute brains and skill for obstinacy or insanity....If we could credibly arrange it so that we had to carry out the threat, whether we wished to or not, we would not even be crazy to arrange it so -- if we could be sure the Soviets understood the ineluctible consequences of infringing the rules and would have control over themselves. By arranging it so that we might have to blow up the world, we would not have to....What we have to do is to get ourselves into a position where we cannot fail to react as we said we would -- where we just cannot help it -- or where we would be obliged by some overwhelming cost of not reacting in the manner we had declared.[9]

**Crisis Stability:** In a crisis that might escalate to nuclear warfare, government leaders should find that the configuration of forces on both sides encourages moderation and unhurried, careful decision making. The force configurations should not encourage rapid or major escalations or quick decisions....It is well understood by now that both the content of the decisions that leaders make in a crisis, and the rationality of the process by which they formulate and make their decision, are heavily influenced by the characteristics of the forces on both sides. For example, one or both sides may have important forces that are vulnerable to attack....Once fighting has begun, leaders may feel strong pressure to employ those forces quickly, to "use them or lose them." But often using them would mean escalating the crisis and perhaps triggering a much bigger war. The goal of crisis stability means creating, ahead of time, forces that will not generate this or similar kinds of escalation pressures.[10]

One of the most important American strategic objectives has been the maintenance of a strategic balance that provides for crisis stability: a balance in which neither side has any incentive to strike first in time of crisis. Ideally, this entails a balance in which neither side can see an difference between striking first or striking second, either in terms of the destruction it could cause the enemy or in terms of the destruction it would receive itself. In reality, of course, there will always be some gain from striking the first blow, if only for the disruption it would bring to the other side's capabilities for $C^3$. Nonetheless, in an age of parity, the United States has everything to gain from a balance which permits the Soviets to believe that, however probable war may seem in time of crisis, they have nothing to lose by waiting, that time (and further negotiation, even at the risk of an American first strike) will not work against them.

Throughout the 1970s, the concern of the United States for crisis stability has been focussed on the issue of the prelaunch survivability of its fixed-site ICBMs.[11] See Escalation Dominance.

**Cruise Missile:** a guided missile (air, sea, or ground-launched) that uses aero-dynamic lift to offset gravity and propulsion to counteract drag. A cruise missile's flight path remains within the earth's atmosphere.

**Damage Limitation:** Active and/or passive efforts to restrict the level and/or geographic extent of devastation during war. Includes counterforce and civil defense measures.

**Deterrence:** We have learned that a threat has to be credible to be efficacious, and that its credibility may depend on the costs and risks associated with fulfillment for the party making the threat. We have developed the idea of making a threat credible by getting ourselves committed to its fulfillment, through a stretching of a "trip wire" across the enemy's path of advance, or by making fulfillment a matter of national honor and prestige....We have recognized that a readiness to fight limited war in particular areas may detract from the threat of massive retaliation, by preserving the choice of a lesser evil if the contingency arises. We have considered the possibility that a retaliatory threat may be more credible if the means of carrying it out and the responsibility for retaliation are placed in the hands of those whose resolution is strongest, as in recent suggestions for "nuclear sharing." We have observed that the rationality of the adversary is pertinent to the efficacy of a threat, and that madmen, like small children, can often not be controlled by threats. We have recognized that the efficacy of the threat may depend on what alternatives are available to the potential enemy, who, if he is not to react like a trapped lion, must be left some tolerable recourse. We have come to realize that a threat of all-out retaliation gives the enemy every incentive, in the event he should choose not be heed the threat, to initiate his transgression with an all-out strike at us; it eliminates lesser courses of action and forces him to choose between extremes. We have learned that the threat of massive destruction may deter an enemy only if there is a corresponding implicit promise of nondestruction in the event he complies, so that we must consider whether too great a capacity to strike him by surprise may induce him to strike first to avoid being disarmed by a first strike from us.[12]

**Deterrence vs. Compellence:** Deterrence means to turn aside or discourage through fear; hence, to prevent from action by fear of consequences....Deterrence involves setting the stage - by announcement, by rigging the trip-wire, by incurring the obligation - and waiting. The overt act is up to the opponent. The stage-setting can often be nonintrusive, nonhostile, nonprovocative. The act that is intrusive, hostile, or provocative is usually the one to be deterred; the deterrent threat only changes the consequences if the act in question—the one to be deterred—is then taken. Compellence, in contrast, usually involves initiating an action (or an irrevocable commitment to action) that can cease, or become harmless, only if the opponent responds. The overt act, the first step, is up to the side that makes the compellent threat. To deter, one digs in, or lays a minefield, and waits—in the interest of inaction. To compel, one gets up enough momentum (figuratively, but sometimes literally) to make the other act to avoid collision.[13]

**Deterrence vs. Defense or Denial:** Essentially, deterrence means discouraging the enemy from taking military action by posing for him a prospect of cost and risk which outweighs his prospective gain. Defense means reducing our own prospective costs and risks

—120—

in the event that deterrence fails. Deterrence works on the enemy's intentions; the deterrent value of military forces is their effect in reducing the likelihood of enemy military moves. Defense reduces the enemy's capability to damage or deprive us; the defense value of military forces is their effect in mitigating the adverse consequences for us of possible enemy moves, whether such consequences are counted as losses of territory or war damage. The concept of "defense value," therefore, is broader than the mere capacity to hold territory, which might be called "denial capability." Defense value is denial capability plus capacity to alleviate war damage.

It is commonplace, of course, to say that the primary objectives of national security policy are to deter enemy attacks and to defend successfully, at minimum cost, against those attacks which occur. It is less widely recognized that different types of military force contribute in differing proportions to these two objectives. Deterrence does not vary directly with our capacity for fighting wars effectively and cheaply; a particular set of forces might produce strong deterrent effects and not provide a very effective denial and damage-alleviating capability. Conversely, forces effective for defense might be less potent deterrents than other forces which were less efficient for holding territory and which might involve extremely high war costs if used.[14] See MAD.

There is a difference between taking what you want and making someone give it to you, between fending off assault and making someone afraid to assault you, between losing what someone can forcibly take and giving it up to avoid risk or damage. It is the difference between defense and deterrence, between brute force and intimidation, between conquest and black mail, between action and threats....To exploit a capacity for hurting and inflicting damage one needs to know what an adversary treasures and what scares him and one needs the adversary to understand what behavior of his will cause the violence to be inflicted and what will cause it to be withheld. The victim has to know what is wanted, and he may have to be assured of what is not wanted. The pain and suffering have to appear contingent on his behavior; it is not alone the threat that is effective - the threat of pain or loss if he fails to comply - but the corresponding assurance, possibly an implicit one, that he can avoid the pain or loss if he does comply. The prospect of certain death may stun him, but it gives him no choice.[15]

...nuclear strategy should not be approached from the assumption that there is an inconsistency between deterrence and defense. President Reagan's recent emphasis upon a transition away from sole reliance on offensive nuclear forces is a bold and appropriate progression in U.S. strategic thought. The credibility of a strategic deterrent intended to cover distant allies and interests can only be degraded by the likely inability of the United States to survive the execution of its threat. Consequently, a more balanced approach to offense and defense by the United States should enhance the credibility of the deterrent threat in Soviet eyes. Such a transition should also enhance deterrence by dramatically increasing Soviet uncertainty concerning the feasibility of an effective first strike against the United States.[16] See SDI.

**Deterrence, Requirements of:** First, we must maintain an essential equivalence with the Soviet Union in the basic factors that determine force effectiveness. Because of uncertainty about the future and the shape that the strategic competition could take, we cannot allow major asymmetries to develop in throw-weight, accuracy, yield-to-weight ratios, reliability and other such factors that contribute to the effectiveness of strategic weapons and to the perceptions of the non-superpower nations. At the same time, our own forces should promote nuclear stability both by reducing incentives for a first use of nuclear weapons and by deterring and avoiding increased nuclear deployments by other powers.

The second requirement is for a highly survivable force that can be withheld at all times and targeted against the economic base of an opponent so as to deter coercive or desperation attacks on the economic and population targets of the United States and its allies.

The third requirement is for a force that, in response to Soviet actions, could implement a variety of limited preplanned options and react rapidly to retargeting orders so as to deter any range of further attacks that a potential enemy might contemplate. This force should have some ability to destroy hard targets, even though we would prefer to see both sides avoid major counterforce capabilities....It should also have the accuracy to attack - with low-yield weapons - soft point targets without causing large-scale collateral damage. And it should be supported by a program of fallout shelters and population relocation to offer protection to our population primarily in the event that military targets become the object of attack.

The fourth requirement is for a range and magnitude of capabilities such that everyone - friend, foe and domestic audience alike - will perceive that we are the equal of our strongest competitors. We should not take the chance that in this most hazardous of areas, misperceptions could lead to miscalculation, confrontation, and crisis.[17]

....the nuclear forces of the United States must serve at least the following four purposes: 1) to deter nuclear attack on the United States or its allies; 2) to help deter major conventional attack against U.S. forces and our allies; 3) to impose termination of a major war, on terms favorable to the United States and our allies, even if nuclear weapons have been used - and in particular to deter escalation in the level of hostilities; and 4) to negate possible Soviet nuclear blackmail against the United States or its allies. It is the purpose of the U.S. nuclear forces and strategy to prevent nuclear attack in all possible contexts and from all possible causes. We can never neglect the risk of a surprise attack "out of the blue" - a risk that imposes severe requirements on the survivability of our retaliatory forces and their supporting command, control and communications systems.[18]

**Escalation:** In a typical escalation situation, there is likely to be a "competition in risk-taking" or at least resolve, and a matching of local resources, in some form of limited conflict between two sides: Usually, either side could win by increasing its efforts in some way, provided that the other side did not negate the increase by increasing its own efforts. Furthermore, in many situations it will be clear that if the increase in effort were not matched and thus resulted in victory, the costs of the increased effort would be low in relation to the benefits of victory. Therefore, the fear that the other side may react, indeed overreact, is most likely to deter escalation, and not the undesirability or costs of the escalation itself. It is because of this that the "competition in risk-taking" and resolve takes place.[19]

**Escalation Dominance:** Escalation dominance means that the U.S. should provide an effective deterrent across the spectrum of threat because it could credibly threaten to "up the ante" in response to a limited provocation. The Soviet Union would be forced to decide whether to risk a not incredible American threat to escalate regardless of the level of Soviet attack. In short, escalation dominance would provide Soviet leaders with an overwhelming incentive to prefer conciliation rather than escalation in any conflict where deterrence can operate. Unlike Assured Vulnerability or Flexible Targeting, the Classical Strategy approach to deterrence is predicated upon the capability to pursue a non-suicidal process of war-termination if war occurs and proceeds to a military decision.[20]

**Essential Equivalence:** A force structure standard that demands capabilities approximately equal in overall effectiveness to those of particular opponents, but does not insist on numerical equality in all cases. See Parity.

**First-Strike:** The first offensive move of a war. As applied to general nuclear war, it implies the ability to eliminate effective retaliation by the opposition.

**Flexible Response:** A strategy predicated on meeting aggression at an appropriate level or place with the capability of escalating the level of conflict if required or desired....an ability to: (1) strike back decisively at the entire Soviet target system simultaneously or (2) strike back first at the Soviet bomber bases, missile sites, and other military installations associated with their long-range nuclear forces to reduce the power of any follow-on attack—and then if necessary, strike back at the Soviet urban and industrial complex in a controlled and deliberate way...

It would certainly be in their interest as well as ours to try to limit the terrible consequences of a nuclear exchange. By building into our forces a flexible capability, we at least eliminate the prospect

—123—

that we could strike back in only one way, namely, against the entire Soviet target system including their cities. Such a prospect would give the Soviet Union no incentive to withhold attack against our cities in a first strike. We want to give them a better alternative. Whether they would accept it in the crises of a global nuclear war, no one can say. Considering what is at stake we believe it is worth the additional effort on our part to have this option.[21]

To deter successfully, we must be able—and must be seen to be able—to respond to any potential aggression in such a manner that the costs we will exact will substantially exceed any gains the aggressor might hope to achieve. We, for our part, are under no illusions about the dangers of a nuclear war between the major powers; we believe that neither side could win such a war. But this recognition on *our* part is not sufficient to prevent the outbreak of nuclear war; it is essential that the Soviet leadership understand this as well. We must make sure that the Soviet leadership, in calculating the risks of aggression, recognizes that because of our retaliatory capability, there can be no circumstance in which we could benefit by beginning a nuclear war at any level or of any duration. If the Soviets recognize that our forces can and will deny them their objectives at whatever level of nuclear conflict they contemplate and, in addition, that such a conflict could lead to the destruction of those political, military, and economic assets that they value most highly then deterrence is effective and the risk of war dimished.[22] See Victory Denial and War-Fighting.

**Intercontinental Ballistic Missile (ICBM):** A missile with a range of 3000 nautical miles. A pilotless projectile propelled into space by one or more rocket boosters. Thrust is terminated at some early stage, after which reentry vehicles follow varying trajectories toward pre-selected targets.

**Intermediate Nuclear Forces (INF):** Ballistic missiles with a range of 600-1500 nautical miles.

**Limited Nuclear War/Limited Nuclear Options (LNOs):** Armed encounters, exclusive of incidents, in which one or more major powers or their proxies voluntarily exercise various types and degrees of restraint to prevent unmanageable escalation. Objectives, forces, targets, and geographic areas all can be limited.

Given the power of modern weapons, a nation that relies on all-out war as its chief deterrent imposes a fearful psychological handicap on itself. The most agonizing decision a statesman can face is whether or not to unleash all-out war; all pressures will make for hesitation, short of a direct attack threatening the national existence. In any other situation he will be inhibited by the incommensurability between the cost of the war and the objective in dispute. And he will be confirmed in his hesitations by the conviction that, so long as his retaliatory force remains intact, no shift in the territorial balance is of decisive significance. Thus both the horror and the power of modern weapons tend to paralyze action: the former because it will make few issues seem worth contending for; the latter because it causes many disputes to seem irrelevant to the over-all strategic equation. The psychological equation, therefore, will almost inevitably operate against the side which can extricate itself from a situation *only* by the threat of all-out war....

The key problem of present-day strategy is to devise a spectrum of capabilities with which to resist Soviet challenges. These capabilities should enable us to confront the opponent with contingencies from which he can extricate himself *only* by all-out war, while deterring him from this step by a superior retaliatory capacity. Since the most difficult decision for a statesman is whether to risk the national substance by unleashing an all-out war, the psychological advantage will always be on the side of the power which can shift to its opponent the decision to initiate all-out war. All Soviet moves in the postwar period have had this character. They have faced us with problems which by themselves did not seem worth an all-out war, but with which we could not deal by an alternative capability.[23]

...to believe that the development of contingency plans will increase the probability of nuclear use is to underestimate seriously the gravity of the decision to go to war, especially nuclear war. What is more, to the extent that concern about the nuclear threshold is more than hypothetical, the most effective way of keeping the threshold high is to increase the effectiveness and readiness of our non-nuclear forces. History, I believe, will show that on those rare occasions when the use of nuclear weapons was seriously considered in the past thirty years, it was because of the impression that adequate conventional forces were not available to achieve the desired objectives.

...a nuclear conflict could escalate to cover a wide range of targets, which is one more reason why limited response options are unlikely to lower the nuclear threshold. But I doubt that any responsible policymaker would deliberately want to ensure escalation, and forego the chance for an early end to a conflict, by refusing to consider and plan for responses other than immediate, large-scale attacks on cities. Surely, even if there is only a small probability that limited response options would deter an attack or bring a nuclear war to a rapid conclusion, without large-scale damage to cities, it is a probability which, for the sake of our citizens we should not foreclose.[24] See Flexible Response.

**Massive Retaliation:** The act of countering aggression of any type with tremendous destructive power; particularly a crushing nuclear response to any provocation deemed serious enough to warrant military action.

**Multiple Independently-Targetable Reentry Vehicle (MIRV):** Multiple reentry vehicles carried by a ballistic missile, each of which can be directed to a separate and arbitrarily located target. A

MIRVed missile employs a post-boost vehicle (PBV) or other warhead-dispensing mechanism. The dispensing and targeting mechanism maneuvers to achieve successive desired positions and velocities to dispense each reentry vehicle on a trajectory to attack the desired target, or the RVs might themselves maneuver toward targets after they reenter the atmosphere.

**Mutual Assured Destruction (MAD):** the cornerstone of our strategic policy continues to be to deter deliberate nuclear attack upon the United States, or its allies, by maintaining a highly reliable ability to inflict an unacceptable degree of damage upon any single aggressor, or combination of aggressors, at any time during the course of a strategic nuclear exchange - even after our absorbing a surprise first strike. This can be defined as our "assured destruction capability...." We must possess an actual assured destruction capability. And that actual assured destruction capability must also be credible. Conceivably, our assured destruction capability could be actual, without being credible - in which case it might fail to deter an aggressor. The point is that a potential aggressor must himself believe that our assured destruction capability is in fact actual, and that our will to use it in retaliation to an attack is in fact unwavering...

When calculating the force we require, we must be "conservative" in all our estimates of both a potential aggressor's capabilities, and his intentions. Security depends upon taking a "worst plausible case" - and having the ability to cope with that eventually. In that eventuality, we must be able to absorb the total weight of nuclear attack on our country - on our strike-back forces; on our command and control apparatus; and our industrial capacity; on our cities, and on our population - and still be fully capable of destroying the aggressor to the point that his society is simply no longer viable in any meaningful, twentieth century sense. That is what deterrence to nuclear aggression means. It means the certainty of suicide to the aggressor - not merely to his military forces, but to his society as a whole.[25]

**Mad vs Flexible Reponse/Damage limitation:** One school - for shorthand, called mutual assured destruction (MAD)—views nuclear weapons as so revolutionary that they render traditional strategy obsolete. Once both superpowers have large numbers, the only utility of nuclear weapons is for mutual deterrence; deterrence is best fortified by ensuring that nuclear war remains unthinkable because any attack will draw devastating retaliation against the other's population and economy. The other school—for shorthand, called damage limitation—sees the nuclear revolution as raising the stakes and risks of conflict dramatically, but without eliminating the strategic or political utility of nuclear weapons. If full-scale war is unthinkable, the side willing to take high risks by threatening or executing an attack that drastically reduces the victim's retaliatory options can prevail by making clear that surrender is preferable to retaliation. Deterrence is fragile and best fortified by counterforce capabilities that match or exceed the enemy's to deny him the option of dominating a military exchange.[26]

Proponents of assured destruction argue that the vulnerability of population centers in both the United States and the Soviet Union that comes with mutual second-strike capability has transformed strategy. Because a military advantage no longer assures a decisive victory, old ways of thinking are no longer appropriate. The healthy fear of devastation, which cannot be exorcised short of the attainment of a first-strike capability, makes deterrence relatively easy. Furthermore, because cities cannot be taken out of hostage, the perceived danger of total destruction is crucial at all points in the threat, display, or use of force. Four implications follow. First, because gaining the upper hand in purely military terms cannot protect one's country, various moves in a limited war—such as using large armies, employing tactical nuclear weapons, or even engaging in limited strategic strikes—are less important for influencing the course of the battle than for showing the other side that a continuation of the conflict raises an unacceptable danger that things will get out of hand.

For the advocates of flexible response, the United States must be prepared to fight a war—or rather a variety of wars—in order to gain a better chance of deterring the Soviets from making any military moves, to deter them from escalating if they do move, and to secure as favorable an outcome as possible at any level of violence. In contrast to the assured destruction view, flexible response argues that in the nuclear era, as in earlier times, the absolute amount of armaments on each side is less important than the relative amounts, because each nation's military forces as well as its population centers are potential targets. As decision makers stop thinking that any war must be total and realize that the stability-instability paradox allows a wider range of contingencies of controlled and less self-defeating strikes, the importance of the details of the strategic balance becomes clear.

Much of the difference between the two schools of thought turns on differing ideas about stability. Both groups agree on the overwhelming importance of preserving one's cities. But for the proponents of flexible response, the common interest in avoiding a mutually disastrous outcome can be used as a lever to extract competitive concessions. Either side can take provocative actions because the other cannot credibly threaten to respond by all-out war. Proponents of assured destruction, on the other hand, see stability as broader, and deterrence as covering a wider set of interests, since it follows from the reasonable fear that any challenge to an opponent's vital interest could escalate. Paradoxically, stability is in part the product of the belief that the world is not entirely stable, that things could somehow get out of control.[27]

...MAD is a desirable state of affairs. It may be immoral to hold populations hostage, but it would be less moral if actions by one or both nations to shift away from an assured destruction policy increased the likelihood of nuclear war. A limited nuclear war would not only be destructive but would raise the real danger of escalation to all-out war. Given current and projected technology, MAD appears to be more stable against technological change as well as political misperceptions than other strategic alternatives. Preserving high levels of counterpopulation damage is less difficult than building effective defenses or obtaining meaningful no-city targeting capabilities, for example, and affords a more certain deterrent effect than any of the other alternatives. Furthermore, it may be in our interest to ensure that the Soviet Union retains a confident assured destruction capability—both to reduce the chance of a Soviet preemptive strike against the United States and to minimize the chance that U.S. leaders might believe that nuclear weapons are effective military instruments....

Through maintaining a confident assured destruction capability supplemented by a range of limited response capabilities and the maintenance of overall numerical equality, the risk of deterrence failing will remain extremely low. Although such a strategy cannot guard against irrational actions or nuclear accidents, no strategy is completely foolproof in these respects. Strategic forces under secure command and control and designed for delayed response, however, reduce the risks of accidental or unauthorized firings and offer the possibility of limiting damage through restraint or war termination in the event a nuclear exchange occurs.[28]

No technological distinction exists or can be created between those nuclear weapons endangering the deterrent forces of the opponent in a first or preemptive strike (and thus decreasing stability) and weapons designed to attack the same forces by retaliation. There is no demonstrable break between nuclear weapons designed for limited attacks and those designed for "stragetic" retaliation. Anti-military nuclear attacks of substantial size will almost certainly generate enormous civilian casualties. Whatever plans or technological preparations the United States may make to fight a "controlled" nuclear conflict, there can be no certain method to protect the U.S. population in case the opponent decides to respond with an anti-population attack. Available casualty estimates understate the effects of large-scale nuclear war; such consequences as epidemics aggravated by maldistribution of medical care, fire, starvation, ecological damage and societal breakdown are well-nigh incalculable. From these inescapable conditions it follows, in my judgment, that the only clear demarcation line giving a "fire-break" in the use of weapons in war will continue to be the boundary between non-nuclear and nuclear devices. Mere shifts in policy and strategic doctrine will neither eliminate the hostage role of the populations of the United States and the Soviet Union, nor decrease the danger of nuclear catastrophe through accident or through unauthorized attack.[29]

**Nuclear Winter Hypothesis:** a global nuclear war could have a major impact on climate—manifested by significant surface darkening over many weeks, subfreezing land temperatures persisting for up to several months, large pertubations in global circulation patterns, and dramatic changes in local weather and precipitation rates—a harsh 'nuclear winter' in any season. Greatly accelerated interhemispheric transport of nuclear debris in the stratosphere might also occur....Although the climate disturbances are expected to last more than a year, it seems unlikely that a major long-term climate change, such as an ice age, would be triggered....Relatively large climatic effects could result even from relatively small nuclear exchanges (100 to 1,000 MT) if urban areas were heavily targeted....

The climatic impact of sooty smoke from nuclear fires ignited by air-bursts is expected to be more important than that of dust raised by surface bursts (when both events occur)....Synergisms between long-term nuclear war stresses—such as low light levels, subfreezing temperatures, exposure to intermediate time scale radioactive fallout, heavy pyrogenic air pollution...aggravated by the destruction of medical facilities, food stores, and civil services, could lead to many additional fatalities, and could place severe stress on the global ecosystem...[30]

**Parity:** A force structure standard which demands that capabilities of specific forces and weapons systems be approximately equal in effectiveness to enemy counterparts. See Essential Equivalence.

**Perception and Deterrence:** In light of the dangers inherent in misperceptions, one might expect that statesmen would pay careful attention to how others perceive them. In fact, this is usually not the case. While they are aware that determining others' intentions and predicting others' behavior is difficult, they generally believe that their own intentions—especially when they are not expansionist—are clear. As a result, they rarely try to see the world and their own actions through their adversary's eyes, although doing so would be to their advantage. If a policy is to have the desired impact on its target, it must be perceived as it is intended, if the other's behavior is to be anticipated and the state's policy is a major influence on it, then the state must try to determine how its actions are being perceived....It is hard to find cases of even mild international conflict in which both sides fully grasp the other's views. Yet all too often statesmen assume that their opposite numbers see the world as they see it, fail to devote sufficient resources to determining whether this is actually true, and have much more confidence in their beliefs about the other's perceptions than the evidence warrants.[31]

Military strength is a central factor in the outcome of a military conflict. The perception of military strength can be a critical element in a political confrontation. Perceptions of a military advantage, or even of a trend in relative military capability that reflects a likely future balance, affect the political behavior of potential adversaries and of third parties in contemplating what actions to take in a crisis.[32]

**Second-Strike:** A strategic concept which excludes preemptive and preventive actions before the onset of a war. After an aggressor initiates hostilities, the defender retaliates. In general nuclear war, this implies the ability to survive a surprise first strike and respond effectively.

**Strategic Defense, Critique of:** The first and greatest obstacle is quite simply that these weapons are destructive to a degree that makes them entirely different from any other weapon in history....even a 95% kill rate (from BMD) would be insufficient to save either society from disintegration in the event of general nuclear war....Not only is their destructive power so great that only a kill rate approaching 100% can give protection, but precisely because the weapons are so terrible neither of the two superpowers can tolerate the notion of 'impotence' in the face of the arsenal of the opponent. Thus any prospect of a significantly improved American defense is absolutely certain to stimulate the most energetic Soviet efforts to ensure the continued ability of Soviet warheads to get through....important and enduring (technical) obstacles (also) have been identified....First a Star Wars defense must work perfectly the very first time, since it can never be tested in advance as a full system. Second, it must be triggered almost instantly, because the crucial boost phase of Soviet missiles lasts less than five minutes....(in this time) there must be detection, decision, aim, attack and kill....Any remotely leak-proof defense against strategic missiles will require extensive deployments of many parts of the system in space, both for detection of any Soviet launch and, in most schemes, for transmission of the attack on the missile in its boost phase. Yet no one has been able to offer any hope that it will ever be easier and cheaper to deploy and defend large systems in space than for someone else to destroy them...Finally...(BMD) offers no promise of effective defense against anything but ballistic missiles.[33]

A mixed defense-offense posture designed to deprive the opponent of a first strike capability is likely to look—in motivation and in capability—uncomfortably like a first strike posture. This would be particularly true of a space-based ABM system, where the fragility and vulnerability of the components would make them unreliable except in support of a preemptive strike.[34]

**Strategic Defense Initiative (SDI):** explores the potential of newly emerging technologies to support an effective defense against ballistic missiles—one that would strengthen deterrence and thereby increase our security and that of our allies....Technologies being investigated in the SDI program may offer the possibility of providing a layered defense—that is, a defense that would use various techniques to destroy attacking missiles during each phase of their flight (boost, post-boost, mid-course, and terminal phase).

In order for advanced defenses to strengthen both deterrence and stability, they must, at a minimum, be able to destroy a sufficient portion of an aggressor's attacking forces to deny him confidence in the outcome. The combined effectiveness of the defense provided by the multiple layers would not have to provide total protection in order to enhance deterrence significantly. An aggressor would be much less likely to initiate a nuclear conflict, even in a crisis, if he lacked confidence in his ability to succeed. The defensive system also must be survivable....To discourage the proliferation of ballistic missile forces, the defensive system must be able to maintain effectiveness against the offense at less than the cost of developing offensive countermeasures necessary to overcome it....SDI is a prudent response to the very active Soviet research and development program in strategic defenses; it provides insurance against a possible unilateral Soviet effort to develop and deploy an advanced defensive system.[35]

**Strategic Stability:** an invulnerable configuration of forces such that the structure of the military balance itself precludes a rational decision by either side to strike first. Another category of stability is political....If neither superpower pursues revisionist aims, technical stability of forces is irrelevant. Technical stability may dampen political instability by discouraging provocative behavior, but it does not necessarily do so because the nuclear balance is only one element in the military balance as a whole. If strategic nuclear forces are so technically stable that they neutralize each other, imbalances in other forces may provide coercive bargaining chips to the side with non-nuclear advantages.[36] See Crisis Stability.

For our purposes, a strategic system is stable when stresses or shocks do not tend to produce large and irreversible changes. This does not mean that the system does not react when subjected to stress or shock. For example, a crisis may change strategic forces enormously by putting them on a state of alert. Stability means that the reactions are of a limited, and perhaps predictable, nature, and that they are reversible or lead to a new balance not essentially different from the original. One necessary, but not sufficient, condition for stability is that neither side be under overwhelming pressure to attack because of military requirements based on the nature or deployment of his own or the enemy forces —i.e., that no party be under extreme pressure to act because of the advantage of pre-emption.

Thus, stability is partly, but only partly, measured by the degree of advantage that any side may obtain by acting first, relative to his situation if he is attacked. We have already discussed the classic unstable situation, reciprocal fear of surprise attack, where each side, if it were attacked, would be so very much worse off than if it struck first that there is a motivation on each side to pre-empt because of fear of the known pressure to pre-emption of the other side's fear of its own pressure for pre-emption. Stability would be further enhanced if both sides became indifferent. Stability would become greater still if the difference between first and second strikes remained the same, but the absolute level of the balance of terror were raised. Although this seems true of stability against pre-emption or first strike, stability against other threats may decrease as the level of deterrence increases. Compare, for example, two situations in which 50 per cent of the casualties to be expected if the enemy struck first would probably be prevented by pre-emption. There probably would be more stability against pre-emption if the expected number of casualties from a first strike were 50 million rather than 1 million. Even greater stability would exist if all parties would gain great military advantages from striking second as compared with striking first. This be would obtain theoretically if there were two parties with roughly equal numbers of weapons, and more than one weapon were required to destroy a weapon.[37]

**Sufficiency:** A force structure standard that demands capabilities adequate to attain desired ends without undue waste. Superiority thus is essential in some circumstances; parity/essential equivalence suffices under less demanding conditions; and inferiority, qualitative as well as quantitative, is sometimes acceptable.

**Superiority:** Superiority has a variety of possible meanings, ranging from the ability to dissuade a putative adversary from offering resistance(i.e., deterring a crisis), through the imposition of severe escalation discipline on opponents, to a context wherein one could prosecute actual armed conflict to a successful conclusion. There is certainly no consensus within the United States defense community today over the issue of whether or not any central war outcome is possible which would warrant description as victory. However, a consensus is emerging to the effect that the Soviet Union appears to believe in the possiblity of victory, and that the time is long-overdue for a basic overhaul of our intellectual capital in the nuclear deterrence field. At the very least, most defense analysts would endorse the proposition that it is important for the United States to be able to deny the Soviet Union victory on its own terms.[38]

**Tactical Nuclear Forces, Weapons, Operations:** Nuclear combat power expressly designed for deterrent, offensive, and defensive purposes that contribute to the accomplishment of localized military missions; the threatened or actual application of such power. May be employed in general as well as limited wars.

**Victory Denial:** War should be deterred most reliably when a potential aggressor cannot anticipate success from his resort to arms and when the threat to deny him victory is not incredible. It is important, as senior American officials have argued very explicitly, that the United States have a posture and doctrine that, in Soviet estimation, could deny any success from the resort to strategic nuclear arms. But Soviet estimation of the probability of the United States exercising its strategic nuclear forces for the purpose of victory denial cannot help but be influenced by consideration of the likely American willingness to suffer Soviet retaliation. No quantity or estimated quality of the performance of damage limiting programs should induce reckless behavior on the part of American politicians. But a dedicated and diverse damage limiting capability should encourage the Soviet leadership to accord some credibility to the U.S. extended deterrent threat, and could serve the critical function of saving lives by the tens of millions in the event deterrence should fail.[39]

**War-Fighting:** War fighters are not more interested in fighting wars than proponents of MAD are interested in assuring mutual destruction....The thesis of the balanced approach to deterrence is that it should at least be recognized at the conceptual level that reducing the vulnerability of the American homeland would promote deterrence stability, and in the event deterrence fails, would offer the substantial promise of saving millions of lives.... ·

One important issue is whether the U.S. should endeavor to provide command, control, and communications ($C^3$) facilities suitable for limited nuclear war options and protracted war. A U.S. capability to threaten tailored selective strikes against different kinds of targets and different geogrpahical areas, in the context of major investment in more survivable command, control, and communication, does not plausibly carry the promise of increasing the risk of war. To plan for the flexible employment of strategic forces should be to enhance deterrence stability both through an advertised U.S. determination to counter Soviet strategy, and because the U.S. nuclear striking power withheld from an initial blow should discourage a Soviet counter-response of a kind likely to ensure the destruction of American society.

This discussion is not arguing for the acceptability of nuclear war....Nuclear war, unfortunately, would occur regardless of the most sincere intentions and dedicated efforts to maintain deterrence, and some potential results of nuclear war would be far more unacceptable than others. This is simply to recognize that there are many different possible nuclear war outcomes; that it is incumbant upon the U.S. government to structure its defense capabilities in such a way as to minimize the level of destruction that would be inflicted upon North America should war occur; and that the possibility of achieving a tolerable post-war political settlement should be maximized. The strong likelihood that this approach to nuclear strategy would enhance deterrence stability, and thereby reduce the probability of war, means that there should be not negative net effect flowing from a U.S. movement toward a more damage-limiting approach to deterrence.[40]

*Sources: John M. Collins, *United States/Soviet Military Balance: Frame of Reference for Congress*, (Library of Congress: Congressional Research Service, 1976): 57-69; U.S. Arms Control and Disarmament Agency, *SALT II: Glossary of Terms*, (Washington, D.C., 1980); and additional sources as noted.

# Selected SALT II Terms and Acronyms*

**Aggregate:** The term "aggregate" refers principally to the overall aggregate of ICBM launchers, SLBM launcers, heavy bombers, and ASBMs. SALT II placed an initial ceiling of 2,400 on this aggregate with reductions to 2,250 planned. There were also sublimits of 1,320 on MIRVed ICBM launchers, MIRVed ASBMs, and heavy bombers equipped for cruise missiles capable of a range in excess of 600 kilometers; 1,200 on MIRVed ICBM SLBM launchers, and ASBMs; and 820 on MIRVed ICBM launchers.

**Ballistic Missile:** Missile designated to follow the trajectory that results when it is acted upon predominantly by gravity and aerodynamic drag after thrust is terminated. Ballistic missiles typically operate outside the atmosphere and are unpowered during most of the flight.

**Deliberate Concealment:** The U.S. and U.S.S.R. have agreed not to use deliberate concealment measures which impede verification by National Technical Means (NTM) of compliance with the provisions of SALT. Deliberate concealment measures could include camouflage, use of coverings, or deliberate denial of telemetric information, such as through the use of telemetry encryption, whenever such measures impede verification of compliance with the agreement.

**Encryption:** Encryption is encoding communications for the purpose of concealing information. In SALT II, this term applied to a practice whereby a side alters the manner by which it transmits telemetry from a weapon being tested rendering the information deliberately undecipherable.

**Fractionation:** The division of the payload of a missile into several warheads. The use of a MIRV payload is an example of fractionation.

**Functionally Related Observable Differences (FRODs):** FRODs are the means by which SALT II provided for distinguishing between those aircraft which are capable of performing certain SALT-limited functions and those which are not. FRODs are differences in the observable features of airplanes which specifically determine whether or not these airplanes can perform the mission of a heavy bomber, or whether or not they can perform the mission of a bomber equipped for cruise missiles capable of a range in excess of 600 kilometers, or whether or not they can perform the mission of a bomber equipped for ASBMs

**Heavy (Ballistic) Missile:** Heavy missiles (ICBMs, SLBMs, and ASBMs) are those missiles which have a launch-weight greater or a throw-weight greater than the launch-weight or throw-weight or the Soviet SS-19 ICBM.

**ICBM Silo Launcher:** An ICBM silo launcher, a "hard" fixed launcher, is an underground installation, usually of steel and concrete, housing an ICBM and the equipment for launching it.

**Interference:** The SALT II Treaty provided that each Party could use NTM of verification to provide assurance of compliance with the Treaty. Each Party undertook a commitment not to interfere with the NTM of the other side (e.g. blinding of satellites.)

**Launcher:** Equipment that launches a missile. ICBM launchers are land-based launchers that can be fixed or mobile, SLBM launchers are missile tubes on a ballistic missile submarine. An ASBM launcher is the carrier aircraft. Launchers for cruise missiles can be installed on aircraft, ships, or land-based vehicles or installations.

**Mobile ICBM Launcher:** Equipment which launches an ICBM and which can move or be moved from one location to another. Mobile ICBM launchers could include ICBM launchers on wheeled vehicles, launchers on vehicles which travel on rails, and lauchers which are moved among launch-points which might be "hard" or "soft."

**Modernization:** The process of modifying a weapon system such that its characteristics or components are altered in order to improve the performance capabilities for that weapon system. SALT II provided that, subject to provisions to the contrary, modernization and replacement of strategic offensive arms could be carried out.

**National Technical Means of Verification (NTM):** Assets which are under national control for monitoring compliance with the provisions of an agreement. NTM include photographic reconnaissance satellites, aircraft-based systems (such as radars and optical systems), as well as sea- and ground-based systems (such as radars and antennas for collecting telemetry).

**Penetration Aids:** Devices employed by offensive weapon systems such as ballistic missiles and bombers to increase the probability of penetrating enemy defenses. Frequently designed to simulate or to mask an aircraft or ballistic missile warhead in order to mislead enemy radar and/or divert defensive anti-aircraft or antimissile fire.

**Post-Boost Vehicle (PBV):** Often referred to as a "bus," the PBV is that part of a missile's payload carrying the reentry vehicles, a guidance package, fuel, and thrust devices for altering the ballistic flight path so that the reentry vehicles can be dispensed sequentially toward different targets.

**Standing Consultative Commission (SCC):** A permanent U.S.-Soviet commission first established in accordance with the provisions of SALT I. Its purpose is to promote the objectives and implementation of the provisions of the various SALT agreements achieved between the U.S. and the U.S.S.R. The Commission deals with matters such as questions of compliance with the provisions of the agreements, and the working out of procedures to implement the agreements.

**Throw-Weight:** Ballistic missile throw-weight is the weight which is placed on a trajectory toward the target by the boost stages of the missile. For the purposes of SALT II, throw-weight was defined as the sum of the weight of: the RVs; any PBV for releasing or targeting RVs; and any ABM penetration aids, including release devices.

**Warhead:** That part of a missile, projectile, torpedo, rocket, or other munition which contains the nuclear system, the high-explosive system, the chemical or biological agents, or the inert materials intended to inflict damage.

**Yield:** The energy released in the detonation of a nuclear weapon is generally measured in terms of the Kilotons (KT) or megatons (MT) or TNT required to produce the same energy release.

*Source: U.S. Arms Control and Disarmament Agency (ACDA) *SALT II: Glossary of Terms*, 1980.

# Soviet Strategic Definitions*

**Voyna (war):** A socio-historical phenomenon, characteristic of the antagonistic class society. In its social essence, war is a continuation of the policy of given self-interested powers and the ruling classes within them using forcible means. War is an armed conflict between states (coalitions of states) or between striving antagonistic classes within a state (civil war) to gain their economic and political ends. In the contemporary epoch, war is a complex social phenomenon, affecting all aspects of the life and national activity of the people, putting all their moral, political, economic, military and organization powers to the test. In war, both sides use ideological, economic, diplomatic and other forms and means of strife. According to the politics of the classes concerned, wars may be subdivided into unjust (predatory) wars and just wars. Just wars are waged to protect the interests of the working class and the toiling masses, to liquidate social and national oppression, and to protect national sovereignty against imperialist aggression. The most just wars are those waged in defense of the Socialist fatherland. (p. 48)

**Nachal'Nyy Period Voyny (initial period of a war);** A decisive period of a war, ranging from the outbreak of hostilities to attainment of the short-term strategic goals assigned to the first strategic echelon of the country's armed forces. Under the most favorable conditions the goals of the war may be attained during the initial period of a war. (p. 132)

**Oboronosposobnost' (defensive capability):** The degree of development and readiness of the military, economic, and moral-political forces and potentialities of a country, ensuring reliable defense of the state in modern war, and utter defeat of the aggressor. Defensive capability is determined by the character of the political regime and social order, and depends on the political goals of the war, on the organizational activity of the country's political and military leadership, and on the alertness of the people and the armed forces. The high level of defensive capability in the Soviet Union, and in other countries having a peaceful socialist system, is determined by the guiding role of the Communist and workers' parties. (p. 137)

**Ob'Yektivnyye Zakony Voyny (the objective laws of war):** The substantial, recurrent, and inseparable associations which are organically inherent in war, and which determine its conduct, course, and outcome. Such laws specifically include: the dependence of the course and outcome of a war on the correlation of the military-economic forces and potentialities of the belligerent states, on the correlation of moral-political forces and potentialities of the adversaries, on the correlation of the military potentialities of the parties in conflict, and the quantity and quality of their armed forces; and dependence of the method of waging a war on the method of production, and in particular, on its most mobile element—the means of production, which have a direct impact on change in the means of armed conflict. (p. 138)

**Prevoskhodstvo v Silakh i Sredstvakh (superiority in men and equipment)** —A correlation of men and equipment in which one side is superior to the other, thus enjoying conditions that ensure fulfillment of assigned missions in an operation (or battle). Under present-day conditions, superiority in men and equipment means primarily a pre-eminence in nuclear weapons, and in the means of delivering them any distance, and also in the qualitative and quantitative superiority of the various Services of the armed forces. Superiority in forces and weapons is achieved in individual sectors, or in regions, by the following methods: concentration of forces in the main sector; deep organization of operational formations, ensuring rapid and flexible maneuver of men and equipment from depth; continuous intensification of the force of strikes, especially by nuclear weapons; timely commitment of second echelons and reserves; depriving enemy reserves of freedom of maneuver; destruction of enemy material, and disruption of enemy rear operations. (p. 172)

**Strategicheskoye Nastupleniye (strategic offensive)** —A basic type of military activity used by armed forces to achieve the principal goals and missions of armed conflict. Successful conduct of a strategic offensive results in utter defeat of enemy armed forces, neutralization of his military-economic potential, seizure of the territory of member states of a hostile coalition, and their withdrawal from a war. This leads to radical changes in the military-political situation and the course of a war, and, under present-day conditions, to its rapid conclusion. A strategic offensive reflects the active, decisive character of a state's military doctrine and strategy. It is accomplished by delivering nuclear strikes by strategic means, and by conducting simultaneous and successive strategic offensive operations with the participation of all Services in one or several continental and maritime theaters of operations. (p. 214)

**Raketno-Yadernaya Voyna (nuclear missile warfare)** —Warfare in which the decisive means of attaining victory in battle, in an operation, and in armed conflict as a whole, is the nuclear missile—used without restraint by all Services—and above all, the strategic nuclear weapon. Moreover, final victory, even in nuclear missile warfare, is achieved by the united efforts of all Services, using conventional means of armed conflict as well. [p. 191]

*Source: *Dictionary of Basic Military Terms—A Soviet View* in Soviet Military Thought Series - U.S. Air Force, 1980. (Translations)

# REFERENCES

[1]The following discussion relied on arguments made in Weinberger, *Annual Report to the Congress, FY 1987* February 5, 1986, (Washington: Government Printing Office, 1986); and President's Commission on Strategic Forces Scowcroft Commission), 1983.

[2]President's Report on Continuing the Acquisition of the Peacekeeper (MX) Missile, March 1985, White House Report.

[3]John C. Baker and Joel S. Wit, "Mobile Missiles and Arms Control," *Arms Control Today* (November/December 1985): 12.

[4]Walter B. Slocombe, "Why We Need Counterforce at Sea," *Arms Control Today (September 1985): 11.*

[5]Ashton B. Carter, "Satellites and Anti-Satellites: The Limits of the Possible," *International Security* 10 (Spring 1986): 89-94.

[6]John Steinbruner, "Nuclear Decapitation," *Foreign Policy* (Winter 1981-82): 19.

[7]Thomas Schelling, *Arms & Influence* (New Haven: Yale University Press, 1966): 35.

[8]Harold Brown, *Thinking About National Security,* (Boulder: Westview Press, 1983): 81-82; See also Walter Slocombe, "The Countervailing Strategy, *International Security* 5 (Spring 1981): 20-25; Albert Carnesale and Charles Glaser, "ICBM Vulnerability: Cures Are Worse Than the Disease," *International Security* 7 (Summer 1982): 78-84; and Spurgeon M. Keeny, Jr. and Wolfgang K. H. Panofsky, "MAD Versus NUTS: Can Doctrine or Weaponry Remedy the Mutual Hostage Relationship of the Superpowers?" *Foreign Affairs* 60 (Winter 1981/82): 287-304.

[9]Schelling, 36-37 and 42-43.

[10]Richard Smoke, *National Security and the Nuclear Dilemma,* (Reading, Mass.: Addison-Wesley, 1984): 230.

[11]Warner R. Schilling, "US Strategic Nuclear Concepts in the 1970s," *International Security* 6 (Fall 1984): 68-69.

[12]Schelling, *The Strategy of Conflict,* (New York: Oxford University Press, 1963): 6-7; Lawrence Freedman, *The Evolution of Nuclear Strategy,* (New York: St. Martin's Press, 1983); Samuel Huntington, ed., *The Strategic Imperative: New Policies for American Security,* (Cambridge: Ballinger, 1982); Roman Kolkowicz and Neil Joeck, ed., *Arms Control and International Security,* (Boulder: Westview Press, 1984); and John Reichart and Steven Sturm, *American Defense Policy,* (Baltimore: Johns Hopkins University Press, 1982).

[13]Schelling, *Arms and Influence,* 70-71.

[14]Glenn H. Snyder, *Deterrence and Defence: Toward a Theory of National Security,* (Princeton: Princeton University Press, 1961): 3-4.

[15]Schelling, *Arms and Influence,* 2-4.

[16]Colin S. Gray and Keith Payne, "Nuclear Strategy: Is There a Future?" *Washington Quarterly* 6 (Summer 1983): 57.

[17]James R. Schlesinger, *Annual Defense Department Report, FY 1976 and 1977,* (February 5, 1975): II 13-14.

[18]Fred C. Ikle, "Reagan Defense Program," *Strategic Review* (Spring 1982): 17.

[19]Herman Kahn, *On Escalation: Metaphors and Scenarios,* (New York: Praeger, 1965): 3.

[20]Payne, *Nuclear Deterrence in U.S.-Soviet Relations,* (Boulder: Westview Press, 1982): 198.

[21]Robert S. McNamara, House Armed Services Committee Statement, *The FY 1964-68 Defense Program and Defense Budget,* (January 30, 1961): 28-30.

[22]Weinberger, *Annual Report to the Congress, FY 1984* (February 1983): 51.

[23]Kissinger, *Nuclear Weapons and Foreign Policy,* (New York: Harper): 133 and 144.

[24]Schlesinger, II 6-7.

[25]McNamara, "Limited ABM Deployment," in *American Defense Policy* by Mark E. Smith III and Claude J. Johns, Jr., (Baltimore: Johns Hopkins University Press, 1968): 129.

[26]Richard Betts, "Elusive Equivalence," in *The Strategic Imperative* by Huntington, 102-103.

[27]Robert Jervis, "Why Nuclear Superiority Doesn't Matter," *Political Science Quarterly* 94 (Winter 1979/80): 617-618; see also *The Illogic of American Nuclear Strategy* (Ithaca: Cornell University Press, 1984).

[28]Jerome H. Kahan, *Security in the Nuclear Age,* (Washington: Brookings, 1975): 262.

[29]Panofsky, "Mutual Hostage Relationship Between America and Russia," *Foreign Affairs* 52 (October 1973): 117-118.

[30]Paul R. Ehrlich, et. al., *The Cold and the Dark: The World After Nuclear War,* (New York: Norton, 1984): 181-83.

[31]Jervis, "Deterrence and Perception," *International Security* 7 (Winter 1982/83): 4.

[32]Brown, *Thinking About National Security,* 83.

[33]McGeorge Bundy, et. al., "The President's Choice: Star Wars or Arms Control," *Foreign Affairs* 63 (Winter 1984/85): 266-68.

[34]Sydney D. Drell, et. al., "Preserving the ABM Treaty: Critique of the Reagan Strategic Defense Initiative," *International Security* 9 (Fall 1984): 81.

[35]"The President's Strategic Defense Initiative," *GIST: Department of State,* (March 1985); see also Adam Garfinkle, "Politics of Space Defense," *Orbis* (Summer 1984): 240-255; Ikle, "Nuclear Strategy: Can There Be a Happy Ending?" *Foreign Affairs* (Spring 1985): 810-826; and Leon Sloss, "Return of Strategic Defense," *Strategic Review* 12 (Summer 1984): 37-44.

[36]Betts, "Elusive Equivalence," 109.

[37]Kahn, *On Escalation: Metaphors and Scenarios,* 293.

[38]Gray, "Nuclear Strategy: Case for a Theory of Victory," *International Security* 4 (Summer 1979): 86.

[39]Gray and Payne, "Nuclear Strategy: Is There a Future," 63-64.

[40]Gray and Payne, "Nuclear Strategy: Is There a Future," 57-60.

# CHAPTER IV

# SALT, START, and Stops:
# The Evolution of Arms Control

## Starting With SALT: SALT I and the ABM Treaty

In previous chapters we investigated one of the major foundations of post-war U.S. foreign policy—containing the Soviets via either confrontation or detente or some mix of both. During this period, the threat imposed by nuclear weapons complicated efforts to manage Soviet-U.S. relations peacefully. On the other hand, the very existence of these weapons provided a key to a *modus vivendi* with the Soviets who feared the prospects of nuclear war as much as the U.S. did. Fear of nuclear war spurred efforts at detente to reduce political tensions and arms control to avoid dangerous arms races. In fact, as Nixon and Kissinger argued, the imperative of coexistence, which provided a mutual stake in detente, also lay the foundation for SALT I. Arms agreements, one part of "a broadly-based accommodation of interests" would be "linked organically to a chain of agreements and a broad understanding about international conduct appropriate to the dangers of the nuclear age."[1] Through these agreements, then, Nixon and Kissinger hoped to forge a greater Soviet interest in stability, peaceful competition, and the benefits of relaxation.

Since the SALT process of the 1970s played such an important role in both the fostering and decline of detente, an attempt will be made in the first two sections of this chapter to test SALT I and II as barometers of detente and arms control. If SALT contributed to an improved political climate and reciprocal arms reductions, it may be measured as a successful adjunct to detente. If negotiation over SALT and the resulting Soviet-U.S. interaction were followed by a continuation of the arms buildup and anti-detente behavior, then SALT I and II should be judged partial failures. Let us begin with a brief look at the terms of the 1972 ABM and SALT I treaties and at the number of offensive delivery vehicles.

## A. ABM Treaty (ABMT)

1. Neither side is permitted to deploy a nationwide ABM defense. 2. Each side is permitted to deploy a limited defense of two areas—the national capital and one area containing ICBMs. In each defense area, out to a 150 km radius, each side is permitted up 100 ABM launchers and interceptors and a limited radar base for these interceptors. 3. Neither side is permitted to give ABM capability to non ABM systems, e.g., air defense system. 4. Verification will be by national means. The parties

have agreed not to interfere with these. 5. The treaty will be of unlimited duration. Withdrawal is permitted for supreme interest.

## B. Interim Offensive Agreement

1. Each side is permitted to keep fixed land based ICBM launchers currently operational or under construction. No new fixed land based ICBM launchers may be built. 2. The Soviets may complete the 313 modern large ballistic missile launchers currently operational and under construction. No new ones may be built. 3. Neither side may convert to modern large ballistic missile launchers any other ICBM launchers. 4. Each side may keep any SLBM launchers operational or under construction. Also, newer SLBM launchers may be built as replacements for older SLBM launchers or for older heavy ICBM launchers. 5. Verification will be by national means. The parties have agreed not to interfere with these. 6. The duration of the Agreement is five years. Withdrawal is permitted for supreme interest.

## C. Offensive Forces Summary
## (Department of Defense)

|  | U.S.S.R. | United States |
|---|---|---|
| Modern large ballistic missile launchers (e.g., SS-9) | 313 | 0 |
| Other ICBM launchers not replaceable with SLBM launchers (e.g., for Minuteman and SS-11 class missiles) | 1,096 | 1,000 |
| SLBM launchers and older ICBM launchers replaceable with SLBM launchers | 950 | 710 |
| Missile total | 2,359 | 1,710 |
| Heavy bombers (not limited by the agreement) | 140 | 457 |
| Total, delivery vehicles | 2,499 | 2,167 |

The SALT I or Interim Offensive Agreement, which did not limit Multiple Independently Targetable Re-entry Vehicles (MIRVs), where the U.S. led the Soviets in numbers and quality, allowed the Soviets to deploy 1619 ICBM launchers and 950 SLBM launchers, while the American numbers remained at 1054 ICBM launchers and 710 SLBM launchers. The disparities, according to the administration, compensated the Soviets for American qualitative superiority. Despite evidence of rapid Soviet advancement in weapons technology over the years, Nixon and Kissinger counted on qualitative superiority to provide sufficient protection for American security. However, even the temporary qualitative lead in MIRVs and accuracy did not compensate totally for Soviet quantitative (megatonnage and numerical) advantages. In addition, with the development of more powerful warheads, the Soviets had, by the early 1970s, a 4:1 throw-weight advantage.[2]

William Van Cleave, a critic of SALT and the ABM Treaty, elaborated on their military asymmetries. In his estimation, the Soviet advantages "in ICBMs, deployed ABMs, deployed ABM radars, IR/MRBMs, SLCMs, medium bombers, SAMs, and new offensive weapons development...programs" were protected and in some cases enhanced by the interim agreement.[3] In areas of American strategic advantages, "deployed SLBMs, heavy bombers, MIRV...and the nascent Safeguard ABM program," the Soviets were allowed to bridge the gap with little or "no impediment to surpassing the U.S." In terms of numbers and throw-weight, SALT I provided the Soviets with generous compensations for American warhead and technological superiority. This disparity aroused the Senate, under the impetus of Senator Henry Jackson, to pass an ammendment to SALT I forbidding such asymmetries in future arms agreements.

The ABM agreement permitted the Soviet Union and the U.S. to deploy two ABM systems, one to defend national capitols and one to defend an ICBM field. The 1974 ABM agreement reduced this figure to one ABM site each. With respect to this agreement, the asymmetries include a) disparate geographic buffers for the defense of Moscow, b) a Moscow National Command Authority defense which included ICBM launchers, thereby defending political and population centers simultaneously, c) larger Soviet radar inventories that allowed for rapid expansion in the event of cheating, and d) a SAM defense ten times the size of American Systems.[4]

Kissinger responded to critics of the treaties by highlighting their strategic and political benefits. He justified the ABM freeze in terms of trading limitations in defensive systems, which by the 1970s the Soviets desired most, for limitations in offensive weapons, which the U.S. wanted in order to curb the ominous and growing gap between U.S. and Soviet ICBMs. With respect to the SALT and ABM package, he argued that it enhanced security precisely because of the Soviet agreement to freeze the most destabilizing categories of offensive and defensive weapons. In addition, according to Kissinger, the asymmetrical nature of the freeze was not an unreasonable concession due to the fact that, "Beyond a certain level of sufficiency, differences in number...are not conclusive."[5] Finally, since the agreement did not prohibit on-going or planned strategic offensive programs such as multiple warhead (MIRV) conversion or the B-1 bomber, these contributions to American offensive forces offset Soviet numerical advantages in launchers.

According to Nixon and Kissinger, the significance of SALT transcended specific provisions and went to the heart of the superpower post-war competition.[6] Despite the risks of Soviet cheating, these accords offered an opportunity "to strike a reasonable balance in strategic capabilities and to break with the pattern of...competition...suspicion, hostility, and confrontation that has dominated U.S.-Soviet relations for a generation."[7] Nixon and Kissinger viewed the SALT negotiations as a first step in broadening the Soviet-American political relationship. Kissinger considered the effort to limit strategic weapons competition the most important element in the process of detente, given the destabilizing and ultimately futile efforts to achieve superiority. He also warned that, "Sustaining the buildup requires exhortations by both sides that in time may prove incompatible with restrained international conduct. The very fact of a strategic arms race has a high potential for feeding attitudes of hostility and suspicion on both sides, transforming the fears of those who demand more weapons into self-fulfilling prophecies."[8] Consequently, Kissinger urged reliance on sufficiency, rather than competition for superiority. In sum, in his view, SALT I provided strategic stability by constraining force levels, and in so doing it also perpetuated the tenure of detente.

While Nixon and Kissinger assumed that the Soviets shared an interest in avoiding nuclear war, accepting parity in weapons, and seeking strategic stability and detente through arms limitation agreements, they assured the Soviets that any circumvention of the letter or spirit of the arms agreement would jeopardize the agreement and the emerging political relationship.[9] However, despite wariness over the possibility of Soviet duplicity, the administration expressed satisfaction with SALT and detente. After all, as a result of patient negotiation and a developing sense of what international behavior would be acceptable to each side, the prospects for strategic and political stability after SALT seemed greater than ever.

Despite the administration's enthusiasm, critics found little to cheer about. They questioned the provisions of the treaty, which favored the Soviets in quantitative terms; the American negotiating style, which appeared to allow the Soviets considerable flexibility as the Americans sought more desperately for an agreement; and Soviet violations of the treaties. Before elaborating on the details of these criticisms, which applied to SALT II as well as SALT I, mention should be made of some of the specific violations of SALT I charged against the Soviet Union. According to Van Cleave, these violations included: 1) developing, testing, and deploying mobile ICBMs (not strictly a violation of limits on fixed ICBMs; 2) converting "light ICBMs" into "heavy ICBMs" (not strictly a violation, due to the lack of specificity over the definition of heavy ICBMs and the allowable increases in the size of launchers); 3) building ICBM silos beyond the number permitted (clearly a violation); 4) testing SAM and SAM radars "in an ABM mode" and building a new ABM radar at Krasnoyarsk (a violation of the ABM treaty); and 5) interfering with American means of verification.[10]

These violations in spirit and law indicated that the Soviets sought to exploit SALT I ambiguities. The post 1972 non-SALT limited strategic programs also showed this. Irrespective of minor or major Soviet violations, the vigorous Soviet pursuit of strategic development since SALT I upset the Soviet-U.S. military balance and demonstrated contrasts in Soviet and American objectives. For example, after SALT the Soviets tested, developed, and deployed new missiles and improved the efficiency, reliability, and accuracy of MIRV and Cold Launch techniques. According to former Secretary of Defense Schlesinger, the Soviets by 1974 were in the midst of an unprecedented ICBM development program, a truly massive effort "ahead of rather than in reaction to what the United States has done."[11] He also pointed out that the Soviet's strategic nuclear capability went "far beyond anything required by the theories of minimum or finite deterrence."[12] However, according to Kissinger, this situation of Soviet advantage and strategic momentum would be remedied in SALT II. In addition, as supporters of arms control point out, one should not fault an agreement for not constraining what is allowed.[13] In the meantime, according to both Kissinger and Carter, as long as the SALT process did not upset the rough strategic parity between the superpowers, temporary and limited Soviet advantages were irrelevant. Given this claim, the degree to which the SALT process facilitated parity—or whether it encompassed questionable disparities in the numbers and types of weapons allowed in the agreement—is the main focus of the section on SALT II.

## Not Passing the SALT: The Saga of SALT II.

The Carter administration argued that detente and SALT I and II were interrelated and mutually reinforcing phenomena stimulated by the mutual fear of nuclear war and buttressed by shared Soviet and American interests. However, questions about the degree to which the Soviets shared certain interests arose in the wake of doubts about the wisdom of both SALT and detente. Consequently, when attmpting to evaluate SALT II and establish the relationship between the SALT process and detente, it is useful to compare Soviet and American approaches to negotiation, strategic objectives, and strategic doctrines. Such a comparison reveals striking dichotomies. Critical analysts of the American negotiating approach, for example, described it as basically cooperative, compromise-oriented, and impatient.[14] According to one former SALT negotiator, Americans also assumed that there were peaceful solutions to conflicts and that negotiation was "a non-zero sum game where both sides stand to gain mutually and equally."[15] Americans appeared to consider negotiation a method of communicating objectives, instilling mutual confidence, and facilitating cooperative patterns of interaction. With these assumptions in hand, officials in the Carter administration expected negotiations over SALT II to contribute "to the further development of U.S.-Soviet and overall East-West relations. SALT is the foundation for progress in establishing an enduring political relationship with the Soviets that reduces tensions and sets important visible boundaries to our ideological and political and military competition."[16] This expectation relied heavily on the presumed stabilizing function of the negotiating process itself. However, if the Soviets did not share this attitude, American negotiating objectives could be jeopardized.

In contrast to the American approach, the Soviets, as far as we can tell, consider negotiation competitive, barter-oriented, and a form of political warfare with offensive purposes.[17] They appear to consider conflicts and crises normal, often incapable of peaceful resolution, and ripe for exploitation.[18] Soviet negotiating behavior often has been inflexible, ideological, and obsessed with security via superiority. More specifically the Soviets appear to view arms control negotiations as a form of political struggle and a test of wills.[19] Comparing this with the American perspective suggests certain incompatibilities between Soviet and American expectations for arms control negotiation outside of the basic mutual desire to reduce strategic vulnerability. On the other hand, the Soviets obviously desire the beneficial aspects of arms control agreements and accept notions of tactical retreat, whether in military maneuvers or diplomacy.

More ominously, the Soviets and Americans appeared to differ in their views of the prospect of nuclear war. American adherents of Mutual Assured Destruction (MAD) believe nuclear war unthinkable and unwinnable. (See chapter V for a more elaborate discussion of MAD.) However, Soviet military writers refer to the likelihood of nuclear war, the utility of nuclear weapons, and the resulting imperative of war-fighting and war-winning capability.[20] In fact, given the dynamics of Soviet counterforce and BMD development in the 1970s, we may infer that the Soviets view an offensive war-fighting capability as essential for security.[21]. Evidence of these assumptions also can be seen in Soviet civil defense programs, which indicated the existence of contingency planning for survivability and recovery, and in political references, in the 1960s and early 1970s, to the fact that nuclear war would be more disastrous for the West than for the Soviet Union.

Carter and Vance contested the reality of contrasting Soviet and American approaches. They assumed that the nature of nuclear war prohibited thinking in war-fighting terms and that the Soviets realized this, despite confidence-building bluffs about surviving a nuclear war. In their view, speeches by Brezhnev, referring to the disaster facing both sides in the event of a nuclear war, took precedence over military incantations about the prerequisites for war-fighting and damage limitations.

The debate over the nature of the Soviet view of war relates closely to the debate over the extent to which Soviet and American military doctrines reflect similar objectives. The U.S. bases its strategy on MAD—wherein both the U.S. and the Soviets possess the capacity to level unacceptable damage on the other, even after receiving a nuclear first strike. The *mutual* perception of this "fact of life" deters either side from launching a nuclear war. Given the phenomenon of MAD, both sides, should realize the futility of further arms racing and seek limits on certain types of weapons like BMD or counterforce weapons.

In contrast to these assumptions, Soviet military literature refers to the importance of military superiority, especially as it advances Soviet foreign policy; and, until quite recently, specifically rejected MAD. In fact, the objective of strategic superiority was inseparable from the major political purpose of superiority—to constrain American foreign policy. While the Soviet military and political literature sometimes differed, especially in the 1980s, in terms of support for war-fighting versus deterence based on threats of retaliation, the following excerpts provide evidence of the Soviet stress on the value of superiority and invulnerability.

U.S. leaders are obliged publicly to acknowledge changes in the strategic situation which are unfavorable for the U.S. and to take into account the growth in the U.S.S.R.'s might.

We are all witnesses to the fact that the Central Committee of the Communist Party constantly provides the military-technological means to assure indisputable superiority over the armies of the most powerful capitalist countries...

Thus the struggle for military-technological superiority has now become decisive...

The predominance of the forces of peace and progress—a predominance which has now grown appreciably—gives them the opportunity to determine the channel followed by international politics...

Under the conditions of the Scientific-technical revolution the 'balance of fear' as a guarantee of peace cannot be insured for any length of time by the same level of armaments from either the quantitative or qualitative viewpoints. So a peace based on the 'balance of fear' and on mutual 'deterrence' is doomed to a constant arms race and is not insured against the danger of military conflicts...Thus, taking a broad view, a policy based on the absolutization of military strength and the 'balance of fear' cannot be a guarantee of lasting peace. Modern conditions demand the renunciation of the absolutization of the ideas of the 'balance of fear', 'mutual deterrence' and so forth as the main conditions of the stability of peace and detente. Concepts of this kind are based on the absolutely incorrect premise that aggressiveness is characteristic of each of the sides and that it can be 'restrained' only by the threat of annihilation.[22]

Carter dismissed the Soviet rejection of MAD. Whatever the Soviet rhetoric, the nature and number of nuclear weapons forced each side into accepting the "balance of terror." In addition, according to the administration, the SALT process would protect American security 1) by maintaining a strategic force equality or essential equivalence between the U.S. and the U.S.S.R., which guaranteed MAD regardless of a Soviet "principled rejection," and 2) by providing an atmosphere of improved political relations with the Soviets. On the other hand, while the terms of the agreement gave the appearance of equality in some areas, questions arose about the strategy of MAD and about American concessions in SALT II. Consequently, to determine the soundness of the treaty and whether any flaws in it related to contrasts in Soviet and American strategic conceptualizations, a review of the terms of SALT II and the explanations for American acceptance of disparities in the numbers and types of weapons allowed in the agreement will be addressed next.

With respect to strategic nuclear delivery vehicles, SALT II established an equal ceiling of 2400 launchers to be reduced to 2250 by 1981. Of these, only 1320 could be launchers of MIRVed ballistic missiles and/or heavy bombers with long range cruise missiles. Of these 1320, 1200 could be launchers of MIRVed ballistic missiles and only 820 of these could be launchers of MIRVed ICBMs. According to the administration, these ceilings represented genuine milestones due to a mutual acceptance of equality and to the fact that for the first time the Soviets would reduce their number of launchers. These ceilings also represented a reduction in Soviet warheads and throw-weight, if compared to what the Soviets could deploy without SALT II. However, the administration neglected to mention that the limits only appeared equal because, in counting launchers, the U.S. included 220 B-52s in storage and 4 B-1 prototypes but excluded Soviet Backfire bombers, SS-20 IRBMs (both having potential intercontinental range), and Soviet cruise missiles.* Excluding its obsolete bombers, the U.S. remained below the proposed 1981 ceiling for years, while the Soviets acquired over 2500 missiles and bombers. Although Reagan complained about the high SALT ceilings, he chose not to exceed SALT II limits on launchers until the end of 1986.

Another aspect of this artificial numerical equality represented more than partial numerical disparities. The allowance of 308 Soviet heavy missiles (SS-18s) represented a potentially destabilizing factor in SALT with respect to Soviet advantages in throw-weight (5-1), deliverable megatonnage (5-1), delivery re-entry vehicles (3-1) and counterforce capability (6-1).[23] However, Carter downplayed the importance of the increasing vulnerability of American retaliatory forces inherent in these asymmetries. According to the administration, in exchange for not reducing the number of heavy missiles, the Soviets could not count American aircraft and nuclear systems based in Western Europe.** The administration also argued that this latter concession by the Soviets also justified the exclusion of Soviet SS-20 IRBMs and Backfire bombers from the SALT limits.

According to critics, SALT II concealed, "behind a facade of equality, highly significant military advantages for the U.S.S.R." and a very real potential of a Soviet first strike capability.[24] One example of these advantages was the threat from increased Soviet warhead capacity,

*The Backfire bomber may fly unrefueled from the U.S.S.R. and reach targets in the U.S. As with U.S. B-52's, which require refuelings en-route to the U.S.S.R., the Backfire could land in a third country after an attack. With the addition of an extra boosting stage the SS-20 resembles the SS-16 ICBM. Soviet cruise missiles were not counted due to their system inaccuracies. For SALT II figures see the Memorandum of Understanding Between the United States of America and the Union of Soviet Socialist Republics Regarding the Establishment of a Data Base on the Numbers of Strategic Offensive Arms.

which continued unabated as seen in the Soviet momentum in deploying MIRVed SS-18s. The Carter claim that SALT II blunted Soviet warhead deployment was misleading, since the treaty did not limit warheads per se, and since the Soviets already possessed sufficient warheads to destroy a considerable portion of American retaliatory forces. In fact, the Soviets, by the early 1980s, had the theoretical capability to destroy most U.S. ICBMs by expending only two-thirds of the warheads permitted on the SS-18s by SALT II.[25] The remaining one-third delivery vehicles could strike B-52s on the ground, nuclear submarines in port, Washington, D.C., SAC, NORAD, the largest 100 American urban centers, and all major military bases in the U.S. and Western Europe.[26] The fact that SALT II failed to prevent the Soviets from deploying three times the number of warheads required to destroy most American ICBMs undermined the Carter claim that SALT II limited the potential of additional Soviet warheads.

The treaty might have been more valuable with a lower ceiling on heavy missiles and bans on MIRVing these. However, the Soviets refused to accept these suggestions. Carter's rejoinder to critics who urged compensation for Soviet throw-weight advantages contained in MIRVed heavy ICBMs reiterated a Nixon/Kissinger reference to American superiority: "The Soviet advantage in ICBM throw-weight is currently compensated by significant U.S. advantages in numbers of nuclear warheads, missile accuracy, numbers and capability of heavy bombers, and other factors."[27] Also like the previous administration, Carter assumed that American qualitative superiority (to be limited in SALT II through the bans listed below) offered adequate protection for the U.S. force structure. In addition, limitations on heavy missiles would be attended to in SALT III.

Other treaty provisions included bans on 1) new ICBM launchers and systems, aside from one new type of light ICBM; 2) increasing the number of ballistic missile warheads beyond 10 on ICBMs, 14 on SLBMs, and 10 on ASBMs; 3) increasing the number of long range cruise missiles per bomber beyond 28; 4) increasing the throw-weight of strategic ballistic missiles; 5) a rapid reloading ICBM system; and 6) new types of strategic offensive systems. Bans on new systems would limit the arms race. More importantly, many of the qualitative and warhead limits reduced the chances of strategic instability by reducing the most destabilizing weapons—those that threatened the retaliatory assets of the other side. Following the precepts of MAD, the U.S. should forego the capability to destroy hardened Soviet military targets and abandon defensive or other damage-limiting systems because the Soviets would perceive these as threats to their retaliatory forces. Therefore, Carter opted to ban qualitative developments that might compromise respective retaliatory systems. However, banning new systems also reduced Soviet fear of American technological breakthroughs. In the process, the U.S. limited the one area in which it might enhance stability by balancing Soviet quantitative asymmetries. In the meantime, the persistent Soviet

**The forward-based U.S. F-111 has less than one-half the range of the Backfire, which does not have to be forward-based to reach the U.S.

development of a counterforce capability; i.e., a posture aimed at eroding the invulnerability of American nuclear forces, indicated little concern about the destabilizing impact of threatening American retaliatory forces.

The treaty also provided a number of confidence-building measures such as advance notification of ICBM tests, definitions of limited systems and counting rules, and provisions to monitor verification through national technical means (NTM). Unfortunately, even with modern intelligence techniques, the U.S. could not verify completely the number, location, and identity of Soviet missiles, how many warheads an ICBM carried when emplaced in a silo, the number of missiles with a multiple basing system, nor the range limits for cruise missiles.[28] And Soviet ASAT capability may complicate future intelligence gathering techniques. Given these complications and the secretive nature of the Soviet system critics worry about verification to assure Soviet compliance with SALT and agreements to ban high yield ICBM tests, ASAT tests, or BMD research.

In addition to the base package, the two powers included a Protocol that banned until 1981 deployment and testing of mobile ICBM launchers, ASBMs, and ground and sea-based cruise missiles with ranges over 600 kilometers. Critics at the time feared that this protocol jeopardized a major U.S. advantage in cruise missile technology, something the Soviets sought to blunt because the development of these missiles provided a quantum jump in weapon survivability, accuracy, and versatility. Despite Carter's assurances of U.S. freedom to deploy cruise missiles upon the expiration of the protocol in 1981, critics feared an extension of the ban. However, while the Soviets complained of an American violation of the protocol, with the deployment of Pershing II and cruise missiles in Europe, the Reagan administration reminded the Soviets in 1983 of Western attempts to negotiate the elimination of all INF in Europe and of the expiration of the unratified protocol in 1981.

To refute the criticisms of SALT II, Carter argued that its advantages outweighed the disadvantages. It would reduce the risk of nuclear war and incentives for an unlmited arms race, improve the international political climate, encourage new agreements, and protect U.S. security. Equally important, without the treaty limits the Soviets could deploy more nuclear warheads and missiles; the ability to monitor Soviet testing would be impaired, since there would be no limits on concealment; and the U.S. could not reduce political or military insecurity nor "the inherent instability of an unrestrained, and more costly, strategic arms competition."[29]

These putative advantages deserve careful consideration. Aside from the contribution of SALT to reducing the risk of war, the most compelling arguments are those related to the undesirability of a SALT-free world. First, with respect to Soviet deployments, estimates vary over the likely Soviet increases if SALT disintegrated. Even conservative estimates predict a quick Soviet expansion of warheads and missiles. According to the liberal Arms Control Association (ACA), based on its study of Soviet on-line capabilities and recent flight tests, by the 1990s the Soviets could deploy 7000 new strategic warheads on ballistic missiles and bombers, for a new total of about 17,000.[30] The C.I.A. and the Arms Control and

Disarmament Agency (ACDA) project a doubling of Soviet warheads by the mid 1990s. They also predict a slow growth in U.S. weapons. See figure 1 for a comparison of Soviet and U.S. strategic nuclear forces with and without SALT II constraints.

HOW SALT II AFFECTS THE WARHEAD ARSENAL OF THE USSR*

| | TOTAL WARHEADS | BREAKDOWN OF ALL WARHEADS | | |
| | | ICBM | SLBM | BOMBER |
| --- | --- | --- | --- | --- |
| Current Levels | 10,084 | 6,420 | 2,844 | 820 |
| 1990 Levels within SALT limits | 12,492 | 7,320 | 3,352 | 1,820 |
| 1990 Levels without SALT limits | 16,588 | 9,870 | 3,948 | 2,740 |

*Source: CIA figures and estimates assuming that the Soviets will use as many warheads per weapon as possible under SALT II guidelines.

Second, with respect to the impairment of capabilities to monitor Soviet testing and forces, losing SALT II obligations to allow NTM observations of testing data would create additional intelligence obstacles to the U.S., feed on pre-existing suspicions about Soviet leads in the arms race, and complicate predictability about the nature and direction of the Soviet nuclear threat. Third, the disintegration of the SALT process and the ABM treaty would jeopardize on-going arms control negotiations. In sum according to the ACA, to abandon SALT II, which has constrained the Soviet buildup; forced them to remove over 1000 missiles and 13 missile carrying submarines; and allowed the U.S. to remain within shouting distance of Soviet numbers, would "reduce significantly the prospects for reaching a new U.S.-Soviet strategic arms accord," force the two powers into an accelerated arms race, "increase uncertainty on both sides about the capabilities and intentions of the opponent, heighten U.S.-Soviet tensions, and thus increase the risk of nuclear war."[31]

The ACA urges compliance with SALT II regardless of Soviet violations of its terms, which the ACA deems ambiguous and minor. According to the ACA, the Soviet SS-25, a prohibited second new ICBM, poses no military threat since the Soviets have to dismantle an existing ICBM for each SS-25 it deploys; and Soviet encryption of telemetry from missile testing does not impede verification of SALT II. But Carter's and the ACA's faith in SALT II came under increasing fire by those who doubted that the asymmetrical terms of the treaty and the violations of SALT and the ABM treaty (such as the "unlawful" SS-25, encryption of telemetry in such a way as to impede determination of Soviet compliance with the treaties, and the construction of a prohibited ballistic missile detection radar in Krasnoyarsk), protected U.S. security. (See charts 2-6 for a list of

Soviet-U.S. deactivizations to stay within SALT limits and alleged Soviet and U.S. violations). If SALT II failed to protect security, as critics contend, then the next question concerned the extent to which a flawed treaty derived from contrasts in Soviet and U.S. strategic doctrines and objectives.

Chart 2

## US SALT Deactivations[b]

The Salt agreements have required the U.S. to deactivate 320 ICBMs, 544 SLBMs and 11 nuclear-missile carrying submarines:

- Between 1972-75, the United States removed 260 Minuteman I ICBMs and 60 Minuteman II ICBMs in order to increase the number of Minuteman III ICBMs to 550.
- Since 1972, the United States has replaced 176 Polaris A-3 SLBMs with Poseidon C-3 SLBMs and replaced 192 C-3 SLBMs with Trident C-4 SLBMs on 12 submarines.
- Since 1980, the United States has withdrawn 10 Polaris submarines in preparation for the deployment of Trident subs.
- In 1985 the United States dismantled a Poseidon submarine to remain with the SALT II limits as a new Trident missile-carrying sub began sea trials.

Between 1985-90, SALT II will require the United States to remove or retire a number of older ICBMs, SLBMs or ALCM-carrying bombers as new ones are deployed.

- For every MX deployed, a Minuteman III will have to be removed.
- Because the U.S. has reached the 1,200 ceiling on MIRVed launchers, it will have to dismantle a MIRVed ICBM launcher or MIRVed SLBM launcher for every new MIRVed SLBM deployed.
- Once the number of ALCM-carrying B-52s reaches 120, the U.S. will have to retire either an existing ALCM-carrying B-52G or a MIRVed ICBM or SLBM launcher for each addition al B-52H deployed. (Violated 1986.)

[b]Source: "Countdown on SALT II," *Arms Control Association,* 1985, p. 14.

Chart 3

## Soviet SALT Deactivations[c]

The SALT accords have required the Soviet Union to remove 1,007 ICBMs, 233 SLBMs, and 13 Yankee-class nuclear missile-carrying submarines:

- In order to comply with the SALT I and II "freeze" on "heavy" ICBMs, between 1973-80 the Soviet Union withdrew 288 SS-9 ICBMs as SS-18 ICBMs entered the force. SALT II also prohibited the Soviet Union from testing and deploying a "new" heavy ICBM and limited the extent to which existing heavy ICBMs could be modernized.

- Between 1974-84, the Soviet Union removed 510 SS-11 ICBMs as newer SS-17, SS-18 and SS-19 ICBMs were deployed.
- Between 1975-85, the Soviet Union dismantled the missile-carrying portion of 13 Yankee-class submarines as new Delta- and Typhoon-class subs were added; dismantled 209 SS-7 and SS-8 ICBM launchers to allow for permitted increases in SLBMs; removed 212 SS-N-6 SLBMs as SS-N-18 and SS-N-20 SLBMs were introduced; removed 15 SS-N-5 SLBMs as it increased the number of SS-N-18 SLBMs; and removed six SS-N-8 SLBMs as it increased the number of SS-N-20 SLBMs.
- Had SALT II been ratified, the Soviet Union would have been obligated to reduce its aggregate number of ICBMs, SLBMs, and heavy bombers to 2,400 and then to 2,250 by January 1981.

Between 1985-90, SALT II will require the Soviet Union to remove older ICBMs and SLBMs as new ones are deployed.

- Between 1985-90, the Soviet Union is expected to deploy 250 SS-25 single-warhead ICBMs. For every SS-25 deployed in a silo, an SS-11 or SS-13 ICBM will have to be removed. For every SS-25 deployed in a mobile mode, an SS-11 or SS-13 silo will have to be destroyed. (Recent reports indicate that the Soviet Union has begun dismantling SS-11 silos.)
- Between 1986-90, The Soviet Union is expected to deploy 135 new SS-24 ten-MIRV ICBMs. For every SS-24 deployed in a silo, a MIRVed SS-17, SS-18 or SS-19 will have to be removed. For Every SS-24 deployed in a mobile mode, an SS-17, SS-18, or SS-19 silo will have to be destroyed.
- Between 1985 and 1988, the Soviet Union is expected to continue deployments of its MIRVed SS-NX-23 and SS-N-20 SLBMs. Prior to reaching the 1,200 ceiling on MIRVed launchers, the Soviets will have to remove an existing single-warhead SLBM for each SS-NX-23 or SS-N-20 deployed in order to stay within the overall aggregate of 2,504 launchers.
- Once the 1,200 ceiling on MIRVed launchers is reached, the Soviet Union will be obliged to retire the MIRVed SS-N-18 SLBM or a MIRVed ICBM for every SS-N-20 and SS-NX-23 SLBM deployed.
- Between 1985-90, the Soviet Union is expected to continue deployment of one Delta- and one Typhoon-class sub per year. For every sub deployed, the Soviet Union will have to dismantle the missile-launch section of a Yankee- or Delta-class submarine.

ᶜSource: "Countdown on SALT II," Arms Control Association, 1985, p. 13.

Chart 4

## A Look At Alleged Treaty Violations [d]

|  | Action | Treaty | Basis of Violation | Possible Impact |
|---|---|---|---|---|
| Soviet Union | SS-25 | SALT II | May violate "one new type" rule, or be a legal "modernization" | minor; may be stabilizing |
|  | Encryption | SALT II | Ambiguous language | possibly significant |
|  | Krasnoyarsk radar | ABM Treaty | Location illegal, early warning function legal | minor |
|  | Explosions over 150 kilotons "Sverdlovsk incident" | Threshold Test Ban Treaty Biological convention | Technical interpretation of seismic data is highly debatable. At least procedural noncompliance | very minor |
| United States | Minuteman covers Thule/Fy-lingdales radars | SALT II ABM Treaty | Definite Arguable | none none |
|  | Homing overlay experiment | ABM Treaty | Arguable | minor |
|  | Unwillingness to negotiate CTBT | Non-Prolifera-tion Treaty; Limited Test Ban Treaty | Failure to pursue preambles' call for a comprehensive test ban | unknown |
| Both Countries | Nuclear test venting | Limited Test Ban Treaty | Technical violation | none |

[d]Source: Wolfgang K.H. Panofsky, "Arms Control: Necessary Process," *Bulletin of Atomic Scientists* (March 1986): 37.

Chart 5

## Alleged American Violations and Reagan's Responses [e]

| | |
|---|---|
| Minuteman Covers | ...used to protect construction crews during the winter. After Soviet complaints covers removed. |
| Thule/Fylingdales radars | ...allowable under ABM treaty exclusions for Early Warning System radars. |
| Homing Overlay | BMD research is allowable under the ABM treaty. |

[e]Source: White House fact sheet of May 27, 1986.

Chart 6

## Alleged Soviet Violations and Reagan's Accusations[f]

| | |
|---|---|
| The SS-25 | Testing and deployment of this missile violates a central provision of SALT II which was intended to limit the number of new ICBMs. The agreement permits only one new type of ICBM for each party. The Soviets have informed us that their one new ICBM type will be the SS-X-24, now undergoing testing, and have falsely asserted that the SS-25 is a permitted modernization of their old silo-based SS-13 ICBM. The President also concluded that the technical argument by which the Soviets sought to justify the SS-25, calling it "permitted modernization," is also troublesome as a potential precedent, as the Soviets might seek to apply it to additional prohibited new types of ICBMs in the future. |
| Encryption | Soviet use of encryption impedes U.S. verification of Soviet compliance and thus contravenes the provision of SALT II which prohibits use of deliberate concealment measures, including encryption, which impede verification of compliance by national technical means. This concealment activity...impedes our ability to know whether a type of missile is in compliance with SALT II requirements. It could also make it more difficult to assess accurately the critical parameters of any future missile. |
| Krasnoyarsk Radar | Violates the 1972 ABM Treaty, which prohibits the siting of an ABM radar, or the siting and orienting of a ballistic missile detection and tracking radar, in the way the Krasnoyarsk radar is sited and oriented. Politically...the radar demonstrates that the Soviets are capable of violating arms control obligations and commitments even when they are negotiating with the United States or when they know we will detect a violation. Militarily...the Krasnoyarsk radar violation goes to the heart of the ABM Treaty. Large phased-array radars (LPARs), like that under construction near Krasnoyarsk were recognized during the ABM Treaty negotiations as the critical, |

long lead-time element of a nationwide ABM
defense...the Krasnoyarsk radar has the inherent
potential to contribute to ABM radar coverage of a
significant portion in the central U.S.S.R.

---

ᶠSource: Reagan's Statement on Interim Restraint, in Department of State's *Special Report* #147 (May 27, 1986).

Proponents of SALT II and MAD assume the inherent stability of deterrence based on MAD as long as the U.S. and the Soviet Union possessed a "relatively equal" capacity of retaliating and causing unacceptable damage on an aggressor after receiving a first strike. Awareness of the prospect of such damage deters either side from attacking first. However, this proposition failed to take into account sufficiently the importance of the numerical balance in a situation of rapidly changing weapons technology and short-lived qualitative leads. A deterrent posture relying on the inherent stability of sufficiency and assured destruction might be vulnerable if faced with an enemy committed to superiority and even first strike capability. Unfortunately, American objectives for SALT II depended upon a questionable coincident Soviet interest in strategic balance and mutual vulnerability.

As mentioned earlier, not only did Soviet programs, expenditures, and deployments indicate little subscription to American doctrines, but the Soviets specifically rejected the concepts of parity and deterrence based on mutual vulnerability. The Soviets appeared to hope for superiority and for political benefits deriving from such a position. The denial of these Soviet intentions blinded Carter to the potential erosion of the American deterrent—an erosion facilitated by SALT II. For example, if the U.S. based its strategy on MAD and sufficiency and the Soviet Union based its strategy on achieving superiority, future American decision makers, in the event of a failing deterrent, might have only two options, suicide or surrender. Such a choice reflected the paradox of MAD: "if deterrence should fail it would not be rational to carry out the very threat (assured destruction) upon which deterrence is said to rest. And to the extent that carrying out the retaliatory threat is irrational, the credibility of the entire strategy of deterrence is undermined."[32]

Concern over this paradox prompted recommendations for more effective, flexible, and diversified deterrent strategies as well as a re-examination of the SALT process. Both of these were necessary since strategic stability stemmed from the size, diversity, and invulnerability of strategic forces rather than from arms control in and of itself.[33] In addition, before rushing to an agreement, it was important to know what nuclear weapons were supposed to accomplish, whether they had political-military utility as the Soviets apparently expected, and whether the U.S. should re-evaluate the premises underlying its strategic objectives as well as those of the U.S.S.R.[34] Certainly as long as the U.S. misinterpreted the Soviet strategy, it would face major problems when negotiating arms limitations with them.

In this last respect, according to those who relate flaws in the SALT process to flaws in strategy, the U.S. must also determine whether arms control negotiations 1) are goals in and of themselves; 2) have taken the place of strategy; or 3) are, as the Soviets perceive them, temporary expedients employed to further political as well as military goals. Viewing SALT as a substitute for policy and failing to link arms control and strategic objectives, might facilitate the relinquishing of the American, strategic lead to the U.S.S.R. The Reagan administration accused Carter of taking the U.S. in just this direction. However, Carter had argued that an arms agreements provided a valuable purpose—securing an agreement involving the Soviet Union in a rational assessment of the value of mutual restraint, stability, and an expanded political relationship with the U.S. However, according to the Reagan arms control team, Carter's haste to secure an agreement precipitated considerable damage to American strategic interests and demonstrated the weakness of its negotiating position.

Aside from the potential military dangers deriving from the asymmetry of SALT II and the contrasts in Strategic doctrines, critics noted potential political dangers from a Soviet attempt to use nuclear superiority to acquire military and political benefits via pressure, blackmail, and brinkmanship. The record of Soviet expansion and assertiveness when in an inferior position already provided evidence of a proclivity for disrupting international stability. Despite arguments by Kissinger and Carter about the irrelevance of attempts at marginal advantage and superiority, the Soviet Union continued its exercises of international adventures (in Afghanistan, for example) and its references to the political value of Soviet superiority. And, despite beliefs that SALT II would foster an improved political climate and superpower restraint, the Soviets apparently believed 1) that, in SALT II, the U.S. conceded its unwillingness to forego arms limitation even at the cost of inequity; 2) that pressure tactics, whether in arms negotiation or international crises, yielded considerable rewards; and 3) that the U.S. might not use military means to redress a shifting balance of power favoring the U.S.S.R., respond to Soviet strategic build-ups, nor resist Soviet political challenges as effectively as in the past.

Carter overlooked the extent to which SALT II, the Soviet strategic offensive, and detente all provided avenues of political advancement for the Soviets. In other words, the Soviet objective of political dominance could be obtained in two ways: 1) through arms agreements that neutralize American strategic positions and permitted the Soviets access to superiority; and 2) through a detente that disguised Soviet motives and intentions. Evidence of their intentions may be seen in the massive Soviet effort in strategic development since SALT I (deployment of 5 new ballistic missile systems, rapid expansion in throw weight, substantial improvements in ICBM accuracy, etc.). And as Schlesinger pointed out, the Soviet effort went "far beyond anything required by the theories of minimum or finite deterrence."[35]

This should come as no surprise since the Soviet Union rejects American ideas on stability and mutual vulnerability and desires strategic superiority. It also should be no surprise, then, that Soviet military and political activity after SALT I, Soviet resistance to a more equitable SALT

II, and Soviet military doctrine contributed to a SALT process that did not halt arms competition, guarantee a strategic balance, inspire Soviet acceptance of MAD, nor protect American strategic forces. Reagan hoped to reverse this process of Soviet advantage and exploitation with his advocacy of strategic modernizatin, significant cuts in the most destabilizing offensive weapons, and deterrence based on BMD.

## Stopping with START: Reagan and Arms Control

In 1983 the Soviets walked out of the negotiations on START, INF, and Mutual and Balanced Force Reductions (MBFR). They accused the Reagan administration of rejecting arms control, seeking nuclear superiority, and attemtping to upset the strategic balance in Europe. Convinced of the intractability of the administration's defense intentions and of the preliminary failure of the European anti-nuclear movement to block INF deployment, the Soviets decided on another tack. While hesitant about abandoning the negotiations, the Soviets hoped a dramatic walkout might return the spark to Western anti-nuclear and anti-Reagan sentiments. A Reagan administration put on the defensive might offer important concessions to entice the Soviets back to the negotiating table.

But this did not happen. The administration waited, in an election year, for the Soviets to realize that strategic modernization and INF deployment would continue as would research and development in the Strategic Defense Initiative (SDI). By January 1985, with Constantin Cherenko temporarily at the helm, the Soviets reentered arms control negotiations without the demanding preconditions of American abandonment of "unacceptable" positions and deployments. Before evaluating the current bargaining over INF, START, and SDI, it is necessary to review the recent history of the negotiations between Reagan and the Russians.

In his first years in office, Reagan advised allies, neutrals, and adversaries that the 1980's would begin with reversals in the U.S. military decline of the 1970's. The administration started out with blatantly anti-Soviet and anti-arms control rhetoric. Reagan promised to reject SALT II, redress the INF imbalance, upgrade American strategic capabilities, and provide a solid foundation for persuading the Soviets that the U.S. would resist Soviet attempts at superiority and strategic blackmail. All of these promises depended on healthy and purposeful defense spending. As we saw in previous chapters, while the administration pursued increased spending tenaciously in the early years, the congressional knife soon cut considerable holes in Reagan's budget requests. However, some of the cushion provided by the early increases is still reflected in the eight year procurement record of the administration. In the meantime, the battle over budgets receded in importance somewhat compared to the administration's more general concern for meeting the changing prerequisites of nuclear deterrence in the 1980s.

According to the administration, and all post-war administrations, the U.S. deters war or attack by denying the enemy confidence in victory and by maintaining the ability to counterattack. In the 1960s and 1970s, the U.S. relied on MAD to fulfill these functions. However, the Soviet pursuit of superiority eroded the deterrent value of MAD. To buttress the eroded stability of the balance of terror, the Reagan administration has pursued weapons and defenses intended to enhance the survivability and punch of retaliatory forces. Without an invulnerable and devastating second strike capability, "the Soviet Union would then be in a position to threaten or actually attack us with the knowledge that we would be incapable of responding."[36] Reagan emphasized the necessity of preparing responses for a protracted nuclear conflict and developing improved counterforce, damage limiting, and BMD capabilities. According to supporters of the new approach, the most effective way to deter the Soviets was to convince them that they would not prevail because American strategic forces would have the capability to return fire and deny the Soviets victory in a nuclear war. In other words, a counterforce system (the MX) protected by BMD and thus somewhat invulnerable to a first strike would deter a strike because it could thwart Soviet attempts at winning.[37] (See chapter V for a review of Reagan's contribution to strategy.)

Despite administration assumptions that the capability to prevail would deter rather than provoke the Soviets, many worried about the destabilizing impact of declared interests in war-fighting options. Reagan's critics insisted that attempts at counterforce capability aroused Soviet suspicion of U.S. first strike intentions. According to Garthoff, the administration failed to take into account that the Soviet buildup was an attempt to establish parity with the U.S. and was, in fact, "*less* than the parallel American buildup in MIRVed warheads in the 1970s."[38] Garthoff concluded that, given the U.S. lead and its war-waging concepts (Schlesinger's silo targeting strategy of 1974), the Soviets intended a deterrent rather than war-fighting role for their counterforce capability (SS-18s) against U.S. ICBMs. If this were the case, and if parity already existed within the balance of U.S. warhead and Soviet counterforce advantages, then U.S. attempts at developing counterforce capability were destabilizing. On the other hand, while it is crucial to distinguish between attempts at parity and attempts at superiority, we might be better off assuming that Soviet counterforce capability reflected an interest not merely in deterrence, but also in superiority. If this were the case, deterrence might be better served by deployment of a limited invulnerable counterforce (MX and/or Trident II) that would inhibit Soviet considerations of a first strike to preclude an American counterforce (eliminated by a Soviet first strike) or countervalue (useless against silos) response.

In addition, another purpose might be served. Modernizatin of U.S. strategic nuclear forces and adequate defense spending not only demonstrate the determination to deter, but they also encompass a paradoxical role in persuading the Soviets, who respect nations that bargain from strength, to negotiate seriously on arms control. According to Reagan, "Only if the Soviets recognize the West's determination to modernize its own military forces will they see an incentive to negotiate a verifiable agreement establishing equal, lower levels."[39] Reagan proceeded, then, to undertake several missions: strategic modernization and arms control proposals aimed at enhancing strategic stability, resolving the dilemma of the INF race in Europe," and replacing the shadow of the balance of terror with his vision of a balance of safety to be secured by an eventual transition to BMD.

In terms of the arms control agenda, the administration, while slow off the mark, charged into semi high gear with several proposals regarding limits on offensive strategic and Eurostrategic weapons in 1982 and 1983. However, the administration also carefully spelled out its criteria for judging the merits of arms control agreements. Given the poor record of the SALT negotiations, according to the Reagan arms control team, the administration was determined to reject flawed agreements in favor of those that limited the right weapons and reduced the risk of war. According to Shultz, one of the key tests by which the U.S. judges arms control proposals

> is whether they will enhance strategic stability. The military balance that results from an agreement should be one that reduces the incentive for a first strike. It should enhance deterrence by ensuring that no first strike can succeed, that no one can be tempted by illusions of 'victory.' A stable environment reduces the incentive to build new weapons and enhances the incentive to reduce the level of arms. It defuses the tension and danger of any crisis that may occur. Thus an emphasis on strategic stability goes to the heart of reducing the danger of the outbreak of war.[40]

Other criteria included equality or essential equivalence, radical rather than cosmetic reductions in the most destabilizing weapons, and effective verifiability. With these criteria in mind, the administration sought a dialogue on radical cuts in strategic arms, down to about 5000 ballistic missile warheads on each side, in the START talks.

Reagan initially offered a two-part reduction package with proposed cuts in ballistic missile warheads and throw-weight (destructive capability). Each side would reduce ballistic missile warheads to equal levels one-third below current levels. He later accepted the principle of 50% reductions. Deploying only one-half of these warheads on ICBMs would also reduce throw-weight totals. While such cuts would dismantle more Soviet than American ICBM warheads, since the Soviets place a larger portion of their ballistic missile warheads on ICBMs, the American reduction would entail more of a mixture of ICBM and SLBM cuts. The administration assumed that equal ceilings on ballistic missile warheads "would strengthen deterrence and promote stability by significantly reducing the Soviet lead in ICBMs..." thereby making a preemptive Soviet strike "impossible without expending most of the Soviet force."[41] It is the Soviet's ability to launch a debilitating first strike against American ICBMs that the administration sees as most destabilizing. According to Shultz, "weapons like large, fixed, land-based ICBMs with multiple warheads, capable of destroying missile silos—these are the most powerful strategic weapons, the most rapid, the most provocative, the most capable of carrying out a preemptive strike, the most likely to tempt a hair-trigger response in a crisis."[42]

While the administration agreed to include cruise missile and bomber warheads in the START limits, it considers these slow and unlikely first strike weapons to be less destabilizing than warheads on ICBMs. As a result, it rejected Gorbachev's counter proposal to lump all warheads into one category of "nuclear charges" to be reduced equally. The administration has long sought a Soviet commitment to reduce their SS-18 warheads, which provide them a significant advantage in hard-target (silo) killer ICBMs.

A number of problems with these initial proposals stood out immediately. Implicitly the administration asked the Soviets to make major cuts and de facto alterations in their strategic posture in exchange for equal ceilings in areas in which they were most ahead of the U.S. Another problem concerned the extent to which warhead cuts would actually reduce the vulnerability of American ICBMs.

If each side reduced the number of MIRVed ICBMs, the ratio of Soviet warheads to targeted American ICBMs might be greater after START than before! For example, while the Soviet Union has about 5500 ICBM warheads aimable at 1052 American ICBMs (a 5:1 ratio), after START reductions the Soviet could aim 2500 warheads at approximately 400 American ICBMs—an even greater ratio.[43] Critics also questioned the emphasis on reducing throw-weight, since a main source of American vulnerability resided not in the size of Soviet weapons but rather in the accuracy and number of the warheads.

While these arguments point to important problems, it should be remembered that vulnerability derives not only from a MIRVed and highly accurate attacking force, but also from the sheer blackmail potential of over-abundant heavy Soviet missiles and their excessive concentration of warheads. At reduced Soviet levels under START, and assuming American maintenance of 500 ICBM launchers, the ratio of Soviet warheads to American ICBMs could remain about the same—a favorable 5:1 for them. While START would not reduce the favorable Soviet ratio, the acquisition of a matching American counterforce threat, perhaps fortified by Launch on Warning (LOW) status (undesireably unstable) or BMD systems, might provide a symbolic counter to the Soviets heavy missile capability. In the power politics game between the superpowers, the perception of equality in such things as counterforce ability takes on as much importance as the deterrent value of second strike forces.

The Soviets objected to attempts to redress Soviet strategic advantages; to force Soviet adoption of American notions about strategic stability that highlighted American technological, SLBM, and bomber advantages; and to use "unacceptable" arms control proposals to delay negotiations until the U.S. completed the modernization of its nuclear forces. However, the Soviets know that in bargaining over START, as in past bargaining, proposals are made, compromises accepted, and advantages traded off. Consequently, despite various Soviet objections, they inched toward the American positions. This process accelerated after they became convinced that weapons like MX, Trident II, and the B-1 bomber were being fielded; that military appropriations added resources for new

American weaponry, research, and development (American breakthroughs in BMD, Stealth, and Cruise Missile technologies haunt the Soviets); and that prospects for superiority remained elusive, while prospects of an American-paced arms race were imminent. In addition, the Soviets may have felt constrained economically and hence more willing to participate seriously in START. Finally, since the Soviets have a remarkable history of successful bargaining with the U.S., they could look forward to wringing some concessions from the U.S. in the areas of BMD, cruise missiles, bombers, and FBS. While neither the Soviets nor the Americans have raced to offer concessions to produce START, both recently offered marginally more conciliatory START proposals, toned down accusations of insincerity, and expressed varying concern about the future of arms control and the ramifications of its collapse.

As of January 1988, the two sides have agreed to an overall ceiling of 6000 warheads and 1600 missile launchers and heavy bombers. In addition, progress has occurred in establishing subceilings for total warheads for land and sea-based ballistic missiles (4900), reducing ballistic missile throw-weight by 50% and cutting heavy missiles by 50%. The two sides remain apart on the issues of banning mobile missiles, limiting nuclear cruise missiles, and extending on-site inspections.

Perhaps due to a stalemate over SDI and START, Gorbachev opted to concentrate on INF negotiations. Ever since the 1979 NATO decision to deploy a counter to Soviet INF, the Soviets variously insisted on no U.S. deployment, a freeze on INF, and on compensations for U.S. FBS, Western technological edges, and French and British strategic forces. These demands bore so little fruit that Gorbachev abandoned them almost altogether in his post-Reykyvik campaign to seize the arms control initiative. Before evaluating the nature and purpose of this campaign, let us review the debate over INF in the context of NATO strategy.

Actually, problems concerning INF go back to the initial decades of NATO's existence when the United States withdrew its medium range nuclear forces (regarded as obsolete, given America's intercontinental retaliatory ability) while the Soviet Union began deploying large, land-based intermediate range ballistic missiles (IRBMs), the SS-4s and SS-5s. These limited range and inaccurate IRBMs posed only a limited threat since, in the 1950s and 1960s, deterrence in this theater depended upon persuading the Soviets that any attack on Western Europe would automatically provoke American strategic retaliation. As long as America had nuclear superiority, its promise to incorporate NATO under its nuclear umbrella retained high credibility. However, as this capacity eroded, Western Europeans increasingly speculated about the relability of the American commitment to defend them. The West Germans, in particular, requested more tangible evidence than the mere presence of American troops in Europe.

The traditional way to "couple" American and European defense lay in guaranteeing an American nuclear response to Soviet aggression. The more likely the response, the less the Soviet temptation to initiate a conflict that might escalate into even a "limited" war in Europe. The 1979 NATO decision to deploy INF represented one additional way to meet the requirement of "coupling." As Barry Blechman pointed out,

> Deployment of the American missiles in Europe, it was agreed, would provide an intermediate option, making it possible for the United States to respond to the SS-20 without resorting to its central forces, presumably a less difficult step. It was recognized, of course, that the Soviets would likely react to attacks against their territory, regardless of their origin, by attacking U.S. territory, thereby precipitating a full exchange in any event. But this was the main point. Since all parties would recognize that the full escalation spiral would be facilitated by deployment of NATO missiles, Soviet leaders would be reluctant to undertake that first move—the conventional attack or even the political act which made conventional war likely. Thus, by making the U.S. strategic commitments more credible, deployment of Pershing IIs and GLCMs was intended to strengthen NATO's ability to deter even modest moves towards war in Europe.[44]

Kissinger added to this point about deliberately creating the impression of the automaticity of the American response when he noted that the Soviets could not risk a conventional attack against Europe without first taking out NATO's INF to preclude their use against Soviet command centers. In addition, the Soviet Union "could not seek to destroy the missiles in Europe while leaving our strategic arsenal in America unimpaired for a possible strike against Soviet intercontinental ballistic missiles. Far from giving us the possibility of separating the nuclear defense of Europe from that of the United States, intermediate-range missiles in Europe indissolubly link the two."[45]

The Soviets, of course, objected to any raising of the ante in Western Europe. According to Garthoff, the Soviets *required* INF to counter NATO nuclear forces; *considered* the SS-20 a necessary replacement for their obsolete, vulnerable, and inaccurate IRBMs; and *argued* that the SS-20, which was entirely compatible with SALT I and II and which entailed the stabilizing characteristics of mobility, reliability, invulnerability, and lower throw-weight, contributed to deterrence.[46] Most importantly, it deprived NATO of INF superiority. The latter was especially important to the Soviets who, according to Garthoff, suspected that the NATO INF initiative demonstrated an American desire to achieve military superiority and the capability to launch counterforce first strikes against the Soviet Union, to circumvent SALT II limitations, and to keep war off American territory.[47]

This description of Soviet purposes and assumptions provides useful insight into possible Soviet motivations, but it downplays several important considerations. For example, the Soviet insistence that the several hundred strategic British and French weapons threatened a first strike against the Soviet Union and provided incentive for Soviet IRBMs strains credulity. The West rejected this insistence for a number of reasons:

> First, most of these U.K. and French forces are not, in fact, intermediate-range...they are SLBM forces identical with Soviet and U.S. SLBM forces. Most of the remainder are nuclear-capable

aircraft. The Soviet predominance in intermediate-range, nuclear-capable systems in Europe is so great that there would be no justification for compensation to the Soviet Union for British and French nuclear forces even if they were under NATO command...

This Soviet demand is inappropriate in another way as well. The INF negotiations are bilateral negotiations between the U.S. and the U.S.S.R.; neither the United Kingdom nor France has authorized either the U.S. or the U.S.S.R. to negotiate on their behalf. On the contrary, they have stated their refusal to have their forces limited or compensated for in negotiations between us. From their standpoint, their nuclear forces are strategic; they represent their last line of defense in a potentially threatened position.[48]

While the Pershing II poses a theoretical first strike danger, if used against Soviet Command, Control, and Communication ($C^3$) centers, they are unlikely first strike weapons. To highlight their deterrent rather than offensive function, Christoph Bertram noted that "neither the cruise missiles, which require a flight time of two to three hours to reach their targets, nor the Pershing IIs, which are well below the quantitative levels required for an effective disarming strike against Soviet military installations, provide serious offensive options."[49]

The Soviet accusation about an American determination to use the INF as a way to deflect war from its territory also fails to carry much weight since the use of NATO INF would inevitably force escalation to total war. (See the discussion of "No First Use" (NFU) below.) Finally, with respect to the Soviet demand that European missiles and other FBS be taken into account in INF talks, this reflected their 1983 negotiating advantage—the Soviets had deployed over 350 SS-20s, compared with zero INF for NATO. As Robert W. Tucker caustically noted,

the major reason for Soviet opposition to the missiles is not that it challenges the principle of equality but that it challenges the inequality of the strategic relationship between the Soviet Union and Western Europe accentuated by the SS-20s. It does so because the consequences of this inequality must place increasing strain on the cohesiveness of the Atlantic alliance. Understandably, Moscow resists a change that would deprive it, if only in part, of the great advantage it has long enjoyed and one that has been strengthened in recent years.[50]

Soviet resistance to NATO deployment was not the only impediment. There were serious Western European questions about the deterrent value of these weapons that mixed with the recurrent fear of nuclear war and suspicion of American motives. First there was the problem inherent in NATO strategy ever since flexible response replaced massive retaliation and since superpower parity replaced American nuclear superiority—the credibility of the American promise of a nuclear response to a Soviet conventional attack. In acknowledging the increasing relevance of this consideration, former Secretary of Defense McNamara, who now advocates a NFU strategy for NATO, noted the contrasting nature of general and extended deterrence. On the one hand, the strategy of MAD deterred war because of the expectation that any war, including a limited war would inevitably escalate. But NATO relies on the threat to initiate nuclear war to extend deterrence to cover conventional or nuclear attacks against Western Europe. Proponents of NFU wondered how a threat with such suicidal consequences could be believed. McNamara concluded that, since even limited use of nuclear weapons would inevitably lead to total war, the threat of nuclear use via INF had lost credibility as a deterrent to Soviet conventional aggression.[51] Given this reality, according to No First Users, NATO planners should rely on conventional forces alone to deter conventional attacks.

Several problems with this analysis deserve attention. First, in trying to upgrade conventional capability and in promising no first use, NATO might persuade the Soviets that it would not resort to nuclear weapons in response to an attack. But, in doing so, NATO makes hypothetical Soviet planning for war in Europe a bit easier, in the sense that it reduces the risk to the Soviets in the nuclear dimension. Unfortunately, the strategy of NFU does little to impose a replacement risk in the conventional dimension. In addition, if the Soviets could count on the pledge of No First Use, this might make the prospects for conventional attack against a conventionally defended, but inferior, Western Europe more likely. Since a conventional war in Europe would be almost as deadly as nuclear war, a more suitable deterrent strategy would be to assure the Soviets that NATO would go to any lengths to deny the Soviets victory—even at the risk of mutual suicide. The more convinced the Soviets were of such a risk, made more likely by a First Use strategy and deployments consistent with that strategy, the less willing they might be to attack.

While this promise strains credulity, the strain derives from the perhaps inevitable incoherence in NATO doctrine, which includes the threat of flexible response and the resort to INF as a first step in the process of retaliation. The incoherence resides in the persistent paradox of extended deterrence: the best way to deter nuclear war is to make it suicidal if fought; but the best way to deter conventional attack is to make nuclear initiation, in retaliation, credible.[52] In other words, NATO defense depends on convincing the Soviet Union that alliance commanders might escalate to the use of INF and then American strategic nuclear forces, despite the irrationality of such a response. This strategy depends on pretense and bluff, as NATO planners assume that even the remote possibility of nuclear destruction deters more effectively than conventional deterrence and defense because of the high intensity of this threat.[53]

An equally important problem complicating NATO strategy and decisions to deploy INF concerned the differences between American and European views on East-West relations and extended deterrence. As Stanley Hoffmann pointed out recently, where the U.S. reverted to containment, Western Europeans maintained options on detente; where the U.S. wanted to face the Soviets globally, Europeans preferred a narrower geographic focus; where some in the U.S. emphasized increased conventional capability, most European officials encouraged

"First Use" threats; and where the Europeans and Americans first joined together in support of INF deployment for "coupling" and arms control purposes, some Western Europeans expressed reservations about American commitments to both of these purposes.[54] Hoffmann suggested several remedies for avoiding further exacerbation of the divisions in the alliance due to differences over strategy, policy, and style. He emphasized the responsibility of the American leaders to learn the differences

> ...between restoring America's strength and appearing bellicose; between extending their protection to our friends and taking over; between shedding illusions about arms control and seemingly shedding arms control altogether. (And they must) display greater sensitivity to European fears of war...(develop) a long term policy toward the U.S.S.R....(that avoids) the U.S. tendency to give everywhere priority to the Soviet threat and to want others to give it the same priority...(and) share more fully and far more equally the important military decisions—decisions not only on deployments, but on doctrine and the actual use of nuclear weapons.[55]

Most of this advice about the American attitude toward Europe and strategy is appropriate—especially when one considers the counterproductive results of Reagan's earlier discussion of limited nuclear war, Haig's reference to nuclear shots across the bow, American harping about European responsibility to shoulder more of the defense burden, and the recent Reagan decision to surpass SALT warhead limits. On the other hand, Hoffmann downplayed the dangers that the Soviets still pose in both the European and global context. While the Soviets face economic difficulties and fear the devastation of a general or European nuclear war, they also realize the vulnerability of a Western alliance torn by controversy over issues such as German rearmament, Multi-lateral Forces (MLF), the Neutron bomb, stockpiling of chemical weapons, and INF deployment. European hints of willingness to give in to Soviet demands in arms control negotiations highlighted these vulnerabilities. In addition, a greater American "sensitivity to the European fears of war" raises the spectre of previous fears of war and previous concessions that fostered American and European appeasement and disarmament policies in the 1930's. However, Reagan realizes the need to alleviate the European's fear that it is American weapons that are more destabilizing than Soviet ones, that the U.S. is looking to substitute Europe for an American battlefield, and that American firmness is a deliberate tactic to avoid agreement. Equally important, the U.S. and NATO must alert the public in the West to the fact that, while fear of nuclear war is logical, it is neither good policy nor the central issue. The central issues remain how best to prevent nuclear war and how to prevent the Soviets from exploiting Western fears.

NATO and the U.S. rely on nuclear deterrence and flexible response to prevent war. Occasionally the deterrent capacity needs patching and buttressing. INF deployment was one patch to close a gap opened in the European theater. While the Soviets objected to this counter to their SS-

20s, the decision of whether to, or where to, close the gap could not be based on what was acceptable to the Soviets. If, for example, the West had backed down in the face of Soviet decisions to abandon negotiations, this would have opened the door for Soviet manipulation of the negotiation process. In addition, if the West demonstrated vulnerability to internal pressures to accept Soviet demands, this would open the door even further. In the late 1970s and early 1980s the Western anti nuclear movement, and its supporters in left wing European parties provided a constant reminder to the Soviets of the open doors and exploitable divisions within NATO. Given the Western democracies' sensitivities to public opinion, the louder the rhetoric of anti-nuclear marchers, the more likely it is that Western governments will appease these groups via watered down defense budgets, offers of strategic concessions to the Soviets, and increasing maneuvers away from the U.S. With these demonstrations in mind, the Soviets tried to force the hand of the Reagan administration with their 1983 walk out of all the on-going arms control negotiations. When this failed to generate the hoped for freeze in INF deployments at unequal levels, Gorbachev unveiled a new bargaining tack.

The latest wrinkle in the INF shuffle erupted after Gorbachev's 1987 zero-zero proposal to reduce Long Range INF to zero (except for 100 warheads outside of Europe). Americans and their allies found themselves once again enmeshed in the dilemma of extended deterrence. On the one hand, the allies seek arms control in general and reductions in Soviet weapons that threaten Western Europe. On the other hand, a "denuclearized" Western Europe entails the frightening prospect of NATO facing a Soviet Union with conventional superiority without the deterrent bite of flexible response. The Europeans and the Americans, patently unwilling (and possibly unable) to purchase an equivalent conventional capability and influenced by publics eager for arms control, diminishing defense budget, and detente, would encounter considerable opposition to defense and deterrent oriented remedies to a conventional imbalance and nuclear nakedness. Attempts to install and/or modernize shorter range (40-300 mile) tactical nuclear weapons, increase reliance on French and British strategic forces, transfer INF forces to sea or air-based systems, or improve and expand conventional forces would be no more acceptable to many Europeans than they would be to the Soviets.

The Soviets, of course, seek different objectives than NATO. Gorbachev, with considerable flair, daring, and initiative, seeks to realize a number of long-standing Soviet objectives in the INF negotiations: 1) to reduce the burden of Soviet defense spending, 2) to exploit divisions among Europeans over the best way to deal with the Soviet Union (and the U.S.), 3) to influence Western public opinion to see the Soviets as less threatening than the U.S. and yet maintain the "healthy" European fear of provoking the Soviets, and 4) to undermine NATO deterrent strategies and capabilities. To orchestrate the elimination of long and short range INF, with the logical next step being the elimination of tactical nuclear weapons, would provide a great strategic coup for Gorbachev, who in one or two fell swoops could remove NATO's counter to Soviet conventional superiority. To achieve this, while at the same time receiving the mantle of peacemaker, would represent an even greater political coup. (Recent European polls in Britain and Germany indicate that majorities of respondents see the U.S. as slightly more likely to start a nuclear war than the Soviet Union and Gorbachev as doing more for arms control than Reagan.)

Perhaps some of these rewards for the Soviets are worth the cost to those who desire agreements that actually reduce weapons (the Soviets pledged to abandon 1300 warheads compared to a 300 cut in U.S. warheads.) While NATO faces INF cuts, it would retain thousands of tactical nuclear weapons and the possibility of resolving conventional force disparities through Soviet conventional cuts to be negotiated in the future. If the Soviets seriously embrace the idea of domestic economic priorities and rapprochement in Western Europe, then an agreement over INF would represent a bonus for both sides. Unfortunately things are not always as clear as they seem—hence the never say die controversy within NATO about how and what to negotiate with the Soviets.

The allies, in their multi-headed and multi-thumbed way, agree in principle about the value of eliminating INF, especially since they created the zero option in the first place. However, the West Germans fear, again and always, becoming (remaining) a potential battleground where "only" short range tactical nuclear weapons might be used. The French and the British worry about the potential impact of a de-nuclearized Europe on the U.S. commitment to defend Europe. However, Reagan, who would not object to the Europeans assuming more of the costs for their defense, hesitated to forego a treaty with the Soviets based on the zero option he proposed in 1982. Hard-liner Richard Perle supported the Soviet version of the zero option because it forces greater cuts in Soviet than American weapons and because it validated his argument that a tough U.S. bargaining stance would convince the Soviets to respond with appropriate compromises. And compromise they did.

The breakthrough on an INF treaty (INFT) began with the 1985 and 1986 Reagan-Gorbachev summits, during which they agreed in principle to INF reductions exclusive of French and British strategic systems, and to reductions in Short Range INF (SRINF). In December 1987, Reagan and Gorbachev signed an INFT that will eliminate all Soviet and U.S. INF with a range of 500-5500 kilometers (about 300-3400 miles). The treaty also bans production and flight testing of INF and facilities for their deployment, storage, repair, and production. (See Chart below for specific figures.) The treaty codifies Reagan's zero-option and removes a class of weapons in which the Soviets hold a clear advantage. The treaty does not affect the 4000 or so nuclear warheads on American FBS, including nuclear-capable aircraft, short range missiles, and NATO-dedicated SLBMs. Nor does it include limits on British and French nuclear forces. The most dramatic and unprecedented aspect of the treaty lies in the verification provisions. Each party will be allowed access to on-site inspections of missile sites (128 in the Soviet bloc) and production facilities for up to 13 years after the treaty enters into force.

## Proposed INF Treaty

|  | United States | Soviet Union |
|---|---|---|
| What will be eliminated | | |
| Deployed Missiles | | |
| Intermediate Range (600-3,400 miles) | 429 | 470 |
| Short Range (300-600 Miles) | 0 | 387 |
| Non-deployed Missiles | | |
| Intermediate Range | 260 | 356 |
| Short Range | 170 | 539 |
| Total | 859 | 1,752 |

Verification provisions
- Initial inspection 60 days after the treaty enters into force.
- Close-out inspections after three years to ensure that the missiles have been destroyed.
- 20 short-notice inspections in the first three years; 15 short-notice inspections in the next five years; and 10 short-notice inspections in the following five years.
- U.S. inspectors to be based at a Soviet military factory in Votkinsk for 13 years and Soviet inspectors to be based at a U.S. military factory in Utah for 13 years.

|  | United States | Soviet Union |
|---|---|---|
| What will remain | | |
| Strategic Nuclear Weapons | | |
| Launchers | 2,001 | 2,515 |
| Warheads | 13,002 | 10,595 |
| Nonstrategic Nuclear Weapons (warheads) | | |
| Land-based Battlefield Nuclear Weapons | 7,073 | 9,043 |
| Strategic Defensive Nuclear Warheads | - | 5,100 |
| Naval Battlefield Nuclear Weapons | 3,645 | 2,705 |
| Total (nonstrategic) | 10,718 | 16,848 |

Sources: U.S. Arms Control and Disarmament Agency, Natural Resources Defense Council, and *Wall Street Journal* (Dec. 9, 1987): 22.

Critics point to several flaws in the negotiation process, the treaty, and in the verification stipulations. First, critics worry that the Soviets exploited Reagan's domestic weakness in the wake of economic problems (high trade deficits and international debt, stock market crashes, and four years of defense budget declines since the peak of FY 1985), political setbacks (the Iran-Contra scandal, rising anti-Americanism in the third world *and* Europe, and congressional in-fighting over foreign and domestic policies ripe for attack in an election period), and military failures (failure to see American backed groups succeed, failure to retard the erosion of U.S. overseas military bases, and failure to calm the Persian Gulf war.) Given these problems and given Reagan's obvious eagerness for an arms control agreement, Gorbachev succeeded in capturing the initiative in the arms control process and in harvesting most of the credit for the initiative.

With respect to the INFT, critics maintain that it is not the masterstroke portrayed in the Western media. It limits Soviet missiles that have become obsolete (the SS-24s and on-line replacements for the SS-20s). The mobility of the SS-20s and SS-24s makes it almost impossible to know how many missiles and warheads there are and where they are. It forces greater NATO reliance on its less accurate sea-based and more vulnerable land-based delivery systems. And it raises again the question of decoupling. Finally, the scaled down nuclear commitment is unlikely to be buffered by improved conventional defense due to high costs and dissent among the Western European publics persuaded about the stabilizing impact of arms treaties and unconvinced of the dangers inherent in the inability of the West to counter overwhelming Soviet conventional superiority with Eurostrategic or conventional means.

Concern about these military and psychological considerations drive critics to question the value of the INFT. In a statement that repeats the arguments heard for INF deployment, Jeane Kirkpatrick argues that "because the Pershing IIs and Cruise Missiles are what the Soviets fear most, they have become the centerpiece in deterring Soviet moves against Europe and a symbol of U.S. commitment to the defense of Europe. Their removal has a symbolic as well as military significance."[56] Kissinger fears that "once our missiles are out of Europe, political conditions in the host country won't allow us to put them back, even if they put an SS-20 at the Brandenburg Gate."[57]

Despite the caution of previous detentists like Kissinger and despite the more rabid objections of the American Conservative Caucus which accused Reagan of being "a useful idiot for Soviet propaganda," most Americans (80% in one December 1987 poll) approve of the INFT. It is seen as a part of a revival of the overall arms control process that may well lead to a START agreement and perhaps even an agreement to limit, delay, or eliminate the SDI. Supporters dismiss the decoupling danger since the U.S. still extends deterrence through its nuclear-capable FBS, conventional forces in Europe, and its strategic nuclear forces. The INFT will enhance stability, since it will eliminate weapons that inspired first strike fears in the Soviet Union and that epitomized the "use them or lose them" dilemma for both sides.

They also note that while the treaty may be subject to violations, the Soviets would have little incentive to cheat, since they couldn't test "hidden" missiles without revealing their whereabouts. If they couldn't test them, they couldn't remain confident about their reliability. Supporters also doubt the Soviet need to cheat, since Soviet strategic nuclear forces already cover all targets previously under double coverage with the SS-20. Finally, supporters remind us that the whole impetus of Western INF deployments derived from a Western concern about the psychologically intimidating projection of the Soviet threat embodied in the SS-20. The INFT will eliminate the intimidation value of this weapon, and a few or many SS-20s kept in hiding would not serve this purpose.

While the treaty resolves the SS-20 crisis and nurtures hopes for a follow-up START treaty, the nagging questions of NATO strategy remain the same: how to deter a nuclear and conventional attack without upsetting the military balance, bankrupting NATO economies, and jeopardizing the prospects for detente. The allies remain concerned that the strategy of flexible response—to deter by threat of nuclear retaliation and the risk of escalation—may finally be toppled by the renewed Soviet strategy of de-nuclearizing Europe. While NATO, under the treaty, would retain thousands of battlefield warheads, these may not qualify as deterrent weapons. Their most likely use would be *after war began;* i.e., after deterrence failed! U.S. strategic nuclear forces could threaten the Soviets in the event of movements toward conventional hostilities. However, they also seem unqualified as weapons of extended deterrence, due to the incredibility of their use in the context of a conflict that might well be limited to conventional war in Europe. As Christoph Bertram aptly reminds us, "once the systems in the middle spectrum of the nuclear arsenal are removed, NATO is left with weapons on both extremes—very short-range or strategic—which instead suggest to an attacker that he may either succeed in keeping nuclear war geographically limited or in avoiding a nuclear riposte altogether...The process under way is one of 'de-deterring' (not denuclearization), and this is dangerous for Western security."[58]

To avoid this fate will require patient, long-range, and hard-nosed thinking and actions by NATO. The West must not rush to agreements without providing safeguards in terms of verification procedures. It must re-take the initiative and identify for itself and the Soviets what it considers the prerequisites for a stabilizing and self-perpetuating arms control agenda. To the extent it can agree on how to realize these objectives and persuade Western publics to accept the costs as well as the benefits of flexible response, to that extent it may both deter aggression and pave the way for East-West detente.

But it takes two to tango. So far Gorbachev appears to be the more nimble dancer since his entry into the arms control business in 1985. He offered testing moratoriums, qualified on-site inspections, bans on BMD and the "militarization of space," 50% reductions in "nuclear charges," resolution of the 17 year old stalemate over the MBFR, hints of withdrawal from Afghanistan and even Berlin, and so on, in an inspired Western-oriented public relations blitz. A generally receptive West looks to Reagan for appropriately accommodating responses. Reagan himself is more eager than ever to reach accords with the Soviets. He is well past his earlier knee-jerk aversion to the very concept of arms control, which was reminiscent of the attitude of the "hero" in *Rebel Without a Cause* who when asked, "What kind of rebel are you," responded "Whata ya got?"

## Conclusion: The Hurrier I Go, the Behinder I Get

This discussion of various arms control treaties and proposals points to one of the central problems for the Reagan administration: how to sustain an effective deterrent in the midst of intermittent arms races, fiscal constraints, controversy over nuclear and NATO strategy, and criticism from anti-nuclear advocates. Reagan's determination to provide the funding, equipment, and leadership necessary to overcome these problems, although blunted by cuts in defense appropriations, bans on testing, demands for compliance with SALT II and a narrow interpretation of the ABMT, and the administration's sometimes inarticulate instructions on strategic conceptualizations and its waffling on issues such as the desirability of mobile ICBMs and basing modes for the MX, reflects his concern for maintaining the requirements of strategic deterrence. Despite constant rear guard action shoring up support for defense and deterrent imperatives, and despite temporary setbacks like the 1983 Soivet walkout, the administration refused to allow the Soviets to dictate the terms, timetables, and topics to be negotiated. Although Gorbachev successfully seized the arms control initiative in 1986-7, several of his proposals reflected concessions in line with previous U.S. demands. In addition, they came despite previous insistence that no negotiations would take place if the U.S. deployed INF, proceeded with SDI, or failed to link negotiations over offensive, defensive, theater, and ASAT weapons.

Reagan also refused to acquiesce to the alleged Soviet disregard for some of the obligations under the SALT and ABM agreements. He advocated a "proportionate response" to Soviet violations, including the implementation of his strategic modernization program and the continuation of support for the SDI research program. According to Reagan,

> It is absolutely essential that we maintain full support for these programs. To fail to do so would be the worst response to Soviet noncompliance. It would immediately and seriously undercut our negotiators in Geneva by removing the leverage that they must have to negotiate equitable reductions in both U.S. and Soviet forces. It would send precisely the wrong signal to the leadership of the Soviet Union about the seriousness of our resolve concerning their noncompliance. And it would significantly increase the risk to our security for years to come. Therefore, our highest priority must remain the full implementation of these programs.[59]

However, the administration's challenge lies not only in demonstrating true grit, but also in offering true concessions. An administration successful in establishing a hard line reputation remains a partial failure if its style and rhetoric create formidable barriers to successful negotiations with the Soviets. If the Soviets believe Reagan when he talks tough, but fail to believe his arms control overtures and promises, the U.S. is no better off than if the reverse were true. While it is necessary to convince the Soviets of the American ability to stay the course, through military spending, coherent strategic formulations, and demonstrations of political will, this must be accomplished within a framework of containment and deterrence rather than liberation and compellence. The ability of the administration to maintain the prerequisites of an effective deterrent without renewing the arms race, depends on its success in persuading the Soviet Union that American strength, designed to resist its expansion and exploitation of its military position, does not threaten Soviet security.

Reagan's arms control proposals, across the board support for military spending, and fascination with the prospect of replacing MAD with deterrence based on BMD are intended to buttress deterrence and yet reassure the Soviets that the U.S. poses no first strike threat. As such, his proposals flow from traditional American approaches to the Soviet Union, arms control, and nuclear strategy. We might appreciate the similarities more fully after a review of the evolution in American nuclear strategy that follows in the next chapter.

# REFERENCES

[1]Kissinger, *American Foreign Policy* (New York: Norton, 1974): 143-4.

[2]See International Institute of Strategic Studies (IISS), *The Military Balance,* for annual figures on the military balance. See also Donald G. Brennan, "The Soviet Military Build-up and Its Implications for the Negotiations on Strategic Arms Limitations," *Orbis* (Spring 1977): 107-120.

[3]Van Cleave, "Political and Negotiating Asymmetries: Insult in SALT I," in Robert L. Pfaltzgraff, Jr., ed., *Contrasting Approaches to Arms Control,* (Lexington, Mass.: Lexington Books, 1974): 15.

[4]Van Cleave, "Political and Negotiating Asymmetries: Insult in SALT I," 16.

[5]Kissinger, Briefing, (June 15, 1972): 153.

[6]Nixon, *U.S. Foreign Policy for the 1970s: Shaping a Durable Peace,* Report to Congress, May 3, 1973, Department of State Bulletin *(DOSB)* (June 4, 1973): 734.

[7]Nixon, Report in *DOSB* (June 4, 1973): 735.

[8]Kissinger, Statement, U.S. Congress, Senate Committee on Foreign Relations, *Detente* 93rd Cong., 2nd sess., (1974): 239, 247-248.

[9]Kissinger, Briefing, (June 15, 1972): 144.

[10]Van Cleave, "Political and Negotiating Asymmetries: Insult in SALT I," 51-52.

[11]Schlesinger, *Annual Defense Department Report FY 1975* (Washington: Government Printing Office (GPO), 1975): 32-45; and *Annual Defense Department Report FY 1976* (Washington: (GPO, 1976): II-12.

[12]Schlesinger, *Annual Defense Department Report FY 1986,* p. II-2.

[13]Panofsky, "Arms Control: Necessary Process," *Bulletin of Atomic Scientists* 42 (March 1986): 36.

[14]See Richard Pipes, "Detente and Reciprocity," in George R. Urban, ed., *Detente* (New York: Universe Books, 1976): 174-197; and Uri Ra'anan, "The Changing American-Soviet Strategic Balance," U.S. Congress, Senate, Subcommittee on National Security and International Operations, Committee on Government Operations, *International Negotiation,* 92nd Cong., 2nd Sess., 1976.

[15]Statement by Van Cleave, U.S. Congress, Senate, Subcommittee on National Security and International Operations, Committee on Government Operations, *International Negotiation,* Part 7, 92nd Cong., 2nd Sess., (1972): 200.

[16]Speech by Harold Brown, reprinted in *DOSB* 79, #2026, (May 1979): 53.

[17]See Pipes, "Detente and Reciprocity;" and Ra'anan, "The Changing American-Soviet Strategic Balance."

[18]See Strobe Talbott. *Endgame: The Inside Story of SALT II* (New York, 1979); Van Cleave, "Political and Negotiating Asymmetries: Insult in SALT I," and Thomas Wolfe. *The Salt Experience* (Cambridge: Ballinger, 1979).

[19]Colin S. Gray, "Soviet-American Strategic Competition," in Robert J. Pranger and Roger P. Labrie, *Nuclear Strategy and National Security* (Washington: American Enterprise Institute, 1977): 297; Source: *Long-Range U.S.-U.S.S.R. Competiton-National Security Implications,* National Security Affairs Conference, Washington, (October 1976): 36-53.

[20]For Soviet views on nuclear war see A.A. Grechko, *Armed Forces of the Soviet State* (Moscow: Voyenizdat, 1973); V.D. Sokolovski, *Soviet Military Strategy*, 3rd ed., Harriet F. Scott, ed., (New York: Crane, Russak, 1975), and *Communist of the Armed Forces*, November 1975; trans. in *Soviet World Outlook*, (February 13, 1976): 7; According to this work:

> The premise of Marxism-Leninism on war as a continuation of policy by military means remains true in an atmosphere of fundamental changes in military matters. The attempt of certain bourgeois ideologists to prove that nuclear missile weapons lead war outside of the framework of policy and that nuclear war moves beyond the control of policy, ceases to be an instrument of policy, and does not constitute its continuation is theoretically incorrect and politically reactionary...

For the other side of the picture see Lt. Gen. Mikhail Milshtein's interview in the *International Herald Tribune* (August 28, 1980), in which he stated that the Soviet Union "will never use nuclear weapons unless an aggressor uses them first," that nuclear weapons "are not weapons with which you can achieve foreign policy goals," that some points in Sokolovski's book "have certainly grown obsolete," and that it "is simply not true" that "Soviet military doctrine proclaims the acceptability of nuclear war, calls for efforts to achieve victory in such a way, or prepares for delivery of the first strike." For a similar "clarification" see 'Visily Kulish, "Detente, International Relations, and Military Might," *Coexistence* 14 #2, (1978): 175-195.

[21]Leon Goure, et. al., *War, Survival and Soviet Strategy* (Miami: Center for Advanced Int'l. Studies, 1976).

[22]A. Trofimenko, "Political Realism and the Realistic Deterrence' Strategy," *USA: Economy, Politics, Ideology,* #12, p. 2, Moscow, 1971; General S.L. Sokolov, "Our Revolution Knows How to Defend Itself," *Sovetskaya Rossiya,* (February 23, 1971): 1; 'Colonel S.A. Tyushkhevich, *Marxism-Leninism on War and Army,* in Van Cleave, "Soviet Doctrine & Strategy," Los Alamos Discussion (Unclassified paper), 1975, p. 4; Andrei Gromyko, *Kommunist,* September 1975, trans. in FBIS Daily Report (Soviet Union, (October 22, 1975): R16; and D. Preoktor, "Military Detente—A Paramount Task," *Mezhdunarodnaya Zhizn* #5, April 20, 1976, in *FBIS* Daily Report (Soviet Union), (June 9, 1976): A9.

[23]Jacquelyn K. Davis, et. al., *SALT II and U.S.-Soviet Strategic Forces,* (Cambridge: Institute for Foreign Policy Analysis, June 1979): 9.

[24]James E. Dornan, Jr., "A Strategic Symposium: SALT and U.S. Defense Policy," *Washington Quarterly* (Winter 1979): 64-5.

[25]Dornan, 65.

[26]Davis, et. al., 9-10.

[27]*Strategic Arms Limitation Talks,* Department of State: Special Report 46 (Revised), (May 1979): 11-12.

[28]Davis, et. al., 41-17.

[29]Cyrus R. Vance, "SALT II: Summation," in *Current Policy* #96, pp. 1-2; and Special Report 46 (Revised), p.9.

[30]*Countdown on SALT II* (Washington: Arms Control Association, 1985): 6-9.

[31]*Countdown on SALT II,* 1-10.

[32]Dornan, "A Strategic Symposium: SALT and U.S. Defense Policy," 69.

[33]Gray, "A Strategic Symposium: SALT and U.S. Defense Policy," *Washington Quarterly* (Winter 1970): 80-82.

[34]Pipes, "Nuclear Weapons Policy Questioned," *Aviation Week* (November 6, 1977): 62-63.

[35]Schlesinger, *Annual Defense Department Report FY 1975,* 32-45; and *Annual Defense Department Report FY 1976,* II-2 and II-12.

[36]Weinberger, August 1982 letter to U.S. Newspapers.

[37]Gray, "'Dangerous to Your Health': The Debate Over Nuclear Strategy and War," *Orbis* (Summer 1982): 339-340.

[38]Garthoff, *Perspectives on the Strategic Balance,* (Washington: Brookings, 1983): 15.

[39]Reagan, address to the Los Angeles World Affairs Conference, March 31, 1983.

[40]Shultz, "Arms Control, Strategic Stability, and Global Stability," in *Current Policy* 50 (October 14, 1985): 2.

[41]Eugene Rostow, address to Los Angeles World Affairs Conference, in *Current Policy* 425. (Sept. 10, 1982): 2.

[42]Shultz, "Arms Control, Strategic Stability, and Global Stability," 3.

[43]Jan M. Lodal, "Finishing START," *Foreign Policy* (Fall 1982): 70.

[44]Barry M. Blechman, "Is There a Conventional Defense Option?" *Washington Quarterly* (Summer 1982): 60.

[45]Kissinger, "Nuclear Weapons and the Peace Movement," *Washington Quarterly* (Summer 1982): 34.

[46]Garthoff, "The Soviet SS-20 Decision," *Survival* (May/June 1983): 112-113.

[47]Garthoff, "The Soviet SS-20 Decision," 114-117.

[48]Rostow, *Current Policy*, 2.

[49]Christoph Bertram, "Implications of Theater Nuclear Weapons in Europe," *Foreign Affairs* (Winter 1981/82): 309.

[50]Robert W. Tucker, "Rough Equality is Crucial," *New York Times* (April 8, 1983): 29.

[51]McNamara, "The Military Role of Nuclear Weapons," *Foreign Affairs* (Fall 1983): 71-72.

[52]Betts, "Compound Deterrence vs. No-First-Use: What's Wrong Is What's Right," *Orbis* (Winter 1985): 706.

[53]Betts, 701.

[54]Stanley Hoffmann, "NATO and Nuclear Weapons," *Foreign Affairs* (Winter 1981/82): 331-333.

[55]Hoffmann, 341-344.

[56]Jeane Kirkpatrick, "Good Intentions Aside, INF Will Be Chilling to Europe," *Los Angeles Times* (October 11, 1987): Part V, page 5.

[57]Kissinger, quoted in *Wall Street Journal* (December 2, 1987): 15.

[58]Bertram, "Europe's Security Dilemmas," *Foreign Affairs* 65 (Summer 1987): 952.

[59]Reagan, "Statement on Interim Restraint" in *Current Policy* (May 27, 1986): 2.

# BIBLIOGRAPHY

## Arms Control

Adelman, Kenneth L. "Arms Control With and Without Agreements," *Foreign Affairs* 63 (Winter 1984-85): 240-263.

Bertram, Christoph, ed. *Beyond SALT II.* London: IISS, 1978.

Brown, Harold and Davis, Lynn E. "Nuclear Arms Control: Where Do We Stand?" *Foreign Affairs* 62 (Summer 1984): 1145-1160.

Bull, Hedley, *The Control of the Arms Race.* London: Weidenfeld & Nicolson, 1961.

Chayes, Abram and Wiesner, Jerome, ed. *ABM: An Evaluation of the Decision to Deploy an Anti-Ballistic Missile System.* New York: Harper & Row, 1969.

Garthoff, Raymond. "The Prospects Offered by Gorbachev," *Arms Control Today* 16 (January-February 1986): 3-5.

"Salt I: An Evaluation," *World Politics* 31 (October 1978): 1-25.

Hanrieder, Wolfram F. ed. *Technology, Strategy, and Arms Control.* Boulder: Westview, 1985.

Horelick, Arnold. "U.S.-Soviet Relations: The Return to Arms Control," *Foreign Affairs, America and the World 1984* 63 (1984): 511-537.

Lodal, Jan M. "SALT II and American Security," *Foreign Affairs* 57 (Winter 1978-79): 246-268.

Luttwak, Edward. "Is There an Arms Race? *Washington Quarterly* 2 (Winter 1979): 82-87.

Mandelbaum, Michael. "Uncertainty of the Status Quo," *Bulletin of the Atomic Scientists* 7 (August 1985): 131-135.

Newhouse, John. *Cold Down: The Story of SALT.* New York: Holt, Rinehart, 1973.

Podhoretz, Norman. "Appeasement by Any Other Name," *Commentary*, (July 1983): 25-38.

Salter, Stephen H. "Stopping the Arms Race: A Modest Proposal," *Issues in Science and Technology*, (Winter 1986): 74-82.

Schelling, Thomas C. "What Went Wrong with Arms Control?" *Foreign Affairs*, (Winter 1985): 219-232.

Sienkiewicz, Stanley. "SALT and Soviet Doctrine," *International Security* 2 (Spring 1978): 84-100.

Sigal, Leon V. "Warming to the Freeze," *Foreign Policy* 48 (Fall 1982): 54-65.

Steinbruner, John. "Arms and the Art of Compromise," *Brookings Review*, (Summer 1983): 6-13.
"U.S. and Soviet Security Perspectives," *Bulletin of the Atomic Scientists* 7 (August 1985): 89-93.

Voas, Jeanette. "The Arms-Control Compliance Debate," *Survival* (January-February 1986): 8-31.

Willrich, Mason, and Rhinelander, John B. *SALT: The Moscow Agreements and Beyond.* New York: Free Press, 1974.

# NATO, Europe

Betts, Richard K. "Compound Deterrence vs. No-First-Use: What's Wrong is What's Right," *Orbis*, (Winter 1985): 697-719.
"Cruise Missiles: Technology, Strategy, Politics," *Washington Quarterly* 4 (Winter 1981): 66-80.

Bundy, McGeorge et. al. "Nuclear Weapons and the Atlantic Alliance," *Foreign Affairs* 60 (Spring 1982): 753-768.

Cosgrave, Patrick and Richey, George. *NATO's Strategy: A Case of Outdated Priorities?* London: Institute for European Defense and Strategic Studies, 1985.

Dean, Jonathan. "Beyond First Use," *Foreign Policy* 48 (Fall 1982): 37-53.

Draper, Theodore. "The Western Misalliance," *Washington Quarterly* 4 (Winter 1981): 13-69.

Freedman, Lawrence. "Limited War, Unlimited Protest," *Orbis* 26 (Spring 1982): 89-103.

Gallois, Pierre Marie. *Soviet Military Doctrine and European Deterrence: NATO's Obsolete Concepts.* London: Institute for the Study of Conflict, 1978.

Garthoff, Raymond L. "The Soviet SS-20 Decision," *Survival*, May-June 1983, 110-119.

Haseler, Stephen. "The Euromissile Crisis," *Commentary* 75 (May 1983): 28-32.

Hassner, Pierre. "Western European Perceptions of the USSR," *Daedalus*, (Winter 1979): 113-150.

Holloway, David and Sharp, Jane M.O., ed. *The Warsaw Pact: Alliance in Transition?* Ithaca: Cornell University Press, 1984.

Joffe, Josef. "Europe's American Pacifier," *Foreign Policy* 54 (Spring 1984): 64-82.

Joshua, Wynfred. "Soviet Manipulation of the European Peace Movement," *Strategic Review*, (Winter 1983): 9-18.

Kaiser, Karl et. al. "Nuclear Weapons and the Preservation of Peace: A German Response," *Foreign Affairs* 60 (Summer 1982): 1157-1170.

Kaldor, Mary. "Beyond the Blocs: Defending Europe the Political Way," *World Policy Journal* 1 (Fall 1983): 1-22.

Lellouche, Pierre, "Does NATO Have a Future? A European View," *Washington Quarterly* (Summer 1982): 40-52.

Luttwak, Edward N. "How to Think About Nuclear War," *Commentary* 74 (August 1982): 21-28.

Mearsheimer, John J. *Conventional Deterrence.* Ithaca: Cornell University Press, 1983. "Nuclear Weapons and Deterrence in Europe," *International Security* 9 (Winter 1984-85): 19-46.

Nerlich, Uwe. "Change in Europe: A Secular Trend?" *Daedulus,* (Winter 1981): 71-103.

Osgood, Robert E. *Alliances and American Foreign Policy.* Baltimore: Johns Hopkins University Press, 1968.

Rogers, Bernard W. "The Atlantic Alliance: Prescriptions for a Difficult Decade," *Foreign Affairs* 60 (Summer 1982): 1145-1156.

Serfaty, Simon. "Atlantic Fantasies," *Washington Quarterly* 5 (Summer 1982): 74.

Sigal, Leon V. *Nuclear Forces in Europe: Enduring Dilemmas, Present Prospect.* Washington D.C.: Brookings Institute, 1984.

Sommer, Theo. "Europe and the American Connection," *Foreign Affairs,* (1979 Review Issue): 622-636.

Steinbruner, John D. and Segal, Leon V. *Alliance Security: NATO and No First Use.* Washington D.C.: Brookings Institute, 1983.

Vogel, Heinrich. "Western Security and the Eastern Bloc Economy," *Washington Quarterly* 7 (Spring 1984): 42-49.

Yost, David S. "European-American Relations and NATO's Initial Missile Deployments," *Current History* 83 (April 1984): 145-148.

# CHAPTER V
# Evolution of Strategy:
# Do We Want to Be MAD?

## Deterrence and Defense

Ever since man first took up arms against his fellow man the problems of defense, deterrence, and diplomacy have occupied the attention of war-planners, war-fighters, and war-avoiders. How to defend one's self and deter one's enemies took on apocalyptic proportions in the nuclear age. Distinctions between these two related objectives, and the types of weapons appropriate for their success, have been enumerated, debated, and misunderstood. To understand the distinctions (or similarities), and to evaluate American efforts at deterring a nuclear attack, we need to review the debates over American nuclear strategy since 1945. Such a review also places the strategic priorities of Reagan into historical perspective. His recipe for deterrence based on defensive, rather than offensive, threats brings to full circle the evolution in strategic thought from massive defense (pre-W.W. II), to threats of massive retaliation, and to a preference for deterrence based on BMD, damage limitation and the ability to deny the enemy victory in a nuclear war.

To review and compare past and present strategies and preferences, we must first define deterrence. Unfortunately, the almost mystical concept of deterrence defies easy description, although this ancient term of psychology, bargaining, and the military arts and sciences has been the subject of almost every book, article, and official document on defense since the 1940s. Although this chapter can not provide excerpts from all of the best and brightest of those who study the phenomena of nuclear deterrence, perhaps it can display a representative few who set the scene for two competing strands of thought that contributed to the development of a rather schizophrenic American nuclear strategy that still encompasses the often contradictory requirements of massive retaliation and flexible response, deterrence and defense, punishment and prevention.

Bernard Brodie, a premier figure in the early post-war literature, defined deterrence as a threat of retaliation that depended upon the preservation of striking power under attack for its credibility.[1] Herman Kahn, who often criticized Brodie and who believed that superiority in the ability to execute massive retaliation deterred the best, distinguished between minimum, workable, adequate, reliable, stark, and absolute deterrence. In a controversial book reflecting his research at RAND, he argued that there also existed a crucially important distinction between deterrence and denial or defense:

Deterrence prevents an enemy from doing something by making him fear the consequences that will follow. The prevention, therefore, is psychological, although it may make use of physical or material factors. Denial involves putting a "Physical" barrier in the way of the enemy. A denial policy or capability may contribute to a deterrence policy or capability, and vice versa...Despite the interrelation, the distinction is a real one.[2]

Harvard's Thomas Schelling, who drew on analogies from criminal law, child psychology, and game theory, suggested that deterrence concerned exploiting potential force, "persuading a potential enemy that he should in his own interest avoid certain courses of activity...and influencing the choices that another party will make...by influencing his expectations of how we will behave. It involves confronting him with evidence for believing that our behavior will be determined by his behavior."[3] Glenn Snyder took up these themes of threat and persuasion when he defined deterrence as a means of "discouraging an enemy from taking military action by posing for him the prospect of cost and risk which outweighs his prospective gain" and working "on the enemy's intentions" to reduce "the likelihood of enemy military moves."[4] Snyder highlighted the importance of credibility, since deterrence depended largely on the "opponent's degree of confidence that one intends to fulfill (one's) threat."

As the U.S. and the Soviet Union improved their ability to execute mass destruction over the years and as they lived through decades of mortal threat, absolute vulnerability, and dependence on the other's patience and rationality, there developed a subtle, but mutually reinforcing confidence in the oddly constructed sturdiness of a "balance of terror." This confidence still characterizes contemporary deterrent relations, wherein neither the U.S. nor the Soviet Union dares to risk nuclear war because of the awareness of the suffering to be imposed on the "winner" of a nuclear war because the "winning" side cannot assure victory against retaliation.[5] Schelling, who viewed deterrence as a consequence of prudence rather than terror, recently suggested the following comfortable analogy: "People regularly stand at the curb watching trucks, buses and cars hurtle past at speeds that guarantee injury and threaten death if they so much as attempt to cross against the traffic. They are absolutely deterred. But there is no fear. They just know better."[6] Even those opposed in principle to reliance on nuclear threat and vulnerability, accept the evidence that fear, prudence, or just knowing better seem to have been largely responsible for forty years of "peace" between the superpowers. They question, however, the elevation of this condition to the status of desirable strategy and the assumption of its perpetual or immortal deterring power.

These definitions and explanations, raise more questions than they answer about the dynamics of deterrence. How do we deter or compel actions? How do we make the deterrent threat credible and stabilizing? How do the Soviets view deterrence? And, which of them do we listen to—the officially sanctioned military writers of the 1950s and 1960s who referred to the necessity of superiority, war-fighting capabilities, and preemption in crisis or party leaders who, when negotiating arms agreements with the West, highlighted their perception of the inevitability of nuclear catastrophe in the event of war between the U.S. and the Soviet Union? These questions depend on one other issue: the problem of perceptions. Robert Jervis emphasized the overriding, but often neglected, importance of understanding the other side's intentions and fears in order to determine the most effective deterrent. He concluded that decision makers "err both in their estimates of what the other side intends by its behavior and in their beliefs about how the other is reading their behavior. Severe limits are thus placed on the statesman's ability to determine whether and what kind of deterrence strategy is called for and to influence the other's perceptions in a way in which will allow this strategy to succeed."[7]

Western (and Soviet) officials, strategists, scientists, and philosophers have grappled inconclusively with these problems of strategy and perception for over forty years. Their arguments and government policies have created an interesting history of American deterrent options from the threat of massive retaliation during periods of its superiority, to a promise of flexible response and a mixture of countervalue and counterforce targeting, to an acceptance of MAD and population vulnerability, and finally to Reagan's house approach that insists on war-fighting and damage limitation options in case of deterrence failure.

In the following pages a panorama of American strategies and Soviet responses to them will be presented in a chronological, thematic, and hence somewhat redundant order. Perhaps the only uncontested fact in discussions over nuclear developments concerns the date the atomic age began—August 6, 1945 when, in one of the first ambiguous and disputed lessons of deterrence versus compellence, a nuclear power attacked a non-nuclear country in the midst of a conventional war. This immediately created some fundamental questions about the morality of nuclear threat and use, the relevance of technological advances, the relationship between delivery and basing modes to choices of weapons and targets, the value of symbolic "shots across the bow," distinctions between military and civilian targets, the desirability of avoiding decapitation (no atomic bombs on Tokyo), and the political and psychological impact of demonstrations of strength and resolve. American and Soviet strategists tried to formulate answers to these questions in a post-war period that witnessed an amorphous array of arcane and overlapping strategic orientations. (See chart 1 below for a skeletal outline of these semidistinct orientations and their major proponents.) The first strategies for survival, massive retaliation and graduated deterrence and their nascent replacements, dominated the American scene for over fifteen years.

# AMERICAN STRATEGIC ORIENTATIONS
## 1945—1988

| 1950s-1960s | 1950s | 1960s+ | 1960s+ | 1970s+ |
|---|---|---|---|---|
| *Massive Retaliation* | *Graduated Deterrence* | *Flexible Response* | *M.A.D.* | *Countervailing* |

**Strategic Orientations**

| 1950s-1960s | 1950s | 1960s+ | 1960s+ | 1970s+ |
|---|---|---|---|---|
| Strategic Air Command, strategic bombing | tactical nuclear superiority over conventional capability | SAC and ICBM invulnerability, nuclear weapons to deter strategic war, tactical weapons to deter or fight conventional war, improved conventional capability | emphasize countervalue targets, no BMD, arms control, parity | invulnerability, counterforce and countervalue weapons and targets, Flexible Response, Massive Retaliation, PD-59, and Strategic Defense |

**Major Architects**

| 1950s-1960s | 1950s | 1960s+ | 1960s+ | 1970s+ |
|---|---|---|---|---|
| Dulles Eisenhower | Dulles Eisenhower | McNamara | McNamara | Schlesinger Brown (Harold) Weinberger |

**Major Advocates**

| 1950s-1960s | 1950s | 1960s+ | 1960s+ | 1970s+ |
|---|---|---|---|---|
| Brodie Air Force | Brodie Kaufman Kahn Kissinger Schelling Wohlstetter RAND | Brodie Kaufman Kahn Kissinger Schelling Wohlstetter RAND Army | Betts Brodie Freedman Jervis Keeny Panofsky Quester Schelling Snyder Steinbruner Arms Control Association Brookings RAND Pentagon | Gray Ikle Kahn Kissinger Nitze Payne Wohlstetter American Enterprise Institute Hoover Institution National Strategy Information Center RAND Pentagon |

# Strategies for Survival: 1945-1960

At the end of WW II the U.S. found itself in a position of nuclear superiority, international political influence, and spectacular economic power. It also soon found itself competing with its former ally the Soviet Union, providing economic and military support for its former and new allies in Western Europe, and intervening throughout the post-war world. American decision makers perceived themselves to be engaged in an epic political struggle with the Soviet Union that involved the entire international system. A primary concern was how to defend the U.S. and others from a Soviet Union that appeared to be set on expansion in Europe, Asia, and the Middle East. The military danger would be met by an American counter that relied on a threat of nuclear retaliation to disuade the Soviets from aggression. Unwilling to field a conventional army comparable to the Red Army, American leaders hoped to contain the Soviets by threatening them with nuclear air attacks if they should cross the lines of containment being drawn by the Truman and Eisenhower administrations.

Targets in the early emergency war plans (later called Single Integrated Operational Plan (SIOP) for Nuclear War) included all areas vulnerable to American aircraft—cities, ports, and military support facilities (administrative, communications, supplies, etc.). This mix of what would later be called countervalue and counterforce targets set the stage for future attack priorities. Influenced by the picture (highlighted by the Air Force and support industries) of "successful" strategic bombing during WW II, American war-planners assumed that the capability to destroy cities served a dual purpose of deterring the enemy from aggression in the first place and, if deterrence failed, weakening the military effort by hitting industrial and warmaking facilities. The low accuracy and high collateral damage of bomber delivered nuclear weapons further blurred the distinction between counterforce and countervalue targets. Ironically then, especially in view of later controversies, those constructing SIOP considered the city both a de facto counterforce and countervalue target.

The U.S. relied on the threat to use nuclear weapons because it assumed that fear of the consequences of a nuclear attack would persuade the Soviets not to commit direct aggression. As Richard Smoke described it, since the Soviets would not risk the destruction of their homeland, they would not attack (in Europe, for example) and, since they would not attack, the drastic nuclear response would never have to be implemented.[8] This comforting deterrent scenario lost some of its luster after the Soviets exploded their first atomic bomb in 1949 and began plans for sophisticated delivery systems in the 1950s. (The Soviets tested an intercontinental system—the ICBM—before the U.S. did.) However, the Truman and Eisenhower administrations continued to rely on the threat of massive nuclear retaliation to deter the Soviets. Spurred on by Soviet nuclear efforts and by important pockets of domestic encouragement, the U.S. quickly developed the H-bomb, accelerated programs for launcher and delivery vehicles, and articulated policies (brinkmanship and the NATO "Sword and Shield" strategy that relied on the Strategic Air Command to strike Moscow after an attack on Europe) that would make the American promise of massive retaliation seem all too credible to the Soviets.

However, the problem of incredibility undermined the utility of the threat of massive retaliation. Critics in the 1950s, including Herman Kahn, William Kaufman, Henry Kissinger, Paul Nitze, and Robert Osgood questioned whether the strategy of massive retaliation would deter Soviet (or Chinese) challenges. To what extent did the Soviets believe the U.S. would resort to nuclear weapons against a nuclear-capable adversary over the status of city, border, or country X? If this constituted a weak link in the deterrent, then perhaps the U.S. should develop additional methods of deterrence and defense. Early advocates of flexible response and limited nuclear war options (LNOs) suggested the need for a series of interlocking options rather than a single choice of massive retaliation. If the Soviets dismissed the likelihood of massive retaliation in response to primarily limited challenges, perhaps an American possession of a capability to engage successfully in conventional wars and limited nuclear war, would convince them that the U.S. would respond to even limited Soviet challenges.

During the 1950s and 1960s factions in and out of government debated the prospects for the success of massive retaliation, flexible response, and LNOs. Later debates over MAD, selective targeting, and countervailing rehashed and expanded on these arguments. In essence, the controversies centered around the notion that, if retaliation capabilities eroded in some direct proportion to Soviet progress toward nuclear parity, then decision makers who relied on massive retaliation faced a major problem of credibility. Kissinger summed up this perceptual dilemma in the following way.

> Given the power of modern weapons, a nation that relies on all-out war as its chief deterrent imposes a fearful psychological handicap on itself. The most agonizing decision a statesman can face is whether or not to unlease all-out war; all pressures will make for hesitation, short of a direct attack threatening the national existence. In any other situation he will be inhibited by the incommensurability between the cost of the war and the objective in dispute. And he will be confirmed in his hesitations by the conviction that, so long as his retaliatory force remains intact, no shift in the territorial balance is of decisive significance. Thus both the horror and the power of modern weapons tend to paralyze action: the former because it will make few issues seem worth contending for; the latter because it causes many disputes to seem irrelevant to the over-all strategic equation. The psychological equation, therefore, will almost inevitably operate against the side which can extricate itself from a situation only by the threat of all-out war.[9]

He then suggested a remedy for this built in paralysis. He urged the development of a wilder spectrum of capabilities aimed at preventing the Soviet Union from exploiting the endemic Western hesitation to risk escalation by responding to peripheral, but cumulatively important, Soviet challenges. In his judgment these capabilities

> should enable us to confront the opponent with contingencies from which he can extricate himself only by all-out war, while deterring him from this step by a superior retaliatory capacity. Since the most difficult decision for a statesman is whether to risk the national substance by unleashing an all-out war, the psychological advantage will always be on the side of the power which can shift to its opponent the decision to initiate all-out war. All Soviet moves in the postwar period have had this character. They have faced us with problems which by themselves did not seem worth an all-out war, but with which we could not deal by an alternative capability.[10]

Kissinger wanted to shift the risk of escalation onto the Soviets. In the same vein, Schelling suggested that the U.S. should create a strategic situation, by "irreversible maneuvers or commitments, so that only the enemy's withdrawal can tranquilize the situation; otherwise it may turn out to be a contest of nerves."[11] The nature of irreversible actions and commitments occupied the attention of strategists since the first days of the atomic age.

While Kissinger, Schelling, and others urged consideration of LNOs and flexible response as ways to thrust the onus of nuclear risk onto the Soviets, retention of U.S. superiority throughout the 1950s and early 1960s diluted the immediate impact of the warnings about Western self deterrence. Eisenhower, for example, assumed that retention of nuclear weapons sufficient to devastate Soviet cities deterred nuclear and conventional war. In addition, Eisenhower and Dulles liked the tough sounding and inexpensive deterrent threats of massive retaliation and brinkmanship.

However, as seen in previous chapters, the Soviets called the American bluff several times—Korea, Berlin, and the Cuban missile crisis come to mind. To maintain the credibility of LNOs the Eisenhower administration, perhaps following the advice of Schelling and Kissinger, supplemented forces for massive retaliation with forces for graduated deterrence—wherein the U.S. relied on tactical nuclear superiority to provide the capability to prevail in limited wars should they break out. Possession of these capabilities, and the lack of conventional options should deter the Soviets from launching a conventional or limited nuclear attack that would inevitably invite an LNO response. Such a concentration of forces also guaranteed considerable savings in defense spending, an issue close to Eisenhower's heart.

While Eisenhower intended to keep superiority, which he referred to as sufficiency, (i.e., having weapons sufficient to destroy Soviet cities and hedge against ICBM breakthroughs and increasing U.S. vulnerability), the hypothesizing about flexible response, LNOs, and war-fighting capabilities as a part of a posture of graduated deterrence, was intended to enhance the credibility of a U.S. response in the conventional theater, where the Soviets had numerical advantages. While Eisenhower combined the threats of massive retaliation and graduated response, he rejected going beyond what was necessary for sufficiency or balancing the Soviet's conventional strength. Many in the defense community denounced the notion of sufficiency and argued for more active and invulnerable war-fighting capabilities and an enlarged version of graduated deterrence.

These two suggestions, which found many adherents in the 1960s and 1970s, posed one very important unanswered (and perhaps unanswerable) question—was it possible to keep a nuclear war limited? Critics of graduated response and LNOs assumed the inevitability of escalation in any nuclear context, and insisted that designing war-fighting schemes, of whatever intended scale or duration, undermined general deterrence. They worried about the loss of a taboo against nuclear use. In other words, when all sides implicitly agreed to forego the first resort to nuclear weapons, this reinforced the taboo against use. One breech, such as a limited war with exchanges of tactical nuclear weapons, raised the prospect of escalated use of more and larger weapons. Better not to countenance any use in order to foreclose the danger of going up the ladder of nuclear escalation. This criticism persisted as the controversy over LNOs later became associated with McNamara's NATO-oriented flexible response strategy, Schlesinger's selected targeting doctrine, Carter's Presidential Directive 59 (PD-59), and Reagan's recycling of Carter's countervailing objective.

## Strategies for Survival: McNamara's Plan

Studying the strategies of the 1960s reveals a sophisticated re-working of the two strands of thought already discussed. Deterrence, based on the threat of massive retaliation against a mix of counterforce and countervalue targets in the Soviet Union, still prevailed. On the other hand, decision makers continued to search for a formula that would enhance invulnerability, maintain strategic superiority, and incorporate a capability to respond effectively according to the level, scope, and direction of threat. The problem of realizing these objectives without provoking an arms race remained largely unsolved, despite some rather clever theory building and weapon design and deployment in the 1960s.

The Kennedy administration entered office with its own rhetoric about the "missile gap," the eroding invulnerability of American nuclear forces, and the need for increased attention to LNOs, counterforce, and damage limitation ringing in its ears. It moved quickly to review and refine the doctrines of the 1950s and to re-open the debate over massive versus flexible response. The Kennedy "Whiz Kids" and the Robert McNamara-led Pentagon, driven by suspicion of the limited relevance of the threat of massive retaliation, now that the Soviets could retaliate in a nearly similar fashion, sought an escape from the dilemma of an all or nothing response to a Soviet attack. While reiterating the assumption that fear of retaliation deterred the Soviets, McNamara called for flexible strategic nuclear forces sufficient to: "1) strike back decisively at the entire Soviet target system simultaneously or 2) strike back first at the Soviet bomber bases, missile sites, and other military installations associated with their long-range nuclear forces to reduce the power of any follow-on attack—and then if necessary, strike back at the Soviet urban and industrial complex in a controlled and deliberate way."[12] While the U.S. could not be certain of Soviet strategic objectives, faith in the stability of the balance of terror, and confidence in escalation control, it could assume that the Soviets preferred to examine the possibility of limiting "the terrible consequences of a nuclear exchange." According to McNamara,

> By building into our forces a flexible capability, we at least eliminate the prospect that we could strike back in only one way, namely, against the entire Soviet target system including their cities. Such a prospect would give the Soviet Union no incentive to withhold attack against our cities in a first strike. We want to give them a better alternative. Whether they would accept it in the crises of a global nuclear war, no can say. Considering what

is at stake we believe it is worth the additional effort on our part to have this option.[13]

These and other early statements from the administration revealed a number of premises about flexible response. 1) The U.S. needed to be constantly on guard against the possibility of deterrence failure and therefore preparations for damage limitation rather than damage enhancement were necessary. 2) Ability to use nuclear weapons in a variety of low level contingencies would deter the Soviets from military challenges and from escalation if the initial deterrent failed. 3) Damage to the U.S. could be limited by hitting Soviet military targets (to degrade offensive capability) rather than cities and by instituting active (ABM) and passive (civil defense, hardened silos) defensive systems. 5) The promise and potential of flexible response and damage limitation would provide the Soviets with increased incentives to re-tailor their targeting strategy in a similar manner. (An inability or unwillingness to fight anything short of an all out war would do little to encourage Soviet restraint in the event of war.)[14] 6) Nuclear war might be kept limited and ended on terms favorable to the U.S.

These premises encouraged the Kennedy administration to consider buttressing deterrence, based on American willingness to initiate a mutual suicide arrangement with the Soviet Union (i.e., massive retaliation), with deterrence based on the threat *to risk* nuclear war by having the capability to control successfully a flexible and less than total response to any level Soviet challenge. The Soviets would be deterred in two interlocking stages if they were persuaded first, that the U.S. could win (or defeat Soviet objectives) in any limited war scenario and second, that the risk of escalation (a situation in which they would also lose) obtained in any such scenario.

Whatever the appeal of this strategy to those fearful of American inaction in crisis, those fearful of the opposite prospect warned of its dangerous ramifications. First was the obvious inevitability of escalation. Second, discussion of how to fight limited wars and how to avoid assured destruction undermined the rationale of deterrence based on the threat of massive retaliation. Critics feared that such discussions made war more likely since either power might assume that it could initiate aggression without risking the consequences of what would soon be called MAD. Third, critics asserted that preparations for flexible response and LNOs aroused Soviet fears of an American intention to strike first and would increase incentives to preempt if the Soviets believed themselves to be under immediate threat of such an attack.

Supporters of flexible response offered a number of rejoinders to these criticisms. With respect to the danger of escalation, they doubted that the Soviets, faced with defeat at both the tactical and strategic level, would choose to attack in the first place or escalate in the second. Most importantly, with respect to undermining deterrence, they asked whether the Soviet Union would be any more willing to go to nuclear war if it faced the certainty of defeat and substantial damage than if the outcome of war were likely to be MAD[15] With respect to the instability nurtured by reciprocal fears of first strikes, Richard Betts suggested that as long as the

U.S. did not reach the level of a disarming first strike capability or threaten the assured destruction reserves of the Soviet Union, this criticism remained unpersuasive.[16]

Despite McNamara's early persuasion on these points, the intensity of the criticism of flexible response influenced the Kennedy administration's shift to MAD. In the midst of waffling between flexible response and MAD, McNamara pointed to the overriding objective of deterring "a deliberate nuclear attack upon the U.S. and its allies by maintaining a clear and convincing capability to inflict unacceptable damage on an attacker."[17] In his view, deterrence rested most on the "ability to destroy an attacker...not our ability to partially limit damage to ourselves." To realize these objectives required invulnerable second strike forces and jettisoning (at least in a declaratory fashion) the no-cities targeting plans of the early 1960s since the strategy of MAD emphasized that destroying the Soviet Union meant striking Soviet population and industry in retaliation, rather than taking out military targets selectively as one would in a preemptive move. MAD meant that the destructive capacity embodied in the respective punches that the superpowrs could exchange served as the best guarantee that war was likely to be so horrible as to be unthinkable. There was less sense, then, in planning for "winning" a nuclear war, and hence less need for counterforce targeting, but all the more need for striking countervalue assets—to guarantee the horror of the consequences of deterrence failure. By the mid 1960s, the U.S. moved to MAD, although weapons, targets, and deployments (for example, ICBMs numbers in excess of those required by the objectives of MAD—the capacity to destroy 50% of Soviet industry and 25% of its population) still reflected flexible response capabilities.

This brief review of MAD reveals a number of explicit and implicit hypotheses that dominated American attention for over 20 years (longer if you relate MAD to its half brother, massive retaliation.) 1) Any nuclear engagement will result in total war, and the more this prospect is guaranteed, the more deterrence is fortified. 2) A healthy fear of devastation and escalation make deterrence relatively easy and inherently stable.[18] 3) Hypotheses 1 and 2 dictate the practical irrelevance of military superiority. As long as each side could offer certain amounts of destruction on the other's cities, deterrence prevails.[19] 4) Since general nuclear war remains unlikely because of the above hypotheses, the sturdy balance of terror extends deterrence to include Western Europe and other zones of interest. With nothing worth the risk of a nuclear war and with any limited conflict inevitably involving the risk of escalation, MAD deters minor as well as major challenges. 5) The stability of MAD lies in targeting cities, leaving them unprotected, and thus convincing an opponent that it need not fear a first strike since, under the principles of MAD, each side deliberately eschews protecting cities from an opponent's second strike. Schelling explained this paradox in the following way: "A weapon that can hurt only *people*, and cannot possibly damage the other side's striking force, is profoundly defensive: it provides its possessor no incentive to strike first. It is the weapon that is designed or deployed to destroy "military" targets—to seek out the enemy's missiles and bombers—that *can* exploit the advantage of striking first and consequently provide a temptation to do so."[20]  6) Defensive measures and flexible response, both inconsistent with MAD, are impossible to apply or control.

These hypotheses invited considerable criticism from both the left and right in the mid-to-late 1960s. Those on the left questioned the commitment to MAD, given an American military posture still reflecting counterforce objectives (given ICBM leads, for example) and damage limitation intentions (given persistence in ABM research and funding). Others on the left and right condemned the immorality of threatening millions of civilian hostages. Significant sections of the defense establishment, which feared the passing of American nuclear superiority, rejected MAD which guaranteed that, if deterrence failed, it would assure catastrophe for both sides.

The debate focussed on several conceptual flaws. 1) MAD suggested no effective guidance for what to do if deterrence failed, other than launching a counter attack that would assure destruction of the U.S. along with a not very gratifying posthumous revenge against the Soviets. 2) MAD relied on the deterrent effect of a response that would be suicidal to implement. Did the Soviets believe that the U.S. would exercise so suicidal a response to a peripheral Soviet challenge or even a challenge directed at Europe? 3) MAD depended on both the rationality and irrationality of men and states. Betts pointed to this irony as he discussed the logic of a countervalue retaliation after a Soviet counterforce strike:

> In order to demonstrate why the same prewar logic of mutual vulnerability designed to deter the first counterforce strike does not also apply to deterring the first dedicated countervalue strike (that is, in second-strike retaliation), assured-destruction theorists fall back on the import of uncertainty, or "the rationality of irrationality": because the Russians cannot know that we would not lash back in fury even if doing so is suicidal, they cannot risk the possibility. It is reasonable to bank simultaneously on the aggressor's prudence and rationality, and the victim's unpredictability and potential irrationality. This belief that cold calculation of risks probably would apply more to one side than to the other may be valid, and may cover most potential scenarios. But it is still a leap of faith and does not offer a hedge against some scenarios.[21]

4) MAD had questionable validity if the Soviets did not accept deterrence based on mutual vulnerability. In subsequent years detractors of MAD acquired additional colleagues as the pace and direction of strategic developments increased doubts about Soviet subscription to MAD. The Reagan administration embraced the above criticisms and added a few more related to the putative Soviet acquisition of a counterforce first strike capability and interest in strategic defense and superiority.

The architects of MAD responded to these criticisms in a number of ways. While they acknowledged that deterrence could fail, they argued that the fear of this and of escalation both contributed to deterrence. MAD was credible as long as cities remained vulnerable to attack. Even if not credible per se, it instilled caution because the many uncertainties and the great chance of things getting out of control meant that neither side could contemplate a first strike with any confident expectation of non-retaliation. In other words, MAD "is credible because it is clear that if...fighting began, there would be great confusion and plans drawn up before a war would soon be overtaken by events...with nobody able to promise victory."[22] Finally, the Soviet Union does not have to accept MAD as the basis for its force posture to be deterred by it. If the U.S. conveyed the threat of assured destruction credibly, it would deter the Soviet Union regardless of its declaratory policy.

The Kennedy and Johnson administrations concluded that no rational decision maker would risk nuclear war as long as his adversary maintained a survivable second strike capability to inflict unacceptable damage on his country. Despite this assertion, debate over MAD and flexible response continued and colored U.S. strategic posture, arms control policies, and deployment and targeting decisions throughout the 1960s and 1970s. The mixed reception for SALT and the see-saw decisions on the ABM, B-1s, Trident IIs, MIRVs, Cruise Missiles, MXs, and INF all reflected the schizophrenic American attempts to satisfy the often contradictory targeting and rhetorical requirements of MAD and flexible response. The stubborn contradictions within U.S. strategic thinking are perhaps inevitable due, in part, to what Betts referred to as the phenomenon of "what's wrong is what's right." What is right for deterrence is wrong for defense; what deters nuclear war may invite conventional war; and what is right for MAD may be wrong for flexible response. In the meantime, weapons for all of the above strategies or conditions may be required to cover all the bases in the attempt to construct a viable, evolving, and flexible deterrent package. Unfortunately, but not unexpectedly, attempts at designing "new" doctrines and directives in the 1970s failed to resolve most of these contradictions.

## Strategies for Survival: "New" Doctrines and Directives

By the late 1960s, Soviet strategic advances included a MIRVed counterforce capability, invulnerable second strike forces, and progress toward the "un-MAD" notions of superiority and war-winning. In the judgment of new Secretary of Defense Schlesinger, the U.S. had to counter these by preventing a Soviet unilateral advantage over the U.S. and by assuring the Soviets of American ability and willingness to execute its deterrent threat—whether in a massive or "controlled selective fashion." These objectives related to several weapon and deployment decisions—to match the Soviet counterforce capability, modernize strategic nuclear forces so as to enhance their support of both MAD and flexible response, and forego weapons suitable solely for first strike missions. The administration, as well as its critics, noted the contradiction between decisions 1 and 3.

This not unprecedented contradiction derived from the opposing nature and purpose of MAD and flexible response: MAD—to deter attack against cities—and flexible response—to deter limited attacks on American allies and military forces. Schlesinger argued that a flexible response was especially important during a period of ICBM vulnerability, when Soviet ability to remove American forces without hitting cities might deprive the U.S. of a flexible and controlled response, and might, as a consequence of the ability to retaliate only against Soviet cities with SLBMs (thus assuring escalation) force the U.S. to choose between suicide or surrender. However unlikely this scenario, its consequences could prove catastrophic. The Nixon administration therefore wanted to have a capability to retaliate against silos as well as cities in order to eliminate Soviet expectations that initiating limited challenges or limited nuclear wars could work to their advantage. This capability could also help control escalation, if deterrence should fail, by providing options (and consequently incentives) for both sides to avoid hitting cities. Another reputedly beneficial feature was the hypothetical contribution to extended deterrence. In a crisis, decision makers with options to respond according to the level of challenge, rather than being limited to threats of massive retaliation, could stand fast and threaten with greater credibility. The administration assumed that the Soviets (and Western Europeans) would find this new recipe persuasive.

This version of flexible response encountered updated questions concerning whether and how a nuclear war could be kept limited. How could war remain limited if the Soviets played by different rules? Could the respective $C^3$ systems handle escalating tensions in the midst of city and silo kills? Could either side control the incentive for exploiting military advantages during "limited" exchanges? On the other hand, but equally damaging to the case for flexibility, if the two sides assumed escalation control, might they be tempted to resort to nuclear weapons pre-maturely? Finally, could preparing for various war-fighting contingencies and deploying the mandated hardware appear like a first strike preparation to the Soviets, just as their similar programs appeared destabilizing to proponents of flexible response?

Schlesinger took on the task of answering these questions. He insisted, for example, that to adapt American concepts of deterrence to "the large and growing capability of our rivals" and to be prepared for a wide variety of contingencies did not promote war-fighting, but rather served as prerequisites for the main objective of "deterrence across the spectrum of the nuclear threat." He also argued that the U.S. had had LNOs for more than 20 years without lowering the nuclear threshold and that

> to believe that the development of contingency plans (which, after all, is what the search for options is all about) will increase the probability of nuclear use is to underestimate seriously the gravity of the decision to go to war, especially nuclear war. What is more, to the extent that concern about the nuclear threshold is more than hypothetical, the most effective way of keeping the threshold high is to increase the effectiveness and readiness of our non-nuclear forces. History, I believe, will show that on those rare occasions when the use of nuclear weapons was seriously considered in the past thirty years, it was because of the

impression that adequate conventional forces were not available to achieve the desired objectives.[23] (for a similar statement, see Weinberger's *1987 Report to the Congress* below.)

Schlesinger also dismissed the notion that limited nuclear exchanges would inevitably escalate or be indistinguishable from an all out attack. The very likely prospect of, and therefore fear of, escalation made LNO's unlikely, in themselves, to lower the nuclear threshold. No reasonable leader "would deliberately want to ensure escalation, and forego the chance for an early end to a conflict, by refusing to consider and plan for responses other than immediate, large-scale attacks on cities. Surely, even if there is only a small probability that limited response options would deter an attack or bring a nuclear war to a rapid conclusion, without large-scale damage to cities, it is a probability...we should not foreclose."[24]

The Nixon administration's decision to implement the "new" doctrine(s) unsettled MAD purists as well as pacifists (mad or otherwise) and many in between. However, both the Nixon and Carter administrations pursued the dual and often contradictory objectives of deterrence based on threats of MAD (assuming the impossibility of war-fighting) and threats of selective war-fighting. The Carter administration outlined the provisions *of this latter threat in PD-59, which enthroned, cautiously and secretly at first, its remedies for strategic instability, the imbalance in Soviet and* American counterforce capability, and increased American second strike vulnerability.

In setting the scene for PD-59, Secretary of Defense Harold Brown warned that, while the reality of MAD should deter any rational statesman, all too often leaders have made "wishful, mistaken, and foolish estimates of consequences that have led to catastrophic wars...therefore (deterrence) must present such a certainty of destructive retaliation that no chain of reasoning would allow a decision maker contemplating the initiation of a strategic war to conclude that such as attack would be anything other than the worst possible choice."[25] This "MAD-plus" agenda included the requirement of selective response to any type of Soviet attack. According to Brown,

> This ability to provide measured retaliation in response to less-than-total attacks—and thus to prevent the Soviets from imagining that they can gain meaningful advantage at some level of nuclear conflict—is essential to credible deterrence. Moreover, whatever doubts one may have about whether a nuclear war could be kept limited—and I have severe ones—it would be the height of folly to put the United States in a position in which uncontrolled escalation would be the only course we could follow.[26]

In supporting this latter argument, Brown also repeated the analysis of Schlesinger that, while there was a high probability of an out of control escalation,

> ...it would be highly irresponsible to say that, because we cannot predict how such a war would happen, the United States should make no plans for how it will be fought. Imagine a military

planner or political official who had to tell a President who had asked for options in responding to an actual strategic attack that there were no such plans because such a war had been judged inconceivable or unimaginable. Should a nuclear war begin, it is the responsibility of the political and military authorities to try to limit its damaging effects.[27]

Brown's offer of "measured retaliation" and damaged limitation as solutions to the dilemma of American self-deterrence, if the U.S. relied solely on MAD, constituted one foundation of PD-59. This directive assigned the military the task of maintaining strategic nuclear forces, war plans, and $C^3$ sufficient to "countervail" or to convince the Soviets that victory was impossible. According to Walter Slocombe, Brown's Deputy Under Secretary, "the policy dictated that the United States must have countervailing strategic options such that at a variety of levels of exchange, aggression would either be defeated or would result in unacceptable costs that exceed gains."[28] Slocombe also conjectured that the countervailing strategy made "clear that the United States would not be forced by a Soviet attack on our ICBMs to choose between surrender and suicidal all-out attack on Soviet cities. Instead, the United States would be able to retaliate against a more limited set of Soviet targets, so as to deny the USSR any military advantage from its attack, while retaining a force in reserve capable of still further attacks on a broader set of targets, should the Soviets continue to escalate the conflict."[29]

The objective of countervailing highlighted the concern about the counterforce imbalance, wherein the Soviet Union, using only a portion of its heavy ICBMs (SS-18s) could theoretically wipe out the increasingly vulnerable American ICBMs. To blunt a successful Soviet counterforce first strike plan the U.S. needed a survivable counterforce second strike, or the capacity to pose equivalent military destruction. While the strategy envisioned the possibility of counterforce exchanges, semi-protracted nuclear war, and escalation control, as each side presumably would seek desparately to avoid hitting cities and to save its own cities, it's advocates (many of whom doubted the ability to fully control escalation) predicted that the theoretical ability to conduct these activities would enhance deterrence by demonstrating anew the complications of any Soviet first strike scenario.

Despite this prediction, the criticisms of flexible response and LNOs raised in the 1950s and 1960s applied as well to the countervailing strategy of the Carter administration. To see the full blossoming of this denouncement, we must move to the period of the Reagan administration which saw a new round of the debate over flexible response and a renewed concern for the moral as well as military implications of the objectives, methods, and values of strategies to deter.

## Strategies for Survival: The Reagan Round

The Reagan administration's foray into nuclear strategy encountered approval and criticism from across the spectrum of right to left, hawk to dove, and pacifist to nuclearist. It's determination to modernize strategic nuclear forces encouraged those who favored closing the counterforce gap, broaching the potentialities of BMD, and relying on capabilities for war-fighting as means of securing pre-war and intra-war deterrence. On the other hand, the efforts and exhortations in these directions upset those who feared the destabilizing potentials of such efforts that could appear like first strike preparations to the Soviets. While the administration argued for a strategy that consisted of a mixture of offensive and defensive assignments, critics preferred a strategy that guaranteed disaster should deterrence fail since, in their view, the worse the expected results of nuclear war the less likely the U.S. and the Soviet Union would be to take actions that risked it.

These critics found themselves in the ironic position of fending off accusations about the immorality of their suicidal and homicidal theory coming both from within the administration and the religious community. The latest re-twist of an old problem concerns what the American Catholic Bishops called the appalling paradox of nuclear deterrence—the threat to use nuclear weapons against civilian hostages which, if implemented, would be the ultimate immorality. However, proponents of MAD quickly reasserted the other half of the paradox: MAD is moral in its effect—deterrence of nuclear war. Those who opposed the nuclear bluff for moral reasons failed to appreciate, according to proponents like Charles Krauthammer and George Quester, that deterrence resulted from a combination of the possession of nuclear weapons and the will to use them.[30] However, as far as moralists and pacifists were concerned, the questions involved the lack of distinction between threatening and using nuclear weapons and the pseudo-moral facade for an immoral justification for the end (deterrence) justifying the means (threatening and preparing for massive destruction.) On the other hand, if a threat of MAD causes no death and deters war, because of the fear of retaliation and annihilation, then the strategy of MAD, despite its explicit nuclear threat, is profoundly moral in result because it actually deters use. In other words, as George Quester suggested, while immoral in mechanism, MAD is "contingently acceptable precisely because it deters itself from happening."[31] As accused, Krauthammer and Quester use the "ends justify the means" dynamic to rationalize their conditional approval for the balance of terror stabilized by the mutual fear of the superpowers.

The Reagan administration, however, questioned the relevance of this theory in the age of potential first strike forces, eroding invulnerability, and a questionable Soviet subscription to MAD. In this environment, the threat of use appeared suicidal rather than moral, incredible, and therefore unstable should it invite Soviet doubts about the American ability and will to retaliate. Before evaluating Reagan's plan for replacing MAD with a new version of flexible response, lets iron out one other new wrinkle in the possibly immoral process of "thinking about the unthinkable" that added to the fire and dust of the strategic debate: the nuclear winter hypothesis. According to the hypothesis, a series of nuclear blasts will raise clouds of soot and dust that will create a barrier to sunlight in such a way as to lower earth temperatures and impair the ability of plants and trees to sustain life. Such a climatic and environmental catastrophe adds new horrors to the prospect of even a limited nuclear war.

If the hypothesis were correct, the expected results of nuclear winter would make counterforce planning as suicidal as all out nuclear exchanges.[32] This is actually good news for the advocates of MAD. Already skeptical about the prospects for keeping counterforce wars from escalation, they might now point out that, according to the hypothesis, even if counterforce strikes remained limited, they would trigger nuclear winter. Such a reference would highlight the horribleness and thus "unthinkableness" of nuclear war. In other words, the nuclear winter hypothesis reaffirms the original objective of MAD— to make war so horrible as to be unthinkable. In addition, it also adds persuasiveness to the MAD assumption that the more horrible war appears (now guaranteed to be just as horrible in limited encounters), the less likely it is to occur through deliberate planning.

On the other hand, some express an opposite concern about the room for maneuver opened up in a world vulnerable to nuclear winter. If fear of nuclear winter persuades the public and government in the U.S. about the scale and inevitability of nuclear winter, but not leaders in the Soviet Union, then some interesting scenarios might occur to war planners on both sides. Might it be possible to launch a counterforce strike intended to result in damage below the hypothetical nuclear winter threshold and in an American hesitation to retaliate for fear of such a prospect? While this unlikely scenario imputes highly bizarre and risky planning to the Soviets, another scenario might describe the unstable potential of a partially disarmed world with nuclear weapons kept deliberately below the nuclear winter threshold. Would the world then be safe for major conventional wars and limited nuclear wars well below threshold? It might be better to keep well above the threshold to preclude discussion of successful limited nuclear wars. Finally, if the greatest danger of war resides in an accidental rather than deliberate initiation of a war intended to remain under threshold, then the nuclear winter hypothesis plays a rather small role in enhancing the deterrent value of MAD.

However, some advocates of MAD still embrace the hypothesis as a supplemental argument for their case. Not only does each superpower possess the capacity to wipe out cities, but it also possesses the capacity to engineer nuclear winter and terracide. In view of these possibilities, neither side could envision a first strike without debilitating qualms that not even exemption of cities from direct attack could prevent utter catastrophe. On the other hand, what if the hypothesis proves incorrect, is disbelieved, or influences the two sides to plan for more careful and precise preemptive moves? Dare we rely on the fear of nuclear winter as a sufficient deterrent to a limited or all out Soviet attack?

An administration that rejects MAD as inadequate is unlikely to expect the Soviets to be deterred by conjecture about the effects of smoke and dust on the environment in the aftermath of "X" percentage of exploding warheads on cities. And, given the recent scientific reaction to the questionable techniques and conclusions of the Sagan hypothesis, it seems even more unlikely that the fear of nuclear winter or "nuclear fall" alone will deter war.[33] While there is still much to be explored about the likelihood of nuclear winter, the more immediate concern is to finish the discussion of what deters best, rather than what the level of damage will be if deterrence fails. This remains true even if the added uncertainty about the climatic effects of nuclear winter further complicates the deterrent picture. Whatever the complications, what deters war will deter nuclear winter as well. In the final analysis, we must decide whether to depend on MAD or countervailing and flexible response, which embody the hope of persuading the Soviets that even limited attacks intended to foreclose American retaliation, whether out of fear of escalation or nuclear winter, will fail due to an American capability to blunt attack and respond appropriately. So, the debate between these two options continues almost unaffected by the prospects for nuclear winter.

The Reagan administration, building upon the premise of Carter's countervailing strategy and fearing the military imbalance that emerged with the Soviet advances of the 1970s, called for re-establishing a strategic balance of forces, halting the erosion of the survivability of second strike forces, and providing for a "viable war-fighting defense." Former Defense Secretary Weinberger explained the need for these measures in terms similar to those used by Schlesinger and Brown.

> To deter successfully, we must be able—and must be seen to be able—to respond to any potential aggression in such a manner that the costs we will exact will substantially exceed any gains the aggressor might hope to achieve. We, for our part, are under no illusions about the dangers of a nuclear war between the major powers; we believe that neither side could win such a war. But this recognition on *our* part is not sufficient to prevent the out-break of nuclear war; it is essential that the Soviet leadership understand this as well. We must make sure that the Soviet leadership, in calculating the risks of aggression, recognizes that because of our retaliatory capability, there can be no circumstance in which it could benefit by beginning a nuclear war at any level or of any duration. If the Soviets recognize that our forces can and will deny them their objectives at whatever level of nuclear conflict they contemplate and, in addition, that such a conflict could lead to the destruction of those political, military, and economic assets that they value most highly, then deterrence is effective and the risk of war diminished.[34]

Again using language reminiscent of Brown and Schlesinger, Weinberger urged that, while the U.S. could not predict how the Soviets might challenge deterrence, defend again retaliation, or assure escalation control, "we must plan for flexibility in our forces and in our response options so that there will be the possibility of terminating the conflict and re-establishing deterrence at the lowest possible level of violence, thus avoiding further destruction."[35] Only such ability "to respond appropriately to a wide range of aggressive actions" would help establish credibility and ensure that the threatened American response would not be "perceived as inadequate or contrary to our national interests." This concern over the adequacy and credibility of the nuclear deterrent determined the Reagan administration's distaste for MAD. It preferred flexible response to an incredible (and immoral) strategy that emphasized American retaliation against cities—an action that would invite reciprocal retaliation. According to Weinberger, "such a deterrent strategy is hardly likely to carry conviction as a deterrent, particularly as a deterrent to nuclear—let alone conventional—attack on an ally."

While the Reagan administration reaffirmed the traditional requirements of deterrence (essential equivalence and countervailing), it emphasized the exceptional deterrent value of capabilities for war-fighting and escalation dominance, especially in view of apparent Soviet rejection of MAD and their striving for superiority and defense. This emphasis came from the belief that counterforce capabilities would aid deterrence by complicating the planning and execution of a Soviet first strike. Maintaining a survivable counterforce capability would diminish the probability of a crisis leading to war, since the U.S., with such a capability, would reduce "the potential asymmetry in the outcome of a protracted nuclear war that might have been produced by the Soviet's counterforce superiority."[36] In addition, according to Victor Utgoff, NSC staffer under Carter, counterforce equality would reduce "the probability of the sorts of challenges to U.S. interests that might lead to serious crises," since the Soviets could not assume that the U.S. had more to fear in a protracted war than they did. In other words, counterforce quality would contribute to the capability to participate effectively and precisely in counterforce exchange without necessarily forcing the U.S. to escalate to countervalue targeting and MAD. In addition, it would be more rational to implement counterforce responses than to massively retaliate, if deterrence failed, since this would prevent Soviet escalation dominance, preserve the reserve threat of MAD, and "leave the U.S. with bargaining power for terminatin of hostilities short of mutual annihilation."[37] In sum, the administration, assumed that counterforce equality or flexible response, which embodied the foundation for a countervailing strategy, would provide a possibility for escalation control, deter a Soviet resort to a counterforce attack or coercion in crisis, and deny the Soviets victory in any limited or all-out attack.

Supporters of countervailing begin with a set of assumptions borrowed from earlier advocates of flexible response. In their view, both MAD and countervailing rely on certain preparations for war-fighting to increase Soviet uncertainty about the feasibility of attack. According to Gray and Payne, echoing Kahn and Kissinger, nuclear deterrence "ultimately is predicated on threats of nuclear use, and the operational planning for nuclear use must underlie that threat if it is to possess any credibility."[38] In a strident expose of the weakness of a strategy that focused primarily on a punitive offensive approach to deterrence, Gray warned that endorsement of assured vulnerability over preparations for damage limitation guaranteed American paralysis in crisis and suicide in nuclear war.

According to Gray,

War should be deterred most reliably when a potential aggressor cannot anticipate success from his resort to arms and when the threat to deny him victory is not incredible. It is important...that the United States have a posture and doctrine that, in Soviet estimation, could deny any success from the resort to strategic nuclear arms. But Soviet estimation of the probability of the United States exercising its strategic nuclear forces for the purpose of victory denial cannot help but be influenced by consideration of the likely American willingness to suffer Soviet retaliation. No quantity or estimated quality of the performance of damage limiting programs should induce reckless behavior on the part of American politicians. But a dedicated and diverse damage limiting capability should encourage the Soviet leadership to accord some credibility to the U.S. extended deterrent threat, and could serve the critical function of saving lives by the tens of millions in the event deterrence should fail.[39]

In sum, Gray and Payne insisted on a flexible nuclear employment policy and provisions for damage limitations to show the Soviets that the U.S. was not bluffing in its reliance on nuclear retaliation to deter Soviet attack on cities and to deny the Soviets any plausible theory of victory.

They also rejected the assertion that a countervailing strategy decreased security, promoted crisis instability, or assumed a perfect BMD. In their view, while deployment of war-fighting weaponry could fuel a defensive arms race, the U.S. needed to maintain sufficient and varied deterrent *and* defensive forces to ensure that advantages in Soviet war-fighting weaponry would not erode U.S. security. Second, they argued that, while vulnerable first strike weapons increased instability, a *survivable* nuclear force enhanced stability because it denied Soviet war objectives. Third, while they acknowledged the limited perfection of BMD, they suggested that even an imperfect defense "promises to strengthen the stability of deterrence by imposing major new uncertainties upon any potential attack."[40] Silo defense would not have to be perfect to degrade a Soviet capability to effect a successful counterforce first strike.

An additional reason to dispute the critics' claims related to the problems of escalation. While escalation management would impose immense burdens on $C^3$, the solution should not be to abandon attempts at control in the hope that the inevitability of escalation alone would deter both sides equally. If deterrence fails, both adversaries might be well served by plans, however inadequate, to limit damage, signal interest in halting hostilities, and prevent escalation to MAD. In addition, according to Gray and Payne, while limited wars could escalate, "a nuclear arsenal that can not be employed in a controlled fashion for finite political purposes (threat of use must be somewhat credible) is far more likely to deter the deterer than the intended deteree."[41] In sum, supporters of flexible response, war-fighting, and victory denial see these strategies as rational—because they could be implemented below the level of MAD, should deterrence fail; flexible—because they entail responses other than a "no looking back" massive retaliation; and deterring—because they complicate Soviet first strike plans to the point of reducing incentives, no matter how great the crisis, to launch a preemptive attack. With no hope of winning on any level of attack and with the threat of punishment high, the Soviets are deterred.

Despite the passion of true believers like Gray and Payne, many find no comfort in their solutions. Some, like Michael MccGwire, disparage the abstract and arcane style of reasoning, the worst case guesses about Soviet intentions, the punitive tone, and the outdated notions about Soviet aggression that pervade U.S. strategic thinking—especially as articulated by the Reagan administratin which fosters the image of the U.S. as magistrate and the Soviet Union as law breaker.[42] More mainstream authors condemn the administration's misunderstanding of the disparity in American and Soviet security perspectives. The U.S. perspective, whether characterized by McNamara's attempt to instruct the Soviets about the wisdom of mutual vulnerability or Reagan's itch to persuade them about BMD, reflects ethnocentric and selective perception and misperception. For example, as Steinbruner pointed out, the U.S. typically discounts its military strength, exalts its political goals, and imputes to the Soviets highly coherent and hostile purposes.[43] In the meantime, the Soviets impute to the U.S. hostile purposes as reflected in its historical anti-Soviet attitudes, threatening strategies, and persistent military advantages.

In addition to the general condemnation of the style and misperceptions of the Reagan administration, critics objected specifically to its choice of countervailing and/or flexible response. They note the now familiar obstacles to its success: the "reality" of MAD, the inevitability of escalation, the non-utility of nuclear weapons, and the infeasibility and instability of strategic defense. Advocates of MAD fear that attempts to by-pass any one of these realities would place great pressure on the Soviets to counter with an offensive and/or defensive arms race or even with preemption in time of crisis. According to the logic of MAD, given the nature and quantity of nuclear weapons and the impossibility of defenses against them, mankind is "fated" to live in a world in which any nuclear war will lead to an all out one resulting in the destruction of both aggressor and victim and many neutral bystanders. Ironically, this prospect encourages a healthy fear of devastation that makes deterrence, under certain conditions and practices, relatively easy. Equally ironic, devastation is all the more guaranteed, and deterrence all the more viable and stable, the more it is expected that the process of fighting nuclear wars will get out of hand and that statesmen might act irrationally and end up escalating a crisis to a final denouement.[44] Consequently, attempts to avoid this fate by defense, which is impossible against a first strike, or by countervailing strategies, which attempt the impossible assignment of reducing one side's vulnerability by acquiring an equal counterforce capability, are destabilizing and provocative. The ideal deterrence or insurance portfolio would consist of invulnerable second strike forces and deliberate avoidance of weapons and strategies intended to reduce the other side's invulnerability.

As to the problem of escalation, authors like Keeny and Panofsky pointed to the staggering technical problems that would face a country's C[3] system in the midst of even a "limited" war. Fragile command center, electronic and computer failures, and an out-dated, overworked, and unreliable Early Warning System (EWS) all would degrade American response scenarios. Even limited nuclear targeting would encompass massive collateral damage that, in the first stages of a war, might be impossible to distinguish from the first moves in a general nuclear war. Desmond Ball, for example, pointed out the poor suitability of American nuclear forces for LNOs and that the constant reiteration of the need for flexibility and more sophisticated LNOs reflected the constant recognition that, despite the hope for an ability to control the use of nuclear weapons in limited exchanges as a vital part of pre-war and intra-war deterrence, targeting plans and capabilities over the years have shown few prospects for escalation control.[45]

The requirements of $C^3$ and battle management facilities, whether needed for LNOs or counterforce exchanges in a BMD world, seem not only technologically but also psychologically impossible, as men and machines would grapple with an incomprehensible reality of thousands of exploding Hiroshimas and no logical place to stop shooting, no one left in authority to surrender, or no way to signal surrender. Given these inevitable conditions, the powers that flirted with limited exchanges would find themselves unavoidably engaged in an all out, uncontrolled spasm of nuclear death. This prospect alone should warn against anticipating "limited" campaigns which are the most destabilizing elements of a countervailing strategy since they most undermine the effect of the deterrent guarantee of MAD.

Where war-fighters worry about Soviet exploitation of a counterforce advantage and American self-deterrence, advocates of MAD doubt the existence of either exploitability or self-deterrence. They point out that the Soviets, in planning for a counterforce first strike, could never be sure that their forces and controls would function effectively enough to preclude American retaliation.[46] They also see little chance of an effective multilayered deterrence wherein American possession of counterforce weapons might serve as a demonstration of resolve to deny the enemy victory and, if this failed to deter, as an important instrument for taking out Soviet ICBMs, while countervalue weapons might be held in reserve to continue deterrence against attacks on cities. Americans could not be certain that they could execute a successful counterforce second strike or that the Soviets would not respond massively. The decision maker undertaking this endeavor would need great faith in intra-war deterrence and in the Soviet's similar faith!

Finally, advocates of MAD dismiss the possibility of a successful defense-oriented strategy due to the impossible requirements of impermeable and country-wide missile and air defenses. According to Keeny and Panofsky, "any attempt to have a controlled war-fighting capability during a nuclear exchange places tremendous requirements not only on decisions made under incredible pressure by men in senior positions of responsibility but on the technical performance of command, control, communications and intelligence functions."[47] Regardless of whether the U.S. could ever overcome these technological obstacles, strategic defense preparations may be contra-indicated since they may fuel the arms race (in both defensive and offensive weapons) rather than stabilize it. As William Burrows pointed out, "To believe that a (BMD) program would help stabilize the arms race is to believe that the Kremlin would allow the U.S. to make itself invulnerable to attack at the same time that we are perfecting offensive systems which could pulverize Soviet targets with impunity...As the ballistic missile defense takes shape, so too will the means necessary to assure that it will not work as required."[48]

Critics also profiled the first strike pressures expected to flow from a transition to a strategy based on defense. Each side might fear that the other could intend, in times of crisis, to use its first strike forces to degrade the opponent's retaliatory forces and it's BMD to defend against the then weakened response. Since there might appear to be an advantage in going first if one side could limit the damage from retaliation, a move to BMD would heighten instability, do nothing to reduce suspicion, and abandon the only plan known by experience to deter—the threat of MAD.

These criticisms of Reagan's orientations and preferences go to the heart of the divisions between historical supporters of flexible response and MAD: What stabilizes and deters rather than provokes? How many, of which type, weapons provide an adequate defense? Which targets contribute the most to instilling caution on the part of the adversary? Do the concepts of superiority and parity retain significance? While merely raising these questions fails to address all the obstacles and potential solutions discussed over the years, the evolution of the central debate, as reviewed in this chapter, shows several areas of consensus as well as areas of permanent contention. The conclusion below focuses on the key characteristics and the nub of consensus revealed in the forty year debate over deterrence and defense.

## Conclusion: Shoot-outs, Self-Deterrence, Or Stability?

After this display of variations on two strategic themes, what does it all boil down to? Those who urge flexible response warn of the lack of credibility in MAD as a response to limited Soviet challenges. They worry about imbalances in strategic forces, wherein Soviet advantages in counterforce and strategic defense might erode the credibility of an American response. Their solutions to these problems include maintaining multiple retaliation options; essentially equivalent forces; an invulnerable second strike; damage limitation, strategic defense and hardened $C^3$ capabilities; and carefully constructed arms control agreements that enhance stability and equality. These measures will persuade the Soviet Union that if it initiated a limited attack, hoping to avoid the consequences of MAD and perhaps nuclear winter (i.e., hoping for American self-deterrence, since the execution of U.S. assured destruction forces would mean self-annihilation), it would face defeat nonetheless in the form of American LNOs. Attacks would be deterred by a combination of nuclear capabilities, practical plans for their use, and the promise of victory-denial.

On the other hand, those who rely on the reality of MAD warn of the destabilizing impact of discussions of damage limitation, BMD, or using nuclear weapons. They worry about the inevitability of escalation and the fear-inspired and strategy-prompted reciprocal incentives for initiating first strikes in any limited war situation. They insist that not only is there no possibility of defense against nuclear weapons, but that attempts to discover a defense will fuel a defensive arms race, undercut deterrence based on offensive threats, and make first strike attacks appear more feasible to both the potential aggressor and the intended victim. Their solutions to these problems include foregoing counterforce and first strike weapons, abandoning efforts at defending population, and maintaining invulnerable (primarily countervalue) strategic nuclear forces (SLBMs or Midgetman missiles, for example) sufficient for the assignment of guaranteeing that MAD will follow any use of nuclear weapons by the superpowers.

Advocates of MAD fear the repercussions of even thinking about the use of nuclear weapons in flexible response or countervailing scenarios. Presumably, to anticipate moves in some future nuclear exchange makes these moves more likely, despite the reality of MAD and hostaged cities. At a minimum, partisans of MAD advise against tempting fate (or inviting Soviet wrath and irrationality) by disrupting deterrence that has provided peace and stability for 40 years. However, either deterrence is easy or it is not. Why should flexibility detract from the facts of vulnerable cities and second strike forces to hit them, which, according to the logic of MAD, fulfill the requirements of deterrence? Advocates of flexible response suggest that perhaps deterrence is not quite as easy as adherents of MAD proclaim. While a vulnerable population constitutes one ingredient of deterrence, assured second strike capabilities, credibility of response, flexibility, and endurance of $C^3$ (to control responses and to provide the only opportunity to prevent the reality of MAD) also constitute vital ingredients. Some also suggest, to the deep dismay of their critics in the U.S. and Soviet Union, that the next logical step in the strategic equation is a transition to deterrence based on defense rather than offense.

This debate over the extent of the fragility and credibility of deterrence persists because the opponents continue to argue past each other. While no one argues *for* inconsistency between nuclear strategy and targeting doctrine, perhaps we are as "fated" to wander between MAD and flexible response trying to find the most stable and credible deterrent, as we are fated to live in a world that is MAD precisely because we need the capabilities for *both* the ultimate deterrent of assured destruction and the ultimate certainty that the threat-that-serves-as-deterrent would be used if necessary.

One additional point needs to be made here. This is not a debate of deterrence versus war-fighting, but it is a debate over the respective deterrent qualities of MAD versus deterrence based on the ability to respond flexibly to assure the Soviet Union that it could not achieve its objectives at any level of attack. Imagine two gamblers (cosmic in this case) each betting on his winning system. The backer of MAD bets everything on deterrence based on the guarantee of mutual annihilation if war were to break out. He bets that war will not break out because of the fear of the results. The worse and the more inevitable the results seem, the more likely he is to win (deter). The one who bets on flexible response fears deterrence failure. As a result, he hesitates to bet until deterrence is fortified with credible procedures to execute the deterrent threat, minimize damage to himself, and continue elements of the deterrent threat should deterrence fail (intra-war deterrence or escalation dominance.) While the MAD gambler seeks to guarantee that if deterrence fails the superpowers will destroy each other's cities, the "war fighter" seeks to provide the capability to withhold and deter attacks on cities even in the midst of war. The latter prefers to bet that capability to conduct war at various levels and the capability to end war on favorable terms will serve as added deterrents against Soviet attacks.

Many of these gamblers also consider the odds to favor the side that can offer a protective shield around its deterrent forces. On the other hand, MAD advocates believe that strategic defense will only exacerbate the erosion of deterrence already accelerated by the unwise gamble on flexible response and by the discarding of that long time ace in the hole—the ABM Treaty. This new card in the debate over deterrence, the comparative virtues of BMD versus the ABM Treaty, deserves additional attention. The debate over strategy thus continues in the next chapter on Reagan's new deal, his ante of the Strategic Defense Initiative (SDI), undertaken in the hope of winning the hand and helping the U.S. and the Soviet Union escape from the "prision of nuclear terror."

## REFERENCES

[1]Bernard Brodie, ed., *The Absolute Weapon: Atomic Power and World Order*, (New York: Harcourt, 1946): 77.

[2]Kahn, *On Escalation: Metaphors and Scenarios*, 277.

[3]Schelling, *The Strategy of Conflict*, 9 and 13.

[4]Snyder, *Deterrence and Defense: Toward a Theory of National Security*, 3.

[5]George H. Quester, *The Future of Nuclear Deterrence* (Lexington: Lexington Books, 1986): 60.

[6]Schelling, "What Went Wrong With Arms Control?" *Foreign Affairs* (Winter 1985): 233.

[7]Jervis, "Deterrence and Perception," *Internatinal Security* 7 (Winter 1982-83): 28.

[8]Smoke, *National Security and the Nuclear Dilemma*, 53.

[9]Kissinger, *Nuclear Weapons and Foreign Policy*, 133.

[10]Ibid., 144.

[11]Schelling, *Strategy of Conflict*, 194.

[12]Robert S. McNamara, *Annual Report to Congress, FY 1964*, January 30, 1963, (Washington: GPO, 1963): 28-30.

[13]Ibid., 28-30.

[14]Aaron Friedberg, "The 'Evolution of U.S. Strategic 'Doctrine'—1945-1981," in Huntington, *The Strategic Imperative: New Policies for American Security.* 67.

[15]William W. Kaufmann, *The McNamara Strategy* (New York: Harper and Row, 1964): 49-50.

[16]Betts, "Ellusive Equivalence: Political and Military Meaning of the Nuclear Balance," 107.

[17]McNamara, *Statement,* House Armed Services Committee, February 1965, quoted in Kahan, *Security in the Nuclear Age,* 94.

[18]Jervis, "Why Nuclear Superiority Doesn't Matter," *Political Science Quarterly* 94 (Winter 1979/80): 618.

[19]Ibid., 624-625.

[20]Schelling, *Strategy of Conflict,* 233.

[21]Betts, "Elusive Equivalence," 106.

[22]Freedman, *The Evolution of Nuclear Strategy,* 400.

[23]Schlesinger, *Annual Report to Congress, FY 1976,* II-6.

[24]Ibid., II-7.

[25]Brown, *Thinking About Nuclear Strategy,* 50-51.

[26]Brown, Address, in *Current Policy* 79 (May 1970): 2.

[27]Brown, *Thinking About Nucelar Strategy,* 80.

[28]Walter B. Slocombe, "The Countervailing Strategy," *International Security* 5 (Spring 1981): 21.

[29]Ibid., 22.

[30]Charles Krauthammer, "On Nuclear Morality," in R. James Woolsey, ed., *Nuclear Arms: Ethics, Strategy, Politics,* (San Francisco: Institute for Contemporary Studies, 1984): 14. See also National Conference of Catholic Bishops, *The Challenge of Peace: God's Promise and Our Response,* (Washington: 1983); and Douglas MacLean, *The Security Gamble: Deterrence Dilemmas in the Nuclear Age,* (Totowa, NJ: Rowan & Allanheld, 1984).

[31]Quester, *The Future of Nuclear Deterrence,* 142.

[32]See Carl Sagan, "Nuclear War and Climatic Catastrophe: Some Policy Implications," *Foreign Affairs* 62 (Winter 1983/84): 257-292; and responses by Leon Goure, "Nuclear Winter in Soviet Mirrors," *Strategic Review* 13 (Summer 1985): 22-38; Francis P. Hoeber and Robert K. Squire, "The Nuclear Winter Hypothesis: Policy Implications," *Strategic Review* 13 (Summer 1985): 39]46; and Joseph S. Nye, Jr., "Nuclear Winter and Policy Choices," *Survival* (March/April 1986): 119-127.

[33]Starley L. Thompson and Stephen H. Schneider "Nuclear Winter Reappraised," *Foreign Affairs* 64 (Summer 1986): 981-1005.

[34]Weinberger, *Annual Report to the Congress, FY 1983,* February 1983, 51.

[35]Ibid., 52.

[36]Victor Utgoff, "In Defense of Counterforce," *International Security* 6 (Spring 1982): 56.

[37]Betts, "Ellusive Equivalence," 106.

[38]Gray and Payne, "Nuclear Strategy: Is There a Future," *Washington Quarterly* 6 (Summer 1983): 60.

[39]Gray and Payne, "Nuclear Strategy: Is There a Future," 63-64.

[40]Payne and Gray, "Nuclear Policy in the Defense Transition," *Foreign Affairs* 62 (Spring 1984): 842.

[41]Gray, "Dangerous to Your Health: The Debate Over Nuclear Strategy and War," *Orbis* (Summer 1982): 26.

[42]Michael MccGwire, "Deterrence: the problem—not the solution," *International Affairs* 62 (Winter 1985/86): 57-65.

[43]John Steinbruner, "U.S. and Soviet Security Perspectives," *Bulletin of Atomic Scientists* 7 (August 1985): 89-90.

[44]Freedman, *The Evolution of Nuclear Strategy,* 397-400.

[45]Desmond Ball, "U.S. Strategic Forces: How Would They Be Used?" *International Security* 7 (Winter 1982/83): 60.

[46]Carnesale and Glaser, "ICBM Vulnerability: Cures Are Worse Than the Disease," 78-84.

[47]Spurgeon M. Keeny Jr. and Woflgang K. H. Panofsky, "MAD Versus Nuts: Can Doctrine or Weaponry Remedy the Mutual Hostage Relationship of the Superpowers?," 288.

[48]William E. Burrows, "Ballistic Missile Defense: The Illusion of Security," *Foreign Affairs* 62 (Spring 1984): 844.

# Weinberger,
## *Annual Report to Congress FY 1987*, pp 27-88.
## United States Goals, National Security Objectives

The basic defense strategy by which we attempted to implement the military component of containment was deterrence. In essence, that meant maintaining military forces and the determination to use them in ways that would make the costs of aggression against our vital interests substantially greater than any benefit the aggressor could hope to achieve...In the first phase of containment...the U.S. objective was ideological containment: preventing a combination of ideological appeal and internal subversion from seizing power in nations vital to U.S. interests. In 1986, as we watch the embers of communist ideology burning low, this threat has been met. Never since 1917 has communist ideology appealed to less and to fewer, and for better reasons, than it does today. The second phase of containment can be labeled geopolitical containment. Though rarely articulated, U.S. behavior in World Wars I and II reflected our fundamental interest in preventing the Eurasian landmass from being dominated by a hostile power...U.S. vital interests would be jeopardized if the Soviet Union succeeded through intimidation, or outright aggression, in dominating either Europe of Japan.

Today, we face the challenge of the third phase of containment: containment of the Soviets massive military power. Having failed to achieve its ideological or geopolitical ambitions, the Soviet Union in the early 1960s, launched the largest military buildup in world history. By a truly gargantuan effort—now consuming more than 15 percent of its gross national product—the Soviet Union has become a one-dimensional superpower. The issue today is whether the United States and its allies are prepared to permit the Soviet Union to establish military superiority it can use for territorial or political advantage...

United States Defense Strategy: Deterrence

In a word, our basic defense strategy is deterrence...It means that we seek to protect our vital interests by being strong, not to enable us to resort to aggression or war, but to prevent war by our very strength. We seek to prevent war by persuading potential adversaries that the costs of attacking us will exceed any gain they could hope to achieve...

Effective deterrence must meet four tests:

—Survivability: our forces must be able to survive a pre-emptive attack with sufficient strength to threaten losses that outweigh gains;

—Credibility: our threatened response to an attack must be credible; that is, of a form that the potential aggressor believes we could and would carry out;

—Clarity: the action to be deterred must be sufficiently clear to our adversaries that the potential aggressor knows what is prohibited; and

—Safety: the risk of failure through accident, unauthorized use, or miscalculation must be minimized...

U.S. Defense Strategies: Reagan Administration

The principal difference between the Reagan Administration's defense program and its immediate predessor's is our determination to ensure a balance of forces adequate for credible deterrence. The largest problem with the defense posture and strategy we inherited arose from a 20-year Soviet arms buildup that had been accompanied in the decade of the 1970s by a 20 percent reduction in the U.S. defense effort. The global military balance was shifting in favor of the Soviet Union. Through an investment nearly 50 percent larger than our own, the Soviets were buying advantages in virtually every area of comparison—in nuclear forces, in the NATO-Warsaw Pack balance, and in Southwest Asia.

...First, effective deterrence must address not just the objective facts of the military balance sheet, but also Soviet leaders' perceptions of the facts. It is not sufficient for us to believe that the costs we will impose in response to an attack will exceed the benefits the Soviet leadership hopes to achieve. Interpreting the facts within their own frameworks, the Soviet leaders must conclude they cannot advance their objectives by attacking us. Second, risk is the key issue in defense planning. How much should we pay for an "insurance policy" to reduce the risks of a catastrophe? How much risk can we afford? Third, deterrence is multilayered. The layers include defense, escalation, and retaliation...

The United States' conception of the role of nuclear weapons in defense strategy emerged in an era of American nuclear superiority. Now that Soviet nuclear forces are at least equal to our own, and in many dimensions superior, some earlier ideas are outmoded. The Reagan Administration has therefore given highest priority to reducing the threat of nuclear war, reducing reliance upon nuclear weapons, and continuing the development of options that provide the President a range of choices other than surrender in response to a Soviet attack. The President's SDI is not only a natural extension of the search for alternative ways to ensure deterrence; it is the logical culmination of that search...

## Reassessing Our Conceptual Arsenal: Pillars in a Defense Policy for the 1990s and Beyond

Strategic Defense Initiative
and Secure Nuclear Deterrence

Strategic defense represents a natural extension, the capstone of an array of changes in our strategic nuclear forces, motivated by the search for a more secure deterrent. It offers a far safer way to keep the peace. Critics of strategic defense are often proponents of mutual assured destruction (MAD). MAD describes a condition in which after suffering an all-out nuclear first-strike by an adversary, either superpower would retain the nuclear capability to destroy its opponent as a modern society. That is why I call it a mutual suicide pact...According to advocates of MAD, this mutual suicide pact is the bedrock of strategic stability. Because each has the capability to destroy the other's society, it is argued, neither can contemplate war, and war is therefore deterred. Indeed, some MAD proponents advocate actions to make nuclear war as horrible as possible, since that makes it as unthinkable as possible...

Is a nuclear deterrent that simply threatens the end of modern society credible? If the Soviet leadership believed that in response to a nuclear attack by them, we would be forced to choose between suicide and surrender, might they believe that we would not respond to an attack at all? Would deterrence not be weakened? To avoid that dilemma, every president and every secretary of defense since the early 1960s has maintained the capability to respond to a range of possible Soviet attacks with a range of appropriate options. This Administration has continued, indeed accelerated the development of more selective, discriminate, and controlled responses. Such limited options both pose a more credible threat to meet any level of Soviet attack and increase the likelihood that escalation could be controlled and collateral damaged minimized.

Misguided critics have sometimes confused our efforts to create credible response options for the purpose of deterring Soviet aggression with malign intention to fight limited nuclear wars...Nothing could be further from the truth. No one who has received as many briefings on nuclear weapons, or has participated in crisis exercises, as I have, could hold any doubts about the absolute necessity of avoiding nuclear war. It is precisely because of this necessity that the United States must have a secure deterrent. Moreover, the policy of developing selective, discriminate responses is manifestly moral. It is not in our interest to inform the Soviets precisely how we would respond to every possible contingency. Nor is it possible to be certain that our efforts to limit escalation and terminate a conflict once begun would succeed. But it is imperative that we take every step possible both to deter war and to limit the destruction of any conflict. Without credible limited options, our critics' view that any response to a Soviet attack would automatically lead to mutual suicide could become a tragic self-fulfilling prophecy...

The knowledge that any conflict between the United States and the Soviet Union might escalate to nuclear catastrophe is certainly part of deterrence today. But that knowledge also impels us to ask whether there is not a better way to provide for the defense of the West...We hope that strategic defense will eventually render nuclear missiles obsolete. That is our long-range vision. But we have already rendered obsolete one of the concepts of the MAD logic: the belief that deterrence must rest on the threat to destroy a certain high percentage of the Soviet population. We do not, in fact, plan our retaliatory options to maximize Soviet casualties or to attack deliberately the Soviet population. Indeed, we believe such a doctrine...is not prudent because secure deterrence should be based on the threat to destroy what the Soviet leadership values most highly: itself, its military power and political control capabilities, and its industrial ability to wage war. The United States government knows that a nuclear war cannot be won. Our nuclear doctrine is designed to ensure that the Soviet Union's leadership also believes that a nuclear war can never be won—however, they define victory—and, therefore, must never be fought....

A Strategy for Reducing and Controlling Arms

Today, the U.S. stockpile of strategic offensive, defensive, and theater nuclear weapons has some 25 percent fewer weapons than it did in 1967. The megatonnage of this diminished stockpile is approximately 70 percent lower than it was in 1967...the alliance stockpile (is at) the lowest level in 20 years...The Soviets have added more than 7,000 new warheads to their strategic offensive systems since 1967—6,500 of them since 1972, when the SALT I treaty was signed.

Treaty compliance—or noncompliance— is another verse in the same song. Ingnoring Soviet violations of arms control agreements will not make them go away. Indeed, reluctance on our part to respond can only encourage further Soviet noncompliance...arms control violations must be met by firm American reactions. The United States responses should be proportionate (though not necessarily identical in nature), and clearly in the United States' interests. The Soviet leadership must understand that the United States has no intention of accepting one-sided compliance with arms control agreements...

Let me emphasize four key points. First, President Reagan has insisted that we focus steadily on the goal: How to prevent nuclear war and build a more secure world...Second, arms reduction is a component of our larger national security policy—not an isolated objective or independent instrument. Arms reduction is one of the ways in which we pursue our national security objectives. Recognition that arms negotiations and agreements are but a strand in the overall relations between the United States and the Soviet Union brings into sharp focus a major dimension of any effective strategy for achieving arms reductions...In planning U.S. forces and acquiring arms, while simultaneously negotiating with the Soviet Union, it is necessary for us to create incentives for them to reach agreements that meet our interest. Why should the Soviets agree to reductions, if we reduce voluntarily without any corresponding Soviet reduction? Why should they comply, if we previously accepted their violations? Ask yourself: Why is General Secretary Gorbachev now proposing total elimination of nuclear weapons by the year 2000? Quite simply, it is the new strength and resolve we have demonstrated. Not only must we negotiate from strength—this is in fact the only way we can negotiate effectively. It is not Soviet goodwill, but our strength that is bringing about their changes. Third, negotiated, structural arms agreements must...significantly reduce the number of offensive systems, bringing us to parity (measured not just by numbers of warheads but by effectiveness) at much lower levels than each side has now, be effectively verifiable, and contribute to a broad policy of strengthening peace and stability...

## Report of the President's Commission On Strategic Forces (April 1983)

I. Deterrence and Arms Control

The Commission believes that effective arms control is an essential element in diminishing the risk of nuclear war...At the same time the Commission is persuaded that as we consider the threat of mass destruction we must consider simultaneously the threat of aggressive totalitarianism. Both are central to the political dilemmas of our age. For the United States and its allies the essential dual task of statecraft is, and must be, to avoid the first and contain the second...Although the United States and the Soviet Union hold fundamentally incompatible views of history, of the nature of society, and of the individual's place in it, the existence of nuclear weapons imbues that rivalry with peril unprecedented in human history. The temptation is sometimes great to simplify—or oversimplify—the difficult problems that result, either by blinking at the devasting nature of modern full-scale war or by refusing to acknowledge the emptiness of life under modern totalitarianism. But it is naive, false, and dangerous to assume that either of these, today, can be ignored and the other dealt with in isolation. We cannot cope with the efforts of the Soviet Union to extend its power without giving thought to the way nuclear weapons have sharply raised the stakes and changed the nature of warfare. Nor can we struggle against nuclear war or the arms race in some abstract sense without keeping before us the Soviet Union's drive to expand its power, which is what makes those struggles so difficult...

Our words, policies, and actions should all make clear the American conviction that nuclear war, involving few or many nuclear weapons, would be a tragedy of unparalleled scope for humanity...Neither the American people, our allies, nor the Soviets should doubt our abhorrence of nuclear war in any form. By the same token, however, our task as a nation cannot be understood from a position of moral neutrality toward the difference between liberty and totalitarianism...Only if Americans believe that it is worth a sustained effort over the years to preserve liberty in the face of challenge by a system that is the antithesis of liberal values can our task be seen as a just and worthy one in spite of its dangers...

We should, with calm persistence, limit the expansion of...the Soviet Union. We should persuade its leaders that they cannot successfully divert attention from internal problems by resorting to international blackmail, expansion, and militarism—rationalized by alleged threats posed by us or our allies. We should also be ready to encourage the Soviets to begin to settle differences between us, through equitable arms control agreements and other measures. But moral neutrality and indifference or acquiescence in the face of Soviet efforts to expand their military and political power do not hasten such settlements—they delay them, make them less likely, and ultimately increase the risk of war.

Deterrence is central to the calm persistence we must demonstrate in order to reduce these risks. American strategic forces exist to deter attack on the United States or its allies—and the coercion that would be possible if the public or decisionmakers believed that the Soviets might be able to launch a successful attack. Such a policy of deterrence, like the security policy of the West itself, is essentially defensive in nature. The strategic forces that are necessary in order to support such a policy by their very existence help to convince the Soviet Union's leaders: that the West has the military strength and political will to resist aggression; and that, if they should ever choose to attack, they should have no doubt that we can and would respond until we have so damaged the Soviet state that they will unmistakably be far worse off than if they had never begun.

There can be no doubt that the very scope of the possible tragedy of modern nuclear war, and the increased destruction made possible even by modern non-nuclear technology, have changed the nature of war itself. This is not only because massive conventional war with modern weapons could be horrendously destructive...but also because *conventional* war between the world's major power blocs is the most likely way for *nuclear* war to develop. The problem of deterring the threat of nuclear war; in short, cannot be isolated from the overall power balance between East and West. Simply put, it is war that must concern us, not nuclear war alone. Thus we must maintain a balance between our nuclear and conventional forces and we must demonstrate to the Soviets our cohesion and our will...

Deterrence is not, and cannot be, fluff. In order for deterrence to be effective we must not merely have weapons, we must be perceived to be able, and prepared, if necessary, to use them effectively against the key elements of Soviet power. Deterrence is not an abstract notion amenable to simply quantification. Still less is it a mirror image of what would deter ourselves. Deterrence is the set of beliefs in the minds of the Soviet leaders, given their own values and attitudes, about our capabilities and our will. It requires us to determine, as best we can, what would deter them from considering aggression, even in a crisis—not to determine what would deter us...

Arms control can: reduce the risk of war; help limit the spread of nuclear weapons; remove or reduce the risk of misunderstanding of particular events or accidents; seal off wasteful, dangerous, or unhelpful lines of technical development before either side gets too committed to them; help channel modernization into stabilizing rather than destabilizing paths; reduce misunderstanding about the purpose of weapons developments and thus reduce the need to over-insure against worst-case projections; and help make arsenals less destructive and costly. To achieve part or all of these positive and useful goals, we must keep in mind the importance of compliance and adequate verification—difficult problems in light of the nature of the Soviet state—and the consequent importance of patience in order to reach fair and reasonable agreements...stability should be the primary objective both of the modernization of our strategic forces and of our arms control proposals. Our arms control proposals and our strategic arms programs should thus be integrated and be mutually reinforcing. They should work together to permit us, and encourage the Soviets, to move in directions that reduce or eliminate the advantage of aggression and also reduce the risk of war by accident or miscalculation. As we try to enhance stability in this sense, the Commission believes that other objectives should be subordinated to the overall goal of permitting the United States to move—over time—toward more stable strategic deployments, and giving the Soviets the strong incentive to do the same. Consequently it believes, for the reasons set forth below, that it is important to move toward reducing the value and importance of individual strategic targets.

## II. Soviet Objectives and Programs

The Soviets have shown by word and deed that they regard military power, including nuclear weapons, as a useful tool in the projection of their national influence. In the Soviet strategic view, nuclear weapons are closely related to, and are integrated with, their other military and political instruments as a means of advancing their interests. The Soviets have concentrated enormous effort on the development and modernization of nuclear weapons, obviously seeking to achieve what they regard as important advantages in certain areas of nuclear weaponry...Historically the Soviets have not been noted for taking large risks. But one need not take the view that their leaders are eager to launch a nuclear war in order to understand the political advantages that a massive nuclear weapons buildup can hold for a nation seeking to expand its power and influence, or to comprehend the dangers that such a motivation and such a buildup hold for the rest of the world.

# BIBLIOGRAPHY

Allison, Graham T. el al., ed. *Hawks, Doves, and Owls.* New York: W. W. Norton & Co., 1985.

Amster, Warren. "Design for Deterrence," *Bulletin of the Atomic Scientists.* 12 (May 1956).

Ball, Desmond. "Can Nuclear War Be Controlled?" *Adelphi Paper 169. Longon: International Institute for Strategic Studies, October 1981.*
"U.S. Strategic Forces: How Would They Be Used?" *International Security* 7 (Winter 1982-83): 31-61.

Bertram, Christoph, ed. *Strategic Deterrence in a Changing Environment.* Montclaire, N.J.: Gower & Allanheld, Osmun, 1981.

Betts, Richard K. *Surprise Attack: Lessons for Defense Planning.* Washington D.C.: Brookings Institute, 1982.

Bracken, Paul. *The Command and Control of Nuclear Forces. New Haven: Yale University Press, 1983.*

Brodie, Bernard. "The Development of Nuclear Strategy," *International Security.* 2 (Spring 1978): 65-83.
*Strategy in the Missile Age.* Princeton: Princeton University Press, 1959.

Buchan, Alastair. *Problems of Modern Strategy.* London: Chatto & Windus, 1970.

Burt, Richard ed. *Arms Control and Defense Postures in the 1980's* Boulder: Westview, 1982.

Collins, John M. *U.S.-Soviet Military Balance: Concepts and Capabilities:* 1960-1980: New York: McGraw-Hill, 1980.

*DAEDALUS. U.S. Defense Policy in the 1980's.* Entire Issue. (Fall 1980 and Winter 1981).

Dinerstein, Herbert S. *War and the Soviet Union.* New York: Praeger, 1959.

Douglass, Joseph D., Jr. "Strategic Planning and Nuclear Insecurity," *Orbis.* (Fall 1983): 667-694.

Enthoven, Alain C. and Smith, K. Wayne. *How Much is Enough? Shaping the Defense Program 1961-1969.* New York: Harper & Row, 1971.

Erickson, John. "The Chimera of Mutual Deterrence," *Strategic Review,* (Spring 1976): 11-17.

Fallows, James. *National Defense.* New York: Random House, 1981.

George, Alexander and Smoke, Richard. *Deterrence in American Foreign Policy: Theory and Practice.* New York: Columbia University Press, 1974.

Green, Philip. *Deadly Logic: The Theory of Nuclear Deterrence.* Columbus, Ohio: Ohio State University Press, 1966.

Greenwood, Ted and Nacht, Michael. "The New Nuclear Debate: Sense or Nonsense," *Foreign Affairs.* 52 (July 1974).

Halperin, Morton H. *Limited War in the Nuclear Age.* New York: Wiley, 1963.

Howard, Michael. "The Forgotten Dimmensions of Strategy," *Foreign Affairs* 57 (Summer 1979): 976-986.

Huntington, Samuel P. *The Common Defense: Strategic Programs in National Politics.* New York: Columbia University Press, 1961.

Ikle, Fred C. "Can Nuclear Deterrence Last Out the Century?" *Foreign Affairs* 51 (1973): 267-85.
  "Nuclear Strategy: Can There Be a Happy Ending?" *Foreign Affairs.* (Spring 1985): 810-826.

Jastrow, Robert. "Why Strategic Superiority Matters," *Commentary.* (March 1983): 27-32.

Jervis, Robert. *The Illogic of American Nuclear Strategy.* Cornell: Cornell University Press, 1984.
  et al. *Psychology and Deterrence.* Baltimore: John Hopkins University Press, 1985.

Kahn, Herman. *On Thermonuclear War.* Princeton: Princeton University Press, 1960.
  *Thinking About the Unthinkable.* New York: Horizon Press, 1962.

Kaufmann, William, ed. *Military Policy and National Security.* Princeton: Princeton University Press, 1956.
  *A Reasonable Defense.* Washington, Brookings Institute, 1986.

Kegley, Charles W., Jr. and Wittkoph, Eugene R., eds. *The Nuclear Reader: Strategy, Weapons, War.* New York: St. Martin's Press, 1985.

Kennan, George. *The Nuclear Delusion: Soviet American Relations in the Atomic Age.* New York: Pantheon Books, 1982.

Kerr, Donald M. and Kupperman, Robert H. "Nuclear Force Architecture for the 1980's," *Washington Quarterly,* (Winter 1982): 119-129.

Knorr, Klaus. "Controlling Nuclear War." *International Security* 9 (Spring 1985): 79-98.
  and Read, Thorton, eds. *Limited Strategic War.* New York: Praeger, 1962.

Lebow, Richard N. *Between Peace and War: The Nature of International Crisis.* Baltimore: Johns Hopkins University Press, 1981.

Legvold, Robert. "Strategic 'Doctrine' and SALT: Soviet and American Views," *Survival* II (Jan.-Feb. 1979): 8-13.
  *The Problem of Extended Deterrence.* London: International Institute for Strategic Studies, 1981.

McNamara, Robert S. *The Essence of Security: Reflections in Office* London: Hodder & Stoughton, 1968.

Malone, Thomas F. "International Scientists on Nuclear Winter," *Bulletin of the Atomic Scientists* (December 1985): 52-55.

Maxwell, Nancy and Tirman, John, eds. *Toward a New Security: Lessons of the Forty Years Since Trinity.* Cambridge, Mass: Union of the Concerned Scientists, 1985.

May, Michael. "The U.S.-Soviet Approach to Nuclear Weapons," *International Security* 9 (Spring 1985): 140-153.

Morgan, Patrick. *Deterrence: A Conceptual Analysis.* London: Sage Publications, 1977.

Myrdal, Alva. *The Game of disarmament: How the United States and Russia Run the Arms Race.* Manchester: Manchester University Press, 1977.

Nacht, Michael. *The Age of Vulnerability.* Washington, D.C.: Brookings Institute, 1985.

Nitze, Paul. "Assuring Strategic Ability in an Era of Detente," *Foreign Affairs* 54 (January 1976): 207-32.

O'Brien, William and Langan, John, eds., *The Nuclear Dilemma: The Just War Tradition* (Lexington: DC Heath, 1986).

Office of Technology Assessment, *the Effects of Nuclear War* (Washington: GPO, 1979).

Osgood, Robert Endicott. *Limited War: The Challenge to America Strategy.* Chicago: University of Chicago Press, 1957.

Payne, Keith B. "Deterrence, Arms Control, and U.S. Strategic Doctrine," *Orbis,* (Fall 1981): 747-769.

Pipes, Richard. "Why the Soviet Union Thinks it Could Fight and Win a Nuclear War," *Commentary* 64 (July 1977): 21-34.

Prins, Gwyn, ed. *The Nuclear Crisis Reader.* New York: Vintage, 1984.

Schell, Jonathan. *The Fate of the Earth.* New York: Alfred Knopf, 1982.

Schelling, Thomas and Halperin, Morton. *Strategy and Arms Control.* New York: Twentieth Century Fund, 1961.

Schilling, Warner R. "U.S. Strategic Nuclear Concepts in the 1970's," *International Security* 6 (Fall 1981): 48-79.

Scoville, Herbert. "Flexible Madness," *Foreign Policy* 24 (Spring 1974): 164-77.

Segal, Gerald et al. *Nuclear War and Nuclear Peace.* London, MacMillan, 1983.

Sigal, Leon, "The Logic of Deterrence in Theory and Practice," *International Organization* 33 (Autumn 1979): 567-79.

Sloss, Leon and Millot, Marc Dean. "U.S. Nuclear Strategy in Evolution," *Strategic Review,* (Winter 1984): 19-28.

Smoke, Richard. *War: Controlling Escalation.* Cambridge: Harvard University Press, 1977.

Steinbruner, John. "Launch Under Attack," *Scientific American* 250 (January 1984): 37-47.

"Nuclear Decapitation," *Foreign Policy* 45 (Winter 1981-82): 16-28.

Stone, Jeremy. *Strategic Persuasion: Arms Limitation Through Dialogue.* New York: Columbia University Press, 1967.

Thompson, W. Scott, ed. *From Weakness to Strength.* San Francisco: Institute for Contemporary Studies, 1980.

Tucker, Robert W. *The Nuclear Debate: Deterrence and the Lapse of Faith.* New York: Holmes and Neier, 1985.

U.S. Senate. Committee on Armed Services. *Military Implications of the Treaty on the Limitation of Anti-Ballistic Missile Systems and the Interim Agreement on Limitation of Strategic Offensive Arms.* Hearings: 92nd Cong., 2nd Sess., 1972.

Van Cleave, William R. "The Nuclear Weapons Debate," *U.S. Naval Institute Proceedings* 92 (1966): 26-38.

Wohlstetter, Albert. "The Delicate Balance of Terror," *Foreign Affairs* 37 (1959): 211-34.

"Racing Forward? Or Ambling Back?" *Survey* 22 (Summer-Autumn 1976): 163-217.

Wolf, Charles, Jr. "Beyond Containment: Redesigning American Policies," *Washington Quarterly,* (Winter 1982): 107-117.

Woosley, R. James. "The Politics of Vulnerability: 1980-83," *Foreign Affairs* 62 (Spring 1984): 805-819.

York, Herbert. *Race to Oblivion: A Participant's View of the Arms Race.* New York: Simon & Schuster, 1971.

# CHAPTER VI

# Star Wars or What To Do
# If the Empire Strikes First

## Defense, Strategy, and Technology

American nuclear strategy is again undergoing review as strategists, scientists, politicians, and pacifists, debate the wisdom of a transition to a "new" deterrent posture based on defense rather than offense.[1] The Reagan administration itself appears to be divided over its support for two different rationales for missile defense. Reagan wants BMD to initiate a wholly non-nuclear strategy; i.e., to make nuclear weapons obsolete. On the other hand, the administration also acknowledges the crucial importance of an interim objective, a victory denial or flexible response capability.

While advocates of flexible response embrace the latter objective, they differ in the degree of their belief in the possibility of making nuclear weapons obsolete and cities inviolable. While some are committed to city defense, most advocates of flexible response urge reliance on active defenses of American strategic nuclear forces and other targets like $C^3$ facilities. They fear Soviet offensive and defensive capabilities and violations of treaty provisions to limit such capabilities. In sum, they recommend BMD to remedy the perceived imbalance in Soviet-American strategic capability, to insure against Soviet capability to defeat the U.S. in any attack scenario, to limit damage should deterrence fail, and to replace the presumably unstable, incredible, and illogical strategy of MAD.

Advocates of MAD fear that illusions about the value of BMD undermine deterrence and strategic stability. They assume that an attempt to build a BMD system (especially a system devoted to city defense) is technologically impossible and will devour huge resources in a hopeless effort, provoke Soviet countermeasures, escalate an arms race in both defensive and offensive weapons, jeopardize the Anti-Ballistic Missile Treaty (ABMT), complicate NATO strategy, leave other weapons (cruise missiles and bombers, for example) unimpeded, and appear to the Soviets as a part of an American first strike posture. In their view, the Soviets might consider, during some crisis, the comparative advantages and disadvantages of striking first or second against an American BMD too weak to protect against a first strike but tolerably effective against a debilitated Soviet second strike. Worry about such destabilizing incentives for preemption consumes many critics of the SDI.

The issue of technological feasibility occupies much of the attention of strategists and scientists. Critics of the SDI point to technical flaws in almost every stage of a hypothetical system that must defend against

Soviet ICBMs that may evade and/or overwhelm American defenses. In their view, there are just too many uncertainties, vulnerabilities, and unachievable prerequisites for any "perfect" defense to be maintained in a hostile environment of nuclear attack. Technological obstacles include the problems of maintaining $C^3$ reliability and meeting the needs of more perfect Early Warning Systems, missile and warhead interceptors, battle management sensors, computer software, and invulnerable space stations. Finally, a hypothetical BMD response must be triggered almost instantly since the crucial boost-phase of Soviet ICBM's lasts from 3-5 minutes, in which time there must be detection, tracking, aiming, decision, interception, destruction, and damage assessment. One possible way to anticipate such a performance is to place BMD on "automated response." This would raise additional doubts about the sophistication and war-time reliability of untested computers and vulnerable space stations. Even if scientists could overcome the overwhelming technical obstacles, there could be little assurance of the perpetual perfection of defenses, which would be sensitive to the offensive improvements and ASAT technology of the adversary.

While the critics may be correct in the short run, their conclusions seem premature. We cannot rule out, categorically, the possibility and cost-effectiveness of all future defenses. This is especially unwise in view of Soviet research and development in BMD and the Soviet potential for an ABMT breakout that could significantly affect strategic stability. Even a partial Soviet BMD, in combination with a robust counterforce capability (SS-18) targeted against increasingly vulnerable American ICBM silos (Minuteman or MX filled), poses a major danger of Soviet nuclear advantage. While some analysts are confident enough about the technical infeasibility of BMD to urge the U.S. to forego research in this area, it may be more prudent to hedge our bets by keeping defensive options open, especially in the area of silo defense. Whether the U.S. bases its strategy on MAD or defense, preparations to keep ICBMs invulnerable and to make a Soviet first strike futile remain high priority requirements.

This chapter will investigate the feasibility of BMD, as well as its desirability in strategic and political terms. Soviet and NATO reactions to BMD also demand attention. Nearly all analysts assume that the Soviets will respond to an American BMD with both offensive and defensive countermeasures at first. The debate focuses of three questions: is the SDI a useful hedge against a possible Soviet initial advantage in BMD, is a prolonged two-pronged arms race inevitable, and if the Soviets choose a defensive arms race, how poor a choice would this be. Analysts also agree that NATO allies display a conspicuous coolness towards BMD because of anxiety about its potential decoupling effect, the resulting ineffectiveness of Eurostrategic forces against a Soviet BMD, and the prospect of superpower willingness to risk outbreaks of local wars (including wars in Europe) in the face of their newly achieved invulnerability. Considerable debate remains, however, over the validity of these fears.

One additional question needs to be answered: What would be the impact of space-based BMD testing and deployment on the ABMT? Many analysts anticipate that BMD research alone jeopardizes the existence of the ABMT. However, they differ in their evaluations of the inherent value of the treaty and the effect of engaging in negotiations to revise it. If the ABMT is valuable as a safeguard against a Soviet BMD breakout or a new arms race, then nothing should interfere with it. On the other hand, if the ABMT has lost relevance in the 1980s, then the superpowers might consider appropriate revisions. These propositions set the scene for the debate over the extent to which one should be concerned about the fragility of the ABMT. In the rest of the chapter, I will elaborate on these areas of disagreement over BMD and the ABMT.

## Star Wars: Systems and Battle Stations

As noted above, there are two basic schools of thought on BMD: one that condemns it as technologically impossible, impossibly costly, and uniquely provocative; and a second that approves it as technology's answer to strategic vulnerability. A review of the nature of the targets, functions, weapons, Battle Management capabilities, and problems of the system, will enable us to judge the technological merits (and de-merits) of BMD.[2]

ICBMs and warheads come in various packages with varying degrees of speed, camouflage, and attack characteristics. Ballistic missiles consist of four phases. The two most important are the 3-5 minute boost phase, during which space-based sensors can detect the heat of the missile booster's engine, and the equally brief post boost phase, during which the Post Boost Vehicle (PBV) from the booster expels warheads and decoys. During these phases, the ratio of interceptor to incoming object favors the interceptor prior to PBV release. In the 7-15 minute mid course phase, ground and space-based interceptors will attack warheads as they "fall" to their targets. In this phase, sensors will face the complex task of discrimination between the tens of thousands of tiny and "cold" warheads and decoys. In the 30-40 second terminal phase, where the now more easily discernable warheads reenter the atmosphere, warheads could encounter current or near term weapons such as ground-launched, high-speed rockets and other Kinetic Energy Weapons (KEWs). These weapons, while effective for silo defense, would require additional technological breakthroughs in speed, accuracy, and maneuverability to protect the more vulnerable cities from the barage of warheads expected in an all-out attack.

To be effective, a BMD system must fulfill a number of functions and objectives such as: 1) early warning of attack; 2) coordinating information from sensors, computers, and other elements of $C^3$ to engage, track, and destroy boosters, PBVs, and warheads and to discriminate between warheads and decoys (Battle Management function); 3) ensuring the survivability of components; and 4) supplying power sufficient for earth launches and operations in orbit. The first three objectives require precision sensors, weapons, battle stations, and computers. To accomplish the difficult task of discrimination between warheads and decoys, scientists hope to perfect an "imaging" process that obtains a "picture" of objects being released from PBVs, thus enabling sensors to use the "picture" for birth-to-death tracking of warheads. The final objective will require new technologies to generate cheaper and more efficient energy sources.

KEWs and DEWs (Directed Energy Weapons) are under review for use against every stage of missile and warhead flight. KEWs, which harness the energy of motion for destruction, may include hypervelocity or electromagnetic launchers and chemical-fueled rockets, which both thrust homing projectiles (smart rocks or bullets) toward enemy boosters and warheads. Guided by airborne, space-based, or on-board sensors KEWs might attack targets in the midcourse phase. Larger and faster non-nuclear KEWs such as high-acceleration, heat-seeking, ground-launched interceptors are necessary for endoatmospheric intercept. DEWs such as space and ground-based lasers (electrically or chemically driven), X-ray lasers that depend on nuclear explosives, and neutral particle beams, although exotic and primarily still conceptual, show promise as devices to destroy warheads in space with intense beams of light, electrons, X-rays, or atomic particles accelerated to the speed of light. To supplement satellite emplacement for these devices, a "pop-up" mirror system might be employed to "mirror relay" ground-based lasers to assigned destinations.

While major technological stumbling blocks face many of these BMD systems, technological breakthroughs might compensate for some of these. For example, KEWs, some with built-in sensors and guidance systems, and DEWs such as ground-based, non-nuclear lasers with some space-based elements are all hypothetically possible. According to the Pentagon and the SDI organization (SDIO), a "phase one" BMD that could kill 50% of a projected Soviet counterforce striking force could be deployed before the end of the century.[3] Many critics even acknowledge the current availability of the basic technology for this deployment. As for software coding, a variety of studies have concluded that current software technology, designed to be "error tolerant," will suffice for the phase one system. Overall, projections vary from 5-10 years to develop silo defense weapons and from 40-60 years to develop space-based systems that might extend coverage to cities.[4]

However, before arriving at conclusions about the possibilities of these weapons, some of which may also be useful against bombers, SLBMs, and cruise missiles, it is necessary to note again what may be the two most difficult requirements of BMD (especially for city defense): 1) creating a sophisticated and cost effective battle management complex that must remain maintenance and error free for years and 2) ensuring the survivability of its ground, air, and space assets in the midst of missile and ASAT attack. The main obstacles to meeting these requirements remain target discrimination and power generation. Breakthroughs would depend on quantum leaps in the development of software, computer circuit miniturization, space-based nuclear reactor capability, and space-based battle station and "mirror" self-defense capability.

Critics focus on each stage of missile flight and each function of BMD to emphasize the fact that there are just too many vulnerabilities and unachievable prerequisites for any perfect defense to be developed. A

BMD system must overcome obstacles imposed by the short boost and post boost phases, the inpenetrability of the atmosphere, the saturation of tens of thousands of warheads and decoys during the midcourse phase, and the vulnerability of sensors, $C^3$, and other Battle Management facilities.[5] Critics maintain that inherent limitations in sensors and computer software present the most debilitating obstacles to a dependable, self-maintaining, and self-initiating wartime system immune to attack and deception.[6] The Battle Management mechanisms will have to respond to an overwhelming first strike, gather and process data from a great number of vulnerable sources, and initiate responses quickly enough to destroy ICBMs in their first two stages to prevent warhead and decoy saturation in later phases. Those responses, especially crucial for population defense, will depend on largely untested software that will have to perform billions of arithmetic operations per second. Although the Strategic Defense Initiative Organization might dispute this appraisal, the technology necessary for many of these systems and tasks, if possible at all, is decades or more away.

In addition to these complications, the costs for even near term systems and their energy needs will be high. These expenses could greatly exceed the cost to the Soviet Union to overwhelm, outmaneuver, circumvent, or attack a BMD system. Critics assume that defense costs more than offense due to the attacker's flexibility in choosing targets and countermeasures and the defender's requirements of protecting all targets and anticipating all possible countermeasures. Soviet counters may include hardening, spinning, shining, or foil-stripping boosters to deflect laser and beam hits; shortening the boost phase or slowing boosters, both of which would keep the dispersal stage of warheads within the atmosphere and thus less vulnerable to DEWs; increasing the numbers of boosters, warheads, and decoys; upgrading deception techniques (for example, mylar balloons that appear like warheads, decoys that imitate the "wake" of warheads entering the atmosphere, and aerosol sprays that surround warheads in a radar wave-scattering cloud); transferring payloads to maneuvering and low-flying, long range warheads; and confronting the defense itself (ground, air, and space assets) with ASAT weapons, radar homing warheads, and salvage fusion.[7] The Soviets promise to undertake such counters should the U.S. abandon the ABMT.

While this litany of conceptual and engineering flaws and discussion of possible counters to BMD serve us well in advising caution about the prospects of a "perfect" defense, it seems premature to abandon attempts at researching the possibility of developing BMD. As Zbigniew Brzezinski pointed out, science does not have a stellar record in predicting technological developments such as atom splitting, jet propulsion, ICBMs, and so forth.[8] As for the near future, mastering technological challenges imposed by 1) midcourse discrimination (via "imaging" or other forms of adpative optics), 2) precision-guided lasers (with sensors and computers built-in to eliminate the need for vulnerable ground facilities), and 3) particle beams (depending on newly developed "rubber mirrors" to correct for turbulence in the atmosphere and to reduce beam spreading so that small relay mirrors could direct the beam against a target in its boost phase) could enable the U.S. to develop an effective BMD, negate simple countermeasures, and force the Soviets to resort to costly responses.[9]

With respect to the latter two results, the Soviets will face high costs and difficulties in their attempts to counter or attack an American BMD. As Robert Jastrow noted, for example, lead protection for missiles would make them too heavy for liftoff without reductions in payloads, spinning boosters would not defeat lasers sending out energy in sharp pulses, and a shine on booster surfaces to deflect lasers would be tarnished through launch and after exposure to laser heat.[10] Finally, it should be noted that space assets might be defended through hardening, shielding, concealment, proliferation, maneuverability, and deploying guard satellites or "gun" emplacements on satellites. Of course, some of these counters to countermeasures are as exotic as the other systems necessary for an effective BMD.

The debate over the feasibility and costs of weapons, sensors, and countermeasures involves much speculation. Given their doubts about the operational feasibility, cost effectiveness, and robustness of a BMD system, most critics conclude that a perfect BMD is impossible. Supporters, however, point to potential technological breakthroughs (both Soviet and American) as a compelling reason to keep the BMD option open.

## Star Wars: A Strategy for Survival or Superiority?

Regardless of one's judgment of the technological prospects for BMD, questions concerning its potential impact on strategic stability demand more immediate attention. Reagan, in his 1983 address on the SDI, expressed concern about the horrors of nuclear war and his reluctance to rely on a threat of MAD for deterrent purposes. According to the principles of MAD, the U.S. and the Soviet Union leave populations undefended and rely on strategic nuclear forces to threaten devasting retaliation against any attacker. The capability to destroy cities deters a potential attacker, and the greater the guarantee that nuclear war will be horrible, guaranteed by undefended cities, the more stable the deterrent.

Reagan and opponents of MAD question the logic of a strategy that promises absolute destruction if deterrence fails. Would the Soviets, who have rejected MAD explicitly in the past and implicitly (a counterforce build-up targeting silos rather than cities), believe in the American threat to retaliate in response to peripheral or even direct Soviet attacks? Could the Soviets hope that a counterforce first strike against vulnerable silos might result in American paralysis rather than retaliation with SLBMs against Soviet cities, which would then invite Soviet return strikes against American cities? Defending silos might eliminate the suicidal aspects of MAD. With missile defense the U.S. would have two options, if under attack: it could respond with a limited counterforce second strike or a full retaliatory strike. The increased uncertainty about acquiring the ability to eliminate American counterforce second strike forces would deter the Soviets from a preemptive first strike. In sum, according to Weinberger,

"Defense that could deny the Soviet missiles the military objectives of their attack, or deny the Soviets confidence in the achievement of those objectives, would discourage them from even considering such an attack, and thus be a highly effective deterrent."[11] This rationale for BMD reflects Weinberger's interest in a victory denial capability.

If BMD could deny the Soviets a capability to strike first, since Soviet ICBMs would fail against defended targets and would be foolish to use in first strike against cities, then both the threat of retaliation and the futility of attack would jointly deter attack. But Reagan wants to do more than protect silos. He wants to "render nuclear missiles obsolete." A move towards a country-wide BMD would reflect a more complete shift towards deterrence based solely on defense and victory denial, since offensive weapons would eventually be futile against ICBMs and populations. However, the prospect of defending populations is the most challenging technological and strategic task of BMD. If possible, the transformation to deterrence based on defense would be complete. In the meantime, prior to extending full coverage, supporters of BMD, also point to the damage limitation properties of BMD. They argue that deterrence based on defense would not only deter because it could defeat a Soviet attack, but should deterrence fail it might provide some protection for the population, especially if coupled with an arms control agreement to decrease ICBMs. In addition, it might offer some prospect of terminating a nuclear engagement at some stage short of mutual assured destruction, if the missile defense system could seriously degrade a Soviet offensive first strike capability.

Critics argue that the premise that inspires the desire for BMD—the danger from ICBM vulnerability—is flawed as long as SLBMs remain able to retaliate against cities. In addition, they fear that preparing for BMD could appear like first strike and war-fighting preparations to the Soviets, since the same defenses that complicate a Soviet first strike plan would be even more effective against a weakened Soviet second strike. A BMD would exert great pressure on the Soviets to counter with offensive and defensive build-ups or even with preemption. Neither superpower could avoid participation in a dual arms race since each would fear the other's BMD capability against retaliatory forces. Charles Glaser described an incendiary situation in which the U.S. and the U.S.S.R. would increase offensive forces to overcome the other's defenses and defensive forces to offset expected offensive advances of the other side.[12]

Sidney Drell described another scenario in which an imperfect BMD system would guarantee preemptive incentives:

> In a crisis each side would wrestle with the fear that the opponent might strike first, and if war seemed inevitable a preemptive strike would be judged better than awaiting the adversary's initial blow...the preemptive strike would be made not on any calculation of absolute advantage, but solely on one of relative advantage: since a nuclear attack is inevitable anyway, strike first in order to enhance one's own effectiveness and diminish the enemy's as much as possible.[13]

Preemption might also result from superpower assumptions that they could initiate aggression without risking the consequences of MAD. One study concluded that the superpowers, acting under such a false sense of security, could end up with defenses that don't defend and offenses that don't deter.[14] Preparations for BMD and damage limitation, then are not only unnecessary, but they are dangerous as well. They undermine deterrence based on the healthy fear of the futility of defense, the inevitability of escalations, and the guarantee of MAD.

These criticisms, inspired by the credo of the unavoidable reality of MAD, entail some questionable assumptions. In response to the assumption about the irrelevance of ICBM vulnerability, in view of the retaliatory value of SLBMs, it is important to note the transitory nature of this situation. There are several promising developments in Anti-Submarine Warfare (ASW). For example, satellite sensors can detect, with limited but improving degrees of accuracy, the thermal and surface wakes of submarines at sea. Further breakthroughs in ASW that might compromise the ability to rely on SLBMs merit concern. Supporters of BMD, who see considerable relevance in the vulnerability of ICBMs, seek to anticipate and compensate for the potential vulnerability of SLBMs before the triad of ICBMs, SLBMs, and bombers disintegrates one leg at a time.

Let us also examine the major contention that discussion of BMD will undermine deterrence, appear like first strike preparations to the Soviets, lead to preemption, and make war more likely since the superpowers, with their newly found defenses, could undertake riskier international behavior. While one or more of these may unfortunately occur, I doubt whether we can argue all three propositions simultaneously. If the newly defended superpowers felt secure enough to consider risky behavior, they would not be moved to preempt out of fear of the other's first strike. If, on the other hand, they feared the other's first strike, they would not take risks in crises. However, the fear of a casual attitude about initiating a nuclear war is not the main concern, as few analysts anticipate that the superpowers could ever feel secure enough to accept the consequences of even a limited nuclear war. Fear of BMD failure; fear of insufficient first strike success against the other's defended, redundant, and mobile second strike capability; and fear of escalation all serve as powerful deterrents. It is rather the questions of the vitality of deterrence when affected by the projected deployment of BMD that is at issue in the debate between supporters of MAD and defense.

What, then, deters best: 1) the threat of MAD which, while it has apparently worked so far to assure deterrence based on fear of retaliation, may lack credibility in an age of improving warhead accuracy and penetrability, smaller warhead yields, and satellite sensor advances that compromise the invulnerability of mobile or otherwise hard to find nuclear forces; or 2) the capability to defend nuclear forces (and perhaps even populations) which, while it might prevent the success of an opponent's limited first strike, appears better suited as a defense against an opponent's weakened second strike? If one bets on defense, one counts on the guarantee that an enemy's first strike would fail; but one than accepts the possibility that an enemy's BMD may limit the effectiveness of retaliatory forces and the more worrisome risks that defenses may be imperfect, provocative, and destabilizing. To bet on MAD, one counts on the fear of escalation and assured destruction to deter; but one accepts the risk that the threat of MAD may lack credibility, if retaliatory forces become vulnerable.

## The Soviets Stalk SDI

Before resolving the dilemma of defenses that may or may not defend or deter, lets elaborate on the debate over the nature of likely Soviet reactions to BMD. While the Soviets have been active recently in research, development, and testing of various BMD-related radars, $C^3$ mechanisms, and weapons, they officially reject Reagan's overtures regarding a transition to a strategy that relies on defense. They accuse the U.S. of attempting to achieve nuclear superiority and note the destabilizing impact of any BMD.[15] In their view, since any BMD system would be vulnerable to countermeasures and therefore incapable of protecting the U.S. against the first strike, the Soviets could logically conclude that the U.S. intends to use a BMD program, in combination with its counterforce (MX and Trident-II) build-up, to protect against Soviet retaliatory forces debilitated by an American first strike. The Soviets repeatedly warn that anticipation of this probability would force them to abandon the ABMT; accelerate deployment of missiles and bombers; develop new weapons to destroy space-based weapons; and improve the deceptive quality of decoys and warheads; shorten the boost phase and increase the accuracy of ICBMs; and shield and harden launchers.[16] Critics conclude that the inevitability of these Soviet attitudes and responses adds to the already solid case against BMD.

On the other hand, the prospect of a unilateral Soviet BMD deployment concerns those who remind American critics of Soviet violations of the letter and spirit of the ABMT and Soviet activity in BMD research, development, and testing. Secretary Shultz pointed out that Soviet spending on defense (missile, civil, and air), has kept pace with expenditures on strategic offensive weapons for the past 20 years.[17] Soviet interest in their own BMD and concern about the dangers of MAD might indicate susceptibility to persuasion about the benefits of deterrence based on defense. Fred C. Ikle suggested that susceptibility will depend on Soviet estimates of the perfectibility of American BMD systems and of the acceptability of alternative nuclear strategies.[18] He noted the following examples of Soviet decisions to abandon unpromising weapons and strategies and to undertake more promising alternatives:

> When we invested heavily in air defenses in the late 1950s, the Soviet Union ceased building new bombers and instead shifted to ballistic missiles. But when it became clear that we had given up on air defenses, the Soviets again invested in the development and then the production of a new strategic bomber. They decided to build new vehicles to take advantage of the freeway we opened for their bombers. By analogy, if we began to close

the freeway in space that we have preserved for ballistic missiles, the Soviet military might stop investing in new ballistic missiles and instead rely on new bombers and cruise missiles. That in itself would be a great gain. Bombers and cruise missiles, compared with ballistic missiles, are less suited for surprise attack because of their longer time of travel. And bombers are safer as deterrent forces since, by taking to the air, they can be made nearly invulnerable in an alert, yet could safely return to their bases should the warning be false.[19]

Given their past history, then, the Soviets might one day embrace BMD and forego attempts at counterforce superiority in a search for more stable strategic choices. This seems likely however, only if the Soviets anticipate higher costs and dangers in pursuing increased offensive capability, find the prospect of greater invulnerability more likely with BMD, and if the U.S. avoids the appearance of seeking superiority or a first strike capability. This choice could be increasingly stabilizing if each side also cut its arsenal of ICBMs which, due to their short flight time, ever increasing accuracy, vulnerability, and Launch On Warning status, many consider to be the most destabilizing element in the strategic equation.

While this choice remains a possibility, currently the Soviets oppose the SDI, and most analysts assume that they will pursue offensive and defensive countermeasures as an initial response to an American BMD. The Soviets fear that American technology might produce a limited BMD system that would seriously weaken the value of Soviet nuclear forces, escalate the arms race as the two powers would react to each other's offensive and defensive deployments, and jeopardize the ABM treaty. The Soviets who regard Reagan's rush to Star Wars with deep suspicion, have engaged in every arena to convince the Americans and Europeans of the danger that BMD poses for the ABMT, agreements on INF, and the arms control process in general. To judge the ramifications of this danger let us review the linkage between BMD and the ABMT.

## Arms, Anti-Arms, and Arms control

Critics of BMD note the valuable legacy of the 1972 ABM treaty that kept the offensive arms race limited, since neither superpower had to fear defensive deployments, and still protects against a defensive arms race. While acknowledging Soviet violations of the spirit of certain treaty provisions, they downplay the relevance of minor violations that do not portend any near term Soviet breakout or potential for an effective Soviet missile defense. Critics fear much more the loss of the treaty itself which would follow any BMD deployment. If American defense plans create additional complications for arms control negotiations, and if re-negotiating the ABMT would exacerbate Soviet-U.S. relations, the U.S. might be better off delaying or even foregoing research and development of BMD. According to Drell,

Too much is at stake in the present tense state of U.S.-Soviet relations to make it prudent to undermine remaining elements of stability and common understanding before we have something in which we can have more confidence as a replacement. Deterrence has been basic to stability and the prevention of nuclear war. As essential guarantee of deterrence, as recognized and defined in the ABM Treaty, has been reciprocal limitation of ABM defenses. Gradual erosion of the Treaty could imperil deterrence and heighten the risk of nuclear war more quickly than ABM deployment...could restore the balance.[20]

The defensive transition desired by Reagan would require a treaty constraining offensive forces and a prior agreement on allowable strategic defense systems. Both of these would be difficult to arrange given the necessity of retaining offensive forces until the perfection of BMD and given the ambiguity of defensive weapons that could be effective for first, as well as second, strikes and that would always be vulnerable to offensive breakthroughs.[21] Drell concludes that the ABMT constrains the Soviet Union, symbolizes the commitment to MAD, and adds to the deterrent value of SLBMs (which in the absence of BMD can retaliate more effectively).[22] In this perspective, it is the ABMT, rather than BMD, that enhances deterrence and the prospects for additional arms control. The hope for success at the 1988 summit also rests on the "sanctity" of the treaty.

Those who question the contribution of the ABMT to mutually beneficial arms control, strategic stability, and American security and who see no inherent logic in outlawing defense worry more about a unilateral Soviet breakout from the treaty than they do about abandoning or revising a treaty that the Soviets violate in letter and spirit. The Soviet build-up of SS-18 counterforce weapons violated the spirit of the treaty since it brought into question the Soviet commitment to the principle that weapons aimed at silos were unnecessary and provocative—a principle of MAD that undergirded the treaty. Other activities, such as the installation of the Krasnoyarsk BMD radar facility, deployments of Surface-To-Air Missiles with ballistic missile intercept potential, testing of civil and air defense programs, and research and development of KEWs and DEWs also showed that the Soviets take defensive strategies more seriously than they take the continuing credibility of MAD. And this violated what Ikle called "the implied bargain" of the ABMT: abstention from defensive and counterforce weapons. Given these putative violations and the Soviet interest in selective BMD prohibitions (they primarily object to space-based defenses where they lag behind the U.S.), the fragility of the ABM Treaty fails to exercise BMD supporters as much as does the critic's suggestion that the United States forego a chance to develop a perfect defense.

The prospect of perfect defense might even contribute to reductions in offensive forces. For example, a limited silo defense could alleviate verification problems associated with negotiations over the sizeable offensive cuts necessary to have a meaningful impact on the huge arsenals on each side. With high numbers of warheads, a little cheating can not hurt. With fewer numbers, cheating could hurt if one side cheated in the hope of defeating an opponent in a surprise attack. But BMD could help prevent this situation because deception on a very large scale, which could be more easily verified, would be necessary to upset the military balance significantly.[23] With BMD larger cuts could be made since each side would be less vulnerable and therefore less susceptible to danger from minor violations.

In addition, the Soviets might renegotiate the ABM treaty and agree to offensive reductions if they saw greater prospects for increased invulnerability through the ability to limit damage to the Soviet Union (with BMD) than through the ability to level damage (with counter-force) against the U.S.[24] If, on the other hand, the Soviets fear American first strike intentions and an American-driven defensive arms race more than they believe in the chance to defend their ICBMs or populations, then they will not accept arguments about the benefits of a defensive transition.

## Defense, Deterrence, and Decoupling

Another complication flowing from considerations of BMD involves the reaction of NATO allies to the prospect of a defended and invulnerable America and Soviet Union facing each other across a very vulnerable Europe. The NATO allies have historically resisted changes in nuclear strategy, weapons, and deployment characteristics due to fears about the potential erosion in the American commitment to extend deterrence to Western Europe. They have alternated between approving and disapproving INF deployment (and undeployment), flexible response in the 1960s, and even SALT negotiations, which inspired European concern about a decoupling of American and Western European strategies and weapons and about the prospect of the superpowers negotiating alone over the fate of Europe. NATO governments and their publics carry these same anxieties into their evaluations of BMD.

Many NATO governments fear that BMD might undermine the stability of the MAD umbrella, under which they stand protected by the American threat of nuclear retaliation against the Soviet Union for incursions into Western Europe. Stability could be undermined in two very important ways. First, a defended U.S. might be more willing and able to restrict a conflict to Western Europe.[25] In other words, a BMD system might lead to decoupled American and European nuclear forces and to an American capability to opt out of nuclear retaliation for an attack on Western Europe. Stability would also erode if a Soviet BMD degraded the deterrent value of British and French nuclear forces. NATO officials also anticipate a diversion of finite defense funds to research, development, and deployment of BMD at the expense of NATO requirements—both nuclear and conventional. Critics of BMD question the value of increasing European fears that they will be left on their own in exchange for uncertain technological fixes to the problems of deterrence.[26]

While Europeans continue to express doubts about BMD, many hope to share in the economic and technological benefits assumed to accompany BMD research effort. Britain, West Germany, Italy (and Japan) have negotiated agreements with the U.S. for their firms to participate in space defense research. Also, enticing is the prospect of a European based Anti-Tactical Ballistic Missile (ATBM) system. According to Fred Hoffman, a principal SDI consultant, BMD technologies could be applied against late phases of short-range ballistic missiles, whose warheads travel more slowly and are easier to intercept than ICBM warheads.[27] However, despite interest in technology sharing and ATBMs, the general concern about the erosion of the credibility of deterrence remains.

Supporters of BMD note that this erosion began with MAD. Since following the principles of MAD has guaranteed vulnerable populations in the U.S. and Europe, and since delaying a response to the Soviet's counterforce and INF build-up contributed to nuclear force vulnerability, American ability to extend deterrence remains fragile and uncertain. And, the more vulnerable the U.S. is to a Soviet attack, the less credible is its threat to respond to an attack in Western Europe. BMD, by enhancing the invulnerability of strategic nuclear forces, would lower the risk to the U.S. if it should retaliate and thus enhance the credibility of extended deterrence. In other words, the commitment to defend Europe would be believed because the U.S. would have less to fear from Soviet retaliation than in the current situation where retaliation would result in MAD.

While a defended America might be to the advantage of NATO, a defended Soviet Union could counterbalance this advantage because, once again, the American threat to retaliate with a limited nuclear option would be questioned, due to its ineffectiveness against invulnerable Soviet nuclear forces. Thus, according to Payne,

> a key to the current thesis of escalation control, that is, the threat of limited escalation, could no longer suppport extended deterrence. It should be recalled, however, that a primary rationale for limited options, as introduced in the so-called Schlesinger Doctrine of 1974, was to enhance the credibility of the U.S. nuclear umbrella. That credibility had waned in the minds of many (particularly the French) because of U.S. vulnerability to Soviet counterstrikes—the rationale being that the U.S. would be unlikely to initiate a process of escalation on behalf of NATO that could lead to self-destruction. In a defense-dominant strategic environment the credibility of the U.S. commitment to NATO-Europe would be high, even if the U.S. threat of limited strategic counterstrikes were low.[28]

In a situation of two defended superpowers, the nature of the retaliatory threat would differ. Retaliatory targets could include forces outside of the U.S.S.R. such as naval units or an invading army. While threats against these targets do not carry the same paralysing threat of MAD, few would doubt American willingness to implement these threats it under attack. And, as Payne concludes, as long as the Soviet Union could not anticipate an easy victory in Western Europe, it is unlikely to try. "In short, a defense transition would not terminate the U.S. extended deterrent; it would alter the sanctions supporting that deterrent and affect, in a beneficial fashion, Soviet perceptions concerning the likelihood that those sanctions would be imposed...there is little question that an extended deterrent should still function following the transition."[29]

The main dilemma for extended deterrence has been how to convince the Soviet Union of American willingness to risk MAD to defend Western Europe. For over 35 years the U.S. labored to make its retaliatory threat on behalf of Europe more credible—by deploying hostage troops in Europe and by deploying INF there in such a way as to ensure their use in a limited war and thus to guarantee that even a limited nuclear war could escalate to total war and MAD. Such a nearly pre-determined outcome would deter the Soviets from even a conventional attack in Europe. However, with or without INF in Europe, the question of credibility continues to plague Western attempts to deter by threat of massive retaliation. An American BMD could partially remedy this situation by ensuring that the U.S. would not be risking assured destruction in retaliation against limited Soviet incursions in Europe. On the other hand, a Soviet BMD might negate the effect of American retaliation, to say nothing of the retaliation from French or British forces. In the meantime, the question of the possibility of Europe becoming the location of a Soviet-U.S. proxy war arises again in the wake of discussions of BMD that could defend the superpowers but not the Europeans.

Conclusions about the value of BMD in the European context depend on one's views of whether a defended or vulnerable U.S. would be more likely to respond to a Soviet conventional or limited nuclear attack against Europe. One cannot ignore the possibility that even a partially defended U.S. could extend deterrence with more credibility than a vulnerable U.S. On the other hand, since war in Europe might presumably be "safe" in terms of not involving the defended territory of the superpowers, the issue of BMD raises horrible pictures in the minds of Europeans who see their territory very much at risk. The Europeans would prefer to see defensive as well as offensive forces constrained in Soviet-U.S. arms control agreements. While impatient with Reagan's persistent unwillingness to abandon SDI, the Europeans hope that the series of summits over INF and START will pressure Reagan to at least slow the pace of his support for SDI. The steadily diminishing funding for SDI research and development encourages those who expect less support from future administrations.

## Star Wars or Star Gazing?

The degree of approval and disapproval for BMD depends on whether one believes that MAD or defense provides the most effective deterrent. An advocate of MAD warns of the unnecessary and provocative gamble associated with BMD. In this view, a BMD system would undermine deterrence based on offensive retaliation—an especially fatal circumstance if one's defenses were incomplete, vulnerable to attack, and perceived as usable as support for first strike targeting. An inevitable Soviet response of offensive and defensive deployments would excerbate the instability triggered by the American defense plan. BMD, then, guarantees strategic instability, preemptive incentives, and frantic and costly arms races. It also invites debilitating costs and, costly or not, it does not entail the only, nor preferable, alternative strategic solution to the dilemma of vulnerability.

On the other hand, according to critics of MAD, BMD would, in the short run, strengthen deterrence based on an ability to retaliate by enhancing strategic nuclear force invulnerability. And, by shoring up the ability to prevent a Soviet first strike victory, it not only would make a failure of deterrence less likely, but it also would provide some hope for damage limitation should deterrence fail. As for defense of population, if the chance exists to defend populations, without provoking Soviet fears of an American first strike intention, no effort should be spared in discovering the technology necessary for its realization. Supporters of BMD conclude that if both sides could avoid being captured by scenario-mongering vis-a-vis the prospects for first strikes, hypothetically made more possible through perfect defenses, then both might avoid an arms race as they switched to deterrence based on defense.

After this review of the debate over the technological and strategic implications of deterrence based on defense, we may conclude that deployment of BMD will entail numerous obstacles as well as numerous rewards. On the one hand, we fear the prospects of accelerating arms races, faltering deterrent threats, destabilizing weapons, disintegrating remnants of arms control agreements, and deteriorating alliances that might result from BMD deployments. On the other hand, we would welcome the prospect of immunity from attack and extrication from the insane situation of mutual threats of annihilation.

BMD, as seen in the context of these two opposing possibilities, embodies the dilemma of deterrence and defense that has plagued American strategists since the days of the controversy over the value of flexible response versus the value of vulnerability as a fear-inspiring deterrent. On the one hand, BMD may deter more effectively due to the enhanced survivability of retaliatory forces that it provides; on the other, it might encourage an offensive and defensive arms race as each side would scramble to defend itself and yet also reduce incentives for the other to attack first. In an additional quirk in the dilemma, each side in a BMD world might wonder if an ability to negate the effects of retaliation might prompt riskier action by an adversary anxious to exploit potential weaknesses in the other's BMD system. Those who value survivable second strike forces over easy access to undefended targets recommend BMD. Those who value deterrence based on the fear of MAD urge compliance with the ABMT, which permits retaliatory forces to reach their targets unimpeded.

Inevitably, the uncertainties about developing a perfect BMD more than match the uncertainties about deterring nuclear war through MAD. Before making choices about strategies of defense versus MAD we might consider the following interim possibilities: 1) Maintaining research and development in missile defense as a hedge against a unilateral Soviet breakthrough. 2) Deferring attempts at testing and deploying BMD systems until ABMT revision. 3) Using the commitment to BMD as pressure on the Soviets to offer concessions on strategic arms cuts. 4) Absent Soviet cooperation in arms control, deploying BMD for silos. 5) Foregoing attempts at city defense until the Soviets could match this capacity. 6) Investigating the possibility of designing and implementing non-nuclear strategies that might both defend cities and make nuclear weapons obsolete. 7) Last, but not least, integrating the negotiations over START and missile defense.

# Selected Strategic Defense Glossary*
# (Spring 1988)

**ABM-X-3:** A traditional terminal defense system using transportable phased-array radars and both long-range and short-range, high-acceleration intercepters. System was developed and tested in the 1970s.

**Active Defense:** Defense utilizing aircraft, missiles, or other more exotic weapons to intercept attacking enemy weapons in space or in the atmosphere.

**Active Sensor:** A system that includes both a detector and a source of illumination. A camera with a flash attachment is an active sensor.

**Airborne Sensors:** A set ot sensors carried as an airborne optical adjunct to a ground-based radar system designed to detect, track and discriminate incoming warheads. Sensors are typically optical or infrared devices carried in an aircraft stationed above the clouds.

**Air Defense:** Systems designed to destroy attacking aircraft or cruise missiles. These systems are distinct in performance and operation from BMD systems. Usually consist of radar, interceptor aircraft, and surface-to-air missiles (SAM).

**Anti-Satellite Weapons (ASAT):** Weapons designed to destroy space-based satellites. The U.S. and U.S.S.R. include ASAT weapons of limited capability in their arsenal at this time. Since many satellites are used for military communication and early warning of a missile attack, this disruption capability could destablize the strategic balance and weaken the confidence of a superpower in its ability to adequately anticipate or deter a nuclear strike from the other side, or support a nuclear strike against the other side.

**Anti-Tactical Ballistic Missiles (ATBM):** Interceptor missiles designed to destroy medium-and intermediate-range ballistic missiles and cruise missiles.

**Area Defense:** A defensive shield designed to protect a wide geographic area usually containing a nation's vital interest, especially its people, industry, and cities—from nuclear attack. Requires a perfect defense against ballistic missiles, nuclear bomb—carrying aircraft, and cruise missiles.

**Beam Weapons:** Weapons that employ directed-energy beams of either laser light or subatomic particles to destroy targets.

**Boost Phase Interception:** The destruction of ballistic missiles during the stage in which they are being powered by their engines. Stage usually lasts from 3-5 minutes. Success achieved in this stage reduces the size of the attacking forces to be engaged later, because all of the warheads and decoys are destroyed with the missile.

**Birth-To-Death Tracking:** The ability to track a missile and its payload from launch until it is intercepted or destroyed.

**Boost Phase:** Portion of a missile flight during which the payload is accelerated by large rocket motors.

**Chemical Laser:** A laser in which chemical action is used to produce pulses in intense light.

**Chaff:** Bits of metal or other material dispersed around incoming warheads to confuse radar by reflecting multiple signals.

**Damage Limiting Capabilities:** Measures employed to reduce damage to a country from nuclear attack by an adversary. Measures include attacks against the enemy's nuclear weapons, military bases, and $C^3$ as well as active defenses and passive defenses.

**Decoy:** A device that accompanies a nuclear weapon delivery vehicle in order to mislead enemy defensive systems, thereby increasing the probability of penetrating those defenses. It may be designed to simulate an aircraft or a ballistic missile reentry vehicle. An aircraft decoy can simulate a bomber's radar cross-section. An ICBM decoy usually simulates the radar signatures of the RV.

**Directed Energy Weapons:** These intense energy "beam" weapons use the most exotic technologies currently being considered for BMD applications. Included are chemical, excimer, free electron and nuclear bomb-powered x-ray lasers, neutral and charged particle beams, and microwave weapons. They could be earth- or space-based. Potential strategic missions include defense against, or destruction of, aircraft, missiles, and satellites.

**Endoatmospheric:** Within the earth's atmosphere, generally considered altitudes below 100 kilometers.

**Exoatmospheric:** Outside the earth's atmosphere, generally considered altitudes above 100 kilometers.

**Homing Overlay Experiment (HOE):** A successful, experimental, ballistic missile defense interceptor test that demonstrated the capability of a nonnuclear warhead to home in on and destroy an ICBM reentry vehicle in space.

**Infrared Sensor:** A sensor to detect the infrared radiation from a cold body, such as a missile reentry vehicle.

**Kinetic Energy Weapons:** These weapons use high-speed, aimed projectiles with build-in-homing devices to destroy their target. Examples include interceptor missiles, ASAT projectiles and hypervelocity rail guns. The technologies needed for the success of these weapons in a BMD role are much more developed than for beam weapons.

**Laser:** A device for generating intense visible or invisible infrared light.

**Laser Tracking:** Process of using a laser to illuminate a target so that specialized sensors can detect the reflected laser light and track the target.

**Moscow System and Upgrades:** Exoatmospheric system, using early warning and phased-array radars for long-range acquisition. Target and interceptor tracking is performed by mechanically steered dish atennas. The exoatmospheric interceptor, the Galosh, carries a large nuclear warhead. The Moscow System is currently being upgraded with new endoatmospheric and exoatmospheric interceptors, phased-array radars, and a new, large phased-array radar for long-range acquisition and battle management.

**Midcourse Phase:** Long period of a warhead's flight to its target after it has been dispensed from the post-boost vehicle until it reenters the atmosphere over its target.

**Particle Beam:** A stream of atoms or subatomic particles (electrons, protrons or neutrons) accelerated to nearly the speed of light.

**Phased-array Radar:** Radar system that tracks many targets simultaneoulsy by electronically pointing a beam in different directions. Does not move an antenna mechanically. Crucial system for anti-missile battle management mission.

**Outer Space Treaty:** According to this treaty, weapons of mass destruction cannot be placed in orbit around the earth, installed on the moon or any other celestrial body, or otherwide stationed in outer space. Limits the use of the moon and other celestrial bodies exclusively to peaceful purposes and prohibits their being used for establishing military bases, installations, testing weapons of any kind, or conducting military maneuvers.

**Passive Defense:** Defense of population or military facilities by protective shelters, hardening, dispersal, mobility, or other means.

**Rail Gun:** A weapon used to destroy ballistic missiles, post-boost vehicles, reentry vehicles, and satellites. The electromagnetic railgun would be deployed on orbiting platforms. The gun operates by converting electrical energy to magnetic pressure, firing guided projectiles at or near the speed of light.

**Safeguard:** A now deactivated system composed of traditional exoatmospheric terminal defense components developed, tested, and deployed in the late 1960s.

**Sentry:** A traditional terminal defense system oriented toward low-altitude defense of ICBMs. Fixed and transportable versions have been considered. Uses a phased-array radar and a high-acceleration, nuclear-armed interceptor. Essentially the same system was known as the Low-Altitude Defense System (LoADS) in the late 1970s.

**Site Defense:** A traditional terminal defense system oriented toward defense of ICBMs. Used phased-array radars, called Site Defense Radars, and a high-acceleration, nuclear-armed interceptor, the Sprint. The system was studied extensively in the 1970s, as a follow-on to Safeguard and as a hedge against Soviet breakout from the ABMT.

**Soviet ASAT Weapon:** An explosive anti-satellite warhead and its maneuvering engine (together known as the interceptor) launched from a modified SS-9. The interceptor is boosted into an orbit that is about the same as the target and it closes in on the satellite. When close enough, the nonnuclear warhead explodes, firing a shotgunlike blast of metal pellets toward the target. Because the

Soviet ASAT is ground-based, it must wait until the earth turns to bring the target over the launch site. The highest altitude a Soviet interceptor has reached is reported to be 1400 miles, and thus high-orbiting satellites are beyond range. Since the Soviet ASAT booster is used to launch other paylods, some experts believe that it would be easy for the U.S.S.R. to switch payloads to an ASAT weapon, making an ASAT weapons ban difficult to verify.

**Terminal Phase:** Final phase of a ballistic missile trajectory, during which the warheads and penetration aids reenter the atmosphere.

*Sources: National Strategy Information Center (1986); Jeffrey Boutwell and Richard Scribner, *Strategic Defense Initiative*, (American Association for the Advance of Science, 1985); and Carter and Schwartz. *Ballistic Missile Defense.*

## Strategic Defense Initiative*

President Reagan called for an intensive and comprehensive effort to define a long-term research program with the ultimate goal of reducing or even eliminating the threat from ballistic missiles, a vital step toward freeing the world from the fear of nuclear conflict...SDIO (SDI Organization) was established as a research program to investigate the feasibility of advanced defensive technologies to provide a better basis for deterring aggression, strengthening stability, and increasing the security of the United States and our allies. It also seeks to reduce and, if possible, eliminate the threat posed by ballistic missiles...We are considering ways to defend both our territory and that of our allies against the ballistic missile threat...

The Soviet Union has failed to show the type of restraint, in both strategic offensive and defensive forces, on which the ABM treaty was based. Their continuous improvement on ballistic missile forces with enhanced hard target kill capability threatens the viability and credibility of our deterrent capability. At the same time, the Soviet Union has continued to pursue a strategic advantage through the development and improvement of active defenses as well as major hardening of their principal assets. These active and passive defenses give the Soviets increasing potential to counter retaliatory forces, especially if our retaliatory capability were degraded by a Soviet first strike. Their significant expenditures on passive defensive measures aimed at improving the survivability of their forces, military command structures, and national leadership poses a very troublesome situation. In the face of these developments, pursuit of the SDI by the United States is both prudent and necessary.

With the advent of rapidly emerging technologies in fields such as data processing, optics, directed energy, sensors, and other related fields, there is new promise of the possibility of engaging a ballistic missile or its warheads at all points in their flight. The layered defense approach offers a powerful disincentive to a potential aggressor because of the large uncertainties introduced in planning and launching a successful attack. Given the absence of active and passive U.S. defenses today, an attacker must consider only his missile reliability, warhead reliability, yield, and accuracy in seeking to destroy a target. To assure a high probability of success, up to three warheads may be dedicated to a target. When faced with a single layer defense having a 20 percent leakage rate, the number of warheads need be increased by only three to five warheads per target to give the same measure of confidence in destroying the target. However, if faced with a three-layered defense, each layer having an 80 percent effectiveness rate, the attacker would have to deploy literally hundreds of warheads to a single target to obtain the same confidence of success. With a strategic defense potentially having four or more layers, with possible engagement at any point along a trajectory, deterrence is substantially bolstered by this reduction in an attacker's confidence of success. If our objectives of developing reliable defenses are realized, proliferation would be forestalled—given the fact that even prohibitive increases in numbers of Soviet warheads would not change their inability to destroy U.S. targets if the Strategic Defense Initiative proves reliable and feasible. At the same time, strategic defenses will be judged desirable only if they are thoroughly reliable. Survivability, of course, is also vital to maintain stability in time of crisis...

(1) Surveillance, Acquisition, Tracking, and Kill Assessment (SATKA): Among the goals of technology research are: new optical and radar sensors capable of efficiently detecting and tracking multiple objects in a nuclear threat environment; on-board signal and data processing systems capable of performing acquisition, tracking, discimination, and kill assessment on the sensor platform and passing these results to battle management; data on observables from ballistic missiles and their warheads; and experiments to test the integration of these technologies short of ABM components.

(2) Directed Energy Weapons Technology (DEW): DEW research provides technology for two principal missions: interactive discrimination of decoys from reentry vehicles; and boost and post-boost phase intercept. The ability of directed energy systems to "perturb" objects offers a uniquely direct mechanism for performing midcourse discrimination, so essential for the viability of midcourse intercept. For the second mission, directed energy weapons would more fully address the fast time line and depressed trajectory threats and thereby provide critical leverage to reduce the utility of ballistic missiles. The state-of-the-art is being advanced in technologies for: high-power laser and particle beam generation; optics and sensors for correcting and controlling the highpower beam; large, lightweight mirrors and lightweight magnets for focusing the beam on targets; precision acquisition, tracking, and pointing to direct and hold the beam on target; and control measures to capitalize on features unique to directed energy devices such as the ability to measure and control the energy delivered to a target.

(3) Kinetic Energy Weapons Technology (KEW): Technologies relating to precision rocket interceptors and hypervelocity guns will be explored to provide potential nonnuclear kills of ballistic missiles in all phases of flight—boost, midcourse, and terminal. Technology base efforts include: smart seekers to acquire targets rapidly and provide highly accurate terminal homing; advanced guidance and control techniques to control

interceptor maneuvers for direct impact with targets; miniature rocket vehicles for boost and midcourse ballistic missile intercept, as well as satellite defense; and electromagnetic launchers and smart hypervelocity gun projectiles...

(4) Survivability, Lethality, and Key Technologies (SLKT): It includes technology for enhancing survivability, reducing uncertainties regarding kill mechanisms and vulnerabilities, evaluation of countermeasures, investigating the needs of SDI logistics, and improvement of space power. The success of SDI is closely linked to our ability to provide electrical power in space as well as placing, operating, and maintaining systems in space...

(5) Progress: Directed energy research in the field of atmosphere compensation has yielded very promising results in technologies that could support the concept of large, ground-based lasers. Work with free electron lasers has progressed more rapidly than anticipated, increasing the potential for application of this technology years ahead of schedule...An experiment in which the MIRACL chemical laser destroyed a static Titan booster, demonstrated graphically the lethality of such a device. The surveillance and sensor areas have witnessed equally impressive progress...additionally, significant progress has been achieved in technologies for hardening of high density microelectronic processors and infrared focal plane arrays against the effect of nuclear radiation that would be experienced during a nuclear exchange. Electromagnetic launcher, or "rail gun," research in kinetic energy is progressing well...extensive cuts to the SDI budget have led to program delays and reductions to some program efforts. The final result is that overall program success has been put more at risk.

*Source: Weinberger, *Annual Report to Congress, FY 1987*, pp. 286-291.

## A.A. Gromyko, Interview, *Pravda reprinted in Current Digest of Soviet Press* (February 6, 1985): 4-8

...The Soviet Union...believes that it is impossible to leave outer space aside. In the final analysis, one can theoretically imagine a situation in which success would have been achieved on questions of strategic arms and on questions of medium-range nuclear weapons. But an arms race would be taking place in outer space. Space would become increasingly filled with weapons appropriate to the sphere. This would not only nullify but also outdo what had been done on earth. As a result, the balance would be adverse for peace, and the situation would be more complicated and even more dangerous...

The American side characterizes its plan...for a so-called large-scale missile defense, as defensive...There is a rather crafty and, generally speaking, insidious strategem here. Imagine that such a system...is successfully created. In other words, a shield that will deflect missiles is created. After all, they say that they fear a nuclear strike from the Soviet Union, and that therefore they need a shield...They say that this shield is peaceable...intended to destroy missiles, to keep these missiles from reaching their targets...They tell us that the U.S. has no intention of delivering a strike against the Soviet Union: They're talking about intention, I emphasize. We say to them: Well then, is the Soviet Union supposed to rely on your conscience?...These are offensive weapons, and this whole plan, frankly, is aggressive...Let us even suppose—for the sake of theoretical analysis—that the U.S. has created this system but is not using its possibilities to launch missiles against the Soviet Union or to deliver a nuclear strike. But after all, it would have this capability if it had such a shield. Wouldn't this be used for pressure, for blackmail? This fits in with the line of the U.S. administration, which is aimed at obtaining a dominating position in the world— a position that would enable the U.S. to dictate its terms...

## REFERENCES

[1]This chapter is an updated version of Hulett, "From Cold Wars to Star Wars: Debate over Defense," *Defense Analysis* 2 (1986): 69-84. See also Gray, "Nuclear Strategy: Case For a Theory of Victory," *International Security* 4 (Summer 1979): 54-87; James C. Fletcher, *Strategic Defense Initiative: Defensive Technologies Study* (Washington: Department of Defense, March 1984); Fred Hoffman, *Ballistic Missile Defenses and U.S. National Security: Summary Report,* (Washington: Department of Defense, Oct. 1983); Gray, "Nuclear Policy in the Defense Transition," 820-842.

[2]Discussion of BMD technology relies on the following sources: James Abrahamson, *Statement,* Senate Committee on Armed Services, 99th Cong., (Feb. 21, 1985): 1-18; Abrahamson, "The Strategic Defense Initiative," *Defense '84* (August 1984): 3-11; Hans Mark, "War and Peace in Space," *Journal of International Affairs* (Summer 1985): 1-21; Gerald Yonas, "The Strategic Defense Initiative," *Daedalus* (Spring 1985): 73-90: and the *The Christian Science Monitor* (Nov. 4-11), 1985).

[3]George Keyworth, quoted in *Financial Times* (March 14, 1985): 2.

[4]Mark, 12-13; and *Los Angeles Times* (Dec. 29, 1985): 10-11.

[5]See Hans Bethe, et. al., BMD Technologies and Concepts in the 1980s," *Daedalus* (Spring 1985): 53-72; McGeorge Bundy, et. al., "President's Choice: Star Wars or Arms Control," *Foreign Affairs* (Winter 1984/85): 264-278; and Ashton B. Carter and David Schwartz, ed., *Ballistic Missile Defense,* (Brookings, 1984); Richard L. Garwin, "Star Wars: Shield or Threat?" *Journal of International Affairs* (Summer 1985): 31-44; Drell, et. al., "Preserving the ABM Treaty: Critique of the Reagan Strategic Defense Initiative," *International Security* 9 (Fall 1984): 68; Richard Garwin, "Star Wars: Shield or Threat?" *Journal of International Affairs* (Summer 1985): 31-44; and Charles A. Zraket, "Strategic Defense: A Systems Perspective," *Daedalus* (Spring 1985): 118.

[6]Carter, 10-12; Union of Concerned Scientists, "Star Wars: A Critique," in *The Nuclear Reader,* by Charles Kegley, Jr., and Eugene Wittkopf, 219-225.

[7]Union of Concerned Scientists, 215-231; *Wall Street Journal* (Dec. 10, 1985): 1; Drell, 68-80; and Garwin, 34-39. In salvage fusion warheads are arranged to explode as they detect penetration by KEWs or DEWs.

[8]Brzezinski, et. al., in *New York Times Sunday Magazine* (Jan. 27, 1985): 29-30.

[9]Yonas, 87-89; Abrahamson, 6; Mark, 12.

[10]Robert Jastrow, Dartmouth physicist formerly with NASA, in a letter to editors of *Commentary* 6 (March 1985): 23-24.

[11]Weinberger, speech reported in the *Wall Street Journal,* (January 2, 1985): 28.

[12]Glaser, "Why Even Good Defense May Be Bad," *International Security* 9 (Fall 1984): 114.

[13]Drell, 81.

[14]Michael Krepon and D. Geoffrey Peck, "Another Alarm on Soviet ABMs," *Bulletin of Atomic Scientists,* (June/July 1985): 34.

[15]Committee of Soviet Scientists in Defense of Peace and Against the Threat of Nuclear War, *Prospects for Creation of a U.S. Space Ballistic Missile Defense System and Impact on the World Military Political Situation,* (Moscow, 1983).

[16]For more on Soviet counters see notes 5 and 7 and David Holloway, "The Strategic Defense Initiative and the Soviet Union," *Daedalus* (Summer 1985): 257-96; Gary L. Guertner, "What is 'Proof'?" *Foreign Policy* 59 (Summer 1985): 73-84; and Sayre Stevens, "Ballistic Missile Defense in the Soviet Union," *Current History* (October 1985): 311-316 and 344.

[17]Shultz, address, "Arms Control, Strategic Stability, and Global Security," in *Current Policy* 750, (October 1985): 2.

[18]Ikle, "Nuclear Strategy: Can There Be A Happy Ending," 816.

[19]Ikle, 816.

[20]Drell, "Preserving the ABM Treaty," 81.

[21]Drell, 83.

[22]Drell, 84-90.

[23]Payne and Gray, "Nuclear Policy and the Defense Transition," 838 and Kissinger, "Talking Down Arms: Proposal for Mutually Assured Survival," *Los Angeles Times* (Sept. 8, 1985): 1 and 3.

[24]Gray, "Deterrence, Arms Control, and the Defense Transition," *Orbis* (Summer 1984): 230.

[25]Bertram, "Strategic Defense and the Western Alliance," *Daedalus* (Spring 1985): 294; and Yost, "European Anxieties about Ballistic Missile Defense," *Washington Quarterly* 7 (Fall 1984): 112-29.

[26]Bertram, 295.

[27]Hoffman, quoted in *Los Angeles Times* (Dec. 19, 1985): 24.

[28]Payne, "Strategic Defense and Stability," *Orbis* (Summer 1984): 225.

[29]Payne, 225.

# BIBLIOGRAPHY

## Strategic Defense Initiative

Abrahamson, James A. "The Strategic Defense Initiative," *Defense '84*, (August 1984): 3-11.

Bluth, Christoph. "SDI: The Challenge to West Germany," *International Affairs* 62 (Spring 1986).

Boutwell, Jeffrey and Scribner, Richard A. *The Strategic Defense Initiative: Some Arms Control Implications*. Washington: American Association for the Advancement of Science, 1985.

Brown, Harold "Is SDI Technically Feasible?" *Foreign Affairs*. 64 (1985): 435-454.

Chalfont, Alun. *SDI: The Case for the Defense*. London: Institute for European Defense and Strategic Studies, Occasional Paper No. 12, 1985.

Cimbala, Stephen J. "Soviet Nuclear Strategies: Will They Do The Unexpected?" *Strategic Review* (Fall 1985): 67-78.

Committee of Soviet Scientists for Peace Against Nuclear Threat. "Strategic and International-Political Consequences of Creating a Spaced-Based Anti-Missile System Using Directed Energy Weapons." Moscow: 1984.

Congressional Budget Office. *Analysis of the Costs of the Administration's Strategic Defense Initiative, 1985-1989*. CBO Staff Working Paper, May 1984.

Davis, Jacquelyn K. and Pfaltzgraff, Robert L., Jr. *Strategic Defense and Extended Deterrence: New Transatlantic Debate*. Cambridge: Institute for Foreign Policy Analysis, 1986.

Dean, Jonathan. "Will NATO Survive Ballistic Missile Defense?" *Journal of International Affairs* 39 (Summer 1985): 95-114.

Deane, Michael J. *Strategic Defense in Soviet Strategy*. Washington: Advanced International Studies Institute, 1980.

Drell, Sidney D. et. al. "Case Against Strategic Defense: Technical and Strategic Realities," *Issues in Science and Technology*. (Fall 1984): 45-65.

"Forum: The Strategic Defense Initiative," *Orbis*, (Summer 1984): 215-255.

Garwin, Richard L. et. al., "Space Weapons," *Bulletin of the Atomic Scientists*. May 1984, special supplement.

Glaser, Charles. "Do We Want the Missiles We Can Build?" *International Security,* (Summer 1985): 25-57.

Graham, Daniel O. *High Frontier: A National Strategy.* Washington: and Payne, Keith. "Nuclear Policy and the Defense Transition," *Foreign Affairs* 62 (Spring 1984): 820-842.

Hadley, Stephen J. *Thinking About SDI.* Washington: Foreign Policy Institute, Johns Hopkins University, 1986.

Hafner, Donald. "Assessing the President's Vision: Fletcher, Miller, and Hoffman Panels," *Daedalus* 114 (Spring 1985): 91-108.

Hans, Mark. "War and Peace in Space," *Journal of International Affairs,* (June 1985): 1-21.

Hoffman, Fred. "The SDI in U.S. Nuclear Strategy," *International Security.* (Summer 1985): 13-24.

Hough, Jerry F. "Soviet Decision-Making on Defense," *Bulletin of the Atomic Scientists* 7 (August 1985): 84-88.

Jastrow, Robert. *How to Make Nuclear Weapons Obsolete.* Boston: Little, Brown, 1985. "The Technical Feasibility of Ballistic Missile Defense," *Journal of International Affairs* 39 (Summer 1985): 45-56.

Kalish, Jack. "The Technologies of Hard-Site Defense," *Issues of Science and Technologies,* (Winter 1986): 122-133.

Kaltefleiter, Werner. *The Strategic Defense Initiative: Implications for Europe.* London: Institute for European Defense and Strategic Studies, 1985.

Keyworth, George A., II. *Reassessing Strategic Defense.* Washington: Council on Foreign Relations, 1984.

Lebow, Richard Ned. "Assured Strategic Stupidity: Quest for Ballistic Missile Defense," *Journal of International Affairs* 39 (Summer 1985): 57-80.

Longstreth, Thomas K., et. al. *The Impact of US and Soviet Ballistic Missile Defense Program on the ABM Treaty.* Washington: National Campaign to Save the ABM Treaty, 1985.

Panofsky, Wolfgang F.K. "The Strategic Defense Initiative: Perception v. Reality," 38 (June 1985): 34-40.

Payne, Keith B. "The Deterrence Requirement for Defense," *Wshington Quarterly* 9 (Winter 1986): 139-154. "The Soviet Union and Strategic Defense: The Failure and Future of Arms Control," *Orbis* 29 (Winter 1986): 673-709. *Strategic Defense: "Star Wars" in Perspective.* Lanham, MD: Hamilton Press, 1986.

Perle, Richard N. "The Strategic Defense Initiative: Addressing Misconceptions," *Journal of International Affairs* 39 (Summer 1985): 23-30.

Ra'anan, Uri and Pfaltzgraff, Robert L., Jr., ed. *International Security Dimensions of Space.* Hamden, CT: Archon Books, 1984.

Rathjens, George. "The Strategic Defense Initiative: Imperfections of Perfect Defense," *Environment* (June 1984): 6-13.

Rivkin, David B., Jr. "What Does Moscow Think" *Foreign Policy,* (Summer 1985): 85-105.

"The Star Wars Controversy," *Congressional Digest.* (March 1985): 69-96.

Stares, Paul B. "Reagan and the ASAT Issue," *Journal of International Affairs* 39 (Summer 1985): 81-94. "U.S. and Soviet Military Space Programs: A Comparative Assessment," *Daedalus* 114 (Spring 1985): 127-146.

Stevens, Sayre. "The Soviet Factor In SDI," *Orbis* 29 (Winter 1986): 689-700.

Union of Concerned Scientists. *The Fallacy of Star Wars.* New York: Vintage Books, 1984. *Papers on Strategic Defense. Satellite Vulnerability.* 1986.

U.S. Congress. *Implications of the President's Strategic Defense Initiative and Antisatellite Weapons Policy.* Arms Control, International Security and Science Subcommittee of the Foreign Affairs Committee. Washington: GPO, 1985.

U.S. Congress. House. Committee on Armed Services. Joint Hearings, Subcommittee on Space Science and Applications, Committee on Science and Technology and Subcommittee on Research and Development. *Assured Access to Space During the 1990s,* 1986.

# CHAPTER VII
# From Cold Wars To Star Wars
# To No Wars

## Challenges, Containment, and the Communists

We have covered a variety of approaches to Soviet-U.S. relations and to the nuclear dilemma that faces the two superpowers. In tracing the unfolding drama of the post-war period, we have seen American fear of Soviet aggression and dominance catapult the U.S. into a confrontational stance for most of that period. Whether in foreign policy (containment) or nuclear strategy (threats of massive retaliation), the U.S. has largely decided to resist the Soviets and attain the military strength necessary to persuade them to opt for self-containment. Reagan's version of containment, like Truman's emphasized the urgency of restoring American and Western political will and military strength. The stress on will and strength reflected Reagan's assumption that the U.S. faces a Soviet power that hopes to coerce nations who fear the implied threat from its military power. Reagan views this hope as part of a longstanding Soviet plan, which presumably found considerable success in the 1970s, for upsetting the international status quo. In particular, Reagan officials blame the Soviets for exploiting and aggravating tensions in the third world as required in this plan. In view of this perceived danger, the Reagan administration, declared its intentions to counter Soviet aggression and global intervention, support all who oppose communism, and equal the increase in Soviet military power.

Shultz announced this intention in a major address to Congress in 1983. He spoke of the obligation to overturn or undercut Soviet encroachments, the assumption "that the Soviet Union is more likely to be deterred by our actions that make clear the risks their aggression entails than by a delicate web of interdependence," and the "expectation that, faced with demonstration of the West's renewed determination to strengthen its defenses, enchance its political and economic cohesion, and oppose adventurism, the Soviet Union will see restraint as its most attractive, or only, option."[1] His assumption that the U.S. could define Soviet options resembled the assumption of NSC-68 that the proper response to Soviet actions and threats was resistance and the associated willingness to use force when necessary. Not fully satisfied with the reactive quality of this agenda, Shultz also proposed anticipatory vigilance: "Where it was once our goal to contain the Soviet presence within the limits of its immediate post-war reach, now our goal must be to advance our own objectives, where possible foreclosing and when necessary actively countering Soviet challenges wherever they threaten our interests."[2]

This updated containment depended on eschewing isolationism, securing a stable military balance, convincing the Soviets that there "are penalties for aggression and incentives for restraint," and forging an

American consensus on the need to manage Soviet power, defend Western interests, and reestablish an American global presence.[3] In sum, the underlying premises of NSC-68—that the Soviet Union was an expansionist and revolutionary "empire"; that Soviet adventurism faltered when met by resistance; and that Western military power, commitment, and unity of purpose prompted and reinforced Soviet caution—remain in full force in Reagan's policy. For example, the naval, military, and CIA maneuvers near and within the borders of Nicaragua and Cuba, the invasion of Grenada, and direct material support for the Contras provided physical evidence of Reagan's persuasion that explicit warnings in Central America signal the Soviets and their clients (and American friends) that the U.S. intended to act decisively in key areas in the mode of containment. Similar support for rebel forces in Afghanistan, Angola, Ethiopia, Kampuchea, and Mozambique, although more subdued or covert, also indicated the administration's interest in setting up selected obstacles to Soviet expansion in the third world or to expansion through Cuban or Vietnamese proxies.

In Reagan's attempt to rollback Soviet challenges in the third world to restore consensus within the West about the relevance and urgency of these objectives in the 1980s, he envisioned a re-vitalization of America's presence in global affairs and the disintegration of the legitimacy of the Brezhnev Doctrine and the exploitative Soviet version of peaceful coexistence. Reagan intended to transcend the limitations of the retrenchment inherent in the Nixon Doctrine, support the cause of those opposed to communisim, and embrace a military, as well as economic and diplomatic, application of containment. Rejecting a self-paralyzing and over-zealous fastidiousness about the nature or tactics of those signed up on the anti-Soviet team, the Reagan administration adopted a self-described *Realpolitik* approach that accepted the prerequisite of forceful resistance when dealing with expansionist states. According to the Reagan Doctrine, the Soviets respect strength and not concession and respond to retreat with advance, but to counterforce and activism with caution.

The administration anticipated that Soviet challenges on the periphery would, if not met, add up to larger and more central challenges in the future. The cold war battle lines, drawn primarily across the geography of the third world and Central Europe, involved not only physical and direct challenges, but also symbolic and indirect tests of the credibility of America's staying powers. To shirk these tests or responsibilities, in the hope that the Soviets would not exploit tensions and regional conflicts, would invite increased Soviet adventurism and reward those eager to attack fragile new governments, especially pro-Western governments. A unilateral American decision to abstain from involvements might leave the fate of many third world conflicts to be decided by the Soviets, and at a relatively low cost for them. To do so would reflect fatalism or self-delusion rather than morality since, in the administration's view, there is little morality in abandoning those threatened by communism. Shultz warned against the illusion that the U.S., in a world threatened by "ruthless' adversaries whose purposes "are antithetical to our most deeply held principles," can promote human rights, justice and democracy by "aloof self-righteousness" or by merely "wishing" for them.[4]

In the strategic arena this same insistence on resistance, engagement, and participation also prevails. The administration relies on deterrence based on strength and resolve, and it refuses to abandon strategic competition in response to pessimism about Soviet strength or doubts about the priority of strategic over economic concerns. While the MX and Trident II missiles, the B-1B bomber, and the SDI program entail tremendous research and development costs, in the Reagan administration matching Soviet strategic capability, fortifying the American ability to retaliate, and thus deterring aggression or direct attack take precedence over economic conerns.

Beyond this, Reagan hopes to escape the balance of terror arrangement of MAD through an eventual transition to deterrence based on defense. According to Reagan, strategic defense is "the one great hope that we might someday rid the world of the prison of mutual nuclear terror...The only question for the Soviets is, do we move toward strategic defense together or alone?"[5] However, many Americans and Soviets criticize this solution as an extreme example of "pie in the sky" dreaming in the age of accurate, abundant, penetrable, and speedy ballistic missiles and vulnerable and inherently undefendable land and space targets. In the view of critics, the SDI, even if partially successful in discovering ways to defend against ICBMs, is more likely to provoke than deter attack because a capability to defend counterforce or countervalue targets would be considerably more effective against a second strike than a first strike, and thus would appear to the Soviets like an adjunct to an American attempt at a first strike capability. This controversy over Reagan's BMD agenda, which limited the 1986 and 1987 summits, will color and set the tone for all future strategic arms control negotiations with the Soviets who officially reject the administration's rationales for SDI.

The administration soon found itself embroiled in the typical and perhaps unavoidable dilemma of arms control: how to balance the requirements of deterrence (weapons modernization, procurement, and deployment) with the equally important requirements of defusing tensions excerbated by the perennial competition in arms. The administration hoped to demonstrate strength without pushing the other side closer to preemption or unproductive and destabilizing escalations in either offensive or defensive arms races. Reagan, in the final year of his administration, appears to want arms control agreements with the Soviet Union more desparately than ever before. His conciliation on INF to be withdrawn from Europe and in the number of ICBMs to be limited in his START proposals, the apparent willingness to consider a deal on delaying Star Wars, and the warm-up on Soviet-U.S. relations in the various summits with Gorbachev, all suggest considerable sacrifice in the consistence of his hard line in exchange for the opportunity to improve Soviet-U.S. relations.

Despite the euphoric and ebullient expressions of renewed hope for improved superpower relations at the 1987 summit, the adminstration also remains convinced that only unflinching steadfastness in the American determination to maintain military strength, project power where needed, and accept the assignments of containment and strategic deterrence brought the Soviet leaders to the realization that their best interests lay in meeting the U.S. at least half way in both the arms control and the political arena. In sum, the administration insists on strength since, in its view, while "America's weakness makes the world a more dangerous place, American's strength deters aggression and encourages restraint and negotiation. We have seen how the rebuilding of America's defense in the early 1980s gave the Soviets an incentive to return to negotiation on arms control. Our ability to project power abroad has help us protect our vital interests and defend our friends against subversion and aggression."[6]

## Critics, Complaints, and Conclusions

Unfortunately, the administration's promises of anticipatory vigilance and strategic competition also pose the danger of yielding the same results that past containments produced; i.e., bitter and inflamatory cold war atmospherics, peripheral political and military confrontations inherently susceptible to escalation, and destabilizing and costly arms races. Critics remind Reagan that the fruits of containment, which dragged the U.S. into the quagmire of Vietnam, led the Nixon and Carter administrations to search for alternatives like detente and SALT. On the other hand, while many question the appropriateness of Reagan's particular application of containment, Americans for years have accepted, with varying degrees of enthusiasm, the need to counter Soviet threats.

Unfortunately, the vague, nebulous, and indirect nature of the threat from the Soviets has been a difficult concept to relay to Western publics fearful of American overcommitment, escalating regional conflicts, and the prospects of nuclear war. Complicating this situation, American officials have had difficulty deciding which issues required a direct response and how to explain such responses to the public. For example, Truman and Acheson wrote South Korea off in 1950 only to find in retrospect that, for the sake of the credibility of other commitments, they had to repulse the North Korean invasion. The Eisenhower administration pursued a primarily rhetorical containment, while sacrificing conventional military strength for a balanced budget and abandoning liberation and rollback after the Soviet invasion of Hungary in 1956. Perhaps more consistence between rhetoric and action might have added more consistency in the pursuit of containment.

On the other hand, for people like Dulles, words were better than nothing. But this was not the case for the Kennedy and Johnson administrations, which seemingly undertook to maintain commitments everywhere for the sake of appearances. However, while their application of containment failed in Vietnam, the failure might be attributed to tactics and public opinion as well as to an indiscriminate containment. And, despite their eagerness to "bear any burden," limitations on the threat and application of force did occur during this period (over Berlin, Laos, Cuba, Czechoslovakia, and in Africa), as did limits on the conduct of the war in Vietnam. Nixon and Kissinger, in their withdrawal from Vietnam and their applications of the Nixon Doctrine, also accepted new found limitations on the American ability to exercise power and influence events. In particular, the policy of detente reflected the awareness that America's ability to influence the Soviet Union depended more on persuasion than coercion and that creating a new direction in America's global and Soviet policy was urgent.

Not all approved of this redirection in U.S. foreign policy. Those on the right disapproved of the pessimism reflected in the abandonment of an active and even aggressive containment. Many on the left questioned the depth of Nixon's and Kissinger's devotion to peaceful coexistence with the Soviet Union or to a scaled down and less interventionist foreign policy. The persistent commitment to Vietnam, defense spending, weapons modernization (including the early flirtation with BMD), repressive third world regimes, and blocking Soviet entry into the global arena obscurred the contrary evidence of a more enlightened American policy. Garthoff, for example, criticized Nixon's mishandling of detente, which resulted, in his view, from a failure to appreciate Soviet preceptions, interests, and expectations.[7] A more open minded approach to the Soviets might have avoided the breakdown of detente that followed Carter's often inept management of Soviet-U.S. relations. Garthoff held little hope that the Reagan administration, which let anti-communist instincts and narrow minded geo-strategy and realpolitik drive its foreign policy, would find an intelligent replacement for detente containment.

Many others share this doubt and disillusionment. In their view, the administration's myopic and obsessive concentration on endangered strategic chokpoints, disintegrating dominos, the avoidable erosion of American prestige, and military solutions to political or economic problems, distorted and undermined American principles and objectives. For example, the administration's lack of discrimination in enlisting international clients continued to link the U.S. with third world dictators of questionable and unsavory reputation, while it simultaneously alienated the U.S. from many friends, allies, and neutrals. This link contributed to the many failures in Reagan's foreign policy. These failures include the unstellar record of influence among allies and non-aligned; the waffling over when and how to abandon clients like Marcos, Pinochet, Zia, the military in South Korea, and the white government in South Africa; the incoherent Middle Eastern and Persian Gulf policies that show an inability to decide how far to trust Israel vs. the Egyptians or Saudis, how much to back Iraq vs. Iran, and how long to wait for Western European support in the area; and the messy coverup of attempts to pay Iran ransom for hostages and equip surrogate containment forces in Nicaragua. As one solution to Reagan's woes, critics called for more selective choices of clients and intervention based on more narrowly defined interests rather than a simplistic realpolitik and an open-ended and all-inclusive containment-driven foreign policy.

While the critics correctly noted that not every regional conflict involved issues of East versus West nor called for military solutions, many critics suffer from their own obsession with discovering a more "principled" foreign policy. Preferring non-intervention on principle and alliances with only "proven" democracies, and yet also dedicated to assuring guarantees of human rights, many critics fail to offer concrete alternatives to containment, engagement, or realpolitik. All of those seeking alternatives or refinements in approaches need to ask the following questions: Will a reinstituted detente suffice or will it encounter the same fate it met in the 1970s? Will righteous non-intervention suffer the same consequences that American isolation and European appeasement did in the 1930s? Could Kennan's original concept of a more selective containment, if somehow welded to an expanded version of the Marshall Plan, wherein the U.S. would provide economic support for appropriately progressive and humane regimes, eliminate some of the economic and soical causes of the cancer (of the Soviet or communist variety?) Does Reagan's tough minded and uncompromising containment or an enlightened and realistic detente offer the best hope for a stable superpower relationship? Is it possible to temper Reagan's crusading anticommunism with a rapprochement with the Soviet Union without the abuses (by both according to Garthoff or by the Soviets according to Reagan) of the 1970s?

Reagan thinks that containment should give way only to a carefully designed detente that reflects a genuine relaxation of tensions, restraint in the pursuit of objectives, and resolve to pacify regional conflicts. While critics may assail Reagan's strict conditions for accommodation with the Soviets and his application of containment, his approach reflected the same pragmatic understanding of the intrusive strategic, political, and economic realities and constraints that all post-war administrations understood. While Reagan concentrated on rebuilding American military strength, refostering Western allied unity, and reinstituting the notion of the mission of the free world to persuade the Soviets of the benefits of democracy and stability, he also recognized the limits of American power and the need for the U.S. to accept gradual changes in the international balance of power.

This recognition, and actions in line with it, displayed a willingness to coexist peacefully with the Soviets. However, since Soviet strategic and political goals conflict with American objectives of security and a stable world order, a policy aimed at demonstrating that Soviet attempts at strategic superiority, political dominance, and upsetting the status quo will fail and prove costly and counterproductive still appears to the Reagan administration to be a more effective policy than the detente practiced in the 1970s. Only an approach devoid of naive assumptions that nuclear arms freezes and political accommodation alone enhance American security or lead to Soviet moderation will provide reminders that the U.S. is determined to resist Soviet expansion, cold war probings, and unequal arms treaties. To the extent that Reagan convinces both the Soviet Union and public opinion in the West of this determination, to that extent the Soviets may be deterred and contained. On the other hand, the success of Reagan's mission depends on the ability to convince these same audiences of America's flexibility and of its willingness to mix detente and containment, arms control and defense, values and realpolitik.

The U.S. has pursued some combination accommodation and containment ever since 1945 (or perhaps more accurately since the Bolshevik revolution of 1917). While the dizzying and schizophrenic history of setbacks in peaceful coexistence and throwbacks to containment versus isolationism frustrated American policy objectives and confused allies and adversaries, perhaps all of the parties can derive some comfort from the fact that ardent cold warriors have often pursued detente and arms control as vigorously as "detentists." While Reagan is by no means a detentist, his gradual evolution toward a mix of containment and accommodation is not unprecedented and may, in fact, ultimately succeed where Carter's approach failed.

In 1988 Reagan shows every indication of seeking arms control and detente. In fact, some Republicans view Reagan's new eagerness for arms control as a dangerous throwback to Carter's naivete in negotiations with the Soviets. In an interesting turnaround, yet not an unprecedented one, Reagan now encounters the same criticism he pressed against arch-detentist Carter. He faces criticism from the right, just as Carter encountered criticism from the left for his requests for the larger defense budgets he opposed as a presidential candidate and as Truman encountered attacks from hawkish Republicans who deplored the "appeasement" and "immorality" of his policy of "living with" the Soviet Union rather than eliminating it in some sort of liberation or rollback effort. The irony persists, then, as Reagan receives criticism from right-wing sections of his party and cautious praise from long-term opponents who held such little hope concerning Reagan's moderation or enlightenment vis-a-vis the Soviets and arms control. However, as if to re-prove his conservative credentials, Reagan resisted the temptation at recent summits to sign an agreement that compromised his objective of a transition to deterrence based on defense. He refused again to exchange SDI for Soviet reductions in INF and offensive nuclear forces. Despite Soviet and American disappointment about failing to reach an agreement on strategic arms, both powers continue to hint of the possibility of future progress in arms control and detente in yet another replay of the hopeful *danse a deux* choreographed by belligerent yet cautious actors within the confines of the nuclear stage.

## REFERENCES

[1]Shultz, *Testimony,* Senate Foreign Relations Committe, Department of State Delivery Copy, (June 15, 1983): 11 and 35.

[2]Ibid., 11 and 35.

[3]Haig, "American Power and American Purpose," *Current Policy* (April 27, 1982): 2.

[4]Shultz, "Progress, Freedom, and Responsibility," *Current Policy,* (Sept. 5, 1986): 2-3.

[5]Reagan, White House Address, *Current Policy* (September 23, 1986): 1.

[6]Shultz, "Progress, Freedom, and Responsibility, 2-3.

[7]Garthoff, *Detente and Confrontation,* 21 and 1073.

# INDEX